Training In Organizations

Needs Assessment, Development, and Evaluation

3rd EDITION

Other Titles in the Cypress Series in Work and Science
Edited by Frank J. Landy, Pennsylvania State University

Honesty in the Workplace
Kevin M. Murphy, Colorado State University

Performance Management and Appraisal
Robert M. Vance, Pennsylvania State University
Scott C. Brooks, Ohio State University

Training In Organizations

Needs Assessment, Development, and Evaluation

3rd EDITION

Irwin L. Goldstein
University of Maryland at College Park

BROOKS/COLE PUBLISHING COMPANY
Pacific Grove, California

To my wife, Micki,

who lights up the stars wherever she goes

Consulting Editor: *Frank J. Landy*

Brooks/Cole Publishing Company
A division of Wadsworth, Inc.

Printed in the United States of America

10 9 8 7 6 5 4 3 2 1

Library of Congress Cataloging-in-Publication Data

Goldstein, Irwin L.
Training in organizations : needs assessment, development, and evaluation / Irwin L. Goldstein. — 3rd ed.
p. cm.
Includes bibliographical references and indexes.
ISBN 0-534-16452-8
1. Employees—Training of. 2. Employees—Training of—Evaluation. 3. Assessment centers (Personnel management procedure) I. Title.
HF5549.5.T7G543 1992
658.3'12404—dc20

92-3484
CIP

Sponsoring Editor: *Marianne Taflinger*
Editorial Assistant: *Heather L. Graeve*
Production Editor: *Penelope Sky*
Manuscript Editor: *Betty Duncan*
Permissions Editor: *Karen Wootten*
Interior and Cover Design: *Leesa Berman*
Art Coordinator: *Lisa Torri*
Interior Illustration: *John Foster*
Typesetting: *Kachina Typesetting, Inc.*
Printing and Binding: *Malloy Lithographing, Inc.*

THIS BOOK IS PRINTED ON ACID-FREE RECYCLED PAPER

Preface

This is the third revision of a book originally published in 1974. It is written for undergraduate and graduate students, and for practitioners who are concerned with needs assessment, systematic development, and thoughtful evaluation of training programs in a variety of organizational settings. The book provides a framework for examining current efforts and establishing new, viable training programs in education, business, and government environments. It is my goal to capture the excitement of the many research and systems issues that abound, both when training is introduced and considered and when new trainees enter the world of the work organization through training programs.

In the preface to the first edition I noted that there was little to be gained by putting an enormous amount of effort into the development of instructional programs unless there were data to tell the implementers where to revise and where to proceed. Although I retain this viewpoint, I am more confident now that there are models that provide both information and input into program design, thereby increasing the likelihood that they will achieve intended goals. In this new edition my goal is to contribute information and ideas to participants in this process who wish to understand the dynamics involved when an organization says "training is the answer."

Organization

Part One emphasizes the needs assessment and learning processes that are the foundation of training programs. The first chapter was rewritten to address the training issues facing society as we approach the year 2000, such as the changing demographics of the working population, the influence of the shift from manufacturing to service markets, the effects of increasing technology in the workplace, and the dynamics of a multicultural and international environment. Chapter 2 anticipates the book's main topics, presenting a training systems model that includes all the interacting components of needs assessment, design, development, and evaluation of training programs. Chapter 3 describes the needs assessment process, including organizational, task, and person analyses that in turn provide inputs for the consideration and design of training programs. Because many techniques of needs assessment are new, including analysis of how training as a system fits into an organization, this chapter has been almost entirely rewritten for this edition. A section on requirements analysis describes the decisions that need to be considered before the actual needs assessment begins. Chapter 4 considers the learning environment, including material related to the preconditions of learning, significant issues in learning and instruction, the variables that support transfer, and factors that determine a quality training environment. Recent material on cognition and instructional theory as it relates to training is included, so that for the first time the relevance to training issues of such concepts as automaticity, advanced organizers, and novices versus expert learners is explored.

Part Two focuses on the evaluations process. Evaluation is the systematic collection of descriptive and judgmental information in order to make effective training decisions about the selection, adoption, value, and modification of various teaching activities. Instructional programs have numerous goals ranging from trainee progress to organizational improvement. Evaluation is an information-gathering technique that cannot result in decisions that categorize programs as good or bad. Rather, evaluation should capture the dynamics of the training program. Chapter 5 discusses the establishment of criteria to measure the multiple objectives of many training programs. Chapter 6 presents the various evaluation models that provide information for intelligent revisions of training programs. Both of these chapters contain recent material on different models of the evaluation process, including utility, content validity, and individual difference models.

Part Three describes training approaches. Chapter 7 includes updated discussion of programmed instruction, audiovisual techniques, machine simulators, behavior modification, and on-the-job training. A number of techniques, such as computer-assisted instruction, have developed significantly because of advances in technology. New topics include embedded training, team training, and videodisc technology. Chapter 8 covers managerial and interpersonal skills, including behavioral role modeling, McClelland's achievement motivation training, Fiedler's Leader Match, and rater training. This material has also been updated to reflect recent changes in the literature. Chapters 7 and 8 both elaborate on the needs assessment, evaluation, and learning materials presented earlier in the book. Special approaches to training issues are discussed in Chapter 9. It emphasizes topics relating training to larger systems issues, and there are new discussions of training programs in relation to the problems of the hard-core unemployed and persons seeking second careers or trying to avoid obsolescence; discrimination and fair employment practices are also considered. There are new sections on the potential training implications of the American Disabilities Act, on international training issues, and on the difficult problem of training managers who will lead organizations in a very complex society.

Acknowledgments

This volume reflects the efforts of many generous people. I am indebted to all the authors and researchers who took time from their busy schedules to graciously share their articles, data, ideas, and manuscripts. Those of you who are fortunate enough to be involved in the Society for Industrial and Organizational Psychology know what I mean when I say that our members' generosity in sharing ideas and helping each other is overwhelming. In this regard I am indebted to the work of many colleagues and friends, including John Campbell, Wayne Cascio, Bill Howell, Jim Outtz, Erich Prien, Shelly Zedeck, and others too numerous to mention. I am especially indebted to the faculty and graduate students of the industrial-organizational psychology group at Maryland. The excitement of hall talk and classroom conversations has contributed to the vitality of this book. I must especially acknowledge the contributions of Eric Braverman and Harold Goldstein, who are responsible for a significant portion of the new needs assessment model in Chapter 3 (see Goldstein, Braverman, & Goldstein, 1991). I consider myself lucky to be influenced by my good friend and colleague Benjamin Schneider. His specific contributions to this book are important, but his close friendship and way of thinking about issues is critical for my own career development. I must especially thank Paul Thayer for being a sounding board for the past twenty years; he has been continually insightful about training issues. I also express appreciation to Scott Tannenbaum, one of the very thoughtful members of the new generation of writers and researchers contributing to knowledge about training systems. His annual review chapter with Gary Yukl convinced me it was time to write the third edition and his comments on this manuscript were invaluable. I express my affection for Bob Dorfman and Brit Kirwan, respectively Provost and President of the University of Maryland at College Park. They believe that administrators should continue to be active scholars, and my efforts to complete this manuscript were thus strongly supported.

I am indebted to my editor, Marianne Taflinger, for providing support while pushing the project ahead. I am also very pleased to have my book in the new Cypress Book Series, edited by my friend and colleague Frank Landy.

This book is most of all the result of a loving and caring environment designed by my wife, Micki, who literally gave up months of family time so that I could complete this revision. My daughter and son, Beth and Harold, were in grade school when the first edition was published and now they have their own professional careers, Beth as a landscape architect and Harold as an organizational psychologist. They understand what support is, and they specialize in love.

Irwin L. Goldstein

Contents

CHAPTER 2
A Systematic Approach to Training 19

CHAPTER 3
The Needs Assessment Phase 29

Needs Assessment and Learning Environment

1
PART

Introduction

1

CHAPTER

Throughout our lives learning experiences are a potent source of stimulation. This text emphasizes the systematic modes of instruction designed to produce environments that shape behavior to satisfy stated objectives. From this point of view, *training* is defined as the systematic acquisition of skills, rules, concepts, or attitudes that result in improved performance in another environment. Therefore, training programs are planned to produce, for example, a more considerate supervisor, a more competent technician in the workplace, or a dental student who can repair cavities in an office. In some cases, such as on-the-job training, the instructional environment is almost identical to the actual job environment. In other instances, such as a classroom lecture on electronics theory for technicians, the learning environment is far removed from the job situation. However, in both circumstances effective training stems from a learning atmosphere systematically designed to produce changes in the working environment.

As stated in the preface, the purpose of this book is to present the interacting components of training systems, including materials related to the ways in which training needs are assessed and the training effort is evaluated. Information is also presented about different types of training programs and the issues involving needs assessment and evaluation of these programs. In addition, issues are explored that intersect between training and societal concerns, such as training and the hard-core unemployed, training and fair employment practices, or training and the aging worker. In this chapter background information is present about the scope of training in our society, focusing on the status of the training enterprise.

SCOPE OF THE INSTRUCTIONAL PROCESS

Training programs are big business in terms of both the amount of effort expended and the money spent. For example, consider the following illustrations gleaned from a variety of time periods and instructional approaches:

1. An analysis of firms that have more than 100 people indicates that education and training has become a booming business (Gordon, 1988). Industrial corporations spend about $40 billion a year on programs that include training in basic skills such as reading and on programs for the development of managers and executives.

2. In a survey of Fortune 500 firms, 91 percent of the firms provided training for middle management, 75 percent for sales training, 56 percent for secretarial training, 51 percent for executive development, and 44 percent for technical training (Ralphs & Stephen, 1986).

3. The Federal Aviation Agency decided that flight simulators had become so sophisticated that business jet pilots could use the simulator to meet many of their training requirements, thereby not requiring actual flying time in the plane (Caro, 1984).

4. Corporations are being forced to participate in some training activities because many people entering the work force lack basic skills. Thus, Polaroid Corporation spent $700,000 to provide basic courses in English and mathematics for 1000 employees (Gorman, 1988). Domino's Pizza, with a grant from the U.S. Department of Labor, is teaching basic reading and mathematics needed for dough making while the trainee is learning to make pizza dough. One estimate is that half of the Fortune 500 firms are becoming "educators of the last resort" (*Time,* 1988, p. 56).

However, my favorite example stems from the time when I was first becoming interested in training systems. Humorist Art Buchwald discusses a continuing educational plan developed by Irwin Feifer (reprinted in the *Training and Development Journal,* Feifer, 1970, p. 43):

> Mass transportation is definitely one of the major problems of the next decade. The ideal solution would be faster, cleaner and safer transportation for everyone. But since this is impossible, other solutions must be found to make commuting worthwhile. Irwin Feifer, who specializes in manpower problems, has come up with an idea which certainly deserves consideration. Mr. Feifer says that as a commuter of the Long Island Railroad, he has been able to give hours of time to studying the transportation nightmare of the '70s. Each month a true-or-false test would be given by the conductor. Those who received 90 or over would be granted a $5.50 reduction on their commuter ticket for the following months. Those scoring 80 or above would get a $3.25 reduction and those who passed with a 65 would not be given a money reduction, but would be assured a seat on the train for the next four weeks. The Feifer Plan is not necessarily aimed just at people who take railroads (a subway educational plan where people can study while being delayed in tunnels is now being worked out), but could also be applied to people driving

> to work in the morning. Those signing up for credits would listen to lectures on the radio in the morning and evening rush hours, and do their book studying at traffic bottlenecks and red lights.
>
> The driver-students would hand in their tests and toll collectors would grade them as they make change. Most people would not mind traffic delays as it would give them more time to get their homework done.
>
> The Feifer Plan would provide for graduation exercises every six months. In the case of the railroads, the ceremonies would be held at the railroad stations with the Secretary of Transportation handing out the diplomas.
>
> Automobile college graduates would receive their diplomas from the license bureau, and each license plate would indicate how many degrees the driver possessed.
>
> The plan, if put into effect, would make Americans the most educated people in the world. It would also turn train delays and traffic jams into a profit. But more important, with everyone going to school, the generation gap could become a thing of the past.[1]

In a speech several years ago, I presented the Buchwald editorial as an introduction to material on training systems. Much to my surprise, a participant noted that such a program was already in existence. At that time Adelphi University offered a program called "Classroom-on-Wheels," which takes place in special commuter cars equipped with frosted windows, microphones, and blackboards. During a five-year period, the program awarded both BBA and MBA degrees. This example is an illustration of the ingenuity that is possible in the design of instructional systems. Given the difficulties facing corporations involving unskilled youth entering the workplace, this type of creativity may be increasingly needed.

Examining the scope of activities for professionals involved in training and development activities provides further insights into the ever-increasing emphasis on instructional systems. The extent of growth in this area is evidenced by the number of people belonging to only one of the professional societies involved in these activities. The American Society for Training and Development had 15 members in 1943, 5000 members in 1967, 9500 members in 1972, 20,000 members in 1980, and over 29,000 members in 1991. This does not include the many people involved in training activities who may be members of other societies such as the Society for Industrial and Organizational Psychology, the American Psychological Association, the American Psychological Society, the American Educational Research Association, the American Academy of Management, or the Society for Human Resource Management. Pinto and Walker (1978) surveyed American Society for Training and Development members to determine which activities were a significant part of their work. Based on almost 3000 responses, these authors performed a factor analysis, a technique used to determine the common dimensions among the job activities. Table 1.1 presents the activities identi-

[1]From Buchwald, A. *Training on the Train.* Copyright 1970 by the Washington Post Company. Reprinted by permission.

Table 1.1 Training and development practitioner roles

a. Needs Analysis and Diagnosis
Construct questionnaires and conduct interviews for needs analysis, evaluate feedback, etc.

b. Determine Appropriate Training Approach
Evaluate the alternatives of "ready-made" courses or materials, use of programmed instruction, videotape, computer managed and other structured techniques versus a more process-oriented organization development/team-building approach.

c. Program Design and Development
Design program content and structure, apply learning theory, establish objectives, evaluate and select instructional methods.

d. Develop Material Resources (Make)
Prepare scripts, slides, manuals, artwork, copy, programmed learning, and other instructional materials.

e. Manage Internal Resources (Borrow)
Obtain and evaluate internal instructors/program resource persons, train others how to train, supervise their work.

f. Manager External Resources (Buy)
Hire, supervise, and evaluate external instructors/program resource persons; obtain and evaluate outside consultants and vendors.

g. Individual Development Planning and Counseling
Counsel with individuals regarding career development needs and plans; arrange for and maintain records of participation in programs, administer tuition reimbursement, maintain training resource library, keep abreast of EEO.

h. Job/Performance-Related Training
Assist managers and others in on-the-job training and development; analyze job skill and knowledge requirements, determine performance problems.

i. Conduct Classroom Training
Conduct programs, operate audio-visual equipment, lecture, lead discussion, revise materials based on feedback, arrange program logistics.

j. Group and Organization Development
Apply techniques such as team-building, intergroup meetings, behavior modeling, role-playing simulation, laboratory education, discussions, cases, issues.

k. Training Research
Present and interpret statistics and data relating to training; communicate through reports, proposals, speeches, and articles; design data collection.

l. Manage Working Relationships with Managers and Clients
Establish and maintain good relations with managers as clients, counsel with them and explain recommendations for training and development.

m. Manage the Training and Development Function
Prepare budgets, organize, staff, make formal presentations of plans, maintain information on costs, supervise the work of others, project future needs, etc.

n. Professional Self Development
Attend seminars/conferences, and keep abreast of training and development concepts, theories, and techniques; keep abreast of activities in other organizations.

From "What Do Training and Development Professionals Really Do?" by P. R. Pinto and J. W. Walker. In *Training and Development Journal,* July 1978, *28,* pp. 58–64. Copyright 1978 by the American Society for Training and Development, Inc. Reprinted by permission.

fied in the survey. The authors note that, to meet needs for specific learning and behavior changes, program design and development were the most significant parts of the training practitioners' work.

An important area of concern for training developers is ethical consideration. A survey by Clement, Pinto, and Walker in 1979 produced a number of examples of unethical behavior including lack of honesty about the expected outcomes of the results (mainly involving overselling the outcomes) violations of confidentiality concerning performance in training, and even abuses in the treatment of trainees. In an update on these issues, Lowman (1991) quotes from a personal communication from London about ethical concerns of students attending a training-and-development course. They are as follows:

- *Voluntary consent*: Trainers should not implicitly coerce unwilling or skeptical participants into self-revealing or physical activities.
- *Discrimination*: Age, sex, race, or handicaps should not be used as barriers to determine who receives training.
- *Cost effectiveness*: Training activities should be based on demonstrated utility, should show a demonstrated benefit vis-à-vis costs and should not be undertaken simply to spend a training budget.
- *Accurate portrayal*: Claims for the benefits of training need to be accurate, training should be consistent across time and trainers; training materials should be appropriately depicted.
- *Competency in training*: Teaching methods that do not work, such as talking down to audiences, should be avoided.
- *Values*: Trainers should believe in the value of what they teach (pp. 208–209).

A good way of summarizing this material is to note that training is a people-to-people activity. Thus, honesty and respect for the individual will go a long way.

In another analysis of survey results, data are reported about the most frequent reasons for sending managers to training programs (Saari, Johnson, McLaughlin, & Zimmerle, 1988). These data are based on a very comprehensive survey of over 600 U.S. companies, each having more than 1000 employees. As described in Table 1.2, the primary reasons for sending managers to management education and training programs are to broaden the individual and to provide knowledge and skills such as job-specific knowledge and state of the art knowledge. Interestingly, the least indicated reason is to provide training as a reward to managers. Regarding the use of the different types of training settings, Saari et al. report that 90 percent of the over 600 companies responding used external short-course programs, 75 percent used company-specific programs, 31 percent used university residential programs, and 25 percent used executive MBA programs. Also, there is an indication that the larger the company in terms of number of employees, the more likely they were to use formal management training and education programs.

Another set of surveys based on activities for organizations that have more than 100 employees provides information about the most commonly used training methods in their organizations (Gordon, 1988). These results

Table 1.2 Reasons indicated as primary for sending managers to programs

	Program Type			
Reason	*University Residential (%)*	*Executive MBA (%)*	*External Short-Course (%)*	*Company-Specific (%)*
Broaden the individual, gain new perspective	78	74	68	69
Opportunity to interact with other managers	40	35	31	49
Obtain job-specific knowledge/skills	54	60	88	78
Obtain state-of-the-art knowledge/skills	55	56	77	59
Reward to the manager	6	8	4	2
Prepare individual for next job	27	27	17	21
Obtain general management education	48	55	35	51
Cost-effective relative to other programs	9	8	23	57
Obtain quality instruction	53	45	45	62
Understand our company's approach to management	—	—	—	82

From "A Survey of Management Training and Education Practices in Companies" by L. M. Saari, T. R. Johnson, S. D. McLaughlin, D. M. Zimmerele. In *Personal Psychology*, 1988, *41*, pp. 731–743. Copyright © 1988 by Personnel Psychology, Inc. Reprinted by permission.

(Table 1.3) show that the most popular approach to training is the use of videotapes, but other techniques including lectures and role playing are frequently used. The large percentage indicating one-on-one instruction emphasizes the amount of on-the-job instruction that occurs. These techniques are discussed in later chapters of this text. Underlying these data is the fact that professional development and evaluation of training programs is a fairly recent phenomenon and, to some extent, it is still an uphill effort.

THE TRAINING STRUGGLE

The increased emphasis on professional activities presented in Table 1.1 has resulted in the development of many professionals who are capable of designing programs that meet instructional objectives based on clearly specified needs. The types of instructional goals that organizations hope training programs can achieve vary widely but could include producing quality goods in a shorter time period, reducing accidents with a corresponding decrease in insurance premiums, implementing a management system that is more ser-

Table 1.3 Instructional Methods*

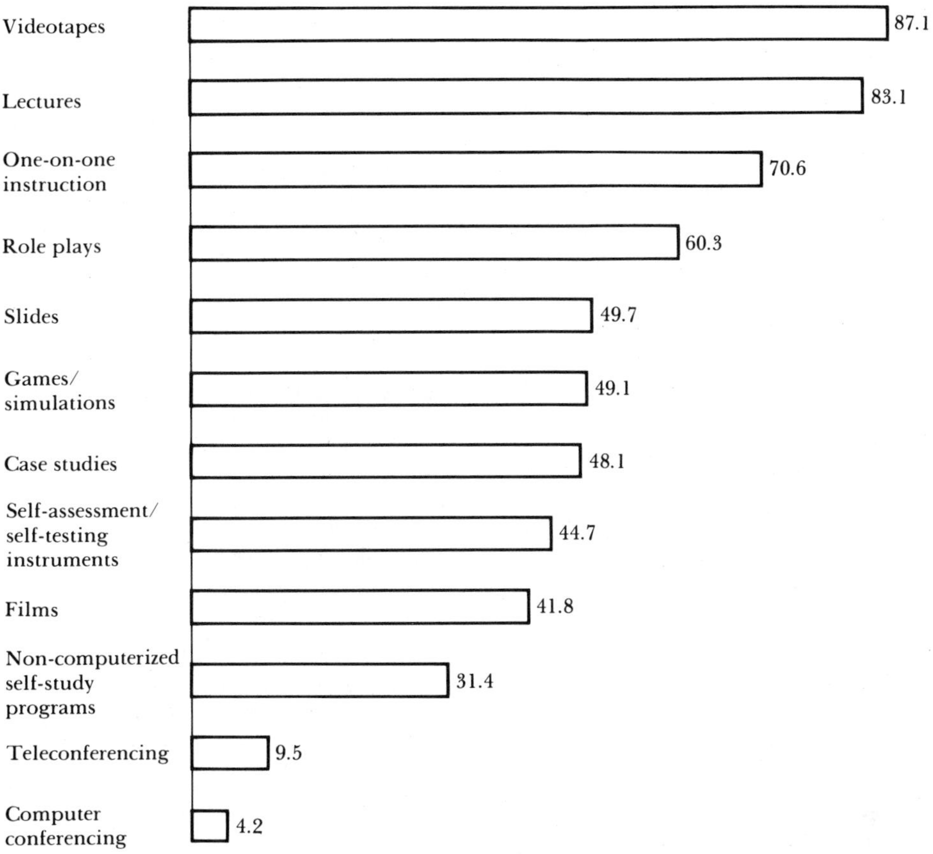

*Percent using these methods for employee training

From "Who is Being Trained To Do What?" by J. Gordon. Reprinted with permission from the Oct. 1988 issue of *TRAINING* Magazine. Copyright 1988. Lakewood Publications Inc., Minneapolis, MN (612) 333-0471. All rights reserved.

vice-oriented toward its customers, and increasing a health-oriented approach to life styles as a way of reducing absenteeism due to illness and stress. The potential number of goals is unlimited. Although training is not a panacea for all societal ills, well-conceived training programs have achieved beneficial results. There certainly appears to be an increasing number of thoughtfully developed programs. This text will present many examples of training programs that work. However, pretending that all programs are either based on appropriate needs assessment or that these programs are even examined to determine the degree to which they achieve their objectives would be unrealistic. Unfortunately, most organizations do not collect the information to determine the utility of their own instructional programs. Their techniques

Table 1.4 How often are the following evaluation methods used in your company?

Almost Always 5	4	3	2	*Almost Never* 1

	5 Only	*4 and 5*
A. Course evaluation form filled out by learner at end of course	73%	86%
B. Course evaluation form filled out by instructor at end of course	12%	23%
C. Evaluation by boss, peers, or subordinate	8%	23%
D. Follow-up evaluation by participants	7%	16%
E. Follow-up questionnaire by participants	5%	14%
F. Use of pre- or post-tests	6%	15%
G. Use of business data records	5%	12%

From "HRD in the Fortune 500" by L. T. Ralphs and E. Stephan, 1986. Reprinted from the *Training and Development Journal*, Copyright 1986 the American Society for Training and Development. Reprinted with permission. All rights reserved.

remain unevaluated, except for the high esteem with which they may be regarded by training personnel. For example, the survey by Ralphs and Stephan (1986) of the Fortune 500 firms provides information about evaluation methods, which are presented in Table 1.4. These results indicate that most evaluations (86 percent) consist of trainee reactions that are written at the end of the course. Relatively few efforts are made to collect information concerning performance changes by means of follow-up on the job, which is when both the trainee and the organization could discover whether the programs are achieving the desired results and when the evaluation could provide clues to the modifications necessary to enable the program to work. Saari et al.'s (1988) survey of over 600 firms found similar results. For example, these companies reported that executive MBA programs were the most expensive management-training approach (averaging about $14,000 for each participant). Yet, 42 percent of the companies reported that they did not conduct any evaluations of their effectiveness. Similarly, only 27 percent of the companies surveyed had a formal procedure designed to conduct needs assessments in order to determine the specific training and education needs of their managers.

Given recent advances in the development of needs assessment and evaluation, which will be emphasized in this text, those survey data are a particularly sad commentary. However, many more outstanding efforts in the training area appeared during the last decade than at any time before. One goal in writing this revision was to say it was time to end the lament about the lack of evaluation and needs assessment, and not include such statements in the text. Perhaps that will be possible in the next revision.

As the next section indicates, this is a particularly critical time. The declining productivity of work organizations is a serious problem for U.S.

Table 1.5 Comparison of job and labor market trends in the 1990s

	Job-Market Needs	*Labor-Market Description*
Industry	Service-oriented	Manufacturing-oriented
Employment	24 million additional jobs—10 million of them don't exist yet	16 million additional workers
Demographics	Younger, skilled, literate	Diverse, older, unskilled, semi-literate
Education	Greater education required	Fewer high-school and college graduates
Job Level	More advanced job opportunities available	Fewer workforce entrants to fill advanced jobs
Job Type	Cognitive and complex jobs	Procedural and predictable jobs
Management	More skilled leaders	More traditional leaders

From "The Challenge of Training in the Nineties" by S. L. Cohen. In *Training and Development,* July, 1991, *45,* pp. 29–35. Copyright © 1991 by the American Society for Training and Development. Reprinted by permission.

organizations, especially as international competition becomes even more intense. The work force is becoming even more diverse in terms of its cultural values because of the entry of more women, minorities, and older persons. In addition, greater variation exists in the educational skills of entry-level workers. Training systems are viewed by both organizations and individuals as a positive step in providing skills and opportunities. For that to occur, training systems must be more carefully designed and more carefully evaluated to ensure that they are meeting the expectations of both the organizations and the individual trainees. It is hoped that this text will also serve as a source for information and techniques necessary to design and evaluate training programs.

THE FUTURE WORKPLACE

Changes that have implications for the use of training systems in the future workplace are described in this section. In the next section, training implications are discussed. In describing both the future workplace and the training implications, articles written by Goldstein and Gilliam (1990) and Goldstein and Goldstein (1990) provide many of the thoughts and ideas. Table 1.5 summarizes many of these ideas.

Changes in Demographics of Entry-Level Persons in the Workforce

Based on the past trends of labor force activity, projecting, with relative accuracy, future trends in labor force participation is possible. Individuals entering the labor force in the year 2000 have already been born, and projections indicate that the work force will have an impact on human resource management in a way never experienced before (Cascio & Zammuto, 1987). In summary, the analyses indicate the following changes will occur (Cascio & Zammuto, 1987; Fullerton, 1985; Offerman & Gowing, 1990):

1. The work force will grow more slowly in the upcoming decade because new entrants—that is, individuals primarily between the ages of sixteen and twenty-four—will decrease substantially. As a result the number of individuals comprising the entry pool will be smaller, and data indicate that many of these people will enter the work force with inadequate basic skills. These factors lead some commentators to state that the entry pool of selectees for industry will be dismal at best (Cascio & Zammuto, 1987).

2. The proportion of the entry-level work force that is white will decline, and the proportion of minority populations will increase significantly.

3. The composition of the work force will also change to include more older workers and more women. Data indicate that individuals between the ages of forty-five and sixty-four years old will increase by at least 25 percent in the coming decades. There are also expectations that women will continue to enter the work force in increasing numbers. However, even with increases in the number of older workers and women, the decline in the entry-level work force will still result in slower overall growth of the work force.

Technology and the World of Work

There is a clear trend toward more highly technologically, sophisticated systems. Klein and Hall (1988) believe that technological developments such as programmable automation will have a dramatic influence on the manufacturing sector of the economy. This includes the use of reprogrammable robots—multifunctional machines that can manipulate materials, parts, tools—and various forms of computer-assisted design and computer-assisted manufacturing. Experts agree that programmable automation will have its greatest impact on semiskilled and unskilled jobs where job loss is likely to be significant. On the other hand, the increases in technology require a highly trained work force to design and operate the systems. However, as discussed in the next section, demographics predict that relatively fewer such people will enter the work force in the years 2000 and beyond.

Shifts from Manufacturing to Service Jobs

There is a shift in our economy from a manufacturing to a service orientation. In the period from 1984–1995, it is expected that nearly nine out of ten new jobs will be in the service-producing industries (Personick, 1985). These jobs are characterized by an increase in the importance of people work, that is, working with customers and clients rather than interacting primarily with co-workers and things (Klein & Hall, 1988). Entry-level service-oriented jobs are also characterized by lower pay levels than the manufacturing sector.

Displaced manufacturing sector workers have unfortunately discovered that they are expected to learn new interpersonal skills for service-oriented jobs, but the pay levels are below what they have previously earned. Interestingly, in some cases advances in technology are also having an impact on service-oriented jobs (for example, the use of automated banking services). In those cases the impact of increased technology is also having a major impact on service jobs.

Organizations and Global Markets

Finally, a future look at jobs and organizations makes increasingly fluid world market arrangements appear quite likely. Many novel strategies are being explored. For example, Klein and Hall (1988) note that some companies are exploring pilot projects involving data-entry jobs in foreign countries because the advantages of low wages and surplus workers outweigh the disadvantages of long-distance electronic data transmission. Most consumers are now aware that it is not unusual for manufacturers to produce products (for example, automobiles) that are partially manufactured in the United States and partially manufactured in a foreign country. Sometimes, these involve arrangements between liaison teams directing the overall efforts between different employees, in different organizations, and in different countries, all contributing to the production of a single final product.

IMPLICATIONS OF THE FUTURE WORKPLACE FOR TRAINING SYSTEMS

A number of important training implications stem from the preceding analyses of the changing workplace. These issues are covered only briefly in this section because they are topics addressed many times in other chapters.

The Problem of Unskilled Youth

The analyses of demographic information concerning people entering the work force compel the consideration of some harsh realities. First, fewer people will be available to enter the work force. Yet, the analyses indicate that the demand for workers will remain high, especially given the development of service-sector jobs. Second, the demographics indicate that many of the individuals who will be available for entry into the work force will be unskilled and undereducated youth. Significant numbers of these individuals will also be members of culturally diverse groups that society has not successfully integrated into the work force. Although many members of minority groups have overcome adversity and have successfully entered professional and technical careers, that so many of the hard-core unemployed are members of minority groups is a sad reflection on our society. In the future, however, society will desperately need their talent in the workplace, but the issues involving training programs are extremely complex. For example, many of these programs are successful to the degree to which the organization itself is willing to make a commitment rather than assuming all the necessary change must come from the entry-level trainee. In addition, organizations are facing difficult choices concerning the need to develop basic entry-level programs, such as literacy training, and/or to arrange partnerships with beleaguered and underfunded school systems. These concerns are discussed further in the final chapter of the text.

Changes in Technology

The kinds of concerns stemming from rapidly changing technologies involve a whole set of individual, organizational, and societal issues. All descriptions of future work organizations characterize them as requiring more complex cognitive skills. For example, executives at the new Mazda plant in Michigan describe their expectations of their workers.

> They want their new employees to be able to work in teams, to rotate through various jobs, to understand how their tasks fit into the entire process, to spot problems in production, to trouble shoot, articulate the problems to others, suggest improvements and write detail charts and memos that serve as a road map in the assembly of the car. (Vobejda, 1987, p. A14)

The implications for training system design are enormous. A report by a commission of the U.S. Department of Labor (1991) notes that a strong back and weak mind will not permit the country to compete in today's marketplace. The commission reports that it is not simply a matter of literacy skills but the need for thinking skills. Included in the required skills are the abilities to assess information, understand work systems, deal with new technologies as the workplace changes, and develop interpersonal skills. Of course, these changes are in addition to the three "Rs" of reading, writing, and arithmetic. The report also notes that unless students learn these skills by the time they leave high school, they face a bleak employment picture. The startling advances in technology and resulting competition make this a necessity.

Paradoxically, the increases in technology and machine responsibility increase the demands on the human being. As noted by Howell and Cooke (1989), increasingly "smart" machines thereby also increase the cognitive complexity for the human being. Instead of simple procedural and predictable tasks, the human becomes responsible for inferences, diagnoses, judgment, and decision making, often under severe time pressure. The dire consequences of failing to provide adequate training were demonstrated in the nuclear power plant accident at Three Mile Island. A major finding of that investigation was that key maintenance personnel did not have adequate training for their jobs (United States President's Commission, 1979). Adding to the complexity of these issues is the rapid technical obsolescence of individuals who previously had very advanced training. Thus, estimates are that an engineer's education has a half-life of five years, meaning that half of what is learned in school is obsolete five years after graduation. Little is known about training and retraining issues. Because individuals are also likely to respond to many job changes, as a result of technology shifts, understanding types of abilities and how transfer of learning across jobs can occur will be important.

Concern for Maximizing Individual Worker Potential

One implication of the decreasing size of the work force is that it will become increasingly necessary to maximize the potential of each individual worker. This means that the future of work organizations will become more dependent on their ability to effectively use all members of society, often by providing training. Despite evidence that indicates the importance of work in the lives of most individuals, a number of difficult realities has existed within the world of work. Many researchers conclude that a contributing factor, which has resulted in lost opportunities for qualified individuals, is the cycle of discrimination plaguing minorities, women, and older workers (Cross, 1986; Rhodes, 1983). As a result of these lost opportunities, increased litigation has focused on organizational decisions involving training opportunities and their lack of availability to members of minority groups, women, older workers, and, more recently, handicapped workers. Training techniques that have not been validated and that are discriminatory in promotional and job opportunities are being struck down by the courts. This is especially the case when completing these training opportunities is required for advancement. Again, this is consistent with individuals viewing training as instrumental in helping them achieve advanced opportunities and the concern they feel when the programs are not made available.

Some believe that as organizations have a greater need for workers, these difficulties will diminish; others are not as confident. In a recent analysis, Reich (1991) notes that many U.S. firms are turning to immigration as a way of gaining skilled workers and that organizations are spending very little of their training budget for helping entry-level workers. These are very complex issues, which will be discussed further in the text. From any perspective, however, these topics clearly have important implications for future training systems.

Managerial Training Implications of a Competitive Environment

It almost seems unnecessary (but I cannot resist!) to suggest that the training implications of all the preceding issues are enormous, especially for training managers who will be working with people. Managers will need to provide on-the-job training to integrate unskilled youth into the work force, while working with job incumbents and other managers who may not have previously been a traditional part of the work force. Supervisors will need to perform these activities at a time when jobs have become increasingly complex and national and international competition more intense. In addition, the increase in service-sector jobs will require managers to work more with people rather than with objects and things from the assembly line. All this will make training in areas such as interpersonal skills even more important in the future workplace. A related impact for training is that there is an increasing emphasis on quality for both service-oriented jobs and manufacturing-oriented jobs. This has important training implications because more employees will need training in quality techniques and processes. However, for the manager the training implications for being able to manage such emphases are enormous. Managers will be expected to understand and manage the processes for achieving quality as well as learning to manage team efforts, which are likely to be emphasized as a way of achieving success. Added to this is the fact that organizations are operating in a more international environment. In discussing the enormous training implications, Ronen notes that the manager given an assignment in a foreign country must possess the "patience of a diplomat, the zeal of a missionary, and the linguistic skill of a U.N. interpreter" (1989, p. 418). Ronen is correct, but the issue is just as complicated for managers working in their own countries because the workplace will need to incorporate individuals who come from environments with very diverse cultures and values. These issues are discussed further in this text.

Accountability

The amount of emphasis concerning evaluation methodology, including information about criterion development, evaluation designs, values and ethics, and problems of performance evaluations in organizations, has exploded. Many organizations are recognizing the important needs that have increased the use of training systems, and they are becoming increasingly concerned about evaluation of training programs as a way of determining whether their goals are being met. With the increased emphasis on quality, training programs are likely to be even more carefully scrutinized to determine the degree to which they are achieving such goals as increased quality service, quality products, or both. The tremendous costs of instructional programs have also resulted in questions about their effectiveness. In many cases during the past several decades, a "fads" approach to instructional design was dominant. This approach emphasized the use of the newest training technique. Indeed, I still regularly receive calls inquiring about the newest training techniques. Campbell (1971) discerns the following pattern to the fads approach:

1. A new technique appears with a group of followers who announce its success.
2. Another group develops modifications of the technique.
3. A few empirical studies appear supporting the technique.
4. There is a backlash. Critics question the usefulness of the new technique but rarely produce any data.
5. The technique survives until a new technique appears. Then, the whole procedure is repeated.

When there are no empirical data to evaluate techniques, the cycle of fads continues. Evaluation must be sold as a tool to provide information rather than as a technique to determine passing and failing. A systematic examination of the training literature indicates the occurrence of many more efforts at assessing the impact of training and of some emphasis on determining which techniques might be best for which behaviors in which situations. However, there is still a need to remember that this is a serious problem. The emphasis on accountability will make it more likely that organizations will correctly insist on understanding the impact of the programs they sponsor.

TRAINING AS A SUBSYSTEM

A text that only considers the technical aspects of needs assessment and evaluation design overlooks most of the dynamics concerning training systems. Training programs exist within organizations. It is unrealistic to think of training systems as if they were in a vacuum. Many investigators have been disappointed with the results of their training programs because they assumed that success would always follow the implementation of a well-conceived program. In some instances supervisors do not permit the employee to use the skills that were acquired in the training program. In other cases training is not the answer. For example, Sheridan (1975) describes, with pointed clarity, the AT&T attempt to comply with a government order to place 19 percent of female employees in outside craft jobs. Despite rigorous recruiting and training efforts, the women they did recruit dropped from training at an average rate of 50 percent. The individuals who completed training usually did not last a full year. Their analysis determined that physical differences between men and women made the job extremely difficult for women to perform. Some of the most serious problems concerned the use of a ladder, which is both long and heavy. Utilizing basic principles of human factors, the job was redesigned so that it could be performed by both men and women. Interestingly enough, the job redesign resulted in a reduction of back injuries for both men and women.

In other instances training analysts have thoughtfully considered the organizational environment to decide what type of program might work. In one of my favorite examples, Thayer and McGehee (1977) describe an instance where the motivation to attend a formal training program was so low that any such program was doomed to failure. Instead of developing such a program, they developed a very difficult open-book test, which was on the topic of the terms of the union contract. As an incentive to do well on the test, they offered a steak dinner for the supervisor who submitted the most correct answers. McGehee encouraged plant managers to wager with each other as to whose supervisor would do best on the test. As a result, managers began to encourage their supervisors to organize group study sessions. The test designer was besieged by phone calls for the entire week following distribution of the very difficult exam; callers argued that there were two or more correct answers to almost every question. By the end of the week, all exams were in and were perfect or near-perfect. Faced with such performance, the company president decided to host a steak dinner for all supervisors and their managers. Interestingly, the exam was the most popular topic during the dinner. Certainly, most "training programs" would have been delighted about the degree of involvement for this "nontraining" approach.

The point is that organizations are very complex systems and training programs are but one subsystem. Thus, changes in the selection system, which can result in people with higher or lower job-relevant skills and abilities, will have a dramatic effect on the level of training required. Changes in jobs as new technologies develop can have similar effects. More effective training programs can also affect all other systems in the work organization. The dynamics of training systems must include the realization that one of the first places to which many new employees are sent is a training program. Similarly, when individuals change positions as a result of a career change or promotion, many enter a training program. It is as important to understand the effects of training experiences as part of the socialization process in entering organizations as it is to evaluate specific training outcomes. The purpose of this text is to provide some understanding of the dynamics of training systems as well as information related to systematic development and evaluation of training programs.

The next chapter presents an instructional model that outlines the various factors to be considered in the design of systematic programs. The description of these interacting components should clearly indicate that no easy technique or gadget can be used in the development of well-conceived programs. Instructional materials will have a profound effect on everyone's life. A great deal of knowledge is presently available and should be used in the development of new programs. A wonderful side benefit is that such efforts can contribute even more information to our existing state of knowledge.

A Systematic Approach to Training

2

CHAPTER

INSTRUCTIONAL TECHNOLOGY

Whereas the term *technology* commonly refers to the development of hardware, *instructional technology* refers to the systematic development of programs in training and education. The systems approach to instruction emphasizes the specification of instructional objectives, precisely controlled learning experiences to achieve these objectives, criteria for performance, and evaluative information. Other characteristics of instructional technology include the following:

1. The systems approach uses feedback to continually modify instructional processes. From this perspective, training programs are never finished products; they are continually adaptive to information that indicates whether the program is meeting its stated objectives.
2. The instructional-systems approach recognizes the complex interaction among the components of the system. For example, one particular medium, like television, might be effective in achieving one set of objectives, whereas another medium might be preferable for a second set of objectives. Similar interactions could involve learning variables and specific individual characteristics of the learner. The systems view stresses a concern with the total system rather than with the objectives of any single component.
3. Systematic analysis provides a frame of reference for planning and remaining on target. In this framework a research approach is necessary to determine which programs are meeting their objectives.

4. The instructional-systems view is just one of a whole set of interacting systems. Training programs interact with and are directly affected by a larger system involving corporate policies (for example, selection and management philosophy). Similarly, educational programs are affected by the social values of society.

The various components of the instructional-systems approach are not new. Evaluation was a byword years before systems approaches were in vogue. Thus, the systems approach cannot be considered a magic wand for all the problems that were unsolved before its inception. If training designers were convinced that their programs worked, a systems approach would be unlikely to convince them that their programs required examination. However, the systems approach does provide a model that emphasizes important components and their interactions, and good evidence exists that this model is an important impetus for the establishment of objectives and evaluation procedures. As such, it is a useful tool that enables designers of instructional programs (as well as authors of books like this one) to examine the total training process.

Figure 2.1 presents one model of an instructional system. Most of the components of this model (for example, derive objectives and develop criteria) are considered important to any instructional system, although the degree of emphasis changes for different programs. The chapters that follow discuss material related to each of these model components. This chapter provides an overview of the complete system and the relationships among the components.

ASSESSMENT PHASE

Assessment of Instructional Need

This phase of the instructional process provides the information necessary to design the entire program. An examination of the model indicates that the training and evaluation phases are dependent on input from the development phase. Unfortunately, many programs are doomed to failure because trainers are more interested in conducting the training program than in assessing the needs of their organizations. Educators have been seduced by computer-assisted instruction and industrial trainers by videodisk technology before they have determined the needs of their organization and the way the techniques will meet those needs. The needs assessment phase consists of organizational analysis; task and knowledge, skill, and ability analysis; and person analysis.

Organizational analysis. Organizational analysis begins with an examination of the short- and long-term goals of the organization, as well as of the trends that are likely to affect these goals. This analysis often requires that upper-level management examine their own expectations concerning their training pro-

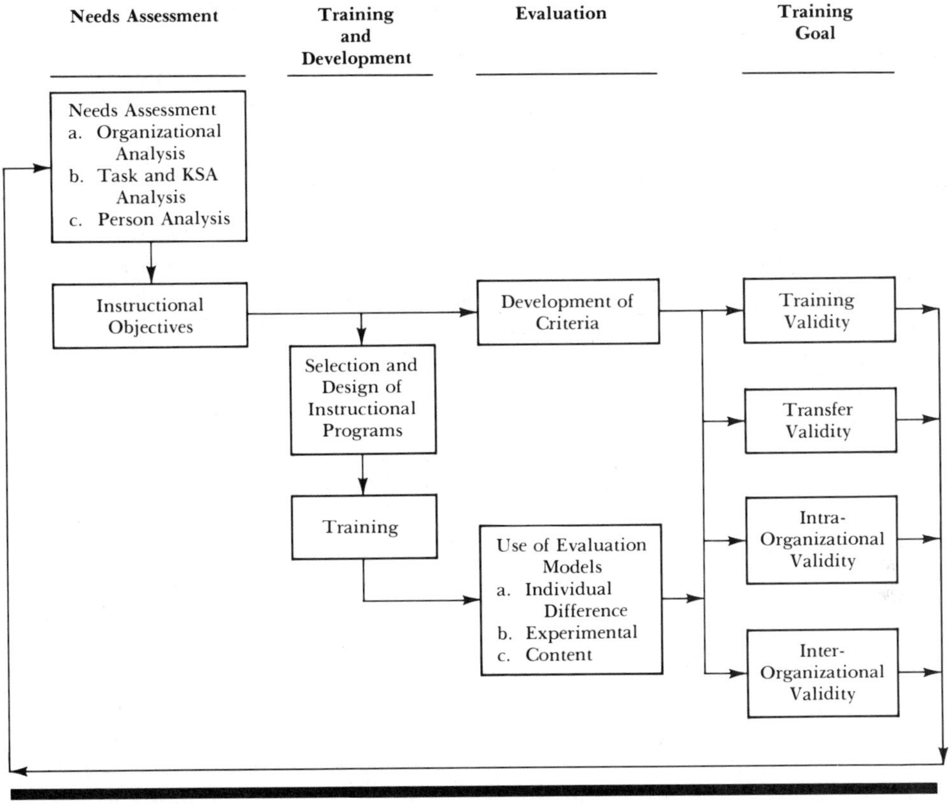

Figure 2.1 An instructional system. There are many other instructional-system models for military, business, and educational systems.

grams. Training designed to produce proficient sales personnel must be structured differently from programs to train sales personnel who are capable of moving up the corporate ladder to managerial positions. When organizational analysis is ignored, planning difficulties abound. Many corporations have spent considerable sums of money retraining personnel because the original training programs and decisions on performance capabilities were based on a system that soon became obsolete. In addition, it is becoming increasingly clear that organizations must ensure that there is a positive climate for trainees to transfer what they have learned in the training program onto the job. Thus, supervisors must ensure that trainees are supported and have the opportunity to use their learned behavior. Otherwise, what is learned in training can rapidly disappear. Another aspect of organizational analysis focuses on training programs and supporting systems—for example, selection, human-factors engineering, and work procedures. Particular problems might best be resolved by changes in selection standards or redesign of the work environment, not necessarily by training changes.

Task and knowledge, skill, and ability analysis. The second part of the needs assessment program is a careful analysis of the job to be performed by trainees upon completion of the training program. The analysis is usually divided into several separate procedures. The first step is a *job description* in behavioral terms; it is *not* a description of the worker. The narrative specifies the individual's duties and the special conditions under which the job is performed. The second procedure, most commonly referred to as *task specification,* further denotes all the tasks required on the job so that eventually the particular skills, knowledge, and attitudes required to perform the job will become clear. For example, a brief description of the job of an airline reservation clerk might indicate that the clerk makes and confirms reservations, determines seat availability, and so on. The task specification would consist of a complete list of tasks providing information about *what* the worker does and *how* the worker does it, to *whom* or *what* and *why*. Thus, a task for the airline reservation clerk might be "inspects availability board to determine seats available for passengers on standby status." Besides developing tasks that describe the job, choices are also made about the collection of information about those tasks. Thus, depending on how the analysis will be used, data might be collected about how important each task is or how frequently it is performed.

Organizational analysis and task analysis provide a picture of the task and the organizational setting in which the task occurs. One critical consideration is missing—that is, the knowledge, skills, and abilities (KSAs) required of the individual who will be in the training program. Task requirements must be translated into the KSAs necessary to perform those tasks. This is a difficult but necessary aspect based on inferences from the tasks. Essentially, we are asking for judgments concerning which KSAs make a difference in the performance of those tasks. For example, to perform the task concerning airline seats available, the airline reservation person might have to learn a number of KSAs. For example, the clerk might need to know the seating plan for the different types of aircraft used by that carrier. Another aspect of the KSA analysis is collecting information that is helpful in making training decisions. For example, it is possible to determine which KSAs are critical to job performance, which you should expect to have before being selected, and which should be learned in training as opposed to on the job.

Person analysis. This analysis is concerned with how well a specific employee is carrying out the tasks that comprise the job (McGehee & Thayer, 1961). As such, this component of the needs assessment is very much related to the determination of the KSAs necessary to perform the tasks. However, here the emphasis is not on determining which KSAs are necessary but on assessing how well the employee actually demonstrates the KSAs required by the job. To perform person analysis, deriving measures of job performance known as *criteria* becomes necessary. (This will be discussed further in the evaluation section.) A very important aspect of person analysis is to determine which necessary KSAs have already been learned by the prospective trainees. Too many training programs are exercises in boredom because they focus on skills already acquired. Determining the actual target population is also necessary. Some training programs are designed for individuals who are already in the system, whereas others are for trainees who are not yet part of the organization. In either case, it is senseless to design the training environment without acknowledging the characteristics of the groups to be trained.

Instructional Objectives

From information obtained in the assessment of instructional needs, a blueprint emerges that describes the objectives to be achieved by the trainee upon completion of the training program. These objectives provide the input for the design of the training program as well as for the measures of success (criteria) that will be used to judge the program's adequacy. One approach to the establishment of instructional objectives is known as *specification of the behavioral objectives* (Mager, 1984). The following is an example of one behavioral objective for a gas-station attendant.

By reading the gasoline pump, the employee can determine the cost of the product and provide correct change to the customer without resorting to paper and pencil for computations. Performance will be judged adequate if the employee

1. Always provides correct change for single items (for example, gas) up to a total of $30.
2. Always provides correct change when the customer pays cash up to $100.
3. Successfully completes twenty trials by providing the correct change.

Similar statements could be designed for instructional systems in a variety of settings. For example, the following behavioral objective is appropriate to the solution of a particular servicing aspect of a photocopier:

> Given a tool kit and a service manual, the technical representative will be able to adjust the registration (black line along paper edges) on a Xerox 2400 duplicator within 20 minutes according to the specifications stated in the manual. (Cicero, 1973, p. 15)

Objectives can also be designed for management jobs. For example, Mager notes the statement "to develop a critical understanding of the importance of effective management" (1984, p. 24) does not begin to express what the learner will be doing when he or she has mastery of the objective. However, the following does give a good idea of what is to be achieved:

> Given all available engineering data regarding a proposed product, be able to write a product profile. The profile must describe and define all of the commercial characteristics of the product appropriate to its introduction to the market, including descriptions of at least three major product uses. (Mager, 1984, p. 25)

Another way of looking at instructional objectives is to ask what, given a particular task and the specification of the KSAs necessary to perform the task, are the effective behaviors that will tell you that the task is being performed correctly? Asking what ineffective behaviors will tell you that the task is not being performed correctly is also possible. Using this approach, Latham and Wexley (1981) have identified various procedures for identifying effective and ineffective behaviors. Some examples of these behaviors for the job of a mechanic in a bowling alley are

> Cleans air conditioning system once a week, for example, vacuums filters.
> Informs others when a machine is not working properly.
> Can make most repairs within 5 minutes because major repairs are minimized through preventive maintenance checks. (pp. 215–218)

Well-written instructional objectives, which are based on tasks and KSAs, specify what the trainee can accomplish when successfully completing the instructional program. They also indicate the conditions under which the performance must be maintained and the standards by which the trainee will be evaluated (Mager, 1984). Thus, objectives communicate the goals of the program to both the learner and the training designer. From these goals the designers can determine the appropriate learning environment and the criteria for examining the achievement of the objectives. Chapter 3 examines the assessment phase, which includes organizational, task, and person analyses as well as the development of behavioral objectives.

TRAINING–DEVELOPMENT PHASE

The Training Environment

Once the tasks, KSAs, and objectives have been specified, the next step is to design the environment to achieve the objectives. This is a delicate process that requires a blend of learning principles and media selection, based on the tasks that the trainee is eventually expected to perform. In 1960 Gilbert described the temptations that often lead to a poor training environment. At that time, the remarks were most appropriate for a teaching machine. Today, they are probably more appropriate for videodisk instructional systems, but in any case they are even more relevant today.

> If you don't have a gadget called a teaching machine, don't get one. Don't buy one; don't borrow one; don't steal one. If you have such a gadget, get rid of it. Don't give it away, for someone else might use it. This is a most practical rule, based on empirical facts from considerable observation. If you begin with a device of any kind, you will try to develop the teaching program to fit that device. (p. 478)

It is important to consider the tasks that are performed and the KSAs necessary to perform those tasks and ask what type of training program will produce the best results. "The best available basis for the needed matching of media with objectives . . . is a rationale by which the kind of learning involved in each educational objective is stated in terms of the learning conditions required" (Briggs, Campeau, Gagné, & May, 1967, p. 3). This is the same process that gardeners use when they choose a certain tool for a certain job. In the same manner, flight trainers choose simulators that create the characteristics of flight in order to teach pilots; however, a simulator is not usually considered appropriate to teach an adult a foreign language. The analysis of job tasks and performance requirements, and the matching of these behaviors to those produced by the training environment, is at this time as much an art as a technology. Although the preceding examples of pilot training and language learning are misleading because they represent obvious differences between tasks, significant improvements in the design of training environments could occur if more emphasis were placed on this matching of training environments to required behaviors.

Learning Principles

In training environments the instructional process involves the acquisition of skills, concepts, and attitudes that are transferred to a second setting (for example, on the job or in another classroom). The acquisition phase emphasizes learning a new task. Performance on the job and in the next environment focuses on transfer of learning to a second setting. Both theoretical and empirical sources of information are available to aid in the design of environments to improve worker performance. Unfortunately, a definitive list of principles from the learning environment that could be adapted to the training setting has not completely emerged. However, recently, theorists have begun to conceptualize the learning and cognitive processes that are relevant to the training process.

In part, this redirection has been based on the kinds of concerns described by Howell and Cooke (1989) in Chapter 1 in the section on the effects of technology. They note that the increasingly "smart" machine being developed put new demands on individuals as they now become responsible for inferences, diagnosis, and judgment, often under severe time pressure. Thus, the learning literature is beginning to focus on "how to make people better diagnosticians, how to increase their available attentional capacity, or how to create appropriate mental models for the complex processes under their control" (p. 125). Although this work is still at an early stage, it is important to explore what has been learned. Theorists have progressed to a stage of development at which it is clear that the choice of the proper learning variable or level of that variable cannot be based on random option. Learning variables interact with the training environment. Thus, it is not appropriate to ignore the information from the learning literature or to accept a particular variable (for example, feedback or knowledge of results) as useful for all tasks. Chapter 4 discusses these aspects of learning and cognitive principles that underlie training processes. The chapter includes discussions about the acquisition and transfer process, as well as about the learning variables that interact with the training environment. It also includes discussions concerning the motivation of the learner and the relationship of motivation to learning performance.

EVALUATION PHASE

Because the development of a training program involves an assessment of needs and a careful design of the training environment, the trainee is expected to perform his or her job at acceptable criterion levels. Unfortunately, this statement of faith displays a sense of self-confidence that is far from justified. Careful examinations of the instructional process disclose numerous pitfalls resulting from mistakes or deficiencies in our present state of knowledge. The assessment of instructional need might have omitted important job components, or the job itself might have changed since the program was designed. In other instances there are uncertainties about the most appropriate training technique to establish the required behaviors.

Unfortunately, few programs are evaluated. Indeed, the word *evaluation* raises all sorts of emotional defense reactions. In many cases the difficulties seem related to a failure to understand that instructional programs are research efforts that must be massaged and treated until the required results are produced. An experience of mine may illuminate this problem. A community agency was offering a program for previously unemployed individuals to help them obtain jobs. A colleague and I were invited to visit and offer suggestions about improvements to the program. Our questions about the success of the program were answered by reference to the excellent curricula and the high attendance rate of the participants. A frank discussion ensued related to the objectives of the program, with particular emphasis on the criteria being utilized to measure the adequacy of the program—that is, how successful the participants were in obtaining and holding jobs. This discussion led to the revelation that the success level simply was not known because such data had never been collected. Of course, it was possible that the program was working successfully, but the information to make such a judgment was unavailable. Thus, there was no way to judge the effectiveness of the program or to provide information that could lead to improvements. Basically, unless there is information about the effectiveness of the programs in helping trainees to find jobs, it was not possible to know whether it made sense to revise or where to place the efforts when revisions were necessary.

The evaluation process centers around two procedures—establishing measures of success (criteria) and using experimental and nonexperimental designs to determine what changes have occurred during the training and transfer process. The criteria are based on the behavioral objectives, which were determined by the assessment of instructional need. As standards of performance, these criteria should describe the behavior required to demonstrate the trainee's skill, the conditions under which the trainee is to perform, and the lowest limit of acceptable performance.

Criteria must be established for both the evaluation of trainees at the conclusion of the training program and the evaluation of on-the-job performance (referred to as transfer validity in the model). In educational settings the criteria must pertain to performance in later courses as well as to performance in the environment where the instructional program was instituted. One classification for this purpose suggests that several different measures are necessary, including reaction of participants, learning of participants in training, behavior changes on the job, and final results of the total program (Kirkpatrick, 1959, 1960). Other serious issues pertain to the integration of the large number of criteria often needed to evaluate a program and to the difficulties (for example, biased estimates of performance) associated with the collection of criterion information. These issues are discussed in Chapter 5.

Besides criterion development the evaluation phase must also focus on the necessary design to assess the training program. As indicated in Figure 2.1, a number of different designs can be used to evaluate training programs, and to some extent the choices are dependent on what you want to obtain information about and the constraints under which you operate. In the last column of the diagram, a number of potential goals are listed:

1. *Training validity*: Did trainees learn during training?
2. *Transfer validity*: Is what has been learned in training transferred as enhanced performance in the work organization?
3. *Intraorganizational validity*: Is the performance for a new group of trainees in the same organization that developed the training program consistent with the performance of the original training group?
4. *Interorganizational validity*: Has the analyst attempted to determine whether a training program validated in one organization can be used successfully in another organization?

As discussed in Chapter 6, these questions often result in different evaluation models or, at the very least, different forms of the same evaluation model. For example, the experimental design model is based on the use of pretests and posttests and uses control groups as a way of accounting for extraneous effects. Some startled trainers have discovered that their control group performed as well as trainees enrolled in an elaborately designed training program. This often occurred because the control groups could not be permitted to do the job without training. Thus, they either had on-the-job training or were instructed through a program that existed before the implementation of the new instructional system. Clearly, if you are interested in transfer validity, the experimental design must include posttest measures not only at the end of training but also at an appropriate time in the work environment or transfer setting.

Besides experimental designs, other approaches to evaluation provide varying degrees of information. For example, individual-differences designs relate individual performance in training to individual performance on the job. It asks whether persons who tend to perform better in training also perform better on the job. If that is the case, the training score can be used to select the better job performers. However, as discussed in Chapter 6, such a model does not tell you very much about the actual quality of the training program. Individuals who do well in training may also do well on the job, even when the training program does not teach as much as it should. Another model also represented in the diagram is content validity. This refers to whether the critical KSAs determined in the needs assessment are emphasized in the training program. That does not assure you that the material was learned; but then again, if the critical KSAs are not included in the training program, there is not much hope for the effort. Chapter 6 stresses that the rigor of the design affects the quality and quantity of information available for evaluation. There are situations in which it is not possible to use the most rigorous design because of cost or because of the particular setting. In these cases it is important to use the best design available and to recognize those factors that affect the validity of the information. A training program should be a closed-loop system in which the evaluation process provides for continual modification of the program. An open-loop system, in contrast, either does not have any feedback or is not responsive to such information. To develop training programs that achieve their purpose, obtaining the evaluative information and using this information for program modifications is necessary. The information may become available at many different stages in the evaluation process. For example, an effective monitoring program might show that the training program has not been implemented as originally planned. In other instances different conclusions might be supported by comparing data obtained from the training evaluation or transfer evaluation. If the participant performs well in training but poorly in the transfer setting, the adequacy of the entire program must be assessed. As indicated by the feedback loops in the model (see Figure 2.1), the information derived from the evaluation process is used to reassess the instructional need, thus creating input for the next stage of development. Even in those instances in which the training program achieves its stated objectives, continual developments can affect the program, including the addition of new media techniques and changes in the characteristics of trainees. These changes often cause previous objectives to become obsolete. The development of training programs must be viewed as a continually evolving process.

Chapters 7 and 8 cover some major training techniques prevalent in education and industry. In these chapters we discuss the objectives of a particular environment, provide illustrations, note the learning principles involved, and discuss the evaluation techniques that are employed to determine the value of these training procedures. Special issues that interrelate societal concerns and training programs are discussed in Chapter 9; for example, training the hard-core unemployed and fair employment practices, training and the older worker, and training in an international environment. In this chapter then, we reflect on many components of the instructional model. We will begin the more comprehensive discussion of the components of instructional programs in the next chapter by examining the first step—assessment of instructional need.

The Needs Assessment Phase

CHAPTER 3

Training programs are designed to achieve goals that meet instructional needs. There is always the temptation to begin training without a thorough analysis of these needs; however, a reexamination of the instructional model introduced in Chapter 2 will emphasize the danger of beginning any program without a complete assessment of tasks, behaviors, and environment. The model shows that the objectives, criteria, and design of the program all stem from these analyses. Goals and objectives are the key steps in determining a training environment, and unless they are specified, there is no way to measure success.

Perhaps the following example will illustrate the dangers of a "let's do it in our heads" approach. This outlandish memo was intercepted by a student as it made the rounds of the federal office buildings in Washington, D.C.

Memorandum for the Director of Personnel
Proposed: Allocation of a position titled: Director of Personnel, Industrial and Agrarian Priorities Description of duties and responsibilities.

1. Without direct or intermediate supervision, and with a broad latitude for independent judgment and discretion, the incumbent directs, controls, and regulates the movement of the wealth of the American economy.

2. The decisions of the incumbent are important since they affect with great finality the movement of agricultural products, forest products, minerals, manufacturer's goods, machine tools, construction equipment, military personnel, defense materials, raw materials and products, finished goods, semi-finished products, small business, large business, public utilities, and government agencies.

3. In the effective implementation of these responsibilities the incumbent must exercise initiative, ingenuity, imagination, intelligence,

industry, and discerning versatility. The incumbent must be able to deal effectively with all types of personalities and all levels of education from college president to industrial tycoon to truck driver. Above all, the incumbent must possess decisiveness and the ability to implement motivation on the part of others consistent with the decision the incumbent had indicated. An erroneous judgment, or a failure to properly appraise the nuance of an unfolding development, could create a complete obfuscation of personnel and equipment generating an untold loss of mental equilibrium on the parts of innumerable personnel of American Industry who are responsible for the formulation of day-to-day policy and guidance implementation of the conveyance of transportation both intra-state and inter-state.

4. In short, on highway construction projects where only one-way traffic is possible, the incumbent waves a red flag and tells which car to go first.

Many analysts insist that job descriptions dictated by this "let's do it in our heads" approach or by a "we know it all already" approach can be just as far from practical application as our illustration. Certainly, designing a training program based on the flowing descriptors in this document would be difficult. Carefully described objectives that set forth required behavior are needed to plan effective training programs; moreover, there should be a direct relationship between these objectives and the type of instruction. Physicians diagnose illness using X-ray film and laboratory tests before they attempt to prescribe a cure through medication, surgery, or other techniques. The training analyst also makes a diagnosis using needs assessment techniques to determine if a cure is necessary and which cure is most likely to produce the desired result. A needs assessment is the diagnostic X-ray film for the training analyst. Figure 3.1 presents a model of the components of the needs assessment process. Most of this chapter will be devoted to a discussion of these components. However, because many of the various parts described in Figure 3.1 are dependent on each other, a short description of each component will be helpful before beginning a more thorough discussion.

The first column, organizational support, recognizes the fact that a needs assessment is an intervention into the lives of employees. Thus, it is necessary to have explicit understanding of what is going to be accomplished by the needs assessment, who is going to participate, and who is going to be responsible for which components.

The second column, organizational analysis, recognizes the important fact that training systems operate within organizations. Training managers must clearly understand the strategic direction of their organization. To design training systems that do not fit into the organization's goals and plans would not make sense. For example, failing to develop training programs for a major technology shift in operations is not a way for the training department to endear itself to top management. In addition, the context is extremely important. Few people would want to design a training program that would be in violation of safety and health regulations or a program that might result in charges of employment discrimination. Similarly, it does not make sense to design a training program that is unacceptable to current supervisors.

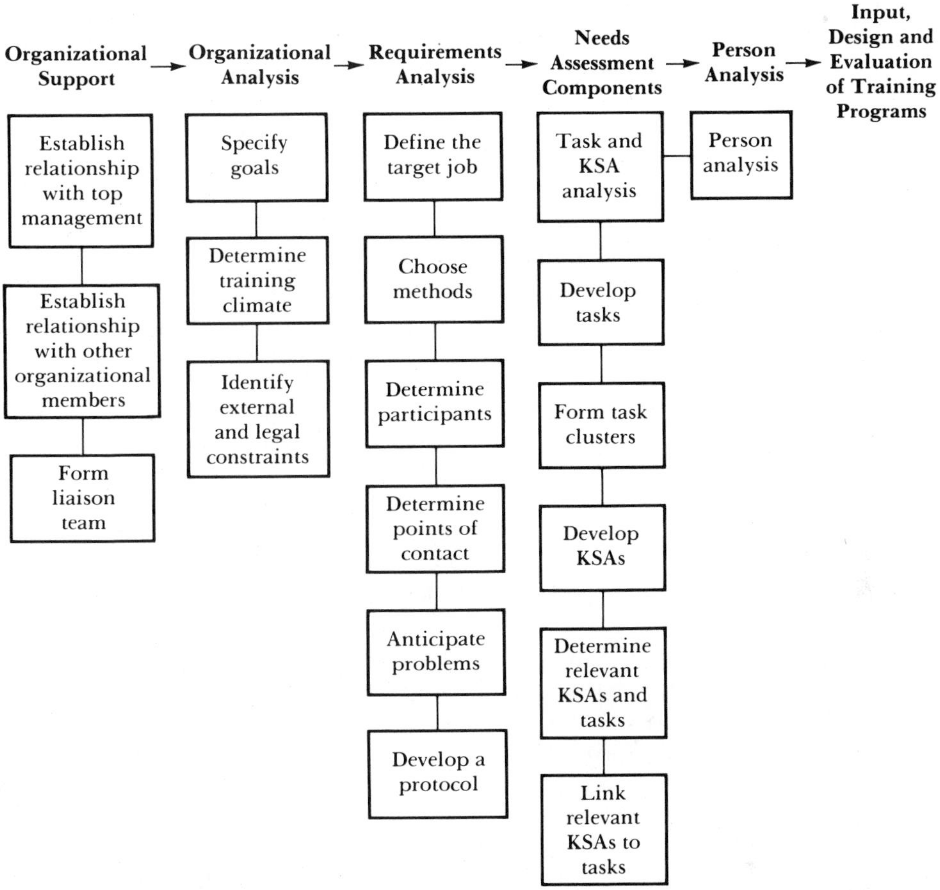

Figure 3.1 A model of the needs assessment process.

The third column, requirements analysis, describes the steps that must be considered before collecting information concerning the tasks and knowledge, skill, and abilities (KSAs) required to perform the job. It begins with determining the target job being examined. Although that might seem self-evident, jobs that have the same label might vary dramatically when performed in different locations or under different conditions. For example, the job of a firefighter is very different for fires in large high-rise buildings versus fires on the docks of San Francisco Bay. If training is going to be designed for both components of the job, the analyst has to ensure that all are included in the assessment. Defining the target jobs also helps determine what methods will be used in the assessment and who will need to participate in order to successfully describe the job.

The next stage, needs assessment components, consists of the collection of the important tasks and KSAs necessary to perform the job. The task and

KSA components will be the input for the actual design of the training program. The fifth column, person analysis, recognizes the fact that it is critical to analyze the work force to determine which of these competencies need to be the focus of training efforts. For example, it is possible to find that your present work force needs training on particular KSAs, whereas new people coming into the work force need training on other KSAs. The next sections of this chapter will discuss each of these components of needs assessment, but it is always important to remember that there is a strong interaction between each of the parts. Thus, if the wrong target job is selected in the requirements analysis, the wrong KSAs will likely be chosen as the focus of training efforts.

ORGANIZATIONAL SUPPORT FOR THE NEEDS ASSESSMENT PROCESS

The needs assessment process can be thought of as a type of organizational intervention. An *intervention,* such as a needs assessment or training program, is a procedure that interrupts organizational members' daily routines and patterns of work behavior. A carefully designed needs assessment will help ensure that the disruption is minimal. The success of needs assessment largely depends on the extent of the support offered by the organization and its members toward the assessment process. Thus, as presented in Figure 3.1, gaining the support of the organization is a critical step in the needs assessment process.

The needs assessment process will only be effective if the assessor can gain the trust of all parties. The process underlying appropriate analysis suggests an interactive system. To design effective training systems, the training organization needs the information from the working organization. Just as important, the training department must gain the cooperation of the working organization in order to have appropriate support for the training system. This suggests an interactive give-and-take relationship to work out the necessary goals and relationships. It also means that organizational conflicts must be resolved before the instructional program is designed and implemented. Glaser and Taylor (1973) report on case studies that examined the factors determining the success of applied research. One interesting finding, applicable to the design of training systems, is that successful studies are characterized by highly motivated people who developed, early in the program, a two-way communication network. The projects had early and active contacts with all pertinent parties. In many cases, this resolved many conflicts. One particular vignette from these case studies focuses on this issue:

> When a group of people or a team are truly involved and participating . . . they look ahead and conceive of their role in time and space in such a manner that includes what they see themselves doing in relation to the project. They usually attempt to interject their own pet theories and questions. . . . At the

very least there's usually a rather heated discussion to work out the details, whether they be of an administrative nature or concern the ideas embodied in the design. . . . (p. 142)

A critical parameter in these case studies was the behavior of the person heading the team. Successful investigators negotiated differences, cleared up misunderstandings, and strongly discouraged their group members from adopting a "we versus they" attitude. The less successful studies were more insular and were characterized as having "tunnel vision." This point cannot be overemphasized. A lack of trust in the analyst and/or the procedure being followed can have dire consequences. An example of the problems that can be created comes from a recent experience of mine. These issues were especially illuminating because everyone I told about the incident responded with similar types of experiences.

> I was invited by an organization's top management to design a needs assessment package that would be used to establish rating scales for performance appraisal. As part of that process, I requested that the first meeting be with a union–management committee, which I had heard about from top management. The committee had representatives from all parts of the organization. The hostility in the atmosphere at the meeting was made apparent by such questions as "What are you trying to sell us?"; "Did you ever do this type of work before?"; "Are you trying to stick us with a system you developed for someone else?" Finally, after several hours of "conversation," I learned that this committee had, at the request of top management, developed an earlier plan for the project. After countless hours of volunteer time, they submitted a report. On the same day their report was submitted, they were informed that an outside consultant had been asked to perform the same activity. Unfortunately for me, I was the chosen consultant. I decided not even to try to begin the project. Instead, we arranged for meetings between top management, the committee, and our research team to work out everyone's feelings and to establish appropriate roles for each group. Eventually, we proceeded with the project with everyone's cooperation. Months later, members of the committee noted that, if we had not met with them and if we had not resolved these difficulties, no one in the organization would have cooperated during the needs assessment; they had intended to subvert the entire needs assessment process. I have no doubt that they would have accomplished their purpose.

The temptation for the training analyst in these types of situations is to ignore the conflict and hope it will go away. However, conflicts do not usually go away; they usually become more troublesome. Perhaps, more seriously, some intervention programs exacerbate the conflict, and the program itself is blamed for the failure. In many cases, the solution to these types of problems is not training programs but conflict-resolution procedures, which must first be used to resolve such difficulties. This example illustrates the importance of establishing the trust of organizational members. Distrust will, at best, result in inaccurate information concerning the job in question. Besides the questionable quality of the information gathered, the ease with which the information is gathered will also be affected. It is highly improbable that participants who mistrust the process will go out of their way to facilitate the needs assessment procedure. Thus, gaining the trust of the organizational members is an important first step for the assessor. Some of the aspects involved in establishing these relations suggested in Figure 3.1 are discussed next.

Establishing a Relationship with Top-Level Management

At the beginning of the process, establishing communication with the relevant top administrator in the organization is necessary. Bennis (1969) points out the importance of this contact. He states that if top leadership does not clearly understand the goals and strategies of the needs assessment, then the procedure may become vulnerable to the natural ups and downs that accompany any organizational intervention. First, it is necessary to agree on why the needs assessment is being done (that is, to design a new training program, to improve an existing training program, to determine the validity of an existing training program, and so on). Second, the analyst must determine who the other people are in the organization whose cooperation must be obtained. Third, the assessor must establish what expectations are being held by top management. These points are important whether the analyst is an outside consultant or a member of the in-house training staff. Thus, it would not make sense for either an in-house or outside consultant to design a plan for the training department without understanding the organization's future goals, nor would it make sense to proceed with a needs assessment unless it was first determined whose cooperation was needed.

Some expectations that might need clarification are the role of the analyst within the organization, the participation of organizational members involved in the assessment procedure, the type of results that can be expected, and the type of actions that can be implemented.

In some instances, top management may have expectations concerning answers to issues such as the number of dissatisfied employees in their organization. This type of outcome is not usually one of the products of a needs assessment for training and development. If unrealistic expectations exist, then they must be negotiated at the outset of the assessment process or, as Schein (1980) indicates, they may function later as traps or sources of disappointment. Besides delineating top management's expectations, it is important for the analyst to explain his or her own expectations. In this regard, some items that should be discussed might include the following:

1. The discussion should establish whether the organization is ready to lend support, time, and effort toward the successful completion of the needs assessment.
2. Information should be exchanged concerning the methods or procedures by which the analyst will operate, the probable time span of the assessment, and the cost of the process.

3. Information on types of outcomes that can result from the process should be presented so that different expectations can be resolved.
4. Issues concerning the confidentiality of the results for any individual member of the organization should be resolved.

Establishing a Relationship with Members of the Organization

Bennis (1969) emphasizes that it is extremely important to gain a "hierarchical umbrella of acceptance" if the needs assessment process is to succeed. This means that it is critical to involve, advise, and inform all key people in the organization about the procedure and to obtain the commitment of these individuals to the assessment process. The term *key people* in this case refers to all those people that are affected by the needs assessment. These range from top-level managers to first-level managers to the actual job incumbents. One way to achieve this "umbrella of acceptance" is to set up a liaison team. The liaison team consists of a small number of people from the organization who will serve as the primary contact between the assessor and the organization. The needs assessment process can benefit in several ways through the formation of a liaison team.

First, a liaison team can aid an assessor by functioning as a communication pipeline to members of the organization. It is important to remember that the members of the liaison team all have access to data that may be literally unobtainable by the analyst, such as the attitudes and feelings of their fellow employees. Information can flow in both directions along this pipeline. That is, liaison team members can be a source of communication about concerns involving the needs assessment. For example, an analyst may discover concerns regarding how the needs assessment participants are being chosen. In addition, liaison team members will undoubtedly have discussions with other employees concerning their experiences with the assessor. If these discussions reveal to employees that the assessor is honest, candid, and professional, then further support for the assessment process may be gained.

The team can help with many important tasks. For example, the team can make suggestions concerning the characteristics of individuals who should participate, prepare memos to participants explaining the process, and set up meetings with participants. This type of participation results in a sharing of the process, which helps establish the trust necessary to accomplish a successful needs assessment. Thus, the liaison team functions by increasing participation and involvement of organizational members in the assessment procedure and by gaining the support of other employees for the entire process.

Because members of a liaison team serve these important functions, the members of the liaison team should be chosen with care. Also, it is obvious that it will be necessary to enlist the aid of various organizational representatives in helping to choose team members. The following are several criteria that you can use to help you choose team members.

1. Ensure that the various components of the organization are represented. In different organizations, this can include representative components from such groups as the training department, union representation, management, and job incumbents from the affected units.
2. Choose members who are recognized leaders of their respective units; they should have good information concerning their units and be able to communicate effectively with the people in their units.
3. Choose members who are generally in tune with the idea of helping by being a problem solver for the organization.

ORGANIZATIONAL ANALYSIS

People concerned with training are required to face a serious problem. That is, the individuals who participate in training programs must learn something in one environment (training) and then use their acquired KSAs in another environment (on the job in the organization). Thus, the trainee will enter a new environment subject to the effects of all the interaction components that represent organizations today. The nature of the environment called an *organization* can be appreciated from Schein's definition:

> An organization is the planned coordination of the activities of a number of people for the achievement of some common, explicit purpose or goal, through division of labor and function, and through a hierarchy of authority and responsibility. (1980, p. 15)

The problem is that often these goals are *not* explicit, and there is often conflict among individuals about the activities to be performed and the goals to be achieved. When this occurs, the trainee is often left with a bag of knowledge, skills, and abilities that is not usable on the job.

Organizational analysis refers to an examination of systemwide components of the organization that may affect a training program beyond those ordinarily considered in task and person analyses. Task and person analyses are more specific, focusing on job tasks and the required person characteristics (KSAs). Organizational analysis has a much broader scope. It is concerned with the system-wide components of an organization. It includes an examination of organizational goals, resources of the organization, transfer climate for training, and internal and external constraints present in the environment. As implied above, many training programs are judged to be failures because of organizational system constraints. For example, the statements "start training at the top" and "I wish my boss had been exposed to this training program" indicate real differences between the approach or values of the training program and those of upper-level supervisors. However, it is too late to compare the goals of upper-level supervision with those of the training program after the instructional program has been instituted. Training programs that are in conflict with the goals of the organization are likely to produce confused and dissatisfied workers.

A classic study by Fleishman, Harris, and Burtt (1955) was probably the first study to suggest the difficulties that arise when the training program and the working environment promote different values. These researchers designed a training program to increase the amount of consideration (friendship, mutual trust) in supervisors. The initial results, collected at the end of the training program, indicated success (as shown by the training scores). However, a follow-up of the program showed that the consideration factor was not maintained on the job. The researchers discovered that the day-to-day social climate, influenced by the supervisors, was not sympathetic to the new values. This study suggests that the climate on the job is a critical component in determining whether the knowledge and skills gained in the training program will be used on the job. This aspect is one of the important parts of organizational analysis, and it will be discussed further in the next section. The Fleishman study also makes clear why experimental designs that enable researchers to study the effects of learning in training and its transfer onto the job are so important. These designs will be examined in Chapter 6 as a part of the study of evaluation processes.

The actual components of an organizational analysis are dependent on the type of program being instituted and the characteristics of the organization. To be perfectly candid, only recently have industrial-organizational psychologists begun to realize the importance of these issues. For example, little attention has been given to understanding the strategic plans of the organization and the implications of such plans for training efforts. Clearly, if an organizational goal is to pursue quality enhancement, training efforts need to be consistent with that objective. The procedures and issues for accomplishing these types of organizational analyses are not completely understood. Also, the scope of the organizational analysis is probably dependent on a number of variables, including who is to be trained, what type of training is contemplated, the size of the organization, and so on. However, examining some of the concerns and making suggestions about some of the procedures that can be used to collect the necessary information is possible. The following broad categories should be considered.

The Specification of Goals

When organizational goals are not clear, designing or implementing training programs is difficult; as a result, specifying criteria that would be used in the evaluation process is also not possible. Figure 3.2 illustrates this sequence. In this diagram, London (1991) presents a variety of different situations and traces out the implications for various policy decisions concerning training. The situations range from those where the goals to be achieved are either clear or not clear. The policy decisions include the following: issues concerning the selection or development of programs; how the decision process is managed; how the program is implemented; the type of evaluation conducted; and the potential outcomes of the entire effort.

In situations type I and II, London (1991) assumes that the goals the

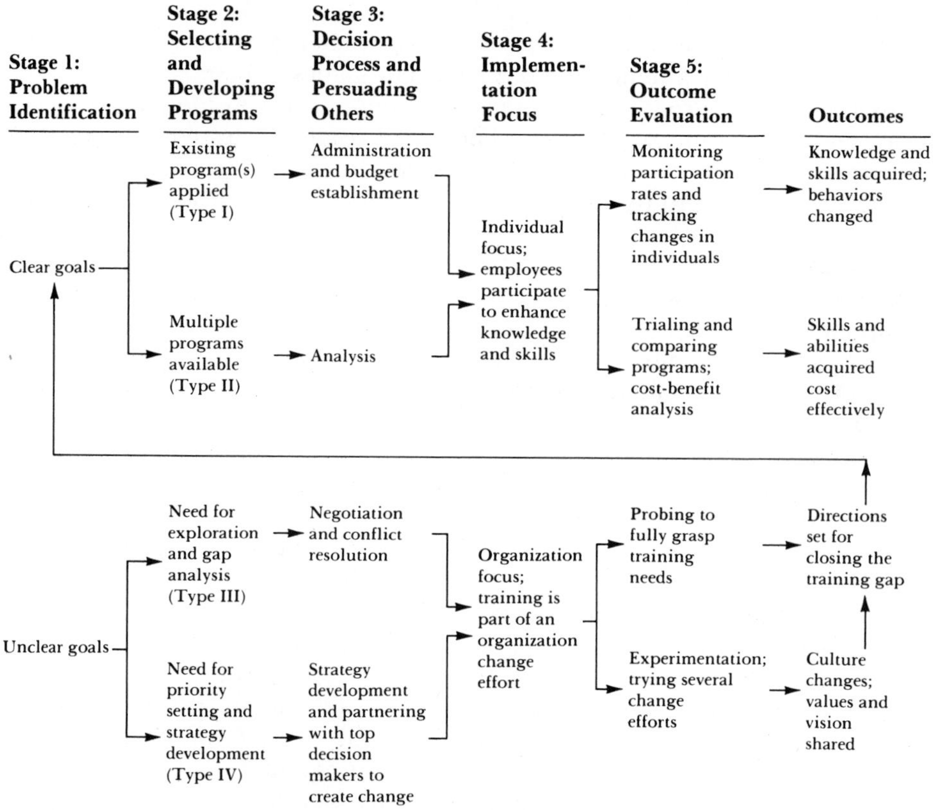

Figure 3.2 Stages of training design and implementation. From "Practice in Training and Development" by M. London, p. 67. In *Working With Organizations and Their People* by D. W. Bray and Associates. Copyright © 1991 by Guilford Press. Reprinted by permission.

organization wishes to achieve are clear. Goals are more likely to be clear when new employees are hired and need to be trained or when new technologies or new products are being implemented. In type I, he describes a situation where the goals to be achieved are not only clear but the training methods already exist. For example, a new technology is introduced with the clear goal that training for the employees is required. London also assumes that an existing training program is supplied by the developer of the technology so that the training method is also specified. In that case, more of the focus would be on training the individuals and then evaluating the programs to ensure that changes have occurred. If the program does not result in effective learning or performance or if the criteria being used to evaluate the program do not appear to be well specified, then the organization still has a problem. Sometimes off-the-shelf programs do not work; thus, it is important for the organization to focus on the evaluation specified in stage 5 of the figure. Depending on the outcome of the evaluation, it might be necessary to redesign the training program or to conduct a needs assessment to determine which new KSAs are required. It should also be clear that an examination of goals requires the organization's support and cooperation. Thus, the previous discussion presenting organizational support considerations (as shown in column 1 of Figure 3.1) is relevant for the performance of any type of analysis, whether it is an organizational analysis, a task analysis, or an evaluation assessment.

In type II, London (1991) describes an instance where the goal is still clear but the choice of how to pursue training is not obvious. For example, new technology might be introduced, but training programs might not be available. Therefore, the program might need to be designed by the training department. Perhaps, customer complaints make it clear that bank tellers need instruction in customer service behaviors. In these cases, a full needs assessment might need to be conducted to determine what types of KSAs need to be learned and what methods are most likely to successfully provide that training. In some cases, alternative methods might be examined and evaluated from a cost-effective viewpoint. Again, it is critical to evaluate the product.

In types III and IV, London (1991) specifies situations where the goals may be unclear. An example could be an instance when two organizations are planning to merge. Another example could be when the organization is changing its focus, such as becoming more globally oriented. This latter example might involve changes in management career-development patterns. In type III, London specifies a condition where, because the goal is unclear, it is first necessary to determine whether it is even a training problem. Here, the training department might even have to be involved in negotiations and discussions to help try to understand the gaps that exist and the causes and solutions. In some of these situations, London notes that the methods might be available in the organization, but before they can become used, the goals must be more clearly specified. For example, the situation described in Chapter 1 included the problem of changing the organization by hiring more women for outside craft jobs. That might include negotiations to clarify a variety of goals including what or who is going to be changed. This could range from training managers who need to be able to accept and work with women to changing equipment so that female workers could perform the job. The specification of these goals is often a critical aspect of organizational analysis. For example, police organizations often spend considerable training time on skill requirements (such as operating a police vehicle or utilizing firearms) or information requirements (knowing the difference between a felony and misdemeanor). However, when public safety organizations become involved in the specification of goals with community associations, they often discover that other objectives—such as interpersonal relationships with the public regardless of race, color, or creed—become salient. Once the goals become clearer, the situation becomes more like a type I or II situation.

In type IV, the goals are also unclear, but the methods for meeting the goals may not be readily obvious or available in the organization. An example of this might be the implementation of changes in the organization to adopt a new corporate culture that would in five years result in the development of a multinational firm. Another example, which is discussed in Chapter 1, might be to shift the organization toward a total quality approach. In these instances, London (1991) notes that the trainer might be participating as a change agent with other team members and organizational leaders to help explore directions for changes and possible experimental ways to facilitate those changes. The questions become broad-scope visions of the ways to achieve organization goals. For example, the teams might need to ask whether it is possible to grow their own managers to participate in the multinational firm or whether they should buy them from other firms. This could result in further analyses including whether it is possible to have a fast-track program for high potential grow your own managers. This could all eventually result in training programs such as the ones described in types I and II, but it is first more likely to result in considerable organizational change efforts.

Besides the importance of specifying goals, Ostroff and Ford (1989) add another important idea. They point out that there are various levels of analysis, such as the individual worker, the work group, and the organization. They indicate that it is important to consider the goals from each operational level. For example, they note that the goals of the unit or department might be used to determine what training is needed. However, at an individual level, the worker might perceive that a training program does not have the potential to help in achieving his or her goals. Thus, the training might not turn out to be useful because the individual is not motivated to learn the material. Or, in the instance discussed earlier, there might be a serious conflict between individual, unit, or organizational goals. The point that Ostroff and Ford make is that it is necessary to determine what level of analysis needs to be examined. Also, it is critical not to generalize from one level to another without having the appropriate data.

The Determination of the Organizational Training Climate

As complex as the specification of systemwide organizational objectives appear to be, the determination of objectives alone will not do the job. Persons who participate in training are faced with a problem; they are required to learn something in one environment (training situation) and use the learning in another environment (on the job). This suggests that another critical aspect of organization analysis is an examination of the systemwide components of the organization that may affect a trainee arriving with newly learned skills. Thus, training programs are often judged to be a failure because of organizational constraints that were not originally intended even to be addressed by the instructional program. As an example, a trainee will have difficulty overcoming a situation where he or she arrives with a set of behaviors that are not consistent with the way the manager prefers to have the job performed. Also, training programs are not likely to be successful when managers are forced to maintain production standards while the employee is sent to a training program.

As noted earlier, Fleishman, Harris, and Burtt (1955) originally noted that there might be difficulties when the values of the training program and the job environment were not the same. Recently, a few authors have made similar suggestions. Michalak (1981) warns us that trainers put too much effort into the portion of training dealing with the acquisition of skill and not enough in what happens afterward. Similarly, Marx (1982) stresses the identification of high-risk situations that the trainee would face and the need for coping skills in those situations. Russell, Terborg, and Powers (1985) evaluated co-worker and supervisory practices to determine whether these personnel were using similar methods as those taught in training. The belief was that if these individuals were behaving in a manner consistent with the training, then trainees will be "reminded" to use such behavior on the job. The results of the study indicate that organizational support is significantly related to organizational performance.

The preceding issues specify the importance of organizational climate issues in transfer of training. However, compared to task and KSA analysis, work in this area is at an early stage. As noted by Goldstein and Thayer (1987), a conceptual model specifying the type of concerns that should be examined is sorely lacking. Rouillier and Goldstein (1990) have worked on research that has identified transfer climate components and classified the components based on an organizational behavior model developed by Luthans and Kreitner (1985). Two major components of transfer climate, situational cues and consequences, were predicted to influence the extent to which transfer would occur. Table 3.1 presents some of the types of items included in each of these categories.

Rouillier and Goldstein (1990) conducted a study investigating their model with a large franchise that owns and operates 102 fast-food restaurants. Surveys were developed that individually measure the transfer climate (situational cues and consequences) of each of the 102 organizational units and the transfer behavior of trainees assigned to the unit. The trainees were assistant managers who completed a nine-week training program and then were assigned on a random basis to one of the 102 organizational units. They found that trainees assigned to units that had a more positive-transfer climate in terms of influencing trainees to use what they've learned (situational cues) and rewarding trainees for doing so (consequences) demonstrated more transfer behavior onto the job. Also, as expected, trainees who had learned more in training performed better on the job, but the interaction between transfer climate and learning was not significant. This provided evidence that the degree of positive-transfer climate affected the degree to which learned behavior was transferred onto the job independent of the degree to which the trainees had learned in the training program. The investigators concluded that transfer climate was a potentially powerful tool that organizations should consider to facilitate training transfer. Certainly, the extent that the training analyst is left with an uneasy feeling of uncertainty in responding to these

Table 3.1 Some examples of organizational items for the assessment of transfer climate

Situational Cues	*Consequences*
Exisiting managers make sure that new managers have the opportunity to use their training immediately.	Existing managers let new managers know they are doing a good job when they use their training.
Existing managers have new managers share their training experience and learning with co-workers on the job.	Existing managers refuse to accept statements or actions from new managers that are different from those learned in training.
The equipment used in training is similar to the equipment found on the job.	More experienced workers ridicule the use of techniques taught in training (reverse scored).
Existing managers assign an experienced co-worker to help trainees as needed back on the job.	Existing managers do not notice new managers who are using their training (reverse scored).
Existing managers ease the pressure of work for a short time so new managers have a chance to practice new skills.	New managers who successfully use their training are likely to receive a salary increase.
Training aids are available on the job to support what new managers have learned in training.	New managers who use their training are given preference for new assignments.

From "The Determination of Positive Transfer of Training Climate Through Organizational Analysis" by J. Z. Rouillier and I. L. Goldstein, 1990. Unpublished manuscript.

items suggests that there might be a considerable amount of work needed before it even makes sense to begin training.

The Identification of External and Legal Constraints

The preceding sections on organizational analysis have identified issues related to specifying organizational goals and the establishment of a positive-transfer climate. The issue examined in this section is the importance of the interacting constraints acting on an organization and their effects on training programs. External constraints have become a very serious problem in the design of training programs.

Ledvinka and Scarpello (1991) describe how the legal environment has changed; Figure 3.3 illustrates some of those changes. Ledvinka and Scarpello note that regulation was originally organized by industry. Thus, the trucking industry is regulated by the Interstate Commerce Commission (ICC) and the Food and Drug Administration (FDA) regulates the drug industry. Each industry and sector of the economy, listed at the top of the figure, has a regulatory agency specifically related to it. That type of regulation is known as vertical regulation. More recently, horizontal regulation has been established where an agency has the responsibility for one activity across many

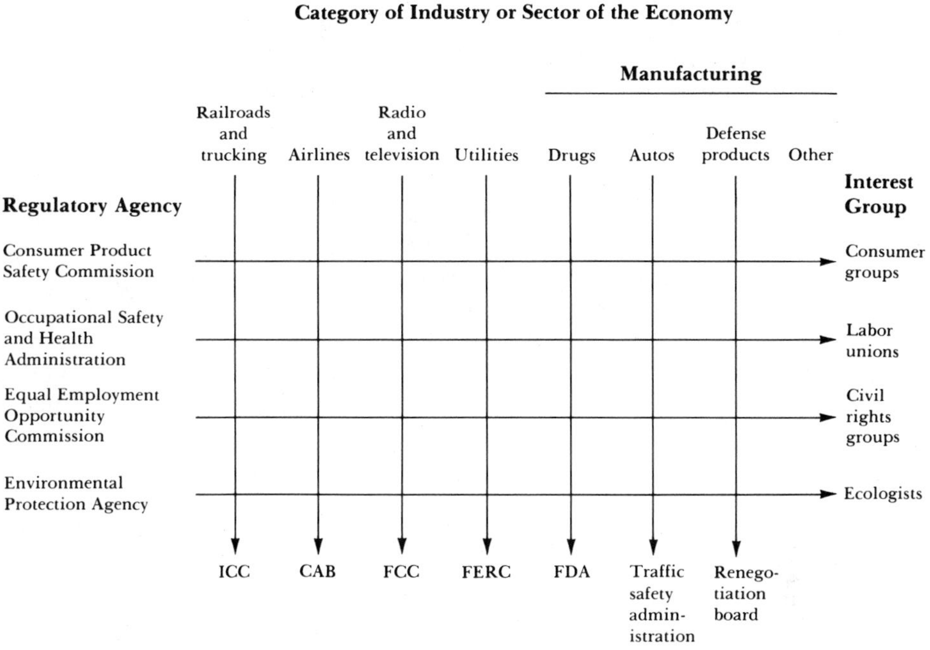

Figure 3.3 Horizontal and vertical regulation. From "The Cost of Government Regulation of Business" by M. L. Weidenbaum. Hearings Before the Subcommittee on Economic Growth and Stabilization of the Joint Economic Commission, 95th Congress, 2d Session, April 11 and 13, 1978, p. 39.

industries or sectors of the economy. The Occupational Safety and Health Administration is concerned with one activity, job safety, in all industries, whereas the Equal Employment Opportunity Commission was created to solve issues related to employment discrimination.

Thus, the older vertical agencies, such as the FDA, were created to solve problems specific to an industry, whereas the newer horizontal agencies were established to solve social problems. As a result, the horizontal agencies have as their constituents the groups concerned with those problems, such as civil rights groups. They are less concerned with the specific mission of the organizations they regulate. The regulations established by the horizontal agencies have had a dramatic effect on practice and research involving human resources in work organizations. Specific aspects related to employment discrimination and training are covered in Chapter 9, but a personal example should make the point clearer. I was asked to design a career-development program to replace an organization's original effort. The original procedure had been found by the courts to discriminate by not making training opportunities available for minorities. Yet, completing the training program was required to be eligible for consideration for promotion. Thus, the court's decision turned out to be a stimulus for the design of a new training effort.

Fair employment practice guidelines have important implications for the needs assessment process, the design of programs, the evaluation of programs, the selection of participants, and even the type of records that must be maintained. It should be noted that fair employment practices are only an illustration of the factors that must be considered. In other cases, the constraint might be new federal or state safety or environmental requirements that affect the objectives of training programs. It would not make much sense to design a training program to teach ways to implement new technology that is in violation of safety and health regulations. Nor would it usually be advisable for a local police agency to teach techniques that were in violation of state or federal regulations. Although the emphasis here has been on legal regulations, external constraints affecting training programs could easily be generalized to other factors. Thus, the culture of different countries makes some job behaviors unacceptable in different places, and training programs teaching those job behaviors must account for that fact.

Resource Analysis

It is difficult to establish working objectives without determining the human and physical resources that are available. This analysis should include a description of the layout of the establishment, the type of equipment available, and the financial resources. More important, human resource needs must include personnel planning that projects future requirements. Too often, organizations respond to personnel needs only in a crisis situation—for example, when they realize they are losing 5 percent of their work force through retirement. Few organizations plan for change within the organization. For example, there is a tremendous increase in the number of computer-controlled machine tools and computer-aided design machines being used by industry. It is estimated that investment in this type of equipment grew at about 15 percent annually from 1983–1989 (Office of Technology Assessment, 1990). At the same time, the use of this technology has dramatic implications for training programs. Thus, if an organization is planning to implement such technology, they would need to do a resource estimate to determine whether they had the people capable of being trained to use the technology.

Also, people leave to take jobs in different organizations, or they retire, or they are promoted within the same organization. Typically, this results in a series of changes in order to fill the jobs that are suddenly available. There is often a frantic search to determine if anyone within the organization has performed similar tasks or if anyone has the KSAs necessary to perform the job. Often decisions are made to move outside the organization or to quickly design a training program to provide instruction for employees to prepare them for the new job. Progression charts, which show who is available for promotion, the KSAs the person has acquired, and the training necessary for performance of the new job are extremely valuable as planning documents. Table 3.2 lists some of the important resource questions that should be asked. Also, recent advances in computerized databases make it much easier to

Table 3.2 Data required for person resource inventory

1. Number of employees in the job classification
2. Number of employees needed in the job classification
3. Age of each employee in the job classification
4. Level of skill required by the job of each employee
5. Level of knowledge required by the job of each employee
6. Attitude of each employee toward job and company
7. Level of job performance, quality and quantity, of each employee
8. Level of skills and knowledge of each employee for other jobs
9. Potential replacements for this job outside company
10. Potential replacements for this job within company
11. Training time required for potential replacements
12. Training time required for a novice
13. Rate of absenteeism from this job
14. Turnover in this job for specified period of time
15. Job specification for the job

maintain information concerning human resources. Kavanagh, Gueutal, and Tannenbaum (1990) provide valuable insights about the advantages of such systems.

PERFORMING A REQUIREMENTS ANALYSIS

Performing a requirements analysis is another critical preliminary step in the needs assessment process. The steps in this process are presented in Figure 3.1. A *requirements analysis* is basically an examination of the details that must be made clear in order for the assessment procedure to function properly. The requirements analysis consists of many specifications that must be completed prior to the collection of tasks and KSAs in order for the assessment procedure to function properly. For example, during this process, it is determined whether a job might be performed differently in different offices or locations. In that case, the needs assessment would have to account for those circumstances. The points that must be addressed in the requirements analysis include the following topics.

Understanding the Job in the Context of the Organization

The first goal of the requirements analysis is to understand the organization so that decisions concerning how the phases of the needs assessment should be conducted can be determined. The best way to accomplish that purpose is to analyze information concerning the organization from available multiple sources. As noted previously, this certainly includes communicating with management and members of the liaison team. Besides the information obtained from participants of the organization, the assessor can use other sources of information. These additional sources of information can be organized into two major categories—previous needs assessment analyses and other documentary materials.

Previous analyses. Information on previous needs assessment of many series of jobs is available from government sources and often from other work organizations. For industrial tasks, the Manpower Administration (U.S. Department of Labor) has extensive materials related to worker functions, task requirements, and worker traits, as well as information related to the proper procedures for performing task analyses. The *Dictionary of Occupational Titles* (U.S. Department of Labor, 1979) presents brief analyses of job tasks and worker requirements for a large number of different occupations. Similar information is available in military and educational technical reports through the National Technical Information Service (for military documents) and the ERIC Clearinghouse on Educational Media and Technology (for educational documents). It is also worth inquiring of other organizations who have similar jobs whether they have needs assessment materials available. Sometimes, these organizations are willing to share information concerning tasks and KSAs, especially with the understanding that any new information gathered would be available to them.

Documentary materials. Besides specific job-analysis materials, there is also a substantial literature describing training programs and other aspects of organizations. It includes catalogs and descriptions prepared by the organization itself; technical literature prepared by trade associations, labor unions, and professional societies; pamphlets and books prepared by federal, state, and municipal departments in the appropriate field (health, education, or labor); and books and pamphlets generally related to the subject.

Previous needs assessment and documentary materials provide useful introductions. However, they are not substitutes for the analyses that must be performed when a training program is designed. Often, analyses of previous jobs do not describe the conditions in the target organization. Sometimes, careful examination shows that only the names of the tasks or the job are the same. Even if the jobs are similar, organizational characteristics may demand a completely different program. These problems are often compounded in the examination of documentary materials in which particular viewpoints may affect the report. Documents published by different organizations (for example, labor or management) may make the same job seem very different. It is important to remember that even if earlier job analyses were actually performed on the targeted job, it does not necessarily indicate how the job is currently performed. On the other hand, if there was actually a needs assessment performed on the job in question, that information should be checked for its accuracy and used to the extent that it is helpful. Thus, these sources provide information that is useful in the initial examination of the job and sometimes reduce the required effort, but the final analysis must be performed with the organization on the jobs of immediate concern.

Defining the Target Job

As presented in Figure 3.1, one of the most critical objectives of the requirements analysis is to identify precisely the job being analyzed. This seemingly simple activity can actually be difficult. The use of a standard job title or generic job name often turns out to be misleading because it often masks a variety of different jobs. For example, the title of administrative aide in hospital management groups often includes a wide variety of different jobs, for example, executive secretary, laboratory assistant, or personnel analyst. In many of these type of instances, it is necessary to determine whether all these activities are to be included in the analysis or whether the intention is to examine particular activities. Similarly, the same job might vary considerably depending on a number of factors, including where or when it is performed. Thus, the same job might be performed differently in various geographical locations or on different work shifts. All these factors need to be determined before the job analysis begins because the determination of which activities will be targeted affects decisions such as which sites are visited and which individuals are chosen to participate.

Choosing the Methods for Conducting a Needs Assessment

It is helpful to think of the needs assessment process as taking a photograph of a job. In this sense, the purpose of the needs assessment process is to take accurate, multiple photographs of the job. It is not a photo of what someone hopes is done on the job. This is an important point. If one of the purposes of the needs assessment is to provide information for the design of training programs, it is necessary to know what is actually done on the job in order to design relevant instruction. Some needs assessment procedures focus on likely future changes that may occur in the job and what new training programs may be needed. Later in the chapter, those type of approaches will be discussed. However, even in those instances, it is first necessary to collect information about the job as it presently exists. Because the purpose of the needs assessment process is to obtain accurate, valid, and reliable information, it is important to develop a method of collecting needs assessment information in a manner that least biases the quality and accuracy of the information. Therefore, focusing attention on the methodology for collecting needs assessment information is necessary.

Learning to select a needs assessment strategy that will produce high-quality information requires effort. There are a number of different methods for collecting task and KSA information. Each method has unique characteristics that can affect both the kind and quality of the information obtained. For example, an interview is dependent on the interviewer's skills and biases, whereas a mail questionnaire can be subject to sampling biases that occur if a substantial number of participants do not return the survey. Steadham (1980) has developed a list of the advantages and disadvantages of various methods, which are presented in Table 3.3.

Table 3.3 Advantages and disadvantages of nine basic needs assessment techniques

	Advantages	*Disadvantages*
Observation • Can be as technical as time-motion studies or as functionally or behaviorally specific as observing a new board or staff member interacting during a meeting. • May be as unstructured as walking through an agency's offices on the lookout for evidence of communication barriers. • Can be used normatively to distinguish between effective and ineffective behaviors, organizational structures, and/or process.	• Minimizes interruption of routine work flow or group activity. • Generates in situ data, highly relevant to the situation where response to identified training needs/interests will impact. • (When combined with a feedback step) provides for important comparison checks between inferences of the observer and the respondent.	• Requires a highly skilled observer with both process and content knowledge (unlike an interviewer who needs, for the most part, only process skill). • Carries limitations that derive from being able to collect data only within the work setting (the other side of the first advantage listed in the preceding column). • Holds potential for respondents to perceive the observation activity as "spying."
Questionnaires • May be in the form of surveys or polls of a random or stratified sample of respondents, or an enumeration of an entire "population." • Can use a variety of question formats: open-ended, projective, forced-choice, priority-ranking. • Can take alternative forms such as Q-sorts, or slip-sorts, rating scales, either pre-designed or self-generated by respondents(s). • May be self-administered (by mail) under controlled or uncontrolled conditions, or may require the presence of an interpreter or assistant.	• Can reach a large number of people in a short time. • Are relatively inexpensive. • Give opportunity of expression without fear of embarrassment. • Yield data easily summarized and reported.	• Make little provision for free expression of unanticipated responses. • Require substantial time (and technical skills, especially in survey model) for development of effective instruments. • Are of limited utility in getting at causes of problems or possible solutions. • Suffer low return rates (mailed), grudging responses, or unintended and/or inappropriate respondents.
Key Consultation • Secures information from those persons who, by virtue of their formal or informal standing, are in a good position to know what the training needs of a particular group are: a. board chairman b. related service providers c. members of professional associations d. individuals from the service population • Once identified, data can be gathered from these consultants by using techniques such as interviews, group discussions, questionnaires.	• Is relatively simple and inexpensive to conduct. • Permits input and interaction of a number of individuals, each with his or her own perspectives of the needs of the area, discipline, group, etc. • Establishes and strengthens lines of communication between participants in the process.	• Carries a built-in bias, since it is based on views of those who tend to see training needs from their own individual or organizational perspective. • May result in only a partial picture of training needs due to the typically non-representative nature (in a statistical sense) of a key informant group.
Print Media • Can include professional journals, legislative news/notes, industry "rags," trade magazines, in-house publications.	• Is an excellent source of information for uncovering and clarifying normative needs. • Provides information that is current, if not forward-looking. • Is readily available and is apt to have already been reviewed by the client group.	• Can be a problem when it comes to the data analysis and synthesis into a useable form (use of clipping service or key consultants can make this type of data more useable).

Interviews • Can be formal or casual, structured or unstructured, or somewhere in between. • May be used with a sample of a particular group (board, staff, committee) or conducted with everyone concerned. • Can be done in person, by phone, at the work site, or away from it.	• Are adept at revealing feelings, causes of and possible solutions to problems which the client is facing (or anticipates); provide maximum opportunity for the client to represent himself spontaneously on his own terms (especially when conducted in an open-ended, non-directive manner).	• Are usually time consuming. • Can be difficult to analyze and quantify results (especially from unstructured formats). • Unless the interviewer is skilled, the client(s) can easily be made to feel self-conscious. • Rely for success on a skillful interviewer who can generate data without making client(s) feel self-conscious, suspicious, etc.
Group Discussion • Resembles face-to-face interview technique, e.g., structured or unstructured, formal or informal, or somewhere in between. • Can be focused on job (role) analysis, group problem analysis, group goal setting, or any number of group tasks or themes, e.g., "leadership training needs of the board." • Uses one or several of the familiar group facilitating techniques: brainstorming, nominal group process, force-fields, consensus rankings, organizational mirroring, simulation, and sculpting.	• Permits on-the-spot synthesis of different viewpoints. • Builds support for the particular service response that is ultimately decided on. • Decreases client's "dependence response" toward the service provider since data analysis is (or can be) a shared function. • Helps participants to become better problem analysts, better listeners, etc.	• Is time consuming (therefore initially expensive) both for the consultant and the agency. • Can produce data that are difficult to synthesize and quantify (more a problem with the less structured techniques).
Tests • Are a hybridized form of questionnaire. • Can be very functionally oriented (like observations) to test a board, staff, or committee member's proficiency. • May be used to sample learned ideas and facts. • Can be administered with or without the presence of an assistant.	• Can be especially helpful in determining whether the cause of a recognized problem is a deficiency in knowledge or skill, or by elimination, attitude. • Results are easily quantifiable and comparable.	• The availabilty of a relatively small number of tests that are validated for a specific situation. • Do not indicate if measured knowledge and skills are actually being used in the on-the-job or "back home group" situation.
Records, Reports • Can consist of organizational charts, planning documents, policy manuals, audits and budget reports. • Employee records (grievance, turnover, accidents, etc.) • Includes minutes of meetings, weekly, monthly program reports, memoranda, agency service records, program evaluation studies.	• Provide excellent clues to trouble spots. • Provide objective evidence of the results of problems within the agency or group. • Can be collected with a minimun of effort and interruption of work flow since it already exists at the work site.	• Causes of problems or possible solutions often do not show up. • Carries perspective that generally reflects the past situation rather than the current one (or recent changes). • Need a skilled data analyst if clear patterns and trends are to emerge from such technical and diffuse raw data.
Work Samples • Are similar to observation but in written form. • Can be products generated in the course of the organization's work, e.g., ad layouts, program proposals, market analyses, letters, training designs. • Written reponses to a hypothetical but relevant case study provided by the consultant.	• Carry most of the advantages of records and reports data. • Are the organization's data (its own output).	• Case study method will take time away from actual work of the organization. • Need specialized content analysts. • Analyst's assessment of strengths/weaknesses disclosed by samples can be challenged as "too subjective."

The steps an assessor should consider in planning which methods to use in the needs assessment process are as follows:

1. An assessor should be aware of the potential problems associated with each of the various methods and designs used in the needs assessment process. Prior knowledge of these potential problems allows the assessor to avoid as many difficulties as possible in planning a needs assessment strategy. For example, it is possible to train interviewers to avoid biases that can contaminate the information being collected.
2. An assessor should use more than one methodology when collecting needs assessment information. Each method has potential biases. One way to alleviate these biases is to use multiple methods. An assessor should select two or more methods in such a way that the advantages of one offset the disadvantages of another. Table 3.3 describes these techniques and their various characteristics.
3. Respondents should represent cross samples of the organization who have relevant information about the job. Multiple perspectives would reveal whether there were alternative viewpoints of the job. For example, it is possible to obtain information from supervisors and top-level management as well as experienced job incumbents. If there are differences in viewpoints, the best approach for the training analyst is to first determine why there are discrepancies rather than simply proceeding with the design of the training program. Only by using these relevant multiple sources of information can the assessor obtain a complete picture of the target job for which he or she will design training programs.
4. It is necessary to design systems that permit the documentation of the information obtained during the needs assessment process. The collection of materials often comes from many different sources and methods over a period of time. For both practical and legal reasons, it is important to document all information obtained in an organized fashion. This is one point that an assessor does not want to learn the hard way.

In addition, it is important for the assessor to decide on the appropriate level of analysis. As noted previously, Ostroff and Ford (1989) carefully note the importance of deciding what level of analysis should be used. If you are collecting information about which tasks are judged to be important, traditionally that information is collected by analyzing the data from all individuals and then assuming the average response reflects the organization. However, in that instance, it might be that different units in the organization have different views, or it might be that different groups of individuals (for example, men and women) have different views. If that is important, the appropriate level of analysis must be chosen to reflect that information.

In conclusion, a general theme in conducting needs assessment is to never do something once when twice will do. This includes multiple methods to collect needs assessment information and using multiple sources of information (for example, supervisors, incumbents, upper-level management). It is also important to avoid having only one person conduct interviews, job observations, or job panels. The use of multiple methods in all aspects of the needs assessment decreases the likelihood of obtaining an inaccurate or biased picture of the job.

Determining the Participants in the Needs Assessment Process

Another step of the requirements analysis is to determine exactly who in the organization will participate in the assessment process. Within organizational constraints, one goal is to try to involve as many relevant organizational members as possible. These constraints can include restrictions such as the budget allotted to the needs assessment, time pressures, and scheduling conflicts. The reasoning behind the idea of involving the maximum number of participants is twofold. First, as mentioned previously, increased involvement and participation in the process builds support. If organizational members believe that their training program was designed with their help and input, they are more likely to lend support for such a program once it is implemented. Second, it is critical to collect information concerning multiple perspectives. Thus, it is important to have a sample that is both representative and large enough to form a complete, accurate picture of the job. In this sense, the analogy of a job analysis to a picture of the job can be extended: Multiple photographs covering multiple perspectives provide the most accurate picture, making it much less likely that the job analyst is fooled by a biased sample of techniques or participants. Several other important points are as follows:

1. One logical way to involve many participants is to have different individuals included in the various stages of the assessment procedure. These stages are described in the next section on the collection of task and KSA information but can include job observations, interviews, panels, and surveys. If this method is followed, the sample of involved individuals builds, with more and more individuals participating and supplying information as the assessment process proceeds. This building process of sample size has a logical progression. Many analysts start with job observations to gain a perspective about the job, switch to panels to obtain descriptions of the tasks and KSAs necessary for the job, and conclude with surveys to collect statistical information such as the importance of the tasks or KSAs.

2. It is important to remember that the number of participants, panels, and other techniques are dependent on the characteristics of the job. Thus, if the job is very different in four geographical sites, one panel in each of four different sites would probably not work. In this instance, it would be the same as conducting one panel for each of four different jobs, which would not give the analyst the multiple perspectives that are necessary.

3. The choice of exactly which groups of people in the organization should participate is complicated. The major criterion is which groups of individuals are most capable of providing the information. Many analysts have discovered that it is best to use job incumbents as participants in the

collection of task statements. The reason for this is that job incumbents find it easy to provide the assessor with information about what tasks they actually perform on the job, whereas supervisors might not have the level of detail to provide that kind of information. Supervisors, on the other hand, can often supply information describing the KSAs that are required on the job because they often think in terms of the abilities of the individuals they supervise.

4. Another issue is exactly which individuals should be selected for participation in the assessment procedure. It is critical that the selection of individuals be representative of the groups of job incumbents or supervisors who either perform or supervise the job. The optimum situation exists when individuals from the organization are selected in a random fashion so that there are no systematic biases operating as to who is selected. Using that type of procedure, the participants are most likely to be representative of the populations being assessed. If the job is found to vary in particular systematic fashions, then the selection should be made randomly within each of those classifications. This is often referred to as random selection within a stratified classification. Besides selecting a representative sample, it is also important to include groups of individuals within the organization who are small in number and thus might not be represented in the usual selection process. Categories of such classification could consist of facets such as minority status and gender. In those instances, it usually makes sense to overrepresent those groups to ensure that the sample size is large enough to be representative of their views of the job. This gives the analyst an opportunity to analyze the needs assessment data to determine whether there are differences in the way the job is viewed by members of these groups.

5. A final issue in the selection of the participants is who selects the individuals. I believe that the analyst should select the individuals using a consistent strategy such as random stratified sampling. As noted above, this makes it more likely that the sample will truly be representative. Another choice is that the analyst can select the individuals according to a set of criteria such as selecting individuals who are good job performers. That is also an acceptable strategy although it is necessary to be careful that the sample is representative. I do not favor having supervisors or members of the organization make the choice unless there is a clear set of guidelines. Otherwise, supervisors might tend to select particular kinds of individuals, which would result in a nonrepresentative sample such as job incumbents who are not needed at work that day. Also, trust is particularly enhanced when it is possible to announce to a panel that the analyst, not their organization, selected them. That type of announcement plus assurances that their individual responses will never be seen by anyone in the organization usually results in a situation where it is possible to collect information in a positive atmosphere.

Determining the Points of Contact in the Organization

Another step in the requirements analysis is to determine points of contact in the organization and the responsibilities of these contacts. It may be that all the organizational contacts are members of the liaison team; but then again, particular needs may require the help of other individuals. It is also important to make sure that the assessor and the organization are in agreement about these roles and responsibilities. This information should be specified so that harmful miscommunication can be avoided. Many an analyst has found some visits resulted in a wasted effort because important groups were not involved in the arrangements.

Anticipating Problems to Be Resolved

Another major step in the needs assessment is to anticipate and plan to resolve problems and issues that can affect the process. This step is also part of the organizational analysis in which the internal and external organizational constraints, which can affect the success of the training program, are determined. However, in this stage of the analysis, the purpose is to determine what factors could be disruptive to the needs assessment process. Examples of the types of issues that can affect the needs assessment procedure are possible organizational strikes, changes in personnel policy or management, and other events. If information about these concerns is obtained, precautions can be taken to avoid problems that could affect the needs assessment. Thus, recognizing particular issues during the panels and explaining their relationship to the needs assessment are possible. For example, I was recently involved in a needs assessment in a telecommunications firm where a department reorganization was being considered. I learned that job incumbents were concerned that the purpose of the needs assessment was secretly a way to redefine a job so that particular job classes could be eliminated. That was not the case, for the purpose of the needs assessment was the design of training programs. That problem was resolved by having the analyst and management discuss the issue at the beginning of each panel discussion. It is important for the analyst to be aware of the fact that these types of organizational issues can have a serious effect on the quality of the information obtained in the needs assessment. The levels of cooperativeness and commitment on the part of the job incumbents is directly dependent on both being aware of the issues and being candid in dealing with the organization's concerns.

Development of a Protocol

Based on the information obtained in the requirements analysis, one final step prior to conducting the needs assessment is to develop a protocol, a script for the assessor to follow in conducting the assessment panels or interviews. The protocol presents the standardized steps to be followed in collecting the needs assessment information. An outline of a protocol can be found in Table 3.4.

The standard protocol includes an introduction, background information on what a job analysis is, and a description of what will be done in the information-gathering session. It also includes guidelines for the analyst on how to conduct the session. The importance of the protocol is that it presents

Table 3.4 Outline of a sample needs assessment protocol

1. Introduce needs assessment team and other participants.
2. Present brief history of project.
3. Explain the general purpose of today's activities.
4. Provide opportunity for questions.
5. Provide background outlining needs assessment process.
   a. Indicate what needs assessment does.
   b. Indicate the various procedures that will be used during the needs assessment phases.
   c. Indicate the type of outcomes that stems from needs assessment.
   d. Indicate the general time lines for the project.
6. Provide specific information on how particpants are selected.
7. Provide information on confidentiality of individual data.
8. Provide specific information on what will be done today.
9. Conduct activities.
10. After conducting activities, indicate how information will be used in the next step.
11. Answer questions and thank participants.

the appropriate steps to be followed and standardizes these steps so that all people involved in the project will conduct their information-gathering sessions in a similar manner. Only an outline of a protocol is presented in Table 3.4 because the information in the script depends on the exact situation of the particular needs assessment.

In conclusion, the key to a successful needs assessment is advanced thought and planning regarding the needs assessment process. It is necessary to consider the variety of methods that can provide useful information and to determine which questions need to be asked. For the needs assessment to be successful, this planning process must be conducted before the actual needs assessment begins.

TASK AND KNOWLEDGE, SKILL, AND ABILITY ANALYSIS

Just as an organizational analysis is necessary to determine the organizational objectives, a *task analysis* is used to determine the instructional objectives that will be related to the performances of particular activities or job operations. The task analysis results in a statement of the activities or work operations performed on the job and the conditions under which the job is performed. It is not a description of the worker but a description of the job. On the other hand, the KSAs describe the knowledge, skills, and abilities necessary to perform these tasks.

As presented in Figure 3.4, Pearlman (1980) shows the various levels of analysis in looking at a job. In the example presented, the tasks performed are the fundamental units of analysis. They determine the groupings at each level in the diagram. Pearlman thus identifies three of the many tasks performed by individuals in the same position in Company A who hold the job of

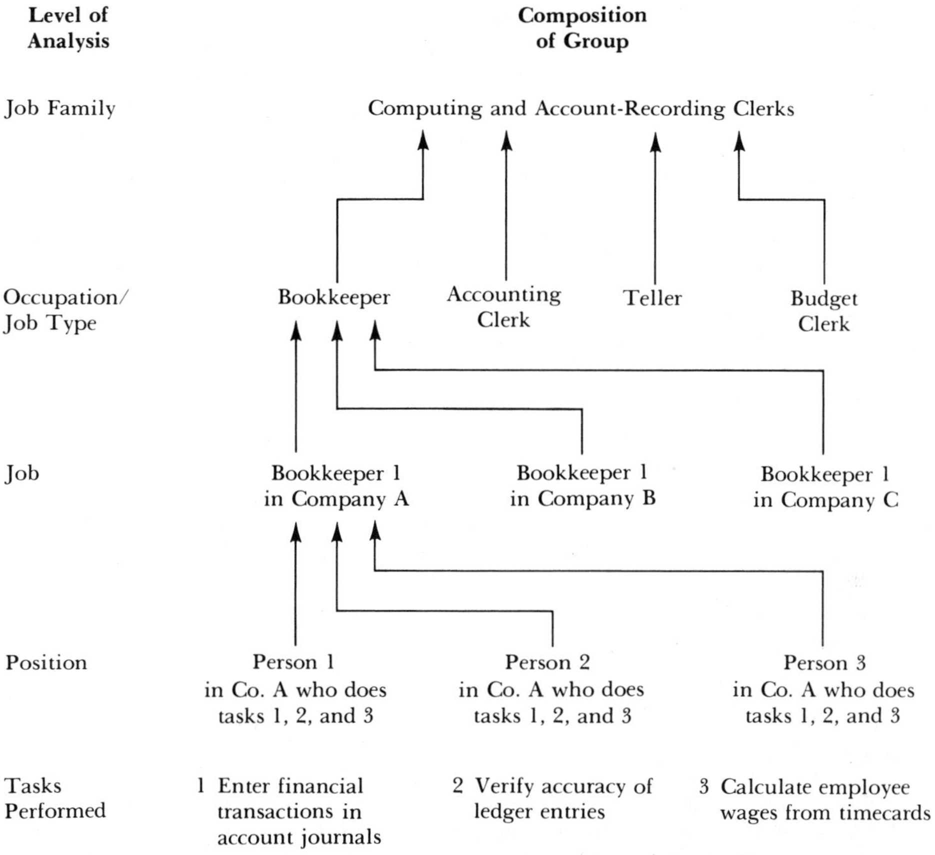

Figure 3.4 Examples of different types of job groupings at different levels of analysis. From "Job Families: A Review and Discussion of Their Implications for Personnel Selection," by K. Pearlman. In *Psychological Bulletin,* 1980, *87,* pp. 1–18. Copyright © 1980 by the American Psychological Association. Reprinted by permission.

Bookkeeper 1. He also labels four of the occupation/job types (bookkeeper, accounting clerk, teller, and budget clerk), which constitute the job family computing and account-recording clerks.

Task analysis consists of several components, each of which further delineates the performance required to succeed at the task. Thus, the analysis begins with a task description, followed by a detailed specification of tasks, and a scaling of tasks on various dimensions such as criticality, frequency of occurrence, and so on.

Task Description

The *task description* serves as a job summary statement describing the major focus and duties of the job. The statement should completely describe all the essential activities of the job, including "worker's actions and the results accomplished; the machines, tools, equipment, and/or work aids used; materials, products, subject matter, or services involved; and the requirements made of the worker" (U.S. Department of Labor, 1972, p. 30). The statement includes the characteristics of the environment (for example, noise or extreme temperature variations) and any special features (for instance, stress) that further delineate the job.

The description should contain material about each kind of activities involved, either in order of their importance or in the chronological order in which they are performed. An interesting example of a job description, presented in the U.S. Department of Labor *Handbook for Analyzing Jobs* (1972), is for the job of manager of a hunt club. The description states that this job consists of the following activities:

> Coordinates hunt activities of hunt club and supervises workers engaged in care and training of horses and hounds used in fox hunting. Purchases feed and supplies for animals. Supervises personnel engaged in training animals, in detection of early stages of animals' illness, and in repairing and repainting stables and kennels. Assists master of foxhounds in setting up obstacles on hunt course, in scenting hunt trail when live quarry is not used, and in staging horse shows. Rides with participants of hunt to control hounds and times horses, using stopwatch. (p. 186)

Another (perhaps more relevant example but not as much fun!) example is for a person who arranges for airline passenger reservations. This description states:

> Makes and confirms reservations for passengers' scheduled airline flights. Arranges reservations and routing for passengers at request of supervisor or customer, using timetables, airline manuals, reference guides and tariff book. Inspects availability board to determine seats available, and prepares reservation card. Telephones customer or supervisor to advise of changes in flight plan to cancel or confirm reservation. (p. 188)

Even in 1972, the handbook was suggesting some of the guidelines that we use today: that the descriptions be terse, in the present tense, and started with an action verb. Each word should give necessary information, and words that have more than one meaning should be avoided.

Development of Task Statements

As presented in Figure 3.1, task and KSA analysis is used to determine the required content of a training program. A task analysis results in a statement of the critical activities or work operations performed on the job and the conditions under which the job is performed. Some examples of task statements from a variety of different jobs can be found in Table 3.5.

The first phase in the task analysis is to specify all tasks performed on the job. The collection of this type of information requires the use of a number of the techniques described in previous sections, including interviewing panels

Table 3.5 Examples of tasks from a variety of jobs

1. Call job candidates to provide feedback and keep them informed during the preemployment selection process.
2. Monitor the implementation/practice of personnel procedures to ensure that provisions of the labor contract (for example, regarding required training, salary schedule) are maintained.
3. Interpret letters from the highway department concerning driver's license revocation in order to verbally advise citizens on the appropriate course of action.
4. Observe and evaluate the performance of job incumbents for the purposes of salary review.
5. Evaluate workloads, priorities, and activity schedules to determine staffing requirements and assignments for area of responsibility.
6. Inspect hospital facilities to determine compliance with government rules and regulations pertaining to health practices.
7. Maintain written records and logs of contacts with customers in order to provide documentation concerning steps taken to resolve their service problem.
8. Provide verbal feedback to first-line supervisors to assist them in critiquing their own performance after incidents in order to help them develop more effective ways of handling future situations.

Note: I thank many of my colleagues in the field of industrial-organizational psychology for the use of some of the materials presented in Tables 3.5–3.10, 3.12, and 3.13. In many cases, it is difficult to determine which iteration produced the actual materials included in the tables. Some of the colleagues involved in projects that resulted in the development of these materials include Wiley Boyles, Wayne Cascio, Joyce Hogan, Frank Landy, Bill Macey, Doris Maye, Jim Outtz, Erich Prien, Paul Sackett, Ben Schneider, Joe Schneider, Neal Schmitt, John Veres, and Shelly Zedeck. I gratefully acknowledge their contributions. All rights for the use of these materials remain the privilege of the researchers who used and developed them.

of job experts (known as subject-matter experts, or SMEs) and observing the job being performed. The rules for the specification of tasks have been evolving for a number of years. The following summary is a synthesis of the work of a number of individuals (Department of Labor, 1972; Ammerman & Pratzner, 1977; Prien, Goldstein, & Macey, 1987; Goldstein, Braverman, & Goldstein, 1991):

1. Use a terse, direct style, avoiding long involved sentences that can confuse the organization. The task statements should be neutral in tone and not refer to either outstanding or poor performance; this is a description of the tasks, not the capabilities of the individual necessary to perform the task. The language should be consistent both in form and level with the language of the people who perform the job.

2. Each sentence should begin with a functional verb that identifies the primary job operation. It is important for the word to describe the type of work to be accomplished. For example, a task statement that says "presents information for the use of supervisors in . . ." does not tell us much about the task. We have no idea whether a report has been written, a conversation is occurring, or a speech is being made. Certainly, the KSAs involved in writing a report for the use of supervisors would be different than the KSAs in giving a speech. Without that information, determining what training needs to be designed is difficult.

3. The statement should describe *what* the worker does, *how* the worker does it, and to *whom/what* and *why* the worker does it. The *why* aspect often becomes a critical part of the task because it forms the foundation for understanding what KSAs may be required. Thus, if a manager has the task of conducting a performance appraisal in order to provide information for advising the job incumbent on needed performance improvement, KSAs needed might include assessing job performance and providing feedback to the individual. However, if the purpose of the performance appraisal is to provide a written recommendation to upper-level management on the promotability of the individual, the KSAs might include assessing job performance but might not include providing feedback to the individual.

The following illustration stems from the job of a secretary:

What:
Sort

To Whom/What?
correspondence, forms, and reports

Why?
in order to facilitate filing them

How?
alphabetically.

The next example comes from the job of a supervisor:

What?
Inform

To Whom/What?
next shift supervisor

Why?
of departmental status

How?
through written reports.

Note by examining the tasks illustrated above and the tasks listed in Table 3.5 that the development of task statements is not limited by the particular type of job.

4. In determining whether multiple tasks should be included in one statement, do not include separate tasks in the same statement unless they are always performed together. If multiple tasks are likely to lead to very different KSAs or very different estimates of the importance of the task, you should consider keeping them separate. Otherwise, latter parts of the job analysis will be adversely affected. For example, if there are several tasks and they are different in how important they are for job performance, it will be difficult for the SMEs to assign an importance rating.

5. The tasks should be stated completely, but they should not be so detailed that it becomes a time-and-motion tideway. For example, a task could be "slides fingertips over machine edges to detect ragged edges and burrs." However, it would not be useful for the identification of tasks to say that the worker raises his or her hand onto table, places fingers on part, presses fingers on part, moves fingers to the right six inches, and so on. Rather, each statement should refer to a whole task that makes sense. Usually, the breaking down of the tasks into a sequence of activities is useful when the task is being taught in the training program. However, that step doesn't occur until the total task domain is identified and it is determined which KSAs need to be taught to perform those tasks. Similarly, trivial tasks should usually be avoided.

Development of Task Clusters

After a full task set is developed from the job analysis, another useful procedure is the development of *task clusters*. Table 3.6 illustrates an example of a task cluster for the job of a customer service representative.

The purpose of clustering is to help organize the task information and to help in the editing of tasks. As such, clustering is usually done following the collection of the complete task set from the job observations, panels, and interviews. It usually involves the following steps:

1. Develop definitions of task clusters that describe job functions. For the job of the customer service representative, the cluster and its definition are for interacting with the customer. Some other clusters, depending on the actual job tasks, might include interacting with technicians or vendors who fix the customer's difficulties and keeping records and logs so that customer information is recorded and maintained.
2. Once a set of task cluster definitions are developed, the next step is to have a group of subject matter experts (SMEs) independently sort each tasks into one of the clusters. The SMEs can be job incumbents or supervisors. Analysts who are involved in conducting the job analyses can also participate in this sorting process. In any case, if the analysts are involved in this process, the outcomes should still be checked by job incumbents and supervisors.
3. Establish a rule that defines agreement on whether a task is successfully clustered. For example, if ten people are performing the clustering, a rule

Table 3.6 Example of a task cluster for the job of a customer service representative

Task cluster title and definition: Interaction with the customer—the tasks involving communication by telephone between the customer service representative and the customer to determine what service difficulties have occurred.

1. Determine what difficulties the customer is having in order to complete a service report.
2. Ask the customer for relevant information in order to provide all information needed by the vendor to service the customer.
3. Call the customer to determine whether the problem has been resolved by the promised date and time.
4. Provide the customer with information so that he or she can follow up the call at a later time to obtain status information.
5. Provide instructions to the customer concerning basic self-checks that can be used to resolve the customer's difficulty.
6. Provide information to the customer about services that are available to resolve the problem.
7. Inform the customer about possible service charges that may be billed to the customer in order to service the customer's equipment.

Note: Please see note for Table 3.5.

might be that seven of ten people must agree on where the task should be clustered.

4. Plan to rework the task cluster definitions. When disagreement occurs on the placement of a task, it usually provides very useful information concerning the development of either the task or the cluster. Usually, disagreement occurs for the following reasons:
   a. The task has more than one work component in it, and different judges focus on different parts of the task.
   b. The task is ambiguous, and different judges interpret the task differently.
   c. The purpose of the task is not clear, and thus different judges place the task in a different cluster.
   d. The clusters themselves are too broad or poorly defined.

   This clustering process usually leads to very useful re-editing of the tasks and the cluster definitions. This typically results in tasks becoming much clearer.

This procedure for organizing clusters is typically known as a *rational clustering exercise.* There are other procedures for clustering, using statistical techniques. However, there seems to be some question about whether factor analytic techniques lead to useful task clusters. Cranny and Doherty (1988) have discovered that the clusters that emerge from such analyses are frequently not interpretable as important job dimensions. Even more serious, SMEs have found that the job dimensions that they deem important may not emerge as factors. At this point, there are no definitive answers to these questions, leading many researchers (for example, Schmitt, 1987) to suggest that research on these issues is badly needed. In any case, although there may still be some questions on the appropriate techniques to use in developing clusters, most researchers agree that it is a useful procedure for the reasons specified above and because the clusters can then be used to provide input for the development of KSAs, which is discussed next.

Knowledge, Skills, and Abilities and Psychological Fidelity

Whereas task analysis provides a critical foundation for any training needs assessment, a task-based system cannot usually provide the entire foundation for a training system. If training is provided on the exact tasks that exist on the job, the training system would have very high physical fidelity. However, in most cases, the goal in training systems design cannot be perfect physical fidelity. The reason for most training systems is that you cannot train an individual on the exact tasks that constitute the job. In some cases, such as flying an airplane, it is simply too dangerous, whereas in other cases the representation of the exact task is too overwhelming for the trainee to learn. Thus, in almost all situations, the task is some simulation of the actual tasks on the job. This includes simulations for learning management techniques such as role playing or learning to fly an airplane in a simulator. The goal usually is

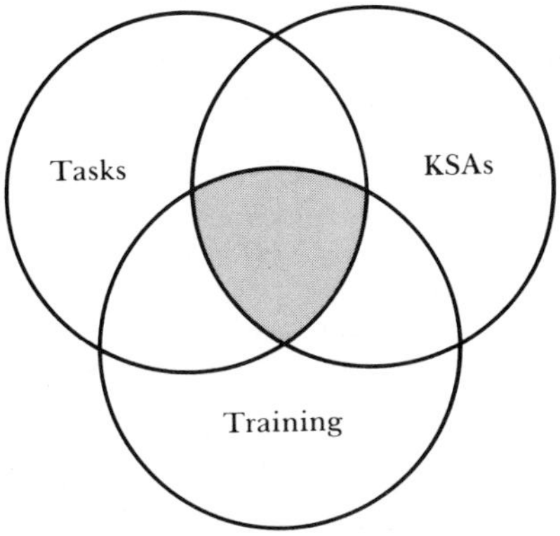

Figure 3.5 Psychological fidelity of training programs.

to choose simulated tasks that permit the calling forth of the skills and abilities that need to be learned. Of course, it is also necessary to specify the knowledges that need to be learned in order to perform the tasks.

This type of training environment is one that has high psychological fidelity in the sense that it sets the stage—for the KSAs that need to be learned to be called forth by the simulated tasks. In that sense, the training program is content-valid to the extent that it is designed so that the appropriate critical tasks are simulated and thus give the opportunity for the relevant KSAs to be demonstrated. This relationship between tasks and KSAs is shown in Figure 3.5. The section of the diagram that models that relationship is shaded; to the degree the training program represents that area, it has psychological fidelity. Too often, trainees are being asked to memorize huge amounts of material for jobs when they never are expected to know the material or don't have to memorize it as part of their job function. In that instance, the problem could have occurred for two reasons: A needs assessment was not properly done to determine what needed to be learned to perform the job, or the training designer did not pay attention to the needs assessment that was available. Thus, the purpose of the needs assessment is to obtain information concerning the critical tasks required to perform on the job and the KSAs necessary to perform those tasks. The next step is the development of KSAs called forth by simulated tasks that give the training program psychological fidelity.

Development of Knowledge, Skill and Ability Analysis

The organizational analysis and the task analysis provide a picture of the task and the environmental setting. However, as noted above, the task analysis provides a specification of the required job operations but does not provide information concerning the KSAs required to perform the tasks. The key issue is determining the human capabilities necessary to effectively perform the job. After these capabilities are specified, then it is possible to analyze the

Table 3.7 Examples of KSAs for a variety of jobs

1. Ability to be able to recognize the strengths and weaknesses of subordinates.
2. Ability to be able to recognize cues in performance of individuals that indicate the need for professional counseling.
3. Ability to be able to organize facts and materials for presentations.
4. Ability to be able to pass on information to subordinates verbally so that the information is understood.
5. Ability to communicate in writing accurately, concisely, and clearly.
6. Ability to organize incoming information for verbal transmission on the radio or telephone.
7. Ability to recognize the usefulness of information made available by others.
8. Skill in transcribing numbers from one document to another.
9. Skill in writing numbers and letters legibly.
10. Skill in adjusting volume and temperature of water spray.
11. Knowledge of map formats and symbols used in reading maps.
12. Knowledge of authority limitations to exceed budget.
13. Knowledge of federal and state laws regarding employee access to company records.

Note: Please see note for Table 3.5.

performance of the target population to determine whether training is necessary. There are several different systems for specifying human capabilities. One system advocated by Goldstein and Prien (for example, Prien, 1977; Goldstein, Macey, & Prien, 1981; Prien, Goldstein, & Macey, 1987) emphasizes the KSAs necessary to effectively perform the tasks developed in the task analysis. Prien defines these categories as follows:

Knowledge (K) is the foundation on which abilities and skills are built. Knowledge refers to an organized body of knowledge, usually of a factual or procedural nature, which, if applied, makes adequate job performance possible. It should be noted that possession of knowledge does not ensure that it will be used.

Skill (S) refers to the capability to perform job operations with ease and precision. Most often skills refer to psychomotor-type activities. The specification of a skill usually implies a performance standard that is usually required for effective job operations.

Ability (A) usually refers to cognitive capabilities necessary to perform a job function. Most often abilities require the application of some knowledge base.

Examples of KSA characteristics are presented in Table 3.7 for a variety of jobs.

The description of KSAs involves inferences about what KSAs people need to perform particular tasks. Often, people who directly supervise the job being analyzed serve as effective SMEs to provide this information because they often think about what a job incumbent needs to know or what skills and abilities are needed to perform the tasks. This is in contrast to the collection of

Table 3.8 KSAs from the task cluster titled customer service representative

1. Ability to explain technical information to the customer in a way that he or she understands.
2. Ability to guide the conversation with the customer in order to obtain the necessary information needed by the vendor to service the customer.
3. Ability to resolve customer problems without having to refer them to the supervisor.
4. Ability to communicate with people from a broad variety of backgrounds.
5. Ability to reflect the company's public service image when speaking with others.
6. Knowledge of the services that can legally be provided by the company.

Note: Please see note for Table 3.5.

task information where the job incumbents themselves often know exactly what tasks they perform on the job.

Thus, one procedure to collect KSA information is to present one of the task clusters (such as that shown in Table 3.6) and ask members of a panel the following types of questions:

1. Describe the characteristics of good and poor employees on (*tasks in cluster*).
2. Think of someone you know who is better than anyone else at (*tasks in cluster of task*). What is the reason he or she does it so well?
3. What does a person need to know in order to (*tasks in cluster*)?
4. Try to recall concrete examples of effective or ineffective performance in performing (*tasks in cluster*). Then recall causes or reasons for effective or ineffective performance of (*tasks in cluster*).
5. If you are going to hire people to perform (*tasks in cluster*), what kind of KSAs would you want them to have?
6. What do you expect people to learn in training that would make them effective at (*tasks in cluster*)?

The KSAs shown in Table 3.7 are a sample of KSAs that stem from a variety of jobs. Some other relevant KSAs that stem from the task cluster for a customer service representative presented in Table 3.6 are offered in Table 3.8.

Some of the guidelines for the development of such KSA statements include:

1. Maintain a reasonable balance between generality and specificity. Exactly how general or specific the KSA statement should be will depend on its intended use. When the information is being used to design a training program, it must be specific enough to indicate what must be learned in training.

2. Avoid simply restating a task or duty statement. Such an approach is redundant and usually provides very little new information about the job. It is necessary to ask what KSAs are necessary to perform the task. For example, a task might be "analyze hiring patterns to determine whether company practices are consistent with fair employment practice guidelines." Clearly, one of the knowledge components for this task will involve "knowledge concerning

federal, state, and local guidelines on fair employment practices." Another component might involve "ability to use statistical procedures appropriate to perform these analyses." Both the knowledge and ability components would have implications in the design of any training program to teach individuals to perform the required task.

3. Avoid the error of including trivial information when writing KSAs. For example, for a supervisor's job, "knowledge of how to order personal office supplies" might be trivial. Usually, it is possible to avoid many trivial items by emphasizing the development of KSAs only for those tasks that have been identified in the task analysis as important for the performance of job operations. However, because the omission of key KSAs is a serious error, borderline examples should be included. At later stages in the process, these KSAs will be eliminated if SMEs judge them to be not important.

4. Ask for knowledge and skills and abilities in order to obtain as much information as possible to determine what is needed to perform the tasks. For example, it is clear that having knowledge about how to hit a golf ball is very important; yet we are all familiar with people who can tell you how to hit the ball but still cannot hit it. Thus, it pays to attempt to delineate all the various KSAs; although at times, deciding what should be listed as a knowledge or skill or ability becomes difficult. In those instances, make sure that the item appears in at least one of the possible ways.

Determination of Relevant Task and KSA Characteristics

Once the tasks and KSAs are specified, obtaining further information about both the tasks and KSAs is important. For example, it is necessary to know which tasks are important and which are frequently performed. Similarly, it is necessary to determine which KSAs are important or which ones are difficult to learn. Designing a training program around KSAs that are not important, not needed for the job, or not difficult to learn would not make much sense. This step typically uses a *survey format* that permits the collection of greater amounts of information than can occur in the job observations, interviews, and panels used in the original collection of tasks and KSAs. The survey format makes it possible to collect data from experienced job incumbents or supervisors across large enough samples to ensure confidence in indicators such as the importance of the task. Also, by checking items such as different geographical locations or different units in the organization, determining whether the job is viewed the same way across the organization is possible. An added benefit is that it permits the analyst to involve more of the organization.

The exact questions asked on the survey vary depending on the purpose. For tasks, it is typically necessary to have information concerning the importance of the task and the frequency with which it is performed. An example of an importance scale for tasks can be found in Table 3.9. Similar scales for the importance of KSAs can be designed. It may also be important in the design of training to know whether general familiarity of the knowledge is required or whether full recall is required for job performance. If that

Table 3.9 A sample importance scale for tasks

IMPORTANCE *How important is this task to effective performance in your position?*

1 = Not Important (Improper task performance results in *no* error or consequences for people, things, or places.)
2 = Slightly Important (Improper task performance may result in *slightly serious* consequences for people or *slightly serious* damages to things and places.)
3 = Important (Improper task performance may result in *moderate* consequences for people or *moderate* damages to things and places.)
4 = Very Important (Improper task performance may result in *serious* consequences for people or *extensive* damages to things and places.)
5 = Crucial (Improper task performance may result in *very serious* consequences for people or *very extensive* damages to things and places.)

Note: Please see note for Table 3.5.

were the case, then you could use the scale presented in Table 3.10. Clearly, the training program would be different for knowledges that only require a general familiarity as compared with full recall. Which scales are most useful depends on the questions that the particular needs assessment is being designed to answer. Some of the questions for which scales can be designed include the following:

For Tasks

1. Is the task performed?
2. How frequently is the task performed compared with other tasks?
3. How important is the task for effective performance on the job?

Table 3.10 Example of recall-level scale for knowledge

Recall-Level Required Day 1	*What level of recall do you need at the time of appointment to apply this knowledge on the job?*
1 = General familiarity	A person must be aware of general principles and be able to efficiently locate pertinent details in source documents and/or seek guidance from others.
2 = Working knowledge	A person must be able to apply general principles and specific details from memory in typically encounterd occurrences, bur refer to source documents or seek guidance from others for applying specifics in unusual occurrences.
3 = Full recall	A person must be able to apply both general principles and specific details in a wide variety of occurrences from memory without referring to source documents or seeking guidance from others.

Note: Please see note for Table 3.5.

For KSAs

1. How important is the KSA for performing the job?
2. How difficult is it to learn the KSA?
3. Where do you expect the KSA to be acquired (before selection, in training, on the job, and so on)?

An example of a page of a questionnaire concerning KSAs asking importance and whether the job incumbent needs the KSAs on day 1 at work is given in Table 3.11. The KSAs presented in the table are for the position of radio operators whose job is to communicate with state troopers by radio in order to provide for the safety of both the trooper and the public.

The data collected can be analyzed to determine average responses, variability, and degree of agreement between different panel members. The analyst can set cutoffs for the determination of which tasks and KSAs would be used in further analyses. Thus, on the scale shown in Table 3.11, a value of 3 and above is associated with tasks that are judged important. Therefore, it might be decided that all tasks that earn an average value of 3 and above are included in the next stage of the needs assessment process. Also, it should be clear that the type of information collected in these analyses is useful for decisions that extend beyond the training program. For example, it is possible to

Table 3.11 Sample questionnaire for KSAs

Importance

1 = Not important
2 = Minor importance
3 = Important
4 = Major importance
5 = Critically important

Necessary Day 1

Y = Yes
N = No

VII. Geographical Visualization
This category includes abilities involved in visualizing the environment (including road names and numbers and compass directions) being encountered, or likely to be encountered, by persons in moving vehicles.

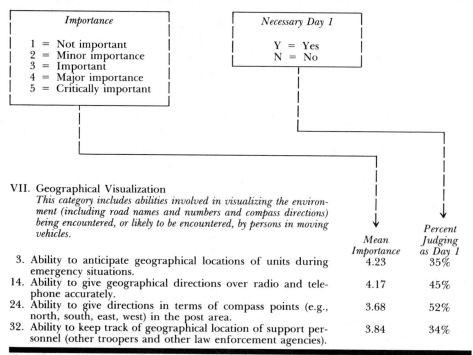

	Mean Importance	*Percent Judging as Day 1*
3. Ability to anticipate geographical locations of units during emergency situations.	4.23	35%
14. Ability to give geographical directions over radio and telephone accurately.	4.17	45%
24. Ability to give directions in terms of compass points (e.g., north, south, east, west) in the post area.	3.68	52%
32. Ability to keep track of geographical location of support personnel (other troopers and other law enforcement agencies).	3.84	34%

Note: Please see note for Table 3.5.

develop questions related to what KSAs individuals need before being selected for the job. Thus the second column indicates the percentage of subject matter experts who indicated that a KSA is needed the first day on the job.

As mentioned previously researchers sometimes discover that different groups of panel members (such as supervisors and employees) do not always agree on what characteristics (for example, tasks) are required to perform the job. In those instances, it would be important to resolve the disagreement before training programs are designed. At the present time, there are not much data about whether different groups within the organization are likely to consistently judge tasks and KSAs differently. One study by Schmitt and Cohen (1989) found very few differences between middle-level managers who were men and women or whites and nonwhites in their judgments concerning tasks. One difference they did find was that nonwhite job incumbents more frequently reported they did not perform a task as compared with their white colleagues. Another study by Landy and Vasey (1991) studied patrol officers with varying experience and found they tended to perform different jobs. Those officers with more than eleven years of experience tend to spend less of their time in traffic activities and more in noncriminal activities than their less experienced colleagues. Their point is that depending on who you choose to help describe the job, you might get different descriptions. These studies reemphasize the point that the samples involved in job analyses must be chosen carefully.

The usefulness of this type of job-analysis data in helping to make judgments about training programs was demonstrated in a study by Mumford, Weeks, Harding, and Fleishman (1987). These investigators used a measure of task-learning time, called the occupational learning difficulty (OLD) index, which are scales used by job analysts to describe the learning time for 600 tasks in forty-eight occupational specialties. They found that the OLD judgments by the job analysts accurately predict a number of important training program characteristics. Thus, when the OLD index indicates that the tasks take more time to learn, the training program for that occupation tends to be longer and have more instructional units. In addition, the programs tend to have smaller faculty–student ratios and more experienced instructors. Essentially, this study confirmed that this type of job-analysis judgment is related to a large number of independent indicators describing the training course. As such, these investigators note that you can use this kind of information about learning difficulty of tasks to help make judgments for new training efforts to determine course length and/or allocation of time for training.

Linking Knowledge, Skill, and Abilities to Tasks

At this point, the analyst has determined which KSAs and tasks are needed for the job and which are important. The next step in developing the needs assessment information base is to determine which KSAs are important for which tasks. To be maximally effective, the training program must be de-

Table 3.12 An example of KSA–task linkage instructions

2 = Essential	This knowledge or ability is essential to the performance of this task. Without this knowledge or ability, you would not be able to perform this task.
1 = Helpful	This knowledge or ability is helpful in performing this task. This task could be performed without this knowledge or ability, although it would be more difficult or time-consuming.
0 = Not Relevant	This knowledge or ability is not needed to perform this task. Having this knowledge or ability would make no difference in the performance of this task.

Note: Please see note for Table 3.5.

signed to help trainees learn the necessary KSAs to perform the tasks important to the job. The actual tasks used in training might be simulations of real-job tasks as long as they can provide the environment necessary for learning the KSAs. Thus, it is critical to develop information on what KSAs are important to perform the critical job tasks.

To be maximally efficient in this step, analysts usually consider only the tasks and KSAs that have met the various criteria, such as a 3 on importance. An example of set of instructions for performing the linking process between the KSAs and tasks is presented in Table 3.12. In this set of instructions, each individual KSA is linked to each individual task. It is important to remember that the only tasks and KSAs being linked are those that have survived the various criteria, such as their importance. Even so, the number of remaining KSAs and tasks sometimes turns out to be quite large. In those cases, some analysts have the individual KSAs first linked to the task cluster (such as the cluster found in Table 3.6). After it is determined which KSAs are linked to which cluster, it is possible to have the SMEs link the KSAs to tasks in the cluster as a way of establishing relevant KSA–task links. This is an easier process because specific links between individual KSAs and individual tasks are established for only those KSAs that were first linked to the cluster.

Some examples of links that might occur for several different jobs are presented in Table 3.13. By looking at the required KSA and noting what types of tasks they are linked to, it is possible to design the training program around simulations of the tasks that actually require that KSA on the job. For example, in the job of customer service representative, the training designer would know from the linkage data that he or she must build training sequences to help the trainee learn to explain technical information concerning basic self-checks and to provide customers information about available services. Of course, all of these linkages are dependent upon SMEs being able to reliably agree on which KSAs are linked to which tasks. Research by Hughes and Prien (1989) indicates that in general SMEs are capable of making such judgments. They found 26 KSA–task linkages where the SMEs agreed. They also found a few instances where the SMEs did not agree. Clearly, training

Table 3.13 Example of KSA–task links form various jobs

Job of Police Radio Operator

KSA—Knowledge of map formats and symbols used in reading maps.

Task Links—Searches maps for geographical information in order to respond to requests from the general public.

Receives information from troopers by phone, such as request for assistance to relay the the closest available trooper.

Receives information from the public by telephone, concerning items such as speeders or accidents, to relay to the trooper responsible for that geographical area.

Job of Customer Service Representative

KSA—Ability to explain technical information to the customer in a way that he or she understands.

Task Links—Provides instructions to the customer concerning basic self checks that can be used to resolve the customer's difficulty.

Provides information to the customer about services that are available to resolve the problem.

Job of a Manager in a Production Plant

KSA—Ability to select, organize, and present pertinent information in logical order.

Task Links—Explains written directives to train subordinates in departmental policies and procedures.

Responds to questions and problems at community meetings in order to resolve community concerns.

Note: Please see note for Table 3.5.

designers would want to focus the design of their programs on instances where there is such agreement. Thus, at the conclusion of the linkage process, the training analyst has information concerning all the required KSAs and for which tasks they are needed. The analyst can also have information on which KSAs are most important, most difficult to learn, and so on. This provides a detailed map for the design of training programs that helps ensure that the training program will be job-relevant.

PERSON ANALYSIS

As stated by McGehee and Thayer (1961), the final step in determining training needs focuses on whether the individual employees need training and exactly what training is required. At this stage, the needs assessment has already accomplished an organizational analysis that permits understanding of where the training systems fit in the work environment and what facilitators and inhibitors exist. Also, the task analysis has determined what important tasks are performed, and the KSA analysis has established which KSAs are important for task performance. The KSA analysis provides considerable information for the person analysis, including data indicating whether the KSA should be learned before entering the job, on the job, during training, and so on. However, in the person analysis, the emphasis is not in determining which KSAs are necessary but rather in assessing how well the actual employees perform the KSAs required by the job. Person analysis asks two questions: Who within the organization needs training, and what kind of instruction do they need? This can be directed at a specific training effort or a program of training for advancement in the organization.

To actually perform a person analysis, it becomes necessary to develop measures of criteria that are indicators of performance. This will be discussed in Chapter 5. However, many of these criteria are very important for a number of purposes in the design of training programs. We can use the criteria to assess performance before training, immediately after training, and on the job. The important point is that the criteria can also be used to determine the capabilities of the people on the job so that training is designed for the particular KSAs needed by those employees. It should be obvious that employees who receive performance appraisal ratings indicating that they need improvement might be candidates for a training program. Of course, it is also the case that negative performance appraisals are not greeted with enthusiasm either by the receiver or by the person who gives the information. Some observers think there might be less resistance to this type of performance appraisal if it is used as a basis to provide learning experiences helpful to the employee; however, this depends on how the whole process is viewed and managed by the organization. There is no solid body of research data on this issue.

Another way of approaching the problem is to have employees perform self-assessments of their abilities for training purposes. Unfortunately, in a review of fifty-five studies in which self-evaluation of ability was compared with measures of performance, Mabe and West (1982) did not find strong relationships between the two measures. Interestingly enough, Mabe and West did find some conditions that maximize the relationship: when the employee expected the self-evaluation to be compared with other evaluations, when the employee had previous experience performing self-evaluation, and when there were guarantees of anonymity. A clear warning on the difficulties researchers are likely to encounter in the use of self-assessments is provided by the work of McEnery and McEnery (1987). They found that self and supervisory needs assessment performed by hospital employees were not related. They also discovered that supervisors tend to project their own needs when they were asked to identify the needs for their subordinates.

Another study, which involves educators participating in an assessment center for high school principals, adds some very important information to the consideration of assessment of training skills (Noe & Schmitt, 1986). In this study, one variable of interest was employee acceptance of assessment of their skills. Noe and Schmitt found that trainees who reacted positively to the needs assessment procedure indicating their skill needs were being met were more likely to be satisfied with the training program content. This type of consideration is important because it not only asks whether we can assess trainee skills in order to determine appropriate training placement but also whether it is possible to determine which variables affect the trainees' willingness to participate and learn from training. In this regard, Noe and Schmitt also found that trainees who had the strongest commitment to job involvement were also the people who were more likely to acquire the key behaviors in the training program. In addition, those employees committed to career planning were the individuals who were more likely to apply training content to their work behavior, resulting in actual on-the-job improvement. These latter points are important for issues concerning motivation and learning (they will be discussed in more detail in Chapter 4).

In summary, an instructional program must be based on the characteristics of the group that will be placed in the training environment. If the program is intended for those people already on the job, the data from the performance, task, and person analysis provide the required information for an analysis of the target population. However, if the target population is a new job or a new group of employees, the analyses are incomplete. Observers have commented on the differences in values between those students entering school and work situations today and those of preceding generations. Such differences must be considered in program design. For example, particular errors may occur on a job due to difficulties related to computer-analysis ability. However, entering trainees may have the prerequisite skills in computer techniques and need less emphasis in that particular area. Thus, the organization may need different training programs for employees and those coming to the job.

Unfortunately, it is sometimes difficult to analyze the incoming target population because they are not presently employed. Potential solutions might consist of examining employees who have recently been hired or consulting with similar organizations that have recently hired trainees. The latter procedure must be performed carefully because small differences between firms can radically change the characteristics of the entering population. Thus, two corporations with the same characteristics but differing locales (for example, rural versus urban) may attract employees with significantly different characteristics. It is necessary to match the characteristics of the target population to the requirements for successful performance. It should also be clear that while this chapter focuses on tasks and KSAs as input to the training process, other aspects to the training process need consideration. Thus, trainees are socialized into the organization by what happens in training. In some cases, they receive realistic job previews not only about their tasks but also about their organization. These issues and their relationship to training design are treated in Chapter 9 in "Organizational Entry, Training, and Socialization."

Summary

In summary, the results of task, KSA, and person analysis can provide critical input information concerning such items as present level of performance, criticality of tasks and KSAs, frequency of occurrence, opportunity to learn, difficulty in learning on the job, and so on. These responses can be organized into composite indices that reflect the different judgments provided for the task and KSA statements. For example, one index can reflect the following logic in the development of training content: The most important tasks to consider are those given the highest priority in the job and for which it is difficult to acquire proficiency. Similarly, the content to be included in the training curriculum can be identified with reference to a composite index identifying the KSAs important for full job performance and for which there is a minimum opportunity to learn on the job. The composite indices are thus evaluated to determine the content and priorities of the training curriculum.

Besides providing input for the design of new instructional programs, the thoughtful application of job-analysis procedures can provide useful input relevant to a variety of training development and evaluation questions. Some of the other potential applications include the following:

1. *Examination of previously designed training programs*: It is possible to compare the emphasis of training programs presently being used with the needs assessment information. This type of comparison could determine whether the emphasis in training is being placed on tasks and KSAs that are important and that are not easily learned on the job.

2. *Design of trainee assessment instruments*: Needs assessment information provides valuable information on the capabilities of trainees to perform the job appropriately. As such, the needs assessment procedures can provide input to design performance-appraisal instruments to assess the capabilities of trainees at the end of training and on the job. It is also possible to design performance-appraisal instruments to determine which employees might need further training.

3. *Input to the interaction between selection systems and training systems*: The determination of the task- and person-element domains can provide input into the selection system by specifying the KSAs required to perform the various job tasks. The degree to which the selection system can identify and hire persons with various KSAs affects the design of the training system. For example, training programs might not need to emphasize those KSAs already in the repertoire of the trainee. Often this results in a training program that is not only more interesting but also less time-consuming.

It is important to emphasize that the choice of a particular methodology should be based on an analysis of the particular application requiring job information. Further, even the choice of questions within a particular methodology is dependent on the application. Thus, in some cases, criticality of performance information is important; in other cases, opportunity to learn or information related to where learning takes place is the key issue. In other instances, a whole variety of questions must be addressed. The critical point is this: Thoughtful planning that considers the variety of methods and applications must precede any needs assessment effort. It is a waste of valuable resources to conduct a needs assessment effort only to discover that the wrong questions have been asked or the wrong problem solved. It is, of course, an even more serious waste of valuable resources to design a training program without a careful needs assessment. Unfortunately, even when needs assessment is performed and the training program is well designed, there appear to be instances when training does not result in learning being transferred onto the job.

As noted earlier, analyses of training programs force consideration of the fact that something learned in one environment (training) will be performed in another (on the job). Thus, the trainee will enter a new environment to be affected by all the interacting components that represent organizations today. Certainly, there are some aspects of the environment that help determine the success or failure of training programs beyond the attributes the trainee must gain as a result of attending the instructional program. The reader is invited to review the organizational analysis section. When the types of issues described in the organizational analysis are ignored, the advantages gained from careful task and person analyses are lost.

EXAMPLES OF NEEDS ASSESSMENT METHODS AND TECHNIQUES

Content-Oriented Job Analysis

The system of job analysis described in the preceding pages by using both a task and KSA approach emphasizes the content of the job that is then used to serve as the input for training. For that reason, a good term to describe the approach is *content-oriented job analysis.* An earlier version of that approach, developed by Prien (see Prien, 1977; Goldstein, Macey, & Prien, 1981), emphasizes tasks, elements, and performance domains. His concept of tasks is consistent with the task analysis described earlier; elements refer to the characteristics of KSAs also previously described. The performance domain refers to incidents that describe the behavior of persons performing the job. These incidents can describe superior or poor performance of an individual using his or her KSAs to perform a task. These incidents often form the basis for rating scales used as criteria to measure the success of employees in performing their jobs. This type of criterion development is discussed in Chapter 5.

Prien, Goldstein, and Macey (1985a) describe a case study where the job-analysis purpose was to determine what should be included in the training program. The setting for the study was a regional bank with a large central organization and many branch offices. Branch offices ranged in size from three employees to full-service operations of several hundred employees. The focus of the study included a broad range of jobs across the locations of bank operations. The management purpose for conducting the job analysis was to examine and evaluate job content to identify opportunities for on-the-job training through selective job-assignment rotation and to differentiate job components requiring classroom training because of few opportunities to learn on the job. These authors indicate that they went through the following phases to complete their study.

Phase 1. They developed a structure, or framework, for organizing and describing the content-domain data acquired through the application of various data-collection procedures. This was achieved through an examination of available training records and materials and direct observation of the work setting and process. The information acquired in this stage provided a general understanding of business operations, terminology, and so on. The outcome of this research phase was a broad framework within which information acquired in later phases of the project could be placed.

Phase 2. The second phase of the job analysis involved a series of interviews with individuals who would qualify as SMEs, drawn from the entire organization. The purpose of these interviews was to collect information about the tasks employees perform and the duty-based KSAs required to perform those tasks. These researchers often found that it was easiest to obtain KSAs by supplying the SMEs with tasks and asking them what KSAs were required to perform those tasks. The result of these interviews was a set of descriptors in the task and element domain. These task- and job-element (KSAs) statements were then evaluated for ambiguity, clarity, and accuracy by the researchers and training representatives to ensure that all content domain was represented.

Phase 3. In this phase of the project, SMEs (including job incumbents, supervisors, and members of management) representing the organization provided further information about the job-content domains. To meet the requirements of identifying training needs, SMEs completed structured questionnaires comprising the task- and job-element statements by providing ratings representing a number of judgments. The two judgments relevant to this illustration are *importance* (ratings of the criticality of KSAs for full job performance), and *opportunity to learn on the job* (ratings of the opportunities to acquire KSAs on the job).

Phase 4. The fourth phase of the needs assessment strategy comprised the data analyses necessary to define the content of the job domain relevant for training purposes. The various components of the job were determined, and importance and opportunity-to-learn indices were computed. For purposes of illustration, a few knowledge and ability items for the construct of customer relations are presented in Table 3.14. The two jobs identified are work done in branch operations and auditing and staff services. Examination of the data in the table reveals that, in general, importance and opportunity-to-learn-on-the-job judgments are quite different for the two job examples. It is possible to compare the data displays for all KSAs and tasks and for all job groups simultaneously on various judgments (for example, criticality). An analysis of all tasks provided the answers to issues related to training content, where training was to be obtained (on the job versus in the classroom), and, for on-the-job training, what assignment would be most appropriate.

Strategic Job Analysis

An area of growing concern is the question of future objectives. As technology continues to change the workplace, training programs are being considered

Table 3.14 Customer relations KSAs

	Group 1— Branch Operations		*Group 2— Auditing/Staff Services*	
	Importance[1]	*Opportunity to*[1] *Learn on Job*	*Importance*[1]	*Opportunity to*[1] *Learn on Job*
Knowlege of bank security investment policies	1.3	1.1	1.1	.6
Knowledge of standard accounting principles and procedures	2.5	1.9	4.1	2.7
Ability to identify key individuals in client organizations	4.1	3.4	.0	.0
Ability to identify areas of inquiry from bank customers which require specialized assistance from individuals outside the bank	3.3	3.1	.3	.1
Ability to explain bank policy and procedure to customers dissatisfied with bank performance	4.8	4.5	.3	.1
Ability to recognize necessity of change in audit procedure from that originally identified in audit program	1.4	1.5	3.4	3.0

[1]The higher the number, the greater the importance and the greater the opportunity to learn.
From "Multi-Method Job Analysis: Methodology and Applications," by E. P. Prien, I. L. Goldstein, and W. H. Macey, Unpublished paper. Memphis, TN: Performance Management Associates, 1985.

for jobs that may not exist. Thus, Hall (1986) describes the importance of establishing a relationship between the future strategic objectives of the organization and the future requirements for their executives. To accomplish this, techniques will need to be developed that permit SMEs to describe explicitly future requirements for their organization. Essentially, a task and KSA analysis of future job requirements is needed. Although this work is still in the developmental stages, Schneider and Konz (1989) describe one possible strategy that they have titled *strategic job analysis*. Their procedure uses similar strategies to those described earlier—obtain tasks, task clusters, and linked KSAs. They also had the job incumbents rate the importance of the task clusters developed by the job-analysis procedures. The task clusters and a very brief description (the actual clusters used had the complete set of tasks presented) are as follows:

Table 3.15 Task cluster importance for present job and future job

Task Cluster	Importance[1] Present Job Mean	Future Job Mean
Goals	4.39	4.80
Plans	3.62	2.66
Informs	3.82	3.77
Monitors	3.18	2.56
Supervises	3.54	3.04
Feedback	4.24	4.73
Appraises	4.53	5.00
Trains	3.64	4.17
Recruits	3.87	4.75
Customer	3.45	2.17

[1]Five-point scale used (1–5) where 1 = not at all important, 2 = slightly, 3 = moderately, 4 = very, 5 = extremely important. Adapted from "Strategic Job Analysis" by B. Schneider and A. M. Konz. In *Human Resources Management,* Spring 1989, *28,* pp. 51–63. Copyright © 1989 by John Wiley & Sons Inc. Reprinted by permission.

1. *Goals:* Sets goals with subordinates.
2. *Plans:* Plans and schedules.
3. *Informs:* Informs and advises subordinates.
4. *Monitors:* Monitors results and updates management.
5. *Supervises:* Supervises staff and resources.
6. *Feedback:* Gives feedback and counsels staff.
7. *Appraises:* Appraises subordinate performance.
8. *Trains:* Trains and develops subordinates.
9. *Staffs:* Staffs the unit (recruits, selects, and terminates).
10. *Customers:* Handles customers.

Then, they used SME panels from upper-level management to develop information on how the job will change and how that will affect the tasks as well as the KSAs required. Some of the changes that managers predicted included computerization of the job, with resulting changes in report-preparation procedures, work group size, competencies required, and personal contact. They also described changes in increased state and federal regulations governing the business, such as increased financial services laws. Based on that discussion, the SMEs rated the clusters, and that data is presented in Table 3.15.

Interestingly, the SMEs indicated a much greater range of importance for the task clusters of the future (from 2.17 to 5.00), as compared to the incumbents, present ratings of importance (from 3.18 to 4.53). They also believed that the clusters titled *goals, feedback, appraises, trains, and staff* would be more important in the future, whereas *plans, monitors, supervises,* and *customers* would be less important. Most interesting is the discussion reported by Schneider and Konz (1989). For example, the reason the SMEs believe that *monitors* will be less important is that a set of tasks will be automated and done by computer. These researchers also collected information about how that might change the KSA requirements and therefore the training programs of the future.

Functional Job Analysis

This system of job analysis is primarily based on the work of Fine (Fine, 1978; Olson, Fine, Myers, & Jennings, 1981). He emphasizes that the whole person is involved in job performance and the method of observation must clearly specify what to look for, record, and emphasize in order to have total coverage. *Functional job analysis* focuses on tasks as the fundamental unit. Fine's format for task statements includes the following questions.

Who?
What action?
To accomplish what immediate results?
With what tools/equipment/work aids?
Upon what instructions? (1978, p. 7)

An example of a task statement using these criteria is presented in Table 3.16, for a person who operates a grader.

Fine's system requires that the tasks be specified thoroughly enough to classify the worker according to the degree of involvement with data, people, and things. The various levels of involvement for each of these are as follows:

Data

6. Synthesizing
5. Coordinating
   Innovating
4. Analyzing
3. Computing
   Compiling
2. Copying
1. Comparing

People

7. Mentoring
6. Negotiating
5. Supervising
4. Consulting
   Instructing
   Treating
3. Coaching
   Persuading
   Diverting
2. Exchanging Information
1. Taking Instructions—
   Helping, Serving

Things

3. Precision Working
   Setting Up
   Operating–Controlling II
2. Manipulating
   Operating–Controlling I
   Driving–Controlling
   Starting Up
1. Handling
   Feeding–Offbearing
   Tending

Table 3.16 Functional job-analysis system for person who operates a grader

Task:
Operates grader manipulating controls to travel forward/back, turn, raise/lower blade; position wheels and blade at correct angles; follows work order, drawing on knowledge and experience, monitoring the performance of the equipment and adapting to the changing situation, constantly alert to the presence and safety of other workers/equipment, in order to perform routine grader tasks such as backfilling, haul road maintenance, snow removal.

TO DO THIS TASK

Performance Standards	*Training Content*
Descriptive Operates equipment properly. Is alert and attentive.	*Functional* How to operate grader. How to do routine grader tasks such as backfilling, scarifying, windrowing, cutting firebreak, maintaining haul road, snow removal.
Numerical All work meets work order requirements. No accidents/damage due to improper operating technique.	*Specific* Knowledge of specific grader. Knowledge of work requirements. Knowledge of specific job site (that is, layout, soil condition, environment).
TO THESE STANDARDS	*THE WORKER NEEDS THIS TRAINING*

From "Contribution of the Job Element and Functional Job Analysis Approaches to Content Validity" by. S. A. Fine. Presented at the International Personnel Management Assessment Council Annual Conference, Atlanta, Georgia, 1978.

The scales are designed to capture all the ways that people function to accomplish their work. Also, each function is designed to include the activities listed below that activity but to exclude those listed above. Thus, on the people scale, a task requiring a person to operate at level 2 (exchanging information) means that the person also performs level 1 functions (taking instruction) but not those functions listed at 3 (coaching) and above. To develop this system, the job analyst would observe both the job and work with SMEs familiar with the particular job. As a result of this analysis, task statements such as the one presented in Table 3.16 would be developed. Then, for that task, the data, people, and thing items would be derived. For example, for the tasks listed in the table, the following types of sample functions were determined.

Data	*People*	*Things*
Determines best procedures for doing work.	Takes continuing instructions from supervisor as necessary.	Adjusts front wheel to counteract side-thrust.
Checks direction of drainage requirements.	Responds to signals from other operators and grade checkers.	Manipulates controls to position blade to desired angle of economic operation.

Based on an analysis of all the data, people, and thing functions, the task is classified. For example, the task of grader (in Table 3.16) is classified as compiling (for data), taking instructions (for people), and for operating-controlling II (for things). Fine also indicates the degree of involvement with each of these functions by assigning 100 points to be spread out among the data, people, and thing functions. For this task, 25 percent is assigned to data, 10 percent to people, and 65 percent to things, indicating the high relative emphasis of the grader task to the kinds of functions found in the things category. On the basis of this type of information, Fine completes the information found in Table 3.16. Thus, he lists the performance standards at a descriptive level that indicates the wholeness of the performance and the numerical standards, which are designed to cover very limited, measurable aspects of performance. From the performance standards, Fine derives the training content. As shown, the functional training content is designed to indicate the general training the person should bring to the job; the specific training content is designed to indicate the specific training necessary for the establishment in which the person is working. It should be noted that the items included in the table are examples and represent only a sample of the material that would appear in a full job analysis of the grader task.

DERIVATION OF OBJECTIVES

The organizational, task, and person analyses provide the information necessary for the assessment of instructional need. This assessment makes it possible to specify the objectives of the training program. The objectives provide direct input for the design of the training program and help specify the criterion measures that will be used to evaluate the performance of the trainee at the end of the training program and in the transfer setting (on the job, in the next program, and so on). The assessment of instructional need tells the trainer where to begin, and the specification of the objectives indicates the completion point of the program.

Mager (1984) describes the characteristics of objectives in the following manner:

1. *Performance:* An objective always states what a learner is expected to be able to do.
2. *Conditions:* An objective always describes the important conditions (if any) under which the performance is to occur.
3. *Criterion:* Wherever possible, an objective describes the criterion of acceptable performance by describing how well the learner must perform to be considered acceptable.

Sound objectives communicate to learners what they are expected to do when they finish the program. Some trainers have suggested (not without a note of sarcasm) that if the instructor communicated these objectives, the success of the program would be assured. The difficulties that can result from not using a system like Mager's to specify behavioral objectives are apparent in expressions like "to appreciate safety." A close examination of this objective indicates that it does not state what the learner is doing when he or she appreciates safety and does not indicate the desired terminal behavior or the conditions under which the behavior will be performed. As a matter of fact, the objective, as stated, would permit any of the following behaviors to be considered as meeting the goal, although it is doubtful that most trainers would consider their course successful if these events occurred:

1. The employee passed a safety knowledge test with a minimum score of 75%.
2. The employee bought a Red Cross handbook on safety.
3. The employee wears safety goggles when the foreman is present.
4. The employee indicates that safety is important on questionnaires handed out by top management. (Goldstein, Tuttle, Wood, & Grether, 1975, p. 48)

Certainly, the design of the training program should be dependent on the definition of appreciation of safety. The following example comes from an analysis of safety problems stemming from persons being injured by grinding wheels. An analysis indicates that this problem occurred when the wheel was warming up, so it was important for individuals not to stand in front of the wheel during warm-up time. The example states

> When the trainee turns on the grinding wheel, the trainee should always tend to stand to the left of the wheel and out of the path of any exploding particles for the 30 seconds necessary for the wheel to reach maximum velocity. (Goldstein et al., 1975, p. 49)

Again, it is important to realize that behavioral objectives can be developed for very complex behaviors. For example, consider Mager's illustration for a course on human relations:

> Be able to prepare within twenty-four hours analyses of any five of the given case studies. These analyses should discuss the cases according to the principles presented during the course and should describe each problem from the points of view of at least two of the participants. References and notes may be used. (1984, p. 36)

Note that the behavioral objective specifies the educational intent, communicates to the learner what he or she will be doing, and describes the terminal behavior, conditions, and criteria of successful performance.

Similar objectives can be written for all important aspects of a training program. In many cases, the trainer will discover that the objectives of the training program are not exactly the same as those for successful job performance. When the job is complex, the trainee cannot be expected to exhibit the same behavior as persons who have been performing the task for many years. Thus, one set of objectives and criteria is designed for the initial training analyses, and other objectives and criteria are designed to be used at a later time on the job. These issues are discussed further in Chapter 5. However, the specification of these different objectives will in itself clear up many misunderstandings about trainee requirements upon completion of the program. Thus far, the objectives discussed have been related to specific aspects of trainee behavior. They represent only one level of analysis. Other objectives are concerned with the performance of a system as a whole, rather than behaviors of individuals.

One specification program, typically called *management by objectives* (MBO), has been recognized by industry for a number of years. Strauss states that

> MBO (at least when it works as it should) requires management to define exactly what it wants to accomplish and to specify all important objectives, especially those commonly ignored. It reduces the emphasis on short-run profits, increases the number of managerial goals and forces the explicit consideration of exactly what steps must be taken if these goals are to be fulfilled. In this way, it helps subordinates learn what is required of them, thus reducing their need for guesswork. As a result, it makes decision-making more rational, for both boss and subordinate. In sum, MBO can become a coordinated process of planning which involves every management level in determining both the goals that it will meet and the means by which they are to be met. (1972, p. 11)

There are several difficulties associated with the MBO process. One group of conflicts is related to the procedures used in implementing the system. There are complaints about the amount of paperwork required, as well as about the great flourish with which objectives and goals are announced—only to be forgotten six months later. These complaints appear to be related to the failure of properly implementing the program. Another more serious criticism is related to who designs the objectives and how the objectives are used—procedures that often lead to conflict between personal and corporate goals. Often the information gathered is used simply to exercise a greater degree of control over the organization. These controversies pertain to participative action in which all individuals have an opportunity to help determine goals and objectives. Whether the system is participative or not, goals and objectives are ultimately designed by someone at the policy level. It is as important to determine the success of the policies as it is to determine the success of an individual worker performing his or her task. Certainly, the specification of goals provides information that can lead to changes in the objectives as well as measures of their achievement.

Conclusions

The purpose of this chapter is to describe the various components of needs assessment, including organizational analysis, task and KSA analysis, and person analysis. The needs assessment provides all the critical input for both the design of the training environment and the evaluation of the actual training program. The needs assessment may provide information indicating that training is not the intervention that is needed or that a number of other programs (for example, conflict resolution between different organizational units) have to be accomplished before training can be considered. In any case, at the conclusion of the needs assessment, the objectives of the training should be apparent: "The best available basis for the needed matching of media with objectives is a rationale by which the kind of learning involved in each educational objective is stated in terms of the learning conditions required" (Briggs, Campeau, Gagné, & May, 1967, p. 3). The process of going from task analysis to systematic identification of the behaviors to be learned remains one of the most difficult phases in the design of training programs. In this regard, some dramatic advances in cognitive psychology have strong implications for instructional design. Also, some of these advances have implications for the design of needs assessment procedures. However, before discussing how this may affect the collection of needs assessment information, it is necessary to understand some of the changes resulting from research in cognitive psychology. This will be discussed in the next chapter.

The other aspect of our training program that follows from the analyses discussed in this chapter is the evaluation process. The criteria and methods for evaluating programs cannot be conveniently added onto the end of the project without disrupting the training program. In addition, some of the data must be collected before and during the training program, as well as some time after the student has completed training. The evaluation design is an integral part of the entire program but is often a neglected function. This will be discussed in Chapters 5 and 6.

The Learning Environment

4

The learning environment discussed in this chapter refers to the dynamics of the instructional setting, with particular emphasis on those components that support learning in the training setting. First, there is consideration of trainee readiness, which is the learning characteristics trainees must bring to the instructional setting. In another section the conditions of instruction and learning are described, including principles that contribute to learning. Then, materials are presented on transfer of learning, with a particular focus on what is necessary to ensure transfer from the learning environment to the on-the-job environment. The chapter concludes with material on the characteristics of an effective environment and effective trainer.

LEARNING AND INSTRUCTION

The basic foundation for instructional programs is learning. The establishment of instructional procedures is based on the belief that it is possible to design an environment in which learning can take place and later be transferred to another setting. The close relationship between learning and instruction is suggested by most learning definitions.: "Learning is a relatively permanent change in knowledge or skill produced by experience" (Weiss, 1990, p. 172).

This definition implies that the change is relatively permanent, but it does not assume that all changes lead to improvements in behavior. Although most learning does lead to improvements, there is clear evidence that people can acquire behavioral tendencies toward drugs or racial hatred that might be injurious. Also, learning is an inferred process that is not directly observable. In some cases, learning becomes immediately observable through performance; in other cases, a considerable period of time passes before learning becomes apparent. The care with which the inference must be established is demonstrated by the effects of alcohol and other drugs on behavior. In many instances, the use of drugs can cause poor performance. However, it should not be inferred that learned behavior has been forgotten. When the effects of drugs have worn off, the performance level can return to normal, without any intervening training (Bower & Hilgard, 1981).

From the preceding discussion, it seems that traditional learning principles applied to modern training or instructional settings would be effective. Thus, the rest of this chapter should be devoted to a review of the learning principles that have been developed in the last 100 years. However, the assumption is invalid. There is a wide gulf separating learning theories and principles from what is actually needed to improve performance. An opening statement discussing a basic gulf between learning theory and its applications is offered by Bruner:

> A theory of instruction must concern itself with the relationship between how things are presented and how they are learned. Though I myself have worked hard and long in the vineyard of learning theory, I can do no better than to start by warning the reader away from it. Learning theory is not a theory of instruction. It describes what happened. A theory of instruction is a guide to what to do in order to achieve certain objectives. Unfortunately, we shall have to start pretty nearly at the beginning, for there is very little literature to guide us in this subtle enterprise. (1963, p. 524)

The views expressed by individuals like Bruner are also supported by empirical analyses. Gagné (1962) examined the utility of laboratory learning principles in the performance of a series of tasks. He found that the best-known principles, including feedback, distribution of practice, and meaningfulness, were "strikingly inadequate to handle the job of designing effective training situations" (p. 85). He reached this conclusion after examining data from a variety of different tasks, including tracking and problem solving. Gagné (1962) suggests that it is necessary to organize the total task into a set of distinct components that mediate final task performance. When these component tasks are present in the instructional program there should be an effective transfer of learning from the instructional setting to the job setting. Thus, the principles of training design would consist of identifying the task components that make up final performance, placing these parts into the instructional program and arranging the learning of these components in an optimal sequence.

In 1971, in the first *Annual Review of Psychology* chapter on training, Campbell noted the importance of Gagné's article, suggesting that this approach specifies a concern with "task analysis, terminal behaviors, component task achievements, the fidelity of training-task components, and sequencing" (p. 567). In 1988 Campbell, again reflecting on Gagné's work, stated that the paper was one of the most important ever published and reflected a paradigm shift. He recommends that all people interested in training be given Gagné's article as required reading. I agree. That paper forced us to begin focusing on the central question—What is to be learned?

During the 1970s, researchers began the task of developing instructional theories, relying on both theoretical and experimental analysis in the laboratory and applied problems taken from instructional settings (Glaser, 1982). These researchers asked questions about the kinds of knowledge necessary to learn to read an instructional manual or to learn a new language (including computer languages). Theories were developed about how the learner organized and integrated information and how information was stored. Glaser notes that a possible difference between people with high and low learning aptitude is the ability of learners to organize and use information in ways that make it possible to transfer it from old to new problems. Glaser makes the goals of instructional theory clear:

> The development that I anticipate is a macro-theory of teaching and instruction: "macro" in the sense that it is concerned with the large practical variables dealt with in schools such as the allocation and efficient use of time, the structure of classroom management, the nature of teacher feedback and reinforcement to the student, the organizational pattern of teacher–student interaction, the relationship between what is taught and what is tested, the degree of classroom flexibility required for adapting to learner background, and the details of curriculum materials as these relate to student achievement. . . . As theory at this level develops, it will be undergirded by the more microstudies of human thinking and problem solving. . . . (1982, p. 299)

Thus began a shift away from a strict behavioristic tradition that emphasized observable behavior and its relationship to traditional conditions of learning, such as the conditions of practice and reinforcement. Rather, there was a growing emphasis on the cognitive learner and mental processes including attention, memory, language, reasoning, and problem solving. In part, this was also driven by the changes in technology. As Howell and Cooke (1989) carefully note, the changes in technology increased demands on the learner who now, instead of performing simple procedural and predictable tasks, must become responsible for inferences, diagnoses, judgments, and decision making, often under severe time pressure. Cognitive tasks suggest cognitively oriented training approaches. Traditional learning had little to say about how to increase attentional capacity, to make for a better diagnosis, or to use a mental model to control all the complex processes that need to be the focus of attention. As Howell and Cooke note, inferences, monitoring, and problem solving will be the work requirements for the future.

Unfortunately, the processes involved in designing instructional systems and the revolution first described by both Gagné and Bruner in the 1960s has only begun to be understood. As Glaser (1990) puts it, it was first necessary to put learning aside and begin to understand human performance. In other words, it was first critical to unravel what makes up competent performance and the differences between the experts and novices. Again, the central question is, What is to be learned? This has led to major advances in areas such as our knowledge of the organization of memory and information-processing requirements. It has even spawned new concepts that have applications for use in training systems, such as advanced organizers, which are discussed later in this chapter. I predict this will eventually be as popular a term to training analysts as part versus whole practice is today. As I examine the first edition of this text (1974), the entire chapter on learning covered classical principles of learning. In the second edition (1986), the idea that instructional and cognitive psychology might have an important influence was introduced, but the chapter still focused on classical principles of learning. In this edition, ideas from instructional and cognitive psychology will be introduced into the sections on learning while still maintaining some of the important classical thoughts. By the next version of this text, perhaps there will be many more important developments to bring to the attention of the reader. Readers interested in good descriptions of the cognitive revolution and its potential relationship to training should consult Campbell (1988), Howell and Cooke (1989), and Weiss (1990).

In the next section, there is first a consideration of trainee readiness, which is the ability, motivation, and other characteristics that must be brought to the instructional setting. In the following section, the conditions of learning are described. Here, various classical principles such as knowledge of results are discussed, as well as some of the principles stemming from instructional psychology, such as aptitude–treatment interactions, automaticity, and advanced organizers. The final component described is the transfer of learning. In this section, material is presented about what is necessary to ensure transfer from the learning environment to the job. The chapter concludes with material on the characteristics of an effective environment and effective trainer.

THE INSTRUCTIONAL ENVIRONMENT

Preconditions of Learning

Before trainees can benefit from any form of training, they must be ready to learn; that is, they must have the particular background experiences necessary for the training program, and they must be motivated. There is reason to believe that individuals perform poorly in training because they either were ill-prepared to enter the program, did not think the program would be useful, or did not want to learn. If these reasons are valid and the cause is not an ill-conceived program, the implementer must be certain that the preconditions for learning are satisfied. Gilbert (1982) describes the complex interaction between the training environment, the individual's prior knowledge and skill, and the incentives necessary to perform by referring to the facets of behavior involved in assembling a tricycle. These facets are presented in Figure 4.1. Gilbert notes that behavior can be changed (or trained) in the following ways:

> The *data* that the manufacturer had provided me as the instructions for assembly, by making them clearer or more confusing. (All manufacturers whose products I have bought wrote confusing instructions.)
> My *skill* in using that data. (My training in reading mechanical instructions was sadly inadequate.)
> The *instruments* to do the job. (Last Christmas the manufacturer forgot to supply the small wrench that its packing list promised.)
> My *capacity* to make the required responses. (My fingers, eyesight and temper are all too short.)
> The *incentive* of a beautifully finished product. (Or sooner or later you'll give up.)
> The *motives* to do the job. (1982, p. 27)

One of the more interesting changes in the research literature in the past five years is a much broader conception of trainee characteristics. As described by Tannenbaum and Yukl (1992) in the most recent *Annual Review* chapter on training, there has been a virtual explosion in the consideration of trainee characteristics including many cognitive characteristics such as self-efficacy and goal orientation. In addition, there is a developing literature on other signals such as expectations about whether training will be useful. First, material related to a trainee's ability will be presented. Then, further material on motivation and other signals and cues will be examined.

Trainee readiness. *Trainee readiness* refers to both maturational and experiential factors in the background of the learner. Because trainee readiness is critical in the learning process, the instructor must be concerned with the ability of the trainee to perform certain tasks. Some psychologists believe that differences in developmental readiness are primarily due to the number and kind of previously learned intellectual skills (Gagné, 1970). Supporters of this view would argue that many of the abstract rules of calculus could be taught to fourth graders if they had first attained the skills (for example, algebra concepts) prerequisite to the form of learning. This point has particular significance for instructors responsible for designing instructional programs involving more mature individuals. Programs will fail if the prerequisite skills necessary to perform successfully are not considered.

These ideas have led researchers to consider various measures to predict who will learn in training situations. Investigators interested in predicting training performance suggest that a person who can demonstrate proficiency in learning to perform on a job sample will learn in training and eventually perform on the job (assuming appropriate training) (Siegel, 1983; Robertson & Downs, 1979, 1989). Thus, the measure consists of a trainability test, which is used to predict later training performance. Note that the trainability test is not the entire training program but a sample of the tasks that reflect some of the required knowledge, skills, and abilities (KSAs) needed for job performance. Clearly, this sample must be based on a careful needs assessment and

Figure 4.1 Six facets of the behavior of assembling a tricycle. From "A Question of Performance—Part 1—The Probe Model" by T. F. Gilbert. In *Training and Development Journal,* 1982, 36(9), pp. 20–30. Copyright © 1982 by the American Society for Training and Development, Inc. Reprinted by permission.

does not serve in lieu of a training program. Rather, the purpose is to use a learning measure based on performance on a relevant sample of tasks, to predict later performance in the training program or on the job.

Most of the trainability test work involves psychomotor performance. A good example of the variety of such tests that have been developed is provided by Robertson and Downs (1979, 1989), who report on over twenty years of research using trainability tests to predict later training performance. They found it possible to predict training success in a large number of jobs including carpentry, welding, sewing, forklift operating, dentistry, and bricklaying. In some studies, they even found that people who performed poorly on the training tests were less likely to turn up for training and more likely to leave in the first month. Thus, the test might have provided some realistic expectations about what the training and job would be like. Robertson and Downs selected relevant sample activities based on what is taught in training. Thus, the carpentry test involved making a certain kind of T-joint, and the welding test consisted of several straight runs along chalk lines on steel. The procedure consisted of the following:

1. Using a standardized procedure, the instructor provides training and demonstrations with the applicant free to ask questions.
2. The applicant is asked to perform the task unaided.
3. The applicant's performance is recorded according to a standardized checklist.

While most of Robertson and Down's trainability tests have a strong psychomotor component, Reilly and Israelski (1988) demonstrate that the same principles work on more knowledge-based tests. They used minicourses that had material representative of training content in order to assess a trainee's ability to acquire knowledge relevant to a full-scale training program.

There is an important distinction between predicting training performance and job performance. Studies that have employed this type of design do not necessarily offer data about the relevance of the training and its relationship to on-the-job performance. Some of these investigators (for example, Siegel, 1983) found, however, they could also use training performance to predict later on-the-job performance. The emphasis here is on trainability. Clearly, the point is that the use of appropriate selection devices to determine who could benefit from training could substantially reduce the cost of instruction. This view is supported by Reilly and Manese (1979), who employed a short, self-paced training course as a sample to predict trainee performance for programs in electronic switching systems for Bell Systems employees. The average cost for this six-month course was $25,000 per trainee.

A related point is that understanding the capabilities of incoming trainees has important implications for the design of training programs. In the last chapter, the point stressed was that the needs assessment provide the information necessary for the design of the instructional program. This information provides the training analyst with information on the characteristics of trainees. Measuring trainees on what they know before they begin training will provide information indicating which trainees may already know this material, which trainees may require remedial work, and which trainees are ready for training. Too often, training analysts think that the only purpose of a training pretest is to compare the results to a posttest to evaluate the instructional program. Pretests also serve the purpose of providing information about trainee readiness.

Trainee Motivation and Other Predispositions

Motivation involves psychological processes that cause arousal, direction, and persistence of behavior (Mitchell, 1982). *Arousal* and *persistence* focus on the time and effort that an individual invests, and *direction* refers directly to the behaviors in which the investment of time and effort are made (Naylor, Pritchard, & Ilgen, 1980). Training analysts are required to recognize a variety of factors that influence motivational levels in human beings and that the factors might not be the same for each individual. As will be indicated in the next section, using as many motivational variables as possible in the instructional setting, in order to enhance learning, is important. On the other hand, individuals who are motivated upon entry into the training program clearly have an advantage from the very beginning. Some interesting data concerning motivation of trainees upon entry were collected in a study of the Navy School for Divers (Ryman & Biersner, 1975). The investigators had trainees fill out a training-confidence scale before training. Some of the motivational items on the scale were

If I have trouble during training, I will try harder.
I will get more from this training than most people.
I volunteered for this training as soon as I could.
Even if I fail, this training will be a valuable experience.

The trainees rated these items on a five-point scale from "disagree strongly" to "agree strongly." The investigators discovered that scores on these items predicted eventual graduation from the program. Thus, the more the pretrainees agreed with these statements, the more likely they were to graduate.

Sanders and Yanouzas (1983) have further developed these ideas in terms of the trainers' ability to socialize trainees to the learning environment. They note that trainees come to the learning environment with certain attitudes and expectations and these may or may not be helpful in the learning process. Table 4.1 describes a number of aspects of the role of a student in the class. Trainees who have expectations that are positive and supportive of these types of activities are more likely to be ready for training. If attitudes are generally negative, then it becomes necessary to determine the source of the difficulties and to correct the problems before training begins. Without such intervention, learning is not likely to occur.

In 1986 Noe described a model specifying some of the motivational as well as other attribute and attitude factors that might affect the trainee's effectiveness in the instructional program. Many of these factors also have

Table 4.1 Indicators of trainee readiness

	SD	D	N	A	SA
As a student in this class, my role is to . . .					
1. Accept personal responsibility for becoming involved in learning experiences.					
2. Be willing to participate actively in classroom analysis of learning activities.					
3. Be willing to engage in self-assessment.					
4. Be willing to learn from classmates.					
5. Believe that information learned will be useful in the future.					
6. Complete assignments and readings prior to class.					

SD Strongly disagreee
D Disagree
N Neutral
A Agree
SA Strongly agree

Adapted from "Socialization to Learning," by P. Sanders and J. N. Yanouzas. In *Training and Development Journal,* 1983, *37,* pp. 14–21. Copyright © 1983 by American Society for Training and Development, Inc. Adapted by permission.

implications for the design of training environments, which will be discussed in the next section. Some factors Noe specified are as follows:

1. Trainees enter a training program because of someone's assessment of their strengths and weaknesses. Achievement will be better to the degree that trainees believe that assessment.

2. The individual's locus of control is likely to affect an individual's motivation and ability to learn. *Locus of control* refers to the degree to which an individual is likely to make internal or external attributions about outcomes. As described in the original theory by Rotter (1966), internals believe that events occurring at work are based on their own behavior and are therefore under their own control. Externals believe that work outcomes are beyond their personal control. Thus, externals attribute work outcomes to factors like luck or the actions of others. Noe postulates that internals are more likely to exhibit high levels of motivation to learn in a training program because they are more likely to accept feedback and take action to correct performance problems.

3. Motivation to learn and achieve will be higher to the degree that trainees feel that they can actually learn the training content. This concept is usually labeled *self-efficacy,* or the belief in one's capability to perform a specific task. As will be discussed below, self-efficacy is a critical concept in social learning theory (Bandura, 1986). In exploring some of the mechanisms involving self-efficacy, Gist (1989) notes that it is possible to actually learn required knowledge and skills, yet self-efficacy perceptions might be so debilitating that trainees are prevented from using the learning.

4. Trainees must perceive that the training environment is designed to be responsive to their efforts. Thus, trainees must feel that achievement has occurred because of their efforts and ability.

5. The outcomes of training must be judged by trainees as relevant or instrumental to job performance.

6. Better job performance must have some value for trainees.

In the time since the introduction of Noe's model, a number of studies have begun to provide preliminary useful information about the model and other similar variables. Although it is not possible to be certain about all these relationships, the following interesting results have emerged:

1. In a training study to improve the administrative and interpersonal skills of educators, Noe and Schmitt (1986) found that trainees who agreed with assessments of their skills and weaknesses are also more likely to perceive the training content as useful.

2. Noe and Schmitt (1986) also found trends suggesting that trainees who are involved in career planning, have a career strategy, and are more job involved are more likely to benefit from training. In a study of entry-level managers in the pharmaceutical industry, Williams, Thayer, and Pond (1991) found that the degree of trainee engagement was related to the individual's motivation to learn in training. The complexity of these issues is demonstrated in a training study designed to enhance proofreading skills (Mathieu, Tannenbaum, & Salas, in press). In this instance, career planning and job involvement are not found to be related to training performance. However, these investigators carefully note that proofreading is only related to the trainees' current job. Thus, individuals with higher career goals are not likely to value training because it was only designed to enhance skills for the present job.

3. In a study of managers being trained in the use of computer software, researchers studied the self-efficacy of trainees entering the program (Gist, 1989; Gist, Schwoerer, & Rosen, 1989). They found that trainees who had higher self-efficacy before and at the midpoint of the program performed better on assessments at the completion of training. Williams and Pond (1991) found a similar relationship with locus of control. That is, individuals who have an internal locus of control also have higher expectancies in terms of effort regarding training performance, which is also linked to higher motivation to learn.

4. A number of researchers provide evidence suggesting a positive relationship exists between a trainee's motivation to learn and scores on learning measures (Noe & Schmitt, 1986; Hicks & Klimoski, 1987; Mathieu, Tannenbaum, & Salas, 1990).

There are probably many other trainee attributes that are related to performance, but these variables are just now being explored. However, this approach certainly seems exciting and promising. Another issue is whether information about trainee attributes can be used to help design more effective training programs. In other words, the emphasis here has been the identification of trainee characteristics, which predicts who will be better performers. Thus, it now appears quite likely that trainees with high self-efficacy will perform better in training. The logical conclusion is that we should select people with higher self-efficacy for our training programs. However, another question is whether it is possible to design an intervention that raises the level of self-efficacy and thus results in raising the general performance level of all trainees. Also, can an intervention be designed to raise the level of expectations of the trainees, the trainers, or both, and does that have benefits? Or, is it possible to develop materials showing how training programs fit career plans, and will this result in trainees understanding the value of the training program and being more highly motivated? These kinds of questions bring us to the design of the training environment. Here issues such as how learning is supported and how the environment can be designed to enhance motivation will be discussed.

THE DESIGN OF TRAINING ENVIRONMENTS

Motivation in the Training Environment

In the preceding section, we described some of Noe's (1986) model and resulting research studies, which specifies some of the factors that are likely to influence an individual's performance in training. The implications of these type of findings for training programs are made clear by the research of Tannenbaum, Mathieu, Salas, and Cannon-Bowers (1991), who investigated the degree to which recruit training in an eight-week socialization program for a U.S. Naval Recruit Training Command was successful. The socialization program focused on learning the required behaviors and supportive attitudes necessary to participate as a part of the organization. They found that training fulfillment, which was the degree to which the training program met trainees' expectations and desires, was positively related to the posttraining commitment to the organization. In another study with important training implications, Hicks and Klimoski (1987) varied pretraining information given to trainees. They found that trainees who received more realistic notice reported greater motivation to learn. Campbell (1988) notes that Noe's model also provides the analyst with a set of issues that must be considered for training design. Thus, it is possible to take these issues and formulate some questions the training designer might consider. In that regard, we offer the following questions:

1. How can the designer increase the trainee's beliefs that training outcomes can be achieved?
2. How can the trainer demonstrate to the trainee the instrumentality of training success for improvements in job performance?
3. How can the trainer positively influence the trainee's beliefs about the value of better job performance?
4. How can the trainer positively influence the level of self-efficacy?

Obviously, an answer to all these questions requires consideration of all issues involved in training systems design. For example, if the needs assessment is not conducted properly, the trainee will learn that the program has not been designed properly and thus has no instrumentality for eventual improvements in job performance. Throughout this text, these types of issues are considered. The emphasis in this particular section will be on motivation and its relationship to the above questions.

As noted earlier, motivation involves psychological processes that cause arousal, direction, and persistence of behavior (Mitchell, 1982). Arousal and persistence focus on the time and effort that an individual invests, and direction refers to the behaviors in which the investment of time and effort are made (Naylor, Pritchard, & Ilgen, 1980). In that sense, motivation is reflected both in the choice of behaviors that individuals decide to engage and the amount of effort devoted to those behaviors (Ilgen & Klein, 1989). For the interested reader, a review of motivational theories and empirical research can be found in Steers and Porter, 1983; Ilgen and Klein, 1989; and Kanfer, 1991. Most of this research is related to performance on the job rather than to learning in the training environment. However, the role of motivation to job performance can provide important insights into performance in training environments. Also, if the motivational level in the transfer, or on-the-job, setting is extremely poor, learning in the instructional setting becomes an academic exercise. Some of the motivational theories that appear particularly relevant to training systems follow.

Social Learning Theory

Early learning theorists argued that a person makes a response to a stimulus and, when that response is reinforced, a connection is formed between the stimulus and response. Eventually, reinforcements of the response strengthen the neural connections so that the behavior will occur in the presence of the stimulus. (Reinforcement theory is discussed in more detail later.) However, many contemporary psychologists think that this explanation for behavior ignores the mental activity going on inside the organism and cannot, by itself, provide explanations for more complex human behavior, such as the cognitive processes involved in actions like thinking and decision making.

As described by Ilgen and Klein (1989), cognitive theories attribute the causes of actions to an individual's processing of information. Thus, the resulting behavior stems from decisions based on the processing of information. Psychologists who espouse the cognitive viewpoint argue that the learner forms structures, or schema, in memory that preserve and organize information about what has been learned. Social learning theory argues that it is "the cognitive representations of future outcomes that generate the motivation for future behavior" (Ilgen & Klein, 1989, p. 151). According to Bandura (1969, 1977), who has been instrumental in the development of social learning theory, people process and weigh information concerning their capabilities and on that basis make choices about their behavior and the effort to bring to the situation. This clearly relates to training in the sense that achievement will be greater to the extent that trainees believe they are capable of mastering the material, the degree to which they have self-efficacy.

Wood and Bandura (1989) describe three particularly relevant aspects of social learning or cognitive theory:

1. The development of the individual's cognitive, social, and behavioral competencies through mastery modeling
2. The development of an individual's beliefs in his or her capabilities, thus enabling high self-efficacy and use of abilities
3. The enhancement of the individual's motivation by the use of goals

Wood and Bandura (1989) note that if an individual could only learn through direct experiences, then human development would be severely retarded. Instead, they propose that individuals can learn by watching another person make a particular response. Bandura states that this observational learning occurs when an observer watches a model exhibit a set of responses. This set of learned behaviors becomes part of the individual's repertoire of potential behavior even though it may not be overtly performed for some time. Bandura believes that these responses, known as modeling, are acquired through symbolic mental processes that function as the observer watches the behavior of a model. Also, there are several other processes including retention of the information, which is an active process aided when people symbolically transform the modeled information into memory codes and mentally rehearse the information. If the strategies result in desired outcomes rather than unrewarding or punishing events, people will produce the desired behavior. These ideas fit in well with another theory, expectancy theory, which states that motivational level is based on a combination of individuals' beliefs that they can achieve certain outcomes from their acts and the value of those outcomes to them. (Expectancy theory is discussed further later.) In addition, social learning theory has provided an important foundation for a training technique appropriately known as behavioral role modeling, which is discussed in Chapter 8.

Wood and Bandura's (1989) second point relates to people's beliefs about efficacy and how it can be strengthened. One way is through mastery experiences. Here, the authors indicate that it is important for the individuals to achieve success and not be discouraged by failure. On the other hand, the experiences must be designed so that people learn to overcome failure. Also, they need to observe proficient models who demonstrate effective strategies. Finally, they must receive realistic encouragement to help them exert greater effort even if they have self-doubts. This last factor is labeled *social persuasion.* Again, many of these points relate to other motivational theories described later. For example, reinforcement theory refers to the importance of the use of positive reinforcement. Also, the implications of social learning theory have resulted in research that is examining various procedures for modifying self-efficacy. Thus, Gist and her colleagues (Gist, 1989; Gist Schwoerer, & Rosen, 1989) have found that by using a modeling approach she can generate higher self-efficacy scores. In addition, it appears that modeling enhances the participants' beliefs about their own capabilities to perform. Thus, modeling might work because it enhances self-efficacy which in turn influences performance. It will take some time to determine whether the results are completely supportive of such an idea.

In a real sense, social learning theory is an overarching model that contains many important aspects of other theories. That becomes even more obvious in the discussion of Wood and Bandura's (1989) third point, which emphasizes goals and their enhancement of an individual's motivation. They describe some of the many relationships between self-efficacy and goals by noting that when there is stronger perceived self-efficacy, individuals set higher goals and have firmer commitments to the goals. The goal systems relate to the belief that individuals have capacities for self-direction and self-motivation. They seek self-satisfaction by fulfilling goals. Thus, goals provide a sense of purpose and direction. Also, by setting these goals, individuals try to sustain the level of effort needed to achieve them. In this way, they also help to build self-confidence. Individuals use goals as standards to measure their progress and their ability. From Wood and Bandura's point of view, motivation is best achieved by setting long-range goals that determine the course an individual will take and by having a series of attainable subgoals that lead and guide the way. Many of the conditions involving the use of goals are specified in goal theory, which is discussed next.

Goal Setting and Motivation

Locke, Latham, and their colleagues (see, for example, Latham & Locke, 1979; Locke, Shaw, Saari, & Latham, 1981) have conducted and reviewed an extensive set of studies describing the effects of setting goals on behavior. In their 1981 review, they found that in 90 percent of the laboratory and field studies, specific and challenging goals lead to higher performance than easy goals, do-your-best goals, or no goals. These authors postulate that goals affect task performance by "directing energy and attention, mobilizing energy expenditure or effort, prolonging effort over time (persistence) and motivating the individual to develop relevant strategies for goal attainment" (Locke et al., 1981, p. 145). These authors have also detailed a number of specific conditions that affect performance:

1. Individuals who are given specific, hard, or challenging goals perform better than those given specific easy goals, do-best goals, or no goals at all.
2. Goals appear to have more predictable effects when they are given in specific terms rather than as a vague set of intentions.
3. The goals must be matched to the ability of the individual such that the person is likely to achieve the goal. Being able to achieve the goal is important for the individual's self-efficacy, for that is how the individual will judge his or her ability to perform well on the tasks. This means

that it is likely that the analyst will need to design intermediate goals to reflect progress in the learning process.

4. Feedback concerning the degree to which the goal is being achieved is necessary for goal setting to have an effect.
5. For goal setting to be effective, the individual has to accept the goal that is assigned or set. Often the acceptance of the goal is related to the degree of support or commitment of the organization to the goal-setting program.

An example of an application of goal-setting techniques is offered by Kim (1984), who had salespeople participatively set goals in terms of specific selling activities and specific sales in dollar terms. Supervisors were given training on how to implement the approach, and feedback on performance was given every two weeks. For departments in which goal setting was introduced, there was significantly higher selling performance than in a control group.

The goal-setting points described above are based on extensive research studies. They suggest a number of ways that training programs can be more effective. The setting of specific challenging goals that are matched to the ability of the individual, followed by feedback on degree of goal achievement, provides a solid foundation for the design of an instructional program. Also, as noted above, the use of goals allows a person to measure his or her capabilities against standards, thereby increasing the sense of self-efficacy and achievement.

Expectancy Theory

Vroom (1964) has developed a process theory of motivation related to the question of how behavior is energized and sustained. The theory is based on cognitive expectancies concerning outcomes that are likely to occur as a result of the participant's behavior and on individual preferences among those outcomes. The expectancy can vary, as can the valence, or strength, of an individual's preference for an outcome. Vroom states that outcomes have a particular valence value because they are instrumental in achieving other outcomes. For instance, money and promotion have potential valence value because they are instrumental in allowing an individual to achieve other outcomes, like an expensive home or a college education for his or her children. The motivational level is based on a combination of an individual's belief that certain outcomes can be achieved from his or her acts and of the value of those outcomes to the individual. Training programs have a valence value for individuals if they believe the programs will permit them to achieve other outcomes. Thus, training becomes a low-level outcome that permits the achievement of higher-level outcomes (such as a job, a promotion, or a raise), which in turn might lead to other outcomes. The theory implies that it will be necessary to show the individual the value of the instructional program in order to properly motivate the person. Programs that appear unrelated to future outcomes will probably not meet the desired objectives. Note that this is a central point in Noe's (1986) proposed model. Also, it is an important aspect in Wood and Bandura's (1989) discussion of social learning theory. If the strategies result in desired outcomes rather than in unrewarding or punishing events, a person will produce the desired behavior. Some other conditions concerning rewards are presented next.

Reinforcement Theory

When the consequence of a response leads to the response being repeated, the consequence is called a *positive reinforcer.* B. F. Skinner, the father of modern programmed-instruction techniques, is the individual most often associated with the development of reinforcement theory. In this form of learning, the person's response is instrumental in gaining a consequence that reinforces, or rewards. The responses can vary in complexity from a person producing a product at work to a rat pressing a bar, and the rewarding stimuli can vary from praise for the person to a pellet of food for the rat. The list of stimuli that have served as reinforcers in various environments is endless but could include praise, gifts, money, and attention. An example of the use of reinforcement principles is illustrated by the work of Pedalino and Gamboa (1974), who were concerned with the reduction of absenteeism and lateness in a manufacturing/distribution plant. These researchers used the following poker game incentive plan as a reinforcement device:

> Each day an employee comes to work and is on time, he is allowed to choose a card from a deck of playing cards. At the end of the five day week, he will have five cards or a normal poker hand. The highest hand wins $20. There will be eight winners, one for approximately each department. (p. 696)

Over a four-month period, the experimental group achieved an 18.27 percent reduction in absenteeism. Unfortunately, the study had to be stopped at this point because sensitive union negotiations were due to begin, which should serve as another reminder of the complexities of organizational factors that reflect life in work organizations. Other researchers, such as Yukl and Latham (1975), have demonstrated the effects of reinforcers on tasks like tree planting.

Some of the aspects that a trainer should consider when using reinforcers include the following points.

Timing of reinforcement. Reinforcement should be given immediately following the appropriate response. Any delay might lead to the reinforcement of extraneous, inappropriate behaviors that are emitted after the correct response is made. For example, a parent may reinforce a child's tantrum by ignoring appropriately made requests but immediately attending to the child's screams. Fortunately, human learners can be reinforced by many stimuli. Thus, a trainee may participate in a learning program to earn a new job or a higher pay rate. In these cases, the learners can be rewarded with feedback concerning their progress until they successfully complete the program and earn the new job. The feedback serves to reinforce correct responses and helps extinguish incorrect responses while the learner works toward a more ultimate reward.

Partial reinforcement. Experiments in the learning laboratory have also produced results that indicate that it is not necessary to reinforce every correct response for learning to take place. This phenomenon is known as partial reinforcement. Skinner and his associates have examined many schedules on which the learner was not reinforced for every correct response, and they have discovered that learning proceeds in an orderly fashion even with intermittent reinforcement. Data indicate that if the learners are reinforced only after a certain number of correct responses, they will perform vigorously and quickly until the required number of responses is achieved. These data also show that responses learned under conditions of partial reinforcement are much more resistant to extinction than those learned under conditions of complete reinforcement. Behavior at slot machines provides a clear illustration of the effects of partial reinforcement. Even though each response is not rewarded with a payoff, the infrequent jackpots maintain the responses. Unscrupulous gamblers often provide one or two payoffs to card players early in the game to hook them and then depend on that partial reinforcement to keep the game going even though the payoffs become less and less frequent. In training settings, it is useful to provide continuous reinforcement until the correct response has been learned. At that point, partial reinforcement will maintain the behavior and make the responses more resistant to extinction. Unfortunately, the same principles apply to undesirable behavior, as illustrated by the difficulties that novices have in learning complex motor skills. For example, tennis beginners using inefficient responses every so often hit a good shot, thus being partially reinforced for poor responses. When the learner decides on formal instruction, it is difficult for the instructor to extinguish these partially reinforced responses.

Punishment. Punishment can be conceptualized as stimuli that the learner would like to avoid. Workers might be penalized for unsafe behavior by losing some of their pay or by being criticized by their supervisor—both aversive stimuli. The implications of punishment are not as well defined as those associated with positive reinforcement, but it is clear that punishment does not always reduce the likelihood of the same response occurring again. Some of the difficulties with aversive stimuli include the following:

1. Often the behavior of the respondent is positively reinforced before punishment occurs. The worker may have performed some unsafe behavior, such as failing to wear uncomfortable safety equipment, but may be positively reinforced by being more comfortable. The positive reinforcement has a strong influence because it follows the inappropriate response more immediately than does the aversive stimulus.
2. Punishment tends to become associated with specific stimuli. The worker learns to wear safety equipment when the supervisor is present but quickly discards it when the supervisor is not there.
3. There is a tendency to be inconsistent in the application of aversive stimuli. Thus, the parent does not punish the child each time the behavior is

inappropriate, and some supervisors look the other way to avoid noticing unsafe behavior, because most individuals do not like to administer punishment. There is also a tendency to feel guilty about the use of punishment, which leads the administrator to follow punishment with positive rewards.

4. Laboratory research suggests that the effects of punishment are largely emotional and only suppress, rather than extinguish, the inappropriate behavior. Once the emotional effects disappear, the behavior reasserts itself.

5. Punishment can lead to undesirable side effects. Anxiety associated with punishment can often create an unfavorable environment for learning and hostile attitudes toward the administrator of the punishment as well as the institutions they represent.

Need Theory and Motivation

A number of content theories emphasizes learned needs as motivators of human behavior. These theories concentrate on the needs that are to be satisfied and do not attempt to specify the exact processes by which these needs motivate behavior. The theories suggest to the training researcher that his or her programs must meet particular needs in order to have a motivated learner. One need theory that has been given considerable attention involves the need for achievement motivation (nAch), which is described by Atkinson and Feather (1966) as a behavioral tendency to strive for success. It is assumed to operate when the environment signals that certain acts on the part of the individual will lead to need achievement.

An illustration of this approach can be found in the studies of Miron and McClelland (1979), which were designed to instill achievement motivation through training programs. They found that participants in their training program were successful in terms of increased sales and profits. (Some of these studies are described in more detail in Chapter 8 in "Achievement Motivation Training.") In another series of studies, combining the approaches of the need and expectancy theories indicates that persons capable of high achievement do not necessarily perform well unless their behavior is viewed as being instrumental for later success (Raynor, 1970; Raynor & Rubin, 1971). Thus, students with high achievement motivation received superior grades when they regarded the grades as important for career success.

Equity Theory

Equity theory is based on the belief that people want to be treated fairly. Thus, individuals compare themselves to other people to see if their treatments are equitable. As stated by Adams, "Inequity exists for a person when he perceives that the ratio of his outcomes to inputs and the ratio of others' outcomes to inputs are unequal" (1965, p. 280). In this definition, *outcomes* include all factors viewed as having value—for example, pay, status, and fringe benefits. *Inputs* include all those factors that people bring with them (such as effort, education, seniority) and perceive as being important for obtaining some benefit (Pritchard, 1969). Inequity is said to create tension that has motivating qualities, requiring the person to reduce or eliminate the discrepancy. This tension is created whether the person compared is perceived as underrewarded or overrewarded.

Although equity theory appears to be especially relevant to the subject of wage factors, it may also have important implications for training. As already noted (Pritchard, 1969), the a priori determination of a variable as input or outcome is not always possible. Training provides such an illustration; that is, instructional programs may be viewed as an input or an output. In the input case, individuals who have acquired the necessary training experiences may view as inequitable promotions and pay raises earned by individuals without equal educational experiences. In the output case, individuals may perceive that they are not given the opportunity to attend advanced training courses. Although there has not been any direct utilization of equity theory in such instances, some interview data suggest that female managers view their opportunities from an equity theory framework (Dachler, 1974). They feel that, given the same training background as men, they do not have equal opportunities for job advancement or for participation in advanced training. Although the results of this situation are difficult to hypothesize, it is interesting to speculate on the behavior expended during the training effort when the trainee perceives that the outcomes are not available. Note again that this proposition is consistent with Noe's (1986) model and with expectancy theory. In addition, job behavior would possibly suffer when the employee perceives that future training and other opportunities are not available.

SIGNIFICANT ISSUES IN LEARNING AND INSTRUCTION

In the same way as the motivation literature, the learning literature reflects a growing emphasis on the cognitive learner and mental processes including attention, memory, language, reasoning, and problem solving. As discussed in the opening section of this chapter, instructional and cognitive theorists have started asking very serious questions about what is to be learned and what are the conditions for learning it. With this emphasis, there is a shift away from strict behavioristic traditions that emphasize observable behavior and traditional conditions of learning, such as the conditions of practice and reinforcement. Traditional learning has little to say about how to increase attentional capacity or make for a better diagnosis, or how to use a mental model to control all the complex processes that need to be the focus of attention. This concern has led to the beginning of the development of instructional theories. As defined by Gagné and Dick, "theories of instruction attempt to relate specified events comprising instruction to learning processes and learning outcomes, drawing upon knowledge generated by learning research and theory" (1983, p. 264). They also note that these theories are often prescriptive in that they identify conditions of instruction that will optimize learning, retention, and transfer. It is everyone's hope that such instructional theories will become the underlying foundation for instructional design procedures that will support learning activities.

In this section, I will attempt to mix what we have learned from the cognitive and instructional theorists with what still seems to be good practice stemming from classical learning theorists. Before beginning those discussions, it is important to understand some of the major shifts stemming from cognitive and instructional theory. The titles of each of these following sections will reflect the various emphases stressed by cognitive and instructional theorists.

What Is to Be Learned

Gagné's instructional theory. One important aspect of the cognitive emphasis is that it focuses on the behavior to be learned and suggests that different approaches might be used to support learning for different behaviors. One good illustration of the emphasis on what is to learned is presented by Gagné's (1984) system. In this model, when teaching an intellectual skill, the trainer is supposed to present an example of the concept or rule; when teaching problem solving, the trainer presents novel problems. In this model, Gagné describes a set of categories of learning outcomes to organize human performance. He then relates those learning outcomes to the conditions necessary to support learning performance. Gagné's learning outcomes are as follows:

1. *Intellectual skills.* These skills include concepts, rules, and procedures. Sometimes this is referred to as *procedural knowledge.* The rules for mathematical computations are a good example of intellectual skills. Some further examples of types of intellectual skills and the tasks they emulate from can be found in Table 4.2.
2. *Verbal information.* This category is also sometimes called *declarative information,* and it refers to the ability of the individual to declare or state something. In Table 4.2, the example is stating the main kinds of fire extinguishers and their uses.
3. *Cognitive strategies.* This refers to the idea that learners bring to a new task not only intellectual skills and verbal information but also a knowledge of how and when to use this information. In a sense, the cognitive strategies form a type of strategic knowledge that enables the learner to know when and how to choose intellectual skills and verbal information.
4. *Motor skills.* This skill refers to one of the more obvious examples of human performance. Examples of motor skills include writing, swimming, using tools, and the like.
5. *Attitudes.* Gagné notes that student preferences for particular activities often reflect differences in attitudes. He points out that people learn to have these preferences and notes that the number of different com-

Table 4.2 Examples of tasks reflected in target objectives and the learning categories they represent

Task	*Learning Category*
Discriminates printed letters *g* and *p*.	*Intellectual skill* (discrimination): perceiving objects as same or different
Identifies *ovate* shape of tree leaves.	*Intellectual skill* (concrete concept): identifying an object property
Classifies *citizens* of a nation, by definition.	*Intellectual skill* (defined concept): using a definition to identify a class
Demonstrates instances of the rule relating pressure and volume of a gas at constant temperature.	*Intellectual skill* (rule): applying a rule to one or more concrete examples
Generates a rule predicting the inflationary effect of decreasing value of currency in international exchange.	*Intellectual skill* (higher-order rule): generating a more complex rule by combining simpler rules
Originates a written composition on the cybernetic features of a bureaucracy.	*Cognitive strategy*: inventing a novel approach to a problem
States the main kinds of fire extinguishers and their uses.	*Information*: communicating organized knowledge in a way that preserves meaning
Chooses reading novels as a leisure-time activity.	*Attitude*: choosing a course of personal action toward a class of events
Executes the tightening of a lag screw with a socket wrench.	*Motor skill*: carrying out a smoothly timed motor performance

mercial messages by which we are bombarded is evidence of the common belief that attitudes are learned.

It would be interesting to know what constitutes a category and why there are five categories instead of seven. Gagné's (1984) rules for the establishment of categories are as follows:

1. Each category should be distinguishable in terms of a formal definition of human performance.
2. The category should include a broad variety of activities that are not dependent on intelligence, age, race, and so on. He excludes (while acknowledging) special categories such as musical virtuosity, wine tasting, and the like.
3. Each category should differ in terms of the basic learning processes, such as information-processing demands.
4. The learning principles should be similar for tasks within a learning outcome category, but it should not be possible to generalize the principles across tasks from different categories.

Thus, Gagné and his colleagues have developed a set of learning categories that permits them to analyze tasks and code behavior into one of the learning outcomes. The most fascinating part of the system is that Gagné and Briggs (1979) have begun to examine each of the outcomes and determine the conditions of learning and instructional events that best support that learning outcome. This system is presented in Table 4.3. The behavioral learning outcomes (intellectual skill, cognitive strategy, and so on) are presented across the top of the table. Down the side of the table are a series of events that are considered important to the instructional system, such as gaining attention of the learner, providing feedback, and so on. The body of the table indicates how each instructional event is manipulated for each learning outcome. Thus, for the event presenting stimulus material, you would present examples of concepts or rules for intellectual skill development, whereas you would present novel problems for the development of cognitive strategies. As more and more is learned about various ways to support learning performance, it is clear that such systems will be very important in helping us design effective training environments. Already, these type of thoughts have led Howell and Cooke (1989) to suggest that we will need a new type of job analysis. They think that it will become necessary to examine the tasks and type of KSAs necessary for the job and then to specify the type of learning required. From that specification, the type of instructional conditions that best supports that type of learning can be designed. As will become obvious, we do not have the information to reach that point yet, but it may not be too far away.

Massed versus spaced practice. Another set of principles comes from the more classical learning literature, but it fits in very nicely with the idea that different principles might apply to different types of learning. Generally, it is considered important to determine whether learners benefit more from as little rest as possible until they have learned their task or from rest intervals within practice sessions. Although the data are not definitive, they suggest that spaced practice for one of Gagné's categories, motor skills, is typically more effective in acquisition and leads to better retention. DeCecco (1968) presents data obtained by Lorge (1930) that examined massed versus spaced practice on a motor skill task. The subjects were required to draw a figure from a mirror image. One group, performing the task under massed-practice conditions, was given twenty trials without any rest periods. The other two groups performed the task under spaced conditions. One group was given one-minute rest periods between trials and the other group one-day rest periods between trials. As Figure 4.2 indicates, there were consistent differences between the spaced-practice groups and the massed-practice group, with the spaced-practice groups demonstrating better performance. Interestingly, a recent review of the training literature by Baldwin and Ford (1988) concludes that these types of results for motor skills are still the norm.

Research exploring the acquisition and retention of verbal skills is not nearly as definitive, although it is still possible to conclude that practice will not be as efficient if the learner has to concentrate for long periods of time without some rest. As most students have discovered, cramming for examinations tends to produce high test scores but rapid forgetting. Because the retention of learned material is important for the transfer process in training settings, spaced practice is the more useful technique. Thus, the literature indicates that distributed practice using reasonable rest periods is the favored technique. There is one important exception. In situations in which the error tendency is high or the learner is likely to forget critical responses, the time between practice must often be shortened or eliminated (DeCecco, 1968). Thus, for problem-solving tasks where the learner must discover the correct answers from a variety of possible solutions, it is necessary to go through a large number of incorrect solutions before arriving at the correct answer. Here, forgetting the previous inappropriate responses would lead to an increase in learning time.

Stages of Learning

One important aspect of cognitive instructional approaches is the idea that learning involves a series of stages and that different types of learning might be important during these stages. The interested reader should consult Glaser (1990), who has reviewed many of the cognitive instructional approaches presented here. The organization of the material in this text will attempt to integrate the cognitive material with information that is still relevant from classical learning theory.

Anderson's ACT* model. Anderson's ACT* model (Anderson, 1987) emphasizes that the major learning mechanism involves a series of stages. The first stage, *declarative learning,* involves obtaining factual knowledge about a task without having learned the conditions of applicability. Thus, in this stage, the person learns facts and instructions, and there is a heavy reliance on memory. Because it is necessary to keep the learning in memory, the learner often uses much verbalization to retain the material. The second stage is *knowledge compilation,* which is the transition process where the learner turns declarative knowledge, which comes from texts or teachers' instructions, into *proceduralized knowledge.* In other words, it is the transition when learners go from knowing "what" into knowing "how."

Anderson's theory assumes that effective knowledge of procedures can only occur by actually being required to use the declarative knowledge. This knowledge-compilation stage is characterized by accelerated performance and less verbalization. As the person gains a high degree of knowledge compilation, it results in automaticity of previously acquired declarative knowledge, freeing the memory for processing of new knowledge and movement toward proceduralized knowledge. The final stage, proceduralization, involves the application and use of knowledge to do something (solving a complex arithmetic problem, playing the piano). Anderson's group has designed complex computer-tutoring programs for a number of complex skills such as programming (Anderson, Farrell, & Sauers, 1984).

Table 4.3 Instructional events and the conditions of learning they imply for five types of learned capabilities

	Type of Capability				
Instructional Event	*Intellectual Skill*	*Cognitive Strategy*	*Information*	*Attitude*	*Motor Skill*
1. Gaining attention	Introduce stimulus change; variations in sensory mode				
2. Informing learner of objective	Provide description and example of the performance to be expected.	Clarify the general nature of the solution expected.	Indicate the kind of verbal question to be answered.	Provide example of the kind of action choice aimed for.	Provide a demonstration of the performance to be expected.
3. Stimulating recall of prerequisites	Stimulate recall of subordinate concepts and rules.	Stimulate recall of task strategies and associated intellectual skills.	Stimulate recall of context of organized information.	Stimulate recall of relevant information, skills, and human model identification.	Stimulate recall of executive sub-routine and part-skills.
4. Presenting the stimulus material	Present examples of concept or rule.	Present novel problems.	Present information in propositional form.	Present human model, demonstrating choice of personal action.	Provide external stimuli for performance, including tools or implements.
5. Providing learning guidance	Provide verbal cues to proper combining sequence.	Provide prompts and hints to novel solution.	Provide verbal links to a larger meaningful context.	Provide for observation of model's choice of action, and of reinforcement received by model.	Provide practice with feedback of performance achievement.
6. Eliciting the performance	Ask learner to apply rule or concept to new examples.	Ask for problem solution.	Ask for information in paraphrase, or in learner's own words.	Ask learner to indicate choices of action in real or simulated situations.	Ask for execution of the performance.
7. Providing feedback	Confirm correctness of rule or concept application.	Confirm originality of problem solution.	Confirm correctness of statement of information.	Provide direct or vicarious reinforcement of action choice.	Provide feedback on degree of accuracy and timing of performance.
8. Assessing performance	Learner demonstrates applicaton of concept or rule.	Learner orginates a novel solution.	Learner restates information in paraphrased form.	Learner makes desired choice of personal action in real or simulated situation.	Learner executes performance of total skill.
9. Enhancing retention and transfer	Provide spaced reviews including a variety of examples.	Provide occasions for a variety of novel problem solutions.	Provide verbal links to additional complexes of information.	Provide additional varied situations for selected choice of action.	Learner continues skill practice.

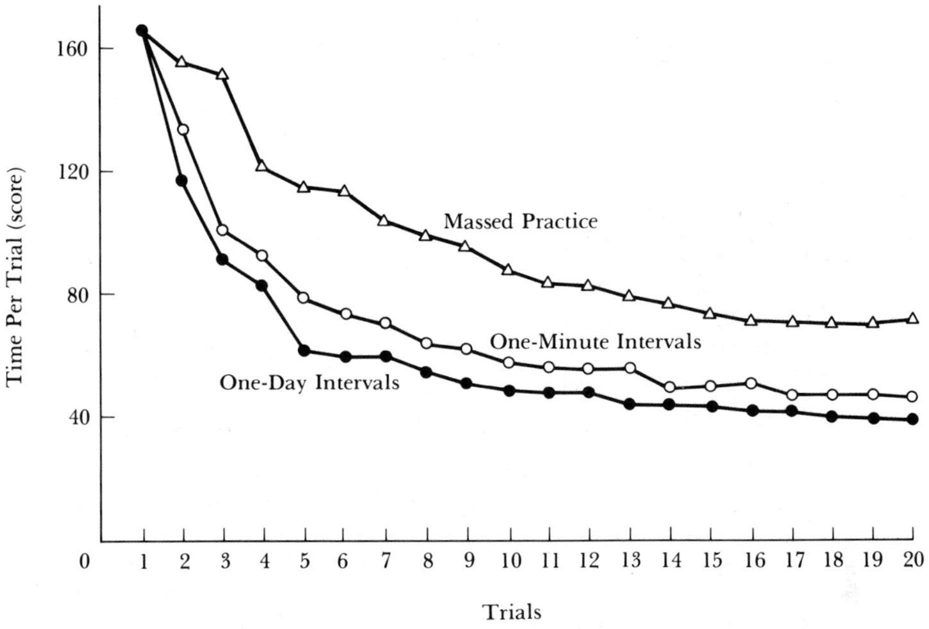

Figure 4.2 The effect of distribution of practice on mirror drawing. Adapted from *Influence of Regularly Interpolated Time Intervals Upon Subsequent Learning* by I. Lorge. Copyright © 1930 by Teachers College, Columbia University.

The reader should consider an example of the potential impact of these ideas for training systems as illustrated by the work of Kanfer and Ackerman (1989). These investigators conducted research using U.S. Air Force trainees who learned an air traffic control simulation task. The trainees learned to accept or land planes on the specified runways, based on a series of rules such as weather conditions and amount of fuel. In the first phase, trainees acquired a basic understanding of the tasks, based on lectures and observations. This is the declarative-knowledge phase, and as indicated above, it has a very high attentional demand. In the second phase, knowledge compilation, the trainee is involved in task practice, trying out methods and using the knowledge gained. As learning continues to occur, the attentional demands of the task are reduced. In the third phase, procedural knowledge, the learner is automating the skill. Here the task is being performed rapidly with minimum attention devoted to the assignment.

Kanfer and Ackerman (1989) conducted a series of experiments where they implemented various goal-setting interventions similar to those discussed in the section on motivation. The results essentially indicate that outcome goals, such as specifying how well you should perform, only have a beneficial result late in the learning process. This confirms the investigators' hypotheses that outcome goal setting would only be helpful late in the process when some of the tasks are being performed more automatically, thus reducing the attentional demands. Earlier in the process, the attentional demands are too high for the goal setting to have an impact. This is an important study that illustrates how our understanding of stages of the learning process, specified by instructional theorists, might interact with other factors such as motivational variables like goal setting.

Ability shifts during stages of learning. Another aspect of the stages of learning relates to the question of whether there are shifts in basic abilities required during different stages of learning. Fleishman (1972) presents considerable research indicating that basic abilities are related to performance in a wide variety of tasks. Examples of a few of the abilities specified by Fleishman include the following:

1. *Reaction time:* speed required to respond to a stimulus
2. *Multilimb coordination:* the coordination of the movement of several limbs in the operation of a control
3. *Gross body equilibrium:* the control of balance with nonvisual cues

Through a variety of studies, Fleishman (1972) found that the particular abilities required to perform a task were systematic and subject to change during practice. For example, Fleishman analyzed a complex tracking task and found that spatial orientation was important early in the task and multilimb coordination was important later in the task. Fleishman used this information in a training program by first presenting special instructions about orientation and later providing information about coordination requirements. The trained group was found to be superior to several other groups when it was examined on the tracking task. As a result of these studies, Fleishman concludes that the importance of general cognitive abilities (for example, verbal and reasoning tests) on motor-type tasks declines with practice. In addition, there was evidence that the need for motor skill abilities increased in importance.

There has been some controversy concerning these studies, but recent analyses by Ackerman (1987) support the original findings that cognitive abilities decline in importance over practice trials while motor skills increase. Further, Ackerman argues that at the beginning of these type of motor skill tasks, people need large stores of cognitive ability to perform well. Thus, tests of cognitive ability are good predictors of performance. However, as time goes on, the required responses based on cognitive ability for the motor skill task become more automated in the same sense that Anderson's theory discusses the automaticity of declarative knowledge. As a result, the influence of individual differences in cognitive ability becomes less important. In addition, Ackerman has demonstrated that in situations designed to make it difficult for the responses to become automated, the influence of cognitive abilities does not diminish over trials. Thus, Fleishman's original approach still presents an important possibility for the specification of particular abilities and their relationship to the most appropriate instructional technique. If it is found in future research that it is possible to train persons in specific abilities and have performance transfer to other tasks that need that same ability, it will have important implications for skill training at different stages of learning. Also, it should be clear from the research of Anderson and of Ackerman that the concept of automaticity has become increasingly important. This will be discussed further in one of the next sections.

Whole versus part learning. This is another classical learning variable that is related to the size of the units practiced during stages of the training session. When whole procedures are employed, the learner practices the task as a single unit. The utilization of part procedures breaks the task into components that are practiced separately. The complexity of the task and the relationship among the components determine the usefulness of whole and part methods (Baldwin & Ford, 1988). Naylor (Naylor, 1962; Blum & Naylor, 1968) originally suggested that the difficulty of any particular subtask (complexity) and the extent to which the subtasks are interrelated (organization) determine total difficulty. He uses the example of a person driving a car to illustrate both the complexity and the organization functions. Driving in rush-hour traffic usually places the greatest strain on forward-velocity control (assuming the driver stays in the same lane), because the operator must continually use the accelerator and brake pedals to maintain varying degrees of speed. When the driver operates the vehicle on a curved section of highway, the steering component becomes the most complex part of the task. Task organization can be illustrated by the interrelationship of forward-velocity control and steering. When the operator desires to make a turn, the two components must be interrelated to properly carry out the turning sequence. Naylor's examination of the part–whole literature supports the following basic training principles concerning part and whole methods: When a task has relatively high organization, an increase in task complexity leads to whole methods being more efficient than part methods; when a task has low organization, an increase in task complexity leads to part methods being more efficient.

The use of part methods suggested by Naylor's analysis does raise some concerns related to the eventual performance of the entire task. The job must be analyzed to discover the important components and to determine the correct sequence for learning the components. In that sense, Naylor was already speculating about the sequencing of learning activities during various stages. During this process, it is necessary to ensure that the trainee has developed the capabilities necessary to proceed to the next part of the task. If the job is properly analyzed and ordered, a progression method can be used. Here, the learner practices one part at the first session. Then, at the next session, a second part is added, and both parts are practiced together. The addition of parts continues until the whole skill is learned.

Automaticity

Automaticity refers to the idea that the performance of tasks can become automated in the sense that they require limited attentional capacity to be performed. One obvious aspect of Anderson's stages and Ackerman's analyses of physical ability data is the point that as the material is learned, it results in automaticity of previously acquired responses that permits the learner to move to the next stage. The concept of automaticity is a crucial point in instructional theory and deserves further explanation. As described in classic studies by Shiffrin and Schneider (1977), processing that once demanded active control can become automatic, thus freeing the learner's limited attentional capacity for other tasks. As described by these investigators, one condition under which this occurs is where there is extensive practice on a task so that responses can become consistently mapped to particular stimuli.

The automatic processes demand little attentional resources, thus becoming easily accomplished while still performing other tasks. They also make the performance of these automatic tasks very quick and efficient. Perhaps the most dramatic example of the use of automated processing as a training procedure involves the vigilance decrement. The *vigilance decrement* refers to the problem of decline in performance over time during a watch-keeping period when the number of signals to be detected are infrequent. Literally, thousands of studies have been devoted to this problem because of its implications for areas of work such as radar signal detection, monitoring of warning signals indicating machine malfunctions (including those in nuclear power plants), and detection involving product quality control on the assembly line. In a dramatic study, Fisk and Schneider (1981) were able to eliminate this decrement by automatizing the activity through a training program that presented the stimulus and then required a response. These pairings went on for over 4000 training trials. In other words, the trainees' responses through this large number of pairings became automated. This meant that much less attentional capacity was needed to perform the task. Later, the trainees performed the real task with only eighteen targets presented over 6000 presentations. Instead of the usual performance decrement occurring, there was virtually no decrement over time because the responses had become automated and thus required very little attentional capacity from the trainee.

Overlearning. Historically, it is also interesting to note that the concept of automaticity has some relationship to the classical concept of overlearning. *Overlearning* is a situation where the learners are presented with a number of extra learning opportunities even after they have demonstrated learning mastery on the task. Overlearning has been judged to be particularly important when the task is not likely to be practiced often or when it is necessary to maintain performance during periods when there will be few practice opportunities. An investigation by Schendel and Hagman (1982) examining psychomotor skills studied the disassembly and assembly of weapons and demonstrated the positive benefits of overlearning. They trained soldiers to criterion and then gave 100 percent overtraining. Thus, if a particular performer took ten trials to perform one errorless disassembly and assembly of the weapon, then he or she received ten additional trials as part of initial training. Another group of soldiers received overtraining, but in this case each person received the particular extra trials midway through the eight-week retention period. This training was referred to as refresher training. At the end of the eight-week interval, both the overtrained and the refresher group performed significantly better than a control group that was given just initial training. The overtrained group was superior to both the refresher group and the control group in terms of the amount retained. Hagman and Rose (1983) found in a review of seventeen studies examining retention on military tasks that task repetition was especially effective in improving retention. They note that repetition both before and after proficiency has been achieved increases the level of acquisition, which in turn is very helpful in maintaining performance during intervals when no practice takes place. They also note that training typically involves combinations where material is presented to be learned and then tests are given to recall information. The experiments they report indicate that repetitions of both the presentation and the testing are effective in promoting retention. The researchers also found that retention was better with spaced rather than massed training, again supporting the basic research literature. They recommend overtraining as a potentially powerful method, especially in those situations where performance must be maintained over long periods without much practice.

The overtraining in this study would not even begin to approach what would be involved in establishing automaticity, but the integration of these two concepts is likely to produce important dividends in the future. Howell and Cooke (1989) note that the training implications for automaticity obviously call for the identification of those elements that are suitable for that type of intervention. Then, the remaining elements that still require controlled processing can use the necessary remaining attentional capacity. They point out that the remaining elements that will benefit from the automation of other components are likely to be the so-called higher mental components such as diagnosis and decision making.

Emphasis on Self-Regulation

Another set of research studies focuses on self-regulatory and performance-control strategies. *Self-regulation* refers to the idea that the experiences of experts seem to enable them to develop skills for checking their performance. As described by Glaser, "experts rapidly check their work, accurately judge its difficulty, apportion their time, assess their progress, and predict the outcomes of their activities" (1990, p. 32). A number of instructional programs have been designed to investigate these skills, such as that by Brown and

Palincsar (1984, 1989) who have designed a program for reading comprehension. Students participating in their program both acquire knowledge and learn strategies that enable them to work independently and yet monitor their behavior. The program involves reciprocal teaching: Students take turns leading the group in the use of strategies that have previously been modeled by the instructor. The procedure includes instruction and practice in executive strategies (questioning, summarizing, clarifying, and predicting), the use of an expert teacher model to initially demonstrate, and a setting where each student contributes to others' learning. Finally, the method teaches what is called a *zone of proximal development* where students are taught to perform within their competence range while being helped to realize higher potential performance levels. This method is also being used to teach sophisticated writing strategies (Scardamalia, Bereiter, & Steinbach, 1984). These approaches are consistent with social learning theory, which emphasizes the development of behavioral competencies through mastery modeling (Wood & Bandura, 1989). That approach was discussed earlier in the section on work motivation.

Emphasis on Mental Models

Another emphasis in the cognitive approach is to understand the mental models that individuals use in performing a task. In part, this involves verbal protocols where individuals actually talk through their thought processes while performing a task. Another aspect of this procedure involves the comparisons of novices with experts. Glaser (1990) notes in his description of structure knowledge for problem solving that as competence is attained in problem solving, elements of knowledge become increasingly interconnected, resulting in the learner having access to coherent chunks of information. The beginner's knowledge is spotty with isolated pieces and definitions. As the learner becomes more of an expert, the pieces become more structured and more integrated with past knowledge. Then, the learner has access from memory to larger and larger units.

The true expert's memory retrieval system is based on the structured content of stored information, and these organizing structures of knowledge are known as *schemata.* The schemata enable experts to grasp the problem and bypass many steps while novices are trying to figure out the surface features. One such program that is attempting to model expert knowledge and to design a tutoring system is titled GUIDON (Clancy, 1986). The system uses as its base the structure for medical diagnosis. The learner directs the diagnosis by implementing inference strategies. If the student fails to generate a link to a solution strategy, the student has to determine what additional knowledge—that is, if it was available—would have prevented the failure. The students keep at this process, continually updating their own knowledge base. Another example of such a program, SCHOLAR, is discussed in Chapter 7 in "Computer-Assisted Instruction."

Experts versus novices. Howell and Cooke (1989) note that the combination of the work on mental models along with exploring differences between experts and novices has profound implications for training programs. These observations are supported by research performed by Gitomer (1988), who studied novice and expert mental models in an electronic troubleshooting task examining the patterns of errors and verbal reports from the participants. Gitomer found that the more expert individuals were guided by mental models that were much more consistent with the true functional properties of the device. Also, the experts' declarative knowledge was more complete and well organized, and they were also better at selecting strategies (procedural knowledge). The study implies that it might be possible to isolate the deficiencies of a trainee's mental model. It might also be possible to determine whether a trainee is having difficulty because of a lack of knowing what to do (procedural) or a lack of access to knowledge (declarative). Another example of this type of work is a study of computer programmers (Cooke & Schvaneveldt, 1988), which resulted in being able to distinguish experts from novices and revealed the misconceptions in novice knowledge. Possibilities here for use in the design of training systems based on expert models and the differences between experts and novices are an important area for future training research. The result could be a prescription on where training needs to focus.

Another area of emphasis for cognitive psychologists examining mental models is the use of strategies to organize and retain information. In many of the situations involving complex cognitive tasks, there is a high demand on memory systems. Yet, a learner involved in short-term memory situations will find it difficult to temporally retain more than seven items of information. The emphasis here has been on research to explore various cognitive schemes to enhance memory systems, such as organizing the material into chunks through mnemonic schemes or analogy systems. Similar principles are being developed and studied (see Howell & Cooke, 1989) for use in storing information for the purposes of long-term memory. This line of work is also consistent with classical learning theory that indicates the more meaningful the material, the more easily it is retained. It is important to properly organize the material and to establish principles to retain information, even if the material appears to be meaningless. Music students are aided in their retention of the musical notes corresponding to the lines and spaces of the staff through the use of coding schemes that organize the information. For example, the lines of the treble staff are the first letters of *Every Good Boy Does Fine,* and the spaces spell *FACE.* Interestingly, in a review of military tasks, Hagman and Rose (1983) did not find that the use of mnemonic techniques helped improve retention. However, in these experiments the task was relatively easy, and the soldiers reported that it was not necessary to have a coding scheme to retain the material.

It is also important to realize that mnemonic schemes are but one way to organize materials. In a fascinating study, Bennett (1983) examined the memorizing strategies used by cocktail waitresses in remembering drink orders. The study found that waitresses were much better at a memory task involving remembering drink orders than students. In addition, the highly accurate memories of the best waitress performers resulted from vivid perceptual interactions at the time of ordering.

Advanced organizers. The use of organizer schemes based on existing knowledge of the learner is now being used in the design of instructional systems themselves. An *organizer* can be any type of cue—including verbal, quantitative, or graphic cues—that is used to present new knowledge by taking advantage of the existing knowledge of the learner. It is called an *advanced organizer* if the material is presented before training and a *comparative organizer* if it is used later in training to clarify later distinctions. In an important series of studies, Mayer and his colleagues (Mayer, 1975; Mayer & Bromage, 1980) used a simplified diagram of the functional structure of a computer to greatly enhance learning of the technical terms and rules in a college course on computer programming. The organizer employed familiar language such as shopping lists and ticket windows in the diagrams. According to Mayer (1989), these organizers (or mental models) help improve learning for several reasons. First, they focus attention on the important components and relationships. Second, they help the trainee organize incoming information. Finally, they help show the relationships between incoming information and existing relevant knowledge. Thus far, there is limited research on this in actual training systems, but the potential seems very apparent.

Production of the Response

Classical learning theory states that it is important for trainees to be active during the learning period. Thus, classical learning theorists would advise students reading materials for an examination to outline, underline, write in the margins, rehearse the materials in some way, and so on. This concept has been further developed by cognitive theorists to emphasize the importance of having the learner actively *produce* whatever capability is to be mastered during training. As Campbell (1988) notes, this is just as critical for knowledge capabilities as it is for a physical or cognitive skill. Too often, the training program does not require the demonstration of the required skill but rather some alternative form that is not necessarily the desired end product. For example, learning the principles of management in working with a complaining employee is not the same as demonstrating the skills necessary to conduct a discussion with the person to resolve the difficulties. A training technique, which will be discussed in Chapter 8, called behavioral role modeling is a procedure for teaching such skills. Also, the interaction of the process of producing the behavior along with many of the active cognitive organizing strategies such as mnemonics should produce strong dividends. Again, however, a lecture on mnemonics would not be helpful by itself as compared to learners demonstrating they have learned the material while using a mnemonic scheme.

Feedback

Holding (1965) traced the series of experiments that established the importance of feedback in the learning process. He notes that one of the earliest studies of *feedback,* or knowledge of results, was provided by E. L. Thorndike (1927), who had two groups of subjects (both blindfolded) draw hundreds of lines measuring three, four, five, or six inches over a period of several days. The members of one group were given feedback that indicated whether their response was right or wrong within the established criterion of a quarter-inch of the target area. The members of the second group were not given any feedback. These data indicate that the group that received the knowledge of results improved considerably in its performance, while the other group continued making errors. A later study repeated this experiment but included a group that received feedback stating the degree of error (Trowbridge & Cason, 1932). The subjects in this group gained even greater accuracy than the group that was just told that the answers were right or wrong. These two studies are examples of the many experiments that have demonstrated the importance of feedback. Researchers suggest that the reason why knowledge of results improves performance can be attributed to motivational and informational functions. The feedback in Thorndike's experiment can be viewed as praise or reproof as well as information about performance on the task.

A study examining training practices in a safety program addressed the issue of feedback (Komaki, Heinzmann, & Lawson, 1980). Komaki et al. specifically asked whether training alone was sufficient or if it was necessary to provide feedback to maintain performance on the job. This study was conducted in the vehicle-maintenance division of a large city's public works department. The researchers selected a department that had high accident rates. The researchers conducted a needs assessment, including examination of safety logs, to determine safety incidents that had occurred. With the help of supervisors and workers, they designed procedures to eliminate accident problems. Thus, if it was found that an accident occurred because a worker had fallen off a jack stand, an item was included in the training program related to the proper use of jacks and jack stands. These training items also formed the basis for a system for observing the effects of performance. The training program involved a number of procedures, including slides depicting posed scenes of unsafe behavior followed by discussions of safety procedures. For example, one slide depicted an employee working under a vehicle without appropriate eye-protection devices. Komaki found that preceding training, employees were performing safely one- to two-thirds of the time. After training, performance improved about 9 percent. Komaki then added another condition, including feedback on a daily basis in the form of a graph showing the safety level of the group and the safety goals that the group was trying to achieve. This extra condition resulted in an improvement of 26 percent over the pre-training phase and 16 percent over the training-only phase. Komaki makes the point that training alone is not sufficient to improve and maintain performance. Rather, training plus feedback provides the most effective strategy.

The study of line drawing discussed previously (Trowbridge & Cason, 1932), which added a group with specific knowledge of results, illustrates the informational function of knowledge of results. Of course, the extra information does not preclude the motivational aspects of the feedback, which were discussed in the section on motivation. In most situations, it is difficult to separate the effects caused by the motivational qualities and the informational aspects of knowledge of results. Even the simple feedback of "right" versus "wrong" conveys some information. The important issue regarding the informational nature of knowledge of results involves specificity. Contrary to popular belief, increased specificity does not necessarily lead to improved performance. It can actually lead to performance deficits. Whereas some increases in specificity may be helpful, a saturation point can be reached at which the information is too much for the subject to handle and which simply leads to confusion. As the subjects become more proficient at a task, they may also learn to integrate more specific feedback. For each task, it is necessary for the trainer to carefully design the feedback to fit that situation and the capabilities of the learner. Additionally, the feedback should be timed so that the information necessary to correct the subject's response is immediately available.

Most training analysts have placed considerable emphasis on the importance of knowledge of results in the learning process. Unfortunately, many of those who emphasize its importance simply assume that any form of feedback with any sort of timing will accomplish the purpose. The preceding discussion indicates that the application of feedback requires real sensitivity for the task and the learner. Ilgen, Fisher, and Taylor (1979) have developed a model describing some important aspects of the processes involved in perceptions of feedback and have summarized some of the conclusions that can be gleaned from the literature. Their discussions suggest important issues that a trainer should consider in attempting to determine how feedback will be perceived. They note the following:

1. There is evidence that feedback must be accurately perceived by the recipient in order to have an effect, and yet it appears that it is often misperceived. In other words, despite the general assumption, feedback is not always perceived correctly and accepted. This seems to be particularly true of negative feedback and may be yet another reason why, as discussed in the section on motivation, it does not always have the expected impact.

2. Results indicate that the accuracy of feedback may be affected by the source of the feedback. For example, they suggest that accuracy varies with the source's credibility. This implies that individuals who wish to use feedback need to work to develop credibility based on their expertise and/or on the basis of a trust relationship.

3. Ilgen and his colleagues also questioned the accepted notion that very high-frequency levels of feedback are always better. The authors suggest that

high frequency of feedback might connote a loss of personal control. It may also lead recipients to excessively rely on feedback and not develop their own capabilities at judging their performance. However, it is also noted that in most work settings, the problem concerning feedback is not too much of it, but rather that it is so infrequent that employees resort to all sorts of methods to try to find out how they are doing.

4. There are also some data to indicate that people delay giving negative feedback because of the unpleasant aspects of giving such information.

5. Their review also notes the importance of taking into account individual differences, a topic which will be covered next. For the purposes of giving feedback, they note that individual needs of the person should be taken into account when choosing feedback. Thus, individuals who are high performers with growth-oriented needs require feedback that emphasizes competency and does not take away from personal initiative. However, poor performers need to be monitored carefully and given very specific feedback. Also, with poor performers, the relationship between feedback and sanctions or rewards must be made very explicit.

Emphasis on Individual Differences

Besides contributions on stages of learning and related processes such as automaticity, another focus of cognitive and instructional theorists is a reexploration of the importance of individual differences and learning. The current emphasis placed on the examination of individual-difference parameters in learning and training represents a merger between two separate camps that previously had rarely recognized each other's existence. Until recently, psychologists concerned with learning and training examined the effects of their treatments and considered individual differences an annoyance that made the establishment of general laws of behavior difficult. On the other hand, differential psychologists ignored treatment effects and busied themselves with the study of individual variability. For example, applied psychologists concerned with selection used measures of individual variability to predict future performance on various measures of success.

Aptitude–treatment interactions. Just as cognitive psychologists have concerned themselves with differences in stages of learning, such as the declarative and procedural stages, they have also been intrigued by the idea that one training program (or treatment) may not work equally well for all trainees. As described originally by Cronbach (1967), this approach has as its goal matching alternate modes of instruction to the different characteristics of the individual so that each person uses the most appropriate learning procedure. This approach is often called *aptitude-treatment interaction* (ATI). Figures 4.3 and 4.4 illustrate two types of ATI relationships. Figure 4.3 shows that all people, regardless of aptitude level, improve with treatment A. In that case, there is no reason to use treatment B; thus, all individuals should be presented with treatment A. Figure 4.4 illustrates an interaction called the *disordinal ATI*. In

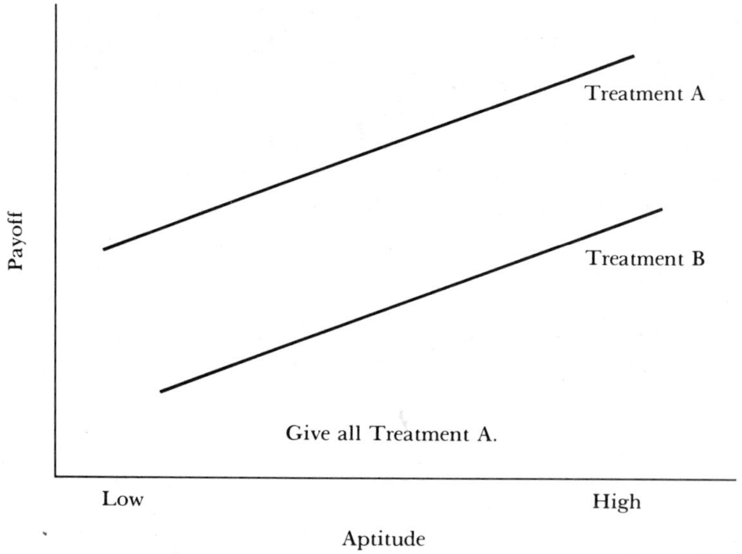

Figure 4.3 Illustration of no aptitude–treatment interaction. From "The Two Disciplines of Scientific Psychology," by L. J. Cronbach. In *American Psychologist,* 1957, *12,* pp. 671–684. Copyright © 1957 by the American Psychological Association.

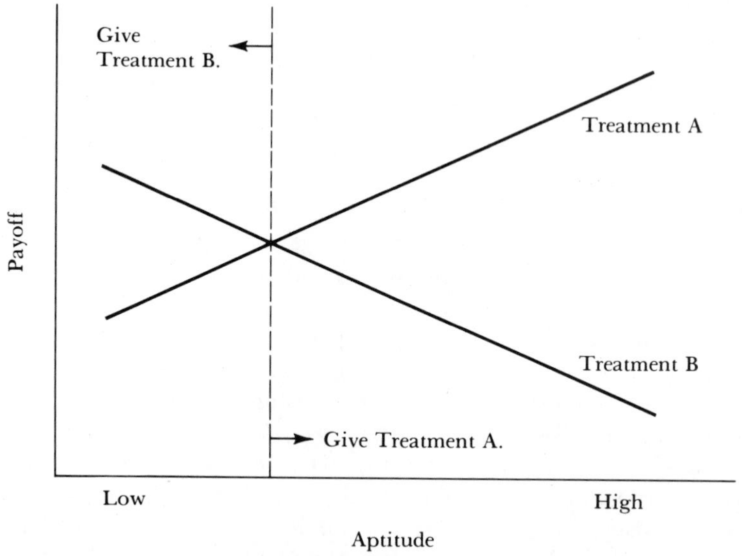

Figure 4.4 Illustration of a disordinal aptitude–treatment interaction. From "The Two Disciplines of Scientific Psychology," by L. J. Cronbach. In *American Psychologist,* 1957, 12, pp. 671–684. Copyright © 1957 by the American Psychological Association.

this case, individuals to the right of the cutoff line (those with higher-aptitude levels) perform best with treatment A. Persons to the left of the cutoff line (those with lower-aptitude levels) perform best with treatment B. Thus, the aptitude level of the individual determines the form of treatment that will lead to superior performance. In these cases, *aptitude* refers to any personal characteristics that relate to learning and thus can include a broad range of variables, such as styles of thought, personality, and various scholastic aptitudes. The variety of factors that have been considered in the aptitude–treatment dimension is illustrated by the following partial list of variables (Howard, 1971):

Aptitude
Scholastic aptitude
Spatial aptitude
Verbal reasoning
Intelligence
Deductive/inductive reasoning
Cognitive style (analytic/nonanalytic)
Mathematics ability
Interests
Ascendancy, dominance
Introversion/extroversion
Need for achievement
Motive to avoid failure
Anxiety
Overachievement/underachievement
Sociability
Attitudes to instruction or subject
Need for autonomy
Miscellaneous personality characteristics

Treatment
Visual presentations
Verbal presentations
PI difficulty or complexity
Multiple-choice versus constructed program instruction (PI) responses
Classroom social change
PI—knowledge of results
PI—overt/covert responding
PI—immediate feedback
Verbal-figural material
Inductive/deductive method
Step size
Praise/blame as reinforcement
Lecture/PI text/teaching machine
Bypassing versus linear programming
PI sequencing (standard/random order)
Rote versus conceptual instruction

As an original illustration of this type of research, we can consider a study of navy technical training made by Edgerton (1958) and reanalyzed by Cronbach and Snow (1969) for ATI effects. Two methods of instruction were used in a course for aviation mechanics. In one method, which was essentially rote learning, the trainees were told to memorize the material and reproduce it on examinations. In the second method, the instructor presented explanations and stimulated students to ask questions. This procedure was dubbed the "why" method. The test predictors taken by the 150 trainees in each group were the Tests of Primary Mental Abilities. The interaction analyses showed that those individuals who scored highly on the verbal-abilities tests were more likely to perform well under the rote treatment. However, a similar relationship was not found for the "why" group. Cronbach and Snow suggest that the explanations in the "why" condition overcame some of the potential learning difficulties for those trainees who scored poorly on the test. On the other hand, the high-ability students did not need that extra information to learn the material. Another interesting interaction was established between scores on an interest test and performance in the course. Those individuals who performed best in the rote treatment had previously expressed interest in the kind of content being taught. There was no relationship between interests and performance in the "why" treatment. In this instance, the more meaningful treatment in the "why" condition may have compensated for whatever handicaps were established by the lack of interest.

Early analyses by some researchers found little evidence for ATI effects illustrated in Edgerton's study (Bracht, 1970). However, those reviews often involved the examination of research where the studies were not planned for an analysis of ATI effects and the control conditions and choice of variables were not consistent with well-planned ATI studies. The problems facing the research community were best characterized by the following quote from Cronbach and Snow:

> The substantive problem before us is to learn which characteristics of the person interact dependably with which features of instructional methods. This is a question of awesome breadth. In principle, it calls for a survey of all the ways in which people differ. It requires that individuality be abstracted into categories or dimensions. Likewise, it calls for abstractions that describe instructional events in one classroom after another. The constructs descriptive of persons and instructional treatments pair up to form literally innumerable ATI hypotheses. It is impossible to search systematically for ATI when the swarm of hypotheses is without order. (1977, p. 493)

These remarks are very important. A long history of trial-and-error empirical studies was not likely to produce any dividends. Rather, it was necessary to examine the processes in the various forms of learning. The choice of aptitude variables can then proceed from an analysis of strategies used in each form of learning rather than from measures of aptitudes that happen to be available. Thus, it is possible to ask which learning processes are used in problem solving and which aptitude variables are likely to interact with those processes.

An important paper by Snow and Lohman (1984) captured some of the promise of ATI effects. This review of their own research as well as their colleagues clearly indicates that a significant interaction exists between general academic ability and the degree of structure in the learning program. These data show that low-ability students benefit much more from high-structure/low-complexity programs. The opposite is true for high-ability students. They benefit much more from low-structure/high-complexity programs. For example, one study (Gray, 1983) examined the effect of reorganizing, elaboration, and grouping systems for studying science-related topics. The intervention strategy increased the ability of lower-aptitude students to work with the materials. However, higher-aptitude students complained that the intervention interfered with the strategies they would ordinarily use. Those data also seem consistent with Edgerton's 1958 study, which indicated that the extra information supplied by the "why" approach was only helpful for low-ability students. Snow and Lohman's review of their own and other studies found consistently similar relationships from instructional method studies, learning strategy studies, and ability-training studies.

While most of this research explored only student performance from grade school through college, other important efforts are concerned with individual differences and actual training performance, which continue to demonstrate the need to consider these issues. Thus, Fleishman and Mumford (1989) found that shorter training programs can be used for trainees who are experienced and have high levels of task-related abilities, whereas less experienced or lower-ability trainees benefit from longer training programs. Again, this can be related to explanations provided by the cognitive theorists. It appears that the less experienced, lower-ability trainees are in an earlier stage of learning such as the declarative stage, which involves a high concentration on gaining knowledge. Thus, it has high attentional demands where it is not possible to do much else. The work described by Snow and Lohman (1984) and by Fleishman and Mumford (1989) provides the type of information that can benefit training programs. It essentially says that analysts should measure the existing ability level of their trainees before beginning training and should tailor the content of the instructional program accordingly. At the very least, research data concerning this issue in a training setting seem very worthwhile exploring.

If this research does begin to produce consistent ATI data, another problem has serious implications for training research. Cronbach and Snow (1969) warn us in their original explorations of these issues that particular training conditions that result in poor performance in one type of short-term treatment should be examined further. The trainer must determine how a particular problem (for example, inability to cope with a discussion method) can be rectified because it is likely to limit the individual in other types of social and work situations. Thus, the problem for the trainer will be to design an instructional program that will allow learners to profit from group discussions so that they will not suffer from that inadequacy in a job setting. In this way, interaction research may eventually offer another important tool by identifying problem areas that require further training.

COGNITIVE STRATEGIES AND NEEDS ASSESSMENT PROCEDURES

One interesting question about the work on cognitive instruction is whether it will eventually lead us to different models of the needs assessment process. In the previous chapter, a number of different needs assessment approaches were presented, but it was difficult to discuss a cognitive approach until the instructional material in this chapter was presented. Howell and Cooke (1989) make the point that it might be necessary to analyze the kinds of tasks and KSAs described in Chapter 3 in terms of their cognitive requirements. For example, in this chapter, it was pointed out that Cooke and Schvaneveldt (1988) were able to determine the misconceptions in novice knowledge. They accomplished this by studying the differences between experts and novices performing the work of computer programmers.

One procedure being studied is a procedural guide to cognitive task analysis, which these researchers have named the PARI methodology (Hall, Gott, & Pokorny, in press). This is an effort by the U.S. Air Force to understand the cognitive task requirements for complex and novel situations. Again, this relates to the appearance of increased technologically sophisticated work centers where it is necessary to perform well in dynamic environments. The PARI procedure uses problem-solving situations where experts use their knowledge to respond to problems. As they choose solutions, the experts are probed for the reasons behind their actions and their interpretations of the results of their actions. The probes become part of an interview process sometimes referred to as a *protocol analysis*. Their interview process uses an instructor expert who poses a problem to a second expert who is naive with respect to the problem's source. The second expert generates a solution step-by-step, and the instructor expert provides the results of each step. Because the first expert does not know the source of the problem, the protocol produces very rich instructional material including the relevant knowledge base and problem-solving strategies.

The authors indicate that the cognitive task analysis develops the psychological underpinnings for the type of task and KSA analyses described in Chapter 3. They would not argue that the task and KSA analysis is unnecessary but rather that the cognitive approach adds the underlying psychological processes and knowledge structures necessary for instruction. They argue their procedures are especially useful in producing knowledge that is usually tacit, such as goals, strategies, and assumptions. Their methodology reveals the difference between such knowledge as how a device works versus strategic knowledge that focuses on how to decide what to do and when. For example, they describe a situation where a particular device failed when a test was being run. The expert did the following:

1. Focused on the components that were active when the test failed, thus avoiding the examination of a large number of irrelevant parts.
2. Determined that the testing equipment was more likely to go bad than the

piece of equipment being analyzed, thus picking the unit with the highest probability of failure.
3. Determined that one piece of equipment was much more difficult to troubleshoot, thus deciding to rule out the easier components first.

Each reason was directly tied to the knowledge of the equipment but involved considerably more knowledge than just how the equipment operated. Interestingly, when novices and experts were compared, they did not seem to differ substantially in their knowledge of troubleshooting procedures (for example, taking measurements or checking connections). However, novices could not formulate the type of strategies described above. Novices tended not to have hypotheses concerning the problem nor expectations concerning what result would occur from the use of their strategies. Often, they tended to focus on the use of outside sources for their strategies, such as deciding to perform a particular operation or test because a book or computer program instructs the learner to try this action. However, the novice learners are uncertain about what they will learn from the test.

This type of approach as applied to training settings is still very new, but these researchers have begun exploring the implications for training program design. In one study, a human tutor posed troubleshooting problems and provided instructions consistent with the type of strategies described above. For example, if trainees had difficulty at a particular stage, they would be provided with information that an expert would have used. Then, they would be asked why the expert would have found that information useful. The initial results of their studies showed dramatic gains in learner performance, especially in terms of efficiently collecting relevant information while conserving time and resources. Future research will likely provide very interesting examples of how these systems can be used both as a needs assessment technique and input to the design of training systems.

THE CONDITIONS OF TRANSFER

The previous sections emphasize instructional principles and initial learning processes. Of course, unless the individual learns during training, the question of transfer to the actual job setting is meaningless. Thus, all discussion ranging from the motivation of the learner to the use of advanced organizers is extremely relevant. If the trainee has not learned, there is not much sense discussing what is going to be transferred. However, issues concerning transfer are paramount, especially for those concerned with instructional programs. Evaluation designs and criteria are chosen to measure performance in the transfer setting as a function of initial learning in the instructional program. Trainees are expected to use the KSAs developed in training in the transfer setting. The main problem is persistence of behavior from the learning setting to another setting. Interestingly, concepts regarding transfer have also changed a great deal in the past ten years. Previously, most of the discussion concerned the learning environment in the training situation. Now, there is discussion about such issues as the degree to which training emphasizes relapse prevention in order to help trainees learn how to maintain their behavior despite obstacles in the training setting. Also, there is discussion about the climate of the organizational setting and whether it helps provide a supportive atmosphere for the trainee to use the skills gained in training. The discussion in this section will first focus on some of the classical ideas in training transfer, and then there will be presentations on some of the new ideas being developed at this time.

The Basic Transfer Design

To determine transfer effects, we might compare an experimental group that learns one task and then transfers to a second task with a control group that performs only the second task. If the experimental group performs significantly better than the control group on the second task, *positive transfer* has occurred. It can be assumed that the learning that occurred in the first task has transferred and aided performance in the second task. This assumption would be valid only if the experiment was properly executed and if it accounted for the various forms of bias and error discussed in the chapters on criteria (Chapter 5) and experimental design (Chapter 6). If the experimental group performs worse than the control group on the second task, *negative transfer* has occurred. The learning of the first task has resulted in poorer performance on the second task. When there are no differences in performance between the experimental and control groups on the second task, there is *zero transfer.*

Although the basic paradigms of transfer of training have been examined for some time, the exact conditions leading to positive or negative transfer are not easily specified because settings outside the experimental laboratory rarely lend themselves to the type of analysis necessary to accurately specify the degree of transfer. However, it is important to understand the theories that predict varying degrees of transfer because they provide information about the type of environment necessary to achieve positive transfer. The two classic viewpoints that describe the conditions necessary for transfer are the identical-elements and the transfer-through-principles theories.

Identical Elements

The *identical-elements theory* was proposed by E. L. Thorndike and R. S. Woodworth (1901). They predicted that transfer would occur as long as there were identical elements in the two situations. These identical elements included aims, methods, and approaches and were later defined in terms of stimuli and responses. Holding (1965) summarizes the work on transfer by detailing the type of transfer expected based on the similarity of the stimuli and responses (Table 4.4).

In the first case, the stimuli and responses are identical. If the tasks are

Table 4.4 Type of transfer—based on stimulus and response similarity

Task Stimuli	*Response Required*	*Transfer*
Same	Same	High positive
Different	Different	None
Different	Same	Positive
Same	Different	Negative

Adapted from *Principles of Training,* by D. H. Holding. © 1965 by Pergamon Press, Ltd. Adapted by permission.

identical in training and transfer, trainees are simply practicing the final task during the training program, and there should be high positive transfer. However, it would be unusual for a training program to have the same characteristics as the transfer setting. The purpose of the training program is to provide an environment for learning because the trainee is not capable of performing the task as it exists in the transfer setting. Perhaps he or she requires special modes of feedback or a permissive atmosphere in which to learn new approaches. As instruction proceeds, many programs attempt to develop environments that are as similar as possible to the transfer surroundings. But some differences, however subtle, almost always remain. For example, airline trainees know that a serious pilot error on a well-designed simulator will not have the same disastrous consequences as a similar error in a real airplane.

The second case assumes that the task characteristics, both stimuli and responses, are so different that practice on one task has no relationship to performance on the transfer task. It would be farfetched, although not impossible, to design a training program that is totally unrelated to the transfer situation. The third case is common to many training programs. The stimuli are somewhat different in training and transfer settings, but the responses are the same. The learner can generalize training from one environment to another. The person who has learned to drive one type of car usually has little difficulty switching to another (assuming the required responses remain the same), even though minor features may be different (for example, dashboard arrangement). The fourth case presents the basic paradigm for negative transfer. A certain response to training stimuli is practiced so that the same response is given each time those stimuli appear. If the response becomes inappropriate, negative transfer results. As technology develops, producing continual modifications in control and display equipment without considering the role of human beings, there are frequent instances of negative transfer. Some airplane accidents provide a clear illustration of this effect (Chapanis, Garner, & Morgan, 1949). In one instance, a pilot attempted to correct for a landing, in which he was about to undershoot the field, by pulling back on the throttle and pushing the stick forward. However, this procedure was exactly opposite to the correct sequence of responses, and the pilot nosed his plane toward the ground. After the accident, the pilot (fortunately) was able to explain that he had been trained with planes in which the throttle was operated with the right hand and the stick with the left hand. In this plane, the positions of these controls were reversed. Thus, he used his left hand on the throttle and his right hand on the stick. When the emergency occurred, the pilot reverted to his old response habits—with disastrous results.

Some trainers have a tendency to ignore stimulus and response elements as being too mechanistic and detailed. They make the assumption that analyses of stimulus and response elements are too difficult and that much of the research stems from the laboratory and therefore is not relevant. Although these are difficulties, that is an unfortunate judgment. A large number of jobs require responses to large, complex displays where such analyses would be extremely useful. An example of this situation is the nuclear power industry where there is extreme concern about transfer issues resulting from nuclear control room modifications. The life cycle of a nuclear power plant is approximately forty years, and in that time period there will be many changes in the control room. The concern is that the changes introduced must be carefully analyzed to avoid negative transfer effects. An analysis of this problem notes that the most serious negative transfer problem was the situation where "new, conflicting responses on the transfer task are required while stimuli identical or similar to those used in the original task are retained" (Sawyer, Pain, Van Cott, & Banks, 1982, p. 6). Sawyer et al. performed an analysis of the potential changes in control room design and designated preferred versus less preferred solutions. An example of one of those situations is shown in Figure 4.5.

Obviously, it would also be preferable to train operators on a display that, if not identical to the one that would be used, is at least as compatible as possible, thus preventing negative transfer. Another important issue is the role of stress in effecting transfer performance. The popular idea is that increments of stress produce regression to prior habits, thus creating situations that are prone to negative transfer. Although this might be true, there is not enough research evidence available to determine the effects of stress on transfer performance in job situations.

Transfer through Principles

Critics of the identical-elements theory have argued that the analysis of transfer need not be limited to those situations in which there are identical elements. Actually, Thorndike and Woodworth did not intend for the identical-element view to be specific to stimulus and response components (Ellis, 1965). Their elements consisted of items like general principles and attitudes, as well as the more specific components. The *transfer-through-principle theory* suggests that training should focus on the general principles necessary to learn a task so that the learner may apply them to solve problems in the transfer task. An interesting experiment by Hendrickson and

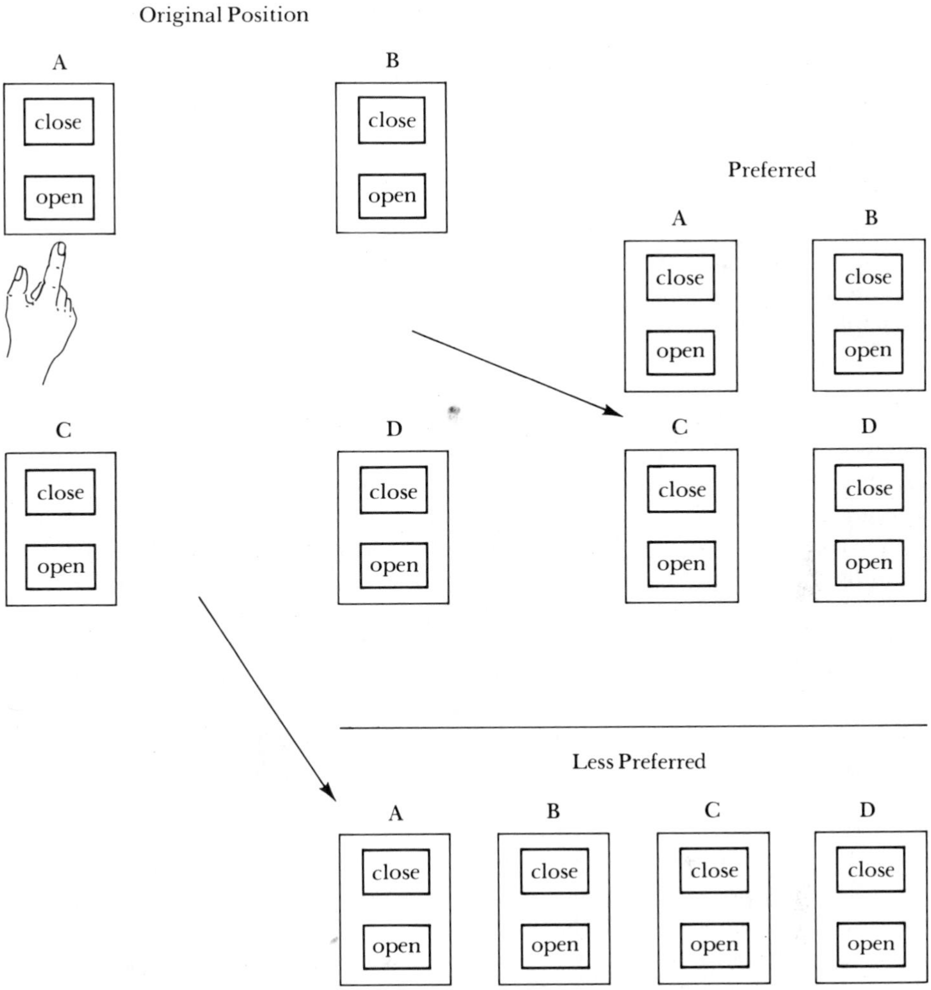

PROBLEM: The top legend-controls are difficult to reach and thus should be lowered.

EXPLANATION: The top alternative is preferable because it retains the basic perceptual relationship among the controls while at the same time moving the top controls within easy reach. Although the bottom alternative is not necessarily a bad one, because of prior experience (conditioning) operators may have some problem identifying the array rapidly.

Figure 4.5 Example of possible control board modification. From "Nuclear Control Room Modifications and the Role of Transfer of Training Principles: A Review of Issues and Research" by C. R. Sawyer, R. F. Pain, H. Van Cott, and W. W. Banks. In *(NUREGGCR-2828, EGG-2211).* Idaho National Engineering Laboratory.

Schroeder (1941) demonstrated the transfer of principles related to the refraction of light. Two groups were given practice shooting at an underwater target until each was able to hit the target consistently. The depth of the target was then changed. One group was taught the principles of refraction of light through water. In the next session of target shooting, this group performed significantly better than the group not taught the principles.

This theory suggests that it is possible to design training environments without too much concern about their similarity to the transfer situation, as long as it is possible to utilize underlying principles. The primary concerns become which environmental design best helps the trainee learn appropriate principles for application in transfer situations (Bass & Vaughan, 1966) and which design best avoids potential negative-transfer effects. In recent years, researchers have begun to ask questions related to the transfer of performance based on improving general abilities through training in related but nonidentical tasks. The idea here is that if it were possible to identify broad abilities, it might be possible to train people in these abilities and have performance transfer to a variety of different tasks, thus avoiding training for each specific task. As noted by Hogan (1978), the research question is whether training on tasks that require a particular ability will result in positive transfer to other tasks that are also known to require the same ability. There is no answer to this question yet.

In a broader context, the concept of occupational adaptability is based on similar ideas. An adaptable individual is defined by Sjogren (1977) "as one who can generalize, transfer, or form associations so that the skills, attitudes, knowledge and personal characteristics that have been learned or developed in one context can be readily used in a different context" (Pratzner, 1978, p. 13). Issues concerning this individual adaptability relate to both opportunities in career development and to opportunities for job transfers. Using this type of model, it is possible to conceptualize how easy or difficult it might be to transfer from one job to another based upon the similarities of the tasks, the KSAs, and the situation. Pratzner has attempted to outline some of these parameters for various jobs. Table 4.5 illustrates this approach. In this table, Pratzner has outlined how three parameters (methods used, content domain, context) change as you consider different jobs. If it were possible to establish measures empirically for each of these parameters and show how they vary from job to job, such a system would be very valuable to persons considering job or career changes.

Transfer and Automaticity

It seems particularly appropriate to close this section on the two classical views of transfer of training by adding a discussion on how the cognitive analyses discussed earlier can affect the consideration of positive transfer of training. As discussed previously, studies by Shiffrin and Schneider (1977) demonstrate that processing can become automatic, thus freeing the learner's limited attentional capacity for other tasks. The condition under which this occurs is

Table 4.5 Examples of changes in job methods, content, and context as a function of changes in jobs

Methods Used (Tasks, Activity)	*Content Domain (Concepts, Objects Acted Upon)*	*Context (Work Situation)*	*Examples*
Same	Same	Same	a. Change in rank from Junior Programmer, to Programmer, to Senior Programmer. b. Change in rank from Associate Professor to Professor. c. Clerk-Steno III to Secretary I.
Same	Same	Different	a. Design Engineer for government research, to Design Engineer for consumer product production, same employer. b. Navy Cook (retired) to Institutional Cook (civilian).
Same	Different	Different	a. Aerospace Systems Analyst for training requirements of new equipment, to Systems Analyst for Public Vocational Education Systems. b. Medical Secretary to Legal Secretary. c. Business Data Programmer to Scientific Data Programmer.
Same	Different	Same	a. Secondary English Teacher to Secondary Social Studies Teacher. b. Flying Instructor (single-engine prop) to Flying Instructor (2-engine jet). c. Truck Driver (light panel) to Truck Driver (heavy tractor-trailer).
Different	Same	Same	a. Skilled Craftsman to Foreman. b. Secondary Teacher to Assistant Principal.
Different	Different	Same	a. Progress upward through key rungs of career ladder, from Orderly, to LPN, to RN, to MD Intern. b. Flight Engineer to Commercial Pilot. c. Bricklayer (house construction) to Real Estate Agent.
Different	Same	Different	a. Liberal Arts Major in Psychology to Salesman. b. Business Major to Auditor
Different	Different	Different	a. Liberal Arts Major in Philosophy to Broker. b. Housewife to Riveter. c. Electronics Technician to Developmental Psychologist.

Source: Frank C. Pratzner, *Occupational Adaptability and Transferable Skills*, Columbus, Ohio: Center on Education and Training for Employment (Formerly NCRVE, Ohio State University). Copyright 1987. Used with permission.

where there is extensive practice on a task so that responses can become consistently mapped to particular stimuli. This results in performance of these automatic tasks in a very quick and efficient way. A particularly vexing problem has been the vigilance decrement that occurs during watch-keeping periods when the number of signals to be detected are infrequent, such as monitoring of warning signals indicating machine malfunctions, or watch-keeping tasks such as early-warning signals of nuclear attack.

As noted earlier, Fisk and Schneider (1981) were able to eliminate this decrement by automatizing the activity through a training program that presented the stimulus and then required a response. These pairings went on for over 4000 training trials, and it is called *consistent mapping.* When the trainees performed the real task with only eighteen targets presented over 6000 presentations (in a fifty-minute period), there was virtually no decrement over time. Another condition of the study involved the same training on 4000 trials, but here the group only received the same number of targets that would occur in the transfer session. This condition was known as *variable mapping* because there was not a consistent mapping of each stimulus and response. When this group transferred to the 6000-trial session, they had the typical 65 percent vigilance decrement over time.

Howell and Cooke's (1989) analysis of this study notes that the ineffective variable-mapping strategy was the procedure that was identical to what occurred in the transfer condition and thus should have produced the best results according to the traditional identical-elements theory. Consistent mapping, which seemed like unrealistic preparation for the transfer tasks, produced the best results. The theoretical explanation for this result is that consistent mapping resulted in automatizing the subjects' detection responses. Again, the point that Howell and Cooke make is that intensive training on certain procedural elements of a task can make them more cognitively automatic and free capacity for other more unpredictable or creative demands. The implications of this for training are enormous, and in the near future it likely will cause us to revise our theories of transfer of training.

Climate for Transfer

In the preceding sections, issues involved in the specification of stimuli and responses and its relationship to the transfer issue were discussed. However, it is critical to remember that transfer of training from an instructional setting (such as a company training program) to a work environment involves all the issues related to the necessity of having a positive-transfer climate in the work organization. These concerns were also discussed in Chapter 3 in "Organizational Analysis." However, it is appropriate to consider the issue again here because it is so clearly related to issues of transfer. I noted that people who participate in training are faced with a problem; they are required to learn something in one environment (training situation) and use the learning in another environment (on the job). This requires an examination of the systemwide components of the organization that may affect a trainee arriving with newly learned skills. Thus, training programs are often judged to be a failure because of organizational constraints that were not originally intended even to be addressed by the instructional program. One study also stresses the importance of a supportive organizational climate. Russell, Terborg, and Powers (1985) evaluated co-worker and supervisory practices to determine whether these personnel were using similar methods as those taught in training. The belief was that if these individuals were behaving in a manner consistent with the training, then trainees will be "reminded" to use such behavior on the job. The results of the study indicate that organizational support is significantly related to performance.

As discussed in "Organizational Analysis" in Chapter 3, there is not much research on this issue. However, Rouillier and Goldstein's (1990) work found two major components of transfer climate, situational cues and consequences, that predicted the extent to which transfer occurred. Some of the types of items included in each of those categories were presented in Table 3.1. This research provides evidence that the degree of positive-transfer climate affects the degree to which learned behavior is transferred onto the job, independent of the degree to which the trainees had learned in the training program. The conclusion is that transfer climate is a potentially powerful tool that organizations should consider in order to facilitate training transfer.

Another important area of research on the transfer-climate issue is the identification of high-risk situations that the trainee would face and the need for coping skills in those situations. The importance of maintaining behavior and overcoming obstacles is clearly detailed in a model developed by Marx (1982). His model is based on another model that was originally designed to examine relapse problems in addictive behavior such as smoking and alcoholism. The model as shown in Figure 4.6 outlines the importance of having coping responses in the repertoire of managers, to prevent relapses in their learned behavior. Thus, as part of his training program, Marx makes managers aware of the relapse process. He also has them diagnose situations that are likely to sabotage their efforts at maintaining their new learning. For example, he notes in the model that if one problem is increased stress resulting from time pressure, then a coping skill such as time-management techniques would be taught. As described in the model, these coping responses result in increased self-efficacy and decreased probability of relapse. The model also describes the situations that occur when no coping response is available. In this situation, the results can lead to giving up on attempts to incorporate new learning. Opportunities for positive transfer then disappear regardless of what has been learned in training. Although many of the ideas in the model remain to be tested, many researchers are beginning to investigate the important issues concerning a positive climate for transfer.

Some general conclusions regarding transfer climate are as follows:

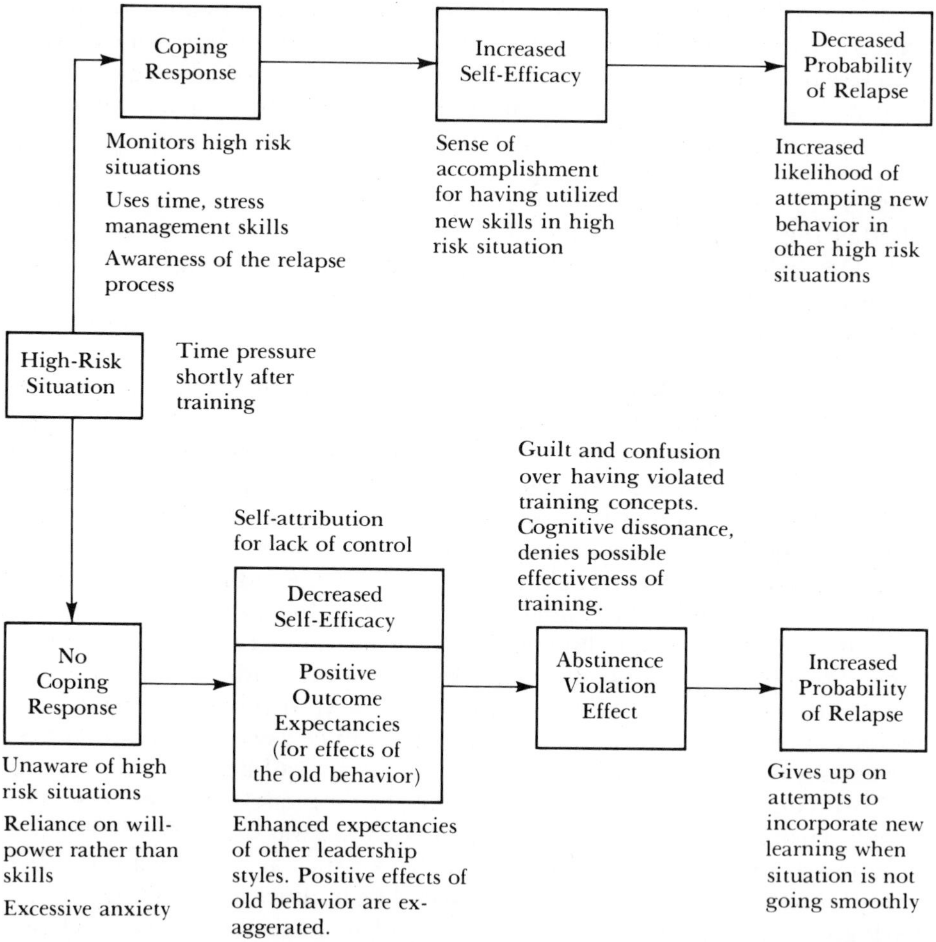

Figure 4.6 Cognitive behavioral model of the relapse process. From "Relapse Prevention for Managerial Training: A Model for Maintenance of Behavioral Change," by R. D. Marx. In *Academy of Management Review,* 1982, 7, pp. 433–441. Copyright 1982 by the Academy of Management. Reprinted by permission.

1. We must have a system that unites trainer, trainee, and manager in the transfer process.
2. Before training, the expectations for the trainee and the manager must be clear.
3. We must identify obstacles to transfer and provide strategies to overcome these problems.
4. We must work with managers to provide opportunities for the maintenance of trainees' learned behavior in the work organizations.
5. Many people believe that we will need to develop a continuous learning

climate so that an atmosphere emerges where employees feel it is important to continually learn and develop. This probably includes support for situations where formal training does not even exist. This point is discussed further in Chapter 9 in "Training Organizational Leaders for a Complex World."

THE TRAINING ENVIRONMENT

Certainly, one point that instructional theorists are trying to make is that our traditional models of learning do not provide enough information for the design of instructional environments. They are *not* saying that feedback is unimportant or that massed versus spaced learning does not make any difference. They are saying that it is necessary to understand the type of learning involved and the instructional event being considered before it is possible to choose the most effective learning procedures. Besides the work of instructional theorists, a number of other researchers have become concerned with various aspects of the instructional environment. To appreciate the complexity of the kinds of issues that make for a successful training program, consider a study by Baldwin, Magjuka, and Loher (1991), which investigated the effects of trainee choice on subsequent motivation and learning. Trainees were randomly assigned to either no choice of training, choice of training but training was not received, or choice of training with choice received. They found that trainees who had a choice and did receive their choice had higher motivation to learn. Trainees allowed to choose but who did not receive their choice ended up with lower motivation and learned less than trainees who were not even given a choice. Other aspects of the training environment are discussed next.

Instructional Quality

A group of researchers at the Navy Personnel Research and Development Center have concentrated on indicators of instructional quality (Wulfeck, Ellis, Richards, Wood, & Merrill, 1978). Utilizing information gained from research in cognitive and instructional theory, they have specified conditions concerning the adequacy of the course objectives, the test consistency, and the presentation consistency. Their work is based on the idea that there is a task dimension and a content dimension to training. The *task dimension* refers to tasks a trainee can perform. The trainee can either remember information or use the information to do something. In addition, the trainee who uses information can either do it unaided, where there are no aids available except for memory, or do it aided, where some form of support is provided.

The *content dimension* is divided into five types of content that can be provided in a training program: facts, concepts, procedures, rules, and principles. A matrix showing the task and content dimensions (with definitions) is shown in Table 4.6. These researchers then use the dimensions to analyze the

Table 4.6 The task-content matrix of the instructional quality inventory

	FACT: *recall or recognize names, parts, dates, places, etc.*	*CONCEPT*: *remember characteristics, or classify objects, events, or ideas according to characteristics*	*PROCEDURE*: *sequence of steps remembered or used in a single situation or on a single piece of equipment*	*RULE*: *remember or use a sequence of steps which apply across situations or across equipments*	*PRINCIPLE*: *remember, or interpret or predict why or how things happen, or cause–effect relationships*
REMEMBER: recall or recognize facts, concept definitions, steps of procedures or rules, statements of principle					
USE-UNAIDED: tasks which require classifying, performing a procedure, using a rule, explaining or predicting with no aids except memory					
USE-AIDED: same as use-unaided, except job aids are available					

From "The Instructional Quality Inventory: I. Introduction and Overview" by W. H. Wulfeck, II, J. A. Ellis, R. E. Richards, N. D. Wood, & M. D. Merrill. In *(NPRDC SR 79-3)*. Navy Personnel Research and Development Center.

objectives, the presentation, and the tests used in a training program in order to establish the instructional quality. An example of their system for analyzing training presentations is shown in Table 4.7. Across the top of the table are content dimensions like facts, concepts, and so on. Along the side are various types of presentation components (statements, examples, and so on). The body of the table gives the appropriate presentation procedure. Thus, when presenting statements in a training program for a concept, all critical characteristics and their combinations are given. Similarly, when presenting statements for a procedure, all steps are given in the correct order. Wulfeck, Ellis, Richards, Wood, and Merrill (1978) present similar rules for analyzing training objectives and training tests. For example, they ask questions concerning the conditions under which student performance is expected for each of the following:

Environment:
Physical (weather, time of day, lighting, and so on)
Social (isolation, individual, team, audience, and so on)
Psychological (fatigue, stress, relaxed, and so on)

Information:
Given information (scenario, formula, values, and so on)
Cues (signals for starting or stopping)
Special instructions

Resources:
Job aids (cards, charts, graphs, checklists, and so on)
Equipment, tools
Technical manuals

Similarly, the Instructional Quality Inventory offers rules for test items. For example, all tests are judged according to the following criteria:

1. Determine whether each item is clear and unambiguous.
2. Determine whether each item is well constructed. For this criterion, separate instructions are given for different types of test items. For example, the following criteria for tests require trainees to list something:
   - The directions should specify the number of things to be listed (if appropriate for the objective and if the number of things is not a hint).
   - The directions should specify whether order is important. If so, the scoring key should score sequence separately.
   - The scoring key should identify allowable synonyms of alternatives and should specify different weights if appropriate.
3. Determine whether each item is free from hints.
4. Determine whether the items permit common errors to be made.
5. Determine whether there are enough items to test objectives adequately and whether they reflect the full range of performance expected on the job.

The development of test items reflects the use of criteria to measure training performance. This is a very important area that must examine a number of issues such as the relevance of the criteria, types of criteria, and so on. Chapter 5 covers this topic.

Besides developing the inventory and handbooks describing its use, these researchers have conducted research studies. They have generally found that when instructional materials have been modified according to the principles stated in the inventory, increases in trainee performance result.

The Role of the Trainer

Designers and trainers must attend to many other instructional considerations when designing training programs. Probably, one of the most important items is the role of the trainer, who typically makes the difference between a successful or unsuccessful learning experience. The potency of the trainer's role has been demonstrated in some very important research conducted by Eden and his colleagues (Eden & Ravid, 1982; Eden & Shani, 1982). In these studies, trainers were informed that they had trainees with very high-success potential attending their course. Learning performance as measured by both weekly performance measures and instructor ratings was significantly higher for the classes with high-success potential as compared to control groups. Interestingly, the control groups in these cases consisted of trainees with the same ability levels as the people in the high-success groups. The only difference was that the trainers were informed that one group had high-success potential. Eden's analyses, which included reports from trainees, indicate that inducing high expectations in trainers similarly enhanced trainee performance. He feels that the high expectations communicated by trainers or immediate superiors leads trainees to expect more of themselves and to perform better. An interesting facet of his data is that several instructors were replaced in the middle of the training program. However, the performance differentials continued unabated. Eden believes that by this time the induction of high-expectancy effects had occurred and the trainees continued to perform at a high level. The researchers have dubbed this the "Pygmalion effect" in honor of George Bernard Shaw's work, which demonstrated the powerful effect our expectations can have on us. Certainly, this research attests to the powerful role that the instructor can have on learning performance. Eden (1990) correctly points out the expectancy effects are part of every training program. He strongly recommends that trainers be made aware of expectation effects and that they use it in a positive manner by helping trainees raise their self-expectations.

The role of the trainer was also explored by Watkins (1990) in interviews with fifty-seven human resource developers at a government agency, a high-technology corporation, and a research hospital. She explored the trainers' beliefs and discovered three themes. One theme is that being able to train is something with which you are born. These people see skillful training as amazing, magical, and something out of reach. As shown in Table 4.8, per-

Table 4.7 Presentation consistency

Presentation Component	*Content Type of the Objective*				
	Fact	*Concept*	*Procedure*	*Rule*	*Principle*
Statement	Complete fact presented	All critical characteristics and their combinations are given.	All steps are given in the correct order.	All steps and branching decisions are given in the correct order.	All causes, effects, and relationships are given.
Practice Remembering	Recall or recognition required	Recall of concept definition required	Recall of all steps in correct order required	Recall of all steps and branch decisions in correct order required	Recall of all causes, effects, relationships required
	For all content types:	Practice Remembering items must be the same as the test item. They must be the same format as the test item. All practice items must include feedback.			
Examples	Not applicable	Examples show all critical characteristics required for classification, non-examples show absence of critical characteristics.	Application of the procedure must be shown in the correct order.	Application of each step or branching decision must be shown in the correct order.	Interpretation or prediction based on causes, effects, and relationships must be shown.
Practice Using	Not applicable	Classification of both examples and non-examples is required.	All steps must be performed in the correct order.	All steps and branching decisions must be performed in the correct order.	Explanation or prediction based on the principle is required.
	For all content types:	Practice Using items must reflect what is to be done on the job or in later training. The task/content level, conditions, and standards must match the test item and objective. The practice item format must be the same as the test item format. All practice items must include feedback.			
	For CONCEPTS, RULES, and PRINCIPLES:	Some practice items should be different than either the test items or the examples. (Common error items might be the same.)			

From "The Instructional Quality Inventory: IV. Job Performance Aid" by J. A. Ellis, W. H. Wulfeck II. In (*NPRDC SR 79-5*). Navy Personnel Research and Development Center, 1978.

Table 4.8 Three beliefs of trainers about training

Framing Orientation and Beliefs of Trainers	*Action Strategies*	*Consequences for the Training Function*	*Possible Consequences for Learning*
Training is magical.	Support the idea that trainers who have "it" don't need training and those who don't couldn't learn anyway. Hold excellent trainers in awe and discount personal capacity to emulate them. Discount technology of training by emphasizing technical expertise over training expertise when choosing own learning activities. Minimize clarifying of outcomes, purposes, time needed for different outcomes and purposes, and cost justification of training. Avoid seeking valid information about performance.	Almost no one can do it "artfully," so few achieve a high level of professionalism. Trainers will not do professional work. Managers have little solid information about how to use training. Training will become expendable.	Learning will not be predictable.
Training is political.	Assume training is a negotiable benefit for self; blame others for holding the same assumption. Delegate determining training needs and methods to supervisors who enact personal or cultural norms about how best to learn. Remain unaware of implicit priority setting when bending rules, setting budgets for training, or compromising educational goals or time frames.	Training is part of the reward and punishment system rather than the task/goal system. Trainers are vulnerable and personally responsible for both means and ends they did not design. Trainers are expendable.	Learning is a political tool. Learning is expendable.
An alternative conception: Training *is* learning.	Trainers actively engage in learning about learning. Trainers encourage different views of training and design ways to test them. Trainers publicly share and test their understandings of human resource development problems. Trainers jointly design and implement solutions with learners. Trainers and learners publicly reflect on results.	Learners and trainers will experience less defensiveness, more trust. Learners and trainers will feel mutually responsible for results. Learners and trainers will feel freer to experiment, to take risks.	Training is more likely to lead to learning and to more organizationally productive results.

From "Tacit Beliefs of Human Resource Developers: Producing Unintended Consequences" by K. E. Watkins. In *Human Resource Development Quarterly,* 1990, *1*, pp. 263–275. Copyright © 1990 by Jossey-Bass, Inc. Reprinted by permission.

sons who view training from this perspective adopt strategies that result in dire consequences as far as training outcomes. A second theme also described in the table is that training is "political." This view states that training cannot be done well because trainers are political pawns. It is reflected by statements that the training staff is where you put misfits who cannot do anything else. It does not take much imagination to state that the magical and political group would not have the type of expectations that would produce Pygmalion effects. Finally, Watkins identified a group that offers a third theme, "training as learning." These individuals focus on learning as a way of being responsive to organizational needs, and they are characterized by people who continually reflect on their practice and engage in self-learning themselves. The types of themes clearly indicate that the organization must take responsibility for what type of training department they are going to have and how the trainers themselves will be trained. The reader should also reread the material presented in Chapter 1 on the discussion of ethical issues involving trainers.

We can next ask, What kinds of characteristics should good trainers have?

Characteristics of Good Trainers

Many opinions are offered about the characteristics that an instructor in a training course should have. Unfortunately, there is not much research related to questions about the role of these characteristics in fostering learning. Most of the research on this topic has evaluated teacher characteristics and the reaction of students in academic classrooms. Although it is not possible to state that all these characteristics would be equally important in training settings, it is probably a good guess that instructors who have these characteristics would positively benefit the learning environment. One such list adapted from Bartlett (1982) includes the following items:

Is well-organized.
Presents an outline of the course.
Designs the sequence of materials for maximum learning.
Emphasizes conceptual understanding.
Gives lectures so well organized they are easy to outline.
Relates lectures to other aspects of course.
Answers questions clearly and thoroughly.
Uses examples.
Sets difficult but attainable goals.
Encourages students to use their talents to achieve.
Points out how materials they are learning can be useful.
Encourages class discussions.
Makes good use of class time.
Gives exams that reveal strengths and weaknesses.
Explains how topics in the course are related to each other.
Is well-prepared.
Encourages students to learn the material.
Treats course participants as adults.

Table 4.9 Instructor preparation-and-planning checklist

Have you:
1. Publicized the program or activity?
2. Informed everyone about the time, place, location and other meeting arrangements?
3. Arranged all details of the meeting room?
4. Checked the physical requirements for conducting the session?
   a. Seating arrangement
   b. Podium
   c. Ashtrays
   d. Drinking water
   e. Coat racks
   f. Ventilation, heat, light, class comfort
   g. Projectors, screens
   h. Blackboard, chart pad, easel
   i. Chalk, crayon, eraser
   j. Papers, pencils
5. Secured necessary aids and equipment?
   a. Charts
   b. Handouts
   c. Demonstration materials
   d. Record-keeping items
   e. Films
   f. Slides
6. Checked to be certain equipment is in working order and familiarized yourself with it?
7. Established the objective for the session?
8. Carefully studied the lesson plan?
   a. Determined important points to be emphasized?
   b. Considered anticipated responses and group reactions?
   c. Considered experiences, examples and stories to be used?
9. Developed enthusiasm for the program?

From "You and Effective Training," by J. S. Randall. In *Training and Development Journal,* 1978, *32,* pp. 10–19. Copyright © 1978 by the American Society for Training and Development, Inc. Reprinted by permission.

Designs course so students demonstrate what they have learned.
Introduces many ideas during each class session.
Allows students to express problems related to the course.
Encourages students to share their relevant knowledge or experiences.
Effectively uses blackboard and/or audio-visual aids.
Accomplishes the goals and objectives of the course.
Shows enthusiasm for the subject.
Stimulates interest in the subject.
Is accessible outside of class.

Another important approach to instructor-quality issues is described by Randall (1978). He emphasizes the importance of instructor preparation. Any of us who have at the last moment discovered that our visual equipment is not available can appreciate the importance of his concerns. Table 4.9 presents an instructor preparation-and-planning checklist. It is hoped that the use of such

"I'm not learning anything. I'm developing cognitive skills."
Reproduced by permission of PUNCH

Figure 4.7

a checklist will improve instruction and result in a more effective learning environment.

Conclusions

The following statement by Glaser reflects the hopes of the investigators exploring the exciting developments in cognitive and instructional theory:

> The technology of cognitive task analysis that has emerged, however, represents crucial progress; the theory underlying task analysis and our understanding of the nature of human competence have been greatly advanced. The study of learning can now take its cure from this knowledge, and principled investigations of instruction can be a tool of major importance for the interactive growth of learning theory and its applications. (1990, p. 38)

Campbell (1988) warns us that designing training methods based on instructional approaches will be successful to the extent that both the theoretical description of the learning process and the functional descriptions of performance are both valid and substantive enough to guide the design of training programs. The conclusion of most persons involved in instructional psychology (for example, Pintrick, Cross, Kozma, & McKeachie, 1986) is that we are not there yet. However, a number of important ideas, such as the

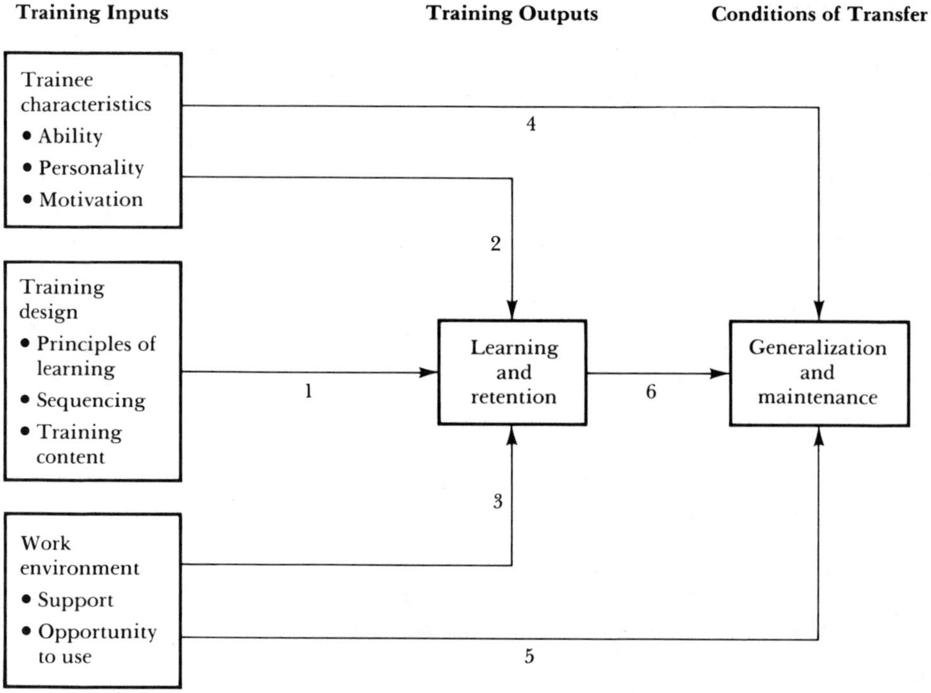

Figure 4.8 A model of the transfer process. From "Transfer of Training: A Review and Directions for Future Research" by T. T. Baldwin and J. K. Ford. In *Personnel Psychology,* 1988, 41, pp. 63–105. Copyright © 1988 by Personnel Psychology, Inc. Reprinted by permission.

differences between declarative and procedural knowledge, are already having an impact. Because cartoons are worth many words, one way the reader can enjoy the impact of cognitive instructional approaches is to consult Figure 4.7.

Finally, to summarize the concepts this chapter has visited, see Figure 4.8. This diagram comes from the work of Baldwin and Ford (1988), who have carefully reviewed the training transfer literature. Their diagram postulates various relationships among the trainee inputs, outputs, and conditions of transfer. Thus, as has also been described in this chapter, all three components are related to what happens in training. That is, there will be good training outcomes with the following types of conditions (these are examples only): good attention to training design (link 1); high trainee ability and motivation (link 2); or the trainee feeling that it makes sense to learn because there is support in the work environment or that training leads to positive outcomes (link 3). Then, if the trainee has learned or retained, there will be an opportunity to perform in transfer onto the job (link 6). If there is motivation and ability to perform, again there will be an impact (link 4). Finally, if the work environment has a positive climate, the transfer is likely to occur and be maintained (link 5).

In conclusion, Tannenbaum and Yukl's (1992) assessment of the learning and cognitive literature led them to propose the following thoughtful guidelines:

> 1. The instructional events that comprise the training method should be consistent with the cognitive, physical, or psychomotor processes that lead to mastery.
> 2. The learner should be induced to actively produce the capability (e.g., practice behaviors, recall information from memory, apply principles in doing a task). The more active the production the greater the retention and transfer.
> 3. All available sources of relevant feedback should be used, and feedback should be accurate, credible, timely, and constructive.
> 4. The instructional process should enhance trainee self-efficacy and trainee expectations that the training will be successful and lead to valued outcomes. For example, training should begin with simple behaviors that can be mastered easily, then progress to more complex behaviors as trainees become more confident.
> 5. Training methods should be adapted to differences in trainee aptitudes and prior knowledge. (p. 404)

Evaluation

2
PART

The Criterion Choices: Introduction to Evaluation

5

CHAPTER

Evaluation is the systematic collection of descriptive and judgmental information necessary to make effective training decisions related to the selection, adoption, value, and modification of various instructional activities. The objectives of instructional programs reflect numerous goals ranging from trainee progress to organizational goals. From this perspective, evaluation is an information-gathering technique that cannot possibly result in decisions that categorize programs as good or bad. Rather, evaluation should capture the dynamic flavor of the training program. Then the necessary information will be available to revise instructional programs to achieve multiple instructional objectives.

There have been many innovations in the development of instructional methodologies in past decades, including techniques like computer-assisted instruction. However, the development of such a system does not guarantee that the appropriate knowledge, skills, and abilities (KSAs) necessary for job performance are being learned and used by trainees on the job. Indeed, as pointed out in preceding chapters, it is possible that the required skills have not been included in the training program or that the required skills taught in the program are not accepted by the supervisor on the job. It is also obvious that the actual designing of training programs is an art. This is true even for instructional programs that are based on careful needs assessment procedures. Evaluation thus permits the systematic collection of information to permit decisions about the selection, adoption, value, and modification of the training program. This philosophy is particularly well stated by Stake:

> Folklore is not a sufficient repository. In our databanks we should document the causes and effects, the congruence of intent and accomplishment, and the panorama of judgments of those concerned. Such records should be kept to promote educational action, not obstruct it. The countenance of evaluation should be one of data gathering that leads to decision making, not to trouble making. (1967, p. 539)

Unfortunately, the past history of evaluation of training programs indicates that much more effort is necessary to acquire the information needed for the decision-making process. One of the first reviews to address the subject found that only one company in forty made any scientific evaluation of supervisory-training programs (French, 1953). There is no question that progress has been made since that time but it is still not possible to conclude that evaluation is considered a norm in the development of training programs. Thus, one survey of 611 companies indicates that 42% of companies did not evaluate the effectiveness of MBA programs and 32% did not evaluate short-course programs (Saari, Johnson, McLaughlin, & Zimmerle, 1988). However, the positive side of those figures indicates a substantial number of organizations did evaluate programs; it turns out that 92% of the companies surveyed did conduct some evaluation of company-specific programs. The less positive side of those numbers is that most of the evaluations focused on trainee reactions to the program rather than determining whether learning had taken place and job performance had been positively impacted.

Grove and Ostroff (1990) describe some of the barriers to training evaluation in work organizations. They include the following points:

1. Top management does not emphasize training evaluation. Although top management is usually interested in evaluating all aspects of business practice, they don't tend to apply the same pressure on training management to evaluate their products. Some people feel that is because top management's fervor in emphasizing the importance of training and career development results in their accepting training on the basis of faith in its value.

2. Training directors often do not have the skills to conduct evaluations. Many directors were direct-line managers or are human resource generalists. Given that training evaluation is a complex enterprise, they often don't have the skills. Further, Grove and Ostroff think that there are few well-written books on how training evaluation should be conducted. Given that these several chapters are devoted to that topic, I won't offer any comments about this point except to hope that some of this material is helpful!

3. It often is not clear to training human resource people what should be evaluated and what questions should be answered by an evaluation. This is the criterion issue, which is discussed in this chapter. Basically, it is difficult for evaluation to be conducted without a clear idea of the objectives to be achieved by the program. Grove and Ostroff note that one manager of a corporate learning center told them he could not match up the objectives with the various course descriptions in his company's own catalog. Also, managers

are not sure whether they are supposed to evaluate trainee reactions, learning, job performance, utility, or all of the above.

4. There is a view that training evaluation can be a risky and expensive enterprise. There is the fear that an evaluation will indicate that a publicly endorsed program is not meeting its objectives. As noted previously, this view is an unfortunate misunderstanding of the purpose of evaluation, which should be to provide the information to help improve programs. The purpose is not to declare programs as good or bad but to gain as much as possible from the effort.

This latter view that evaluation can contribute in a variety of ways is also discussed by Grove and Ostroff (1990). They note the following ways in which training evaluation can make a contribution:

1. Training evaluation can serve as a diagnostic technique to permit the revision of programs to meet the large number of goals and objectives. Thus, the information can be used to select or revise programs. It can also be used to determine whether people liked the program, whether they learned, and whether it positively affected their job performance.

2. Good evaluation information can demonstrate the usefulness of the training enterprise. This type of information can actually show the benefits and the costs gained from training. These data can be very useful when economic realities force difficult decisions on how organizational budgets should be allocated.

3. As discussed in Chapters 1 and 9, legal issues have become important considerations in human resources. Fair employment discrimination lawsuits often question the criteria for entrance into training and the value of training, especially when it is used as a requirement for promotion or job entry. In those cases, evaluation data are required to show the job relatedness of the training program.

4. There have been important advances in the development of evaluation models during the past ten years. Many of these advances have been spurred by demands for accountability in the areas of criminal and civil justice, social welfare, fertility control, mental health, and medical treatment. Many of the evaluation issues facing these evaluators, including the establishment of relevant criteria and innovative experimental designs, are exactly the same concerns facing the training evaluator.

Campbell (1988) states the issue very well. He notes that it is nonsensical to ask the question whether training affects productivity. We all know that it does, and no one would seriously suggest that a pure strategy of trial and error would be a good way to learn the job. On the other hand, it is very difficult to know when the marginal costs of training equal the marginal benefit. There are just too many other variables such as the effectiveness of the selections systems, the effects of new technology, and new incentives. Thus, it is very difficult to specify how resources should be allocated across all these different approaches, especially when they interact with each other.

However, as Campbell notes, a whole host of questions can be answered between those two extremes. They include whether a particular training program leads to better job performance and how much utility results from the program. It is even possible to ask whether the program produced the specific objectives for which it was designed and whether there are particular approaches to training or teaching of skills that are more effective than others.

An evaluation will not solve all training problems, but it is an important step forward. In many instances, the utilization of a simple procedure—for example, giving participants a pretest that can be used in later comparisons—will dramatically improve the validity of the obtained information. The complexities of evaluation should not be underestimated; however, the most serious problem has been the failure to consider evaluation an ordinary part of the instructional design process. The following material focuses on various components of evaluation. The criteria are discussed in this chapter, and in the following chapter methods and designs of evaluation approaches are presented. Clearly, there are numerous interactions between the two topics; the chapters should be treated not as separate entities but as two parts of the same evaluation process.

INTRODUCTION TO CRITERION DEVELOPMENT

Industrial psychologists concerned with the selection of personnel have developed programs based on instruments (for example, paper-and-pencil tests) that predict a standard of success or criterion of the job. The past decade of research has attempted to resolve questions related to these measures of success. Unfortunately, designers of training and educational programs are still faced with the same questions—that is, the choice of measures against which they can determine the viability of their program. In some cases, the training program is the instrument used to predict job success. In this situation, the evaluator attempts to establish the relationship between performance in the training program and performance on the job. In a different model, the training evaluator attempts to determine if people undergoing one form of training perform better on the job than those who have either been trained in another program or simply have been placed on the job. In all these situations, the measures of success are standards by which the value of the program can be judged. The most carefully designed study, employing all the sophisticated methodology that can be mustered, will stand or fall on the basis of the adequacy of the criteria chosen.

In Chapter 3, we traced the development of objectives through the techniques of organizational, task, and person analyses. These objectives state the terminal behavior, the conditions under which the terminal behavior is expected, and the standard below which the performance is unacceptable. In other words, good instructional objectives clearly state the criteria by which the student is judged. At this point, declaring the problem solved and proceeding to the next chapter would be tempting. Unfortunately, that is not possible. First, the choice of criteria is complex. Finding adequate measures of the success of a training program begins with the specification of objectives. Just because there is a measure of success does not mean that it is reliable or free from bias. It is one matter to measure success in a training program that has a degree of control, but quite another to measure success on the job, where the environment often makes the collection of valid criteria a demanding chore.

There is also the question of the relationship between the measures chosen in training and performance on the job. Campion and Campion (1987) describe a carefully designed training program to help people entering the job market learn interviewing skills. The class members responded very positively to the program and demonstrated on an essay test that they had learned the principles being taught. However, interviewer evaluations of behavior produced no differences between trained and untrained groups, and there were also no differences in job offers received by the two groups. The careful evaluation by these researchers produced some reasons why this may have occurred, including the fact that the program may have been too short to produce actual behavior change, even though the candidates could express the principles on a written examination. One of the most important points is that the evaluation gave the researchers information on the impact of the program and what changes should be considered. In addition, these investigators carefully designed their criterion measures to provide the relevant required information. In many instances, problems begin with the choice of criteria as the complex goals represented by organizational objectives that are often difficult to measure. Guion (1961) describes with pointed humor the whole sequence of criterion selection. The following is an abbreviated version:

1. The psychologists have a hunch (or insight) that a problem exists and that they can help solve it.
2. They read a vague, ambiguous description of the job.
3. From these faint stimuli, they formulate a fuzzy concept of an ultimate criterion.
4. They formulate a combination of measures that will give them a satisfactory composite for the criterion they desire.
5. They judge the relevance of this measure—that is, the extent to which it is neither deficient nor contaminated.
6. They then find that the data required for their carefully built composite are not available in the company files, and there is no immediate prospect of having such records reliably kept.
7. Therefore, they select the best available criterion.

Wherry (1957) further warns us that this choice is often dictated by measurement considerations that are no more valid than an arbitrary choice. He notes that selecting a criterion just because it can be measured says, "We don't know what we are doing, but we are doing it very carefully, and hope you are pleased with our unintelligent diligence" (pp. 1–2). Little understanding can be gained by carefully measuring the wrong thing. Thus, these researchers suggest that criteria must also be carefully evaluated so that a good indicant of the impact of our instructional program may be obtained. In the following section we consider these issues of criterion evaluation.

THE EVALUATION OF CRITERIA

Criterion Relevancy

One purpose of the needs assessment is the determination of the KSAs required for successful job performance. As shown in the instructional model developed in Chapter 2, that information must provide direct input into the training program to determine the actual content of the instructional material. The same information concerning the KSAs necessary for successful job performance should also provide the input for the establishment of measures of training success. Logically, we should want our training program to consist of the materials necessary to develop the KSAs to perform successfully on the job. Just as logically, we should determine the success of our training program by developing measures (or criteria) that tell the training evaluator how well the training program does in teaching the trainees the same KSAs necessary for job success. These criteria should be used at the end of the training program to determine how well it is doing. Then, they should be used again later on, when the trainee is on the job, to determine how much of the KSAs learned in training transferred to the actual job.

The chosen criteria are judged relevant to the degree that the components (KSAs) required to succeed in the training program are the same as those required to succeed at the ultimate task (Thorndike, 1949). It is important to recognize that evaluators often choose a criterion because of its immediate availability, so it must be examined for relevance, the fundamental requirement that transcends all other considerations related to criterion development. Accurate job analysis and the ensuing behavioral objectives suggest more clearly the actual criteria to be employed in achieving the behavioral objectives. This relationship between objectives and criteria is an exercise in determining relevance. Figure 5.1 presents the relationship that can exist between items established by the needs assessment and the items represented in the criteria chosen to assess the training program. The degree of overlap between these two sets establishes the relevance of the criteria. The term *criteria* refers to the many measures of success that must be used to evaluate instructional programs and the numerous objectives of training programs. The set on the left side shown in Figure 5.1 refers to KSAs. However, it is just as possible to conceive of organizational goals established from the needs assessment and the degree to which these organizational goals are characterized in the criteria. Again, the degree to which they overlap determines the relevance of the criterion set. These relationships are represented on the right side of Figure 5.1. Most perspectives concerning training

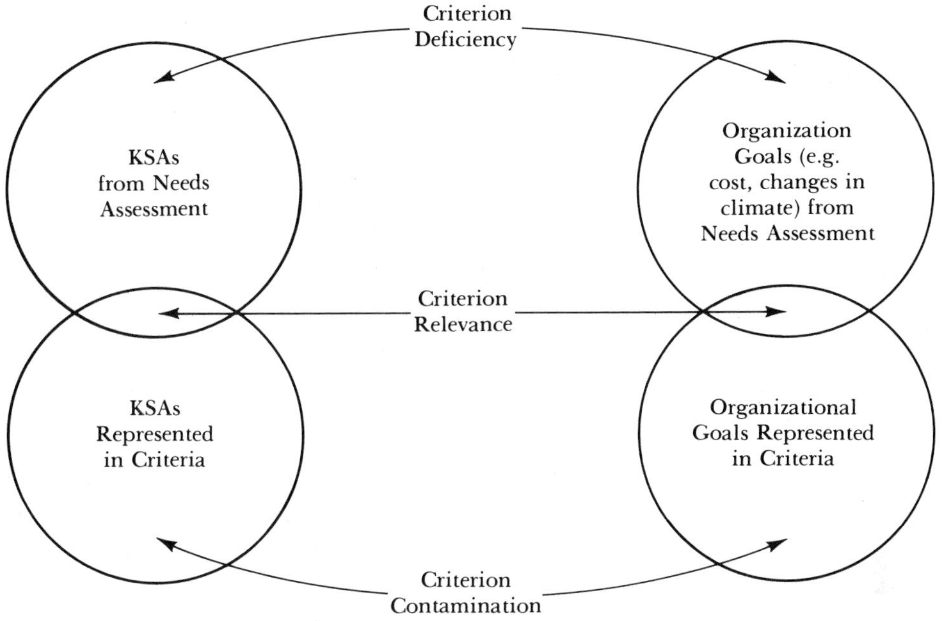

Figure 5.1 The constructs of criterion deficiency, relevance, and contamination.

criteria relate in some way to the trainee performance in learning and using the KSAs stemming from the needs assessment. However, Marx and Hamilton (1991) argue for a much broader multiple perspective of the value of training programs. For example, they note that training often results in other positive benefits such as new networks and coalitions, which can be built between trainees. We might argue that if such a benefit is a goal of the organization, it should be established as a result of the needs assessment so that the programs can be designed to enhance such outcomes. Then, it would be useful to design relevant criteria to determine whether such outcomes occurred and, if necessary, how the program could be modified based on feedback concerning these results.

Another way of conceptualizing these relationships is presented in Figure 5.2. In this case, to simplify the diagram, the relationships are just presented for KSAs. However, the diagram could be redrawn to show the same relationships for organizational goals such as cost. In this diagram, the horizontal axis across the top of the figure represents KSAs determined by the needs assessment. As indicated below that title, there are two possibilities: The KSAs either are or are not represented. Similarly, along the vertical axis, the KSAs are shown as either represented or not represented in the criteria. This results in the four boxes labeled ABCD in Figure 5.2. Using this method of conceptualizing, boxes A and D are labeled criterion relevance. Box D identifies a situation where the KSAs are represented in the needs assessment and the criteria. Box A represents a situation where the KSAs are not identi-

KSA Represented in the Criteria	KSAs Determined by the Needs Assessment: − Not Represented	KSAs Determined by the Needs Assessment: + Represented
− Not Represented	Criterion Relevance A	Criterion Deficiency B
+ Represented	C Criterion Contamination	D Criterion Relevance

Figure 5.2 The relationship between criteria and needs assessment.

fied by the needs assessment as being part of the situation being studied, and thus the criteria appropriately are not designed to represent these KSAs. Essentially, this point of view says that relevance is determined by making sure the criteria contain components that have been determined as relevant for job success. Of course, it is only fair to point out that although we have drawn this diagram as a four-part table, it is actually a continuum. Thus, particular KSAs may be identified by the needs assessment as particularly important, not at all important, a little important, and so on. However, the idea that the criteria should measure those KSAs determined as relevant and not measure those KSAs determined not to be relevant is still the essential point. Of course, the same point can be made about the contents of the training program. It also is supposed to contain materials related to the relevant component and not contain materials that are judged, as a result of the needs assessment, not to be relevant. The kinds of errors that can be made in this process are discussed next.

Criterion Deficiency

Criterion deficiency is the degree to which components are identified in the needs assessment that are not present in the actual criteria. This situation is represented in Figure 5.2 as box B. It is also represented in the upper circles in Figure 5.1. In many cases, it is necessary to make careful judgments about the relationship that is expected between the KSA components established in the needs assessment and the criteria used in the training program.

Actually, there are several kinds of deficiency. The most obvious kind is the type represented in Figure 5.2. That is, an important KSA is identified but omitted from the criterion constructs. It may also be omitted from the training program itself. For example, an organization may expect all middle-level managers to be able to appraise the performance of their employees and provide feedback to the individual so each can improve his or her level of performance. However, as most managers have discovered, their training courses often give them much general information about human relations but do not provide any instructional material on the complex process of appraising the performance of employees. The material is often not only omitted from the training programs but also the criterion-development package; not only is the manager left in the position of not knowing how to perform the task, but the organization does not even know that the manager cannot perform. Sometimes the material is included in the training program, but criteria are still not developed to measure the manager's performance either in training or on the job. This also represents a deficiency. Again, the organization does not know that the manager cannot perform. Even though the organization provided training materials, it has no idea whether the manager has learned the material because no criteria are available to measure the performance. The only solution is to determine, throughout the methodology of needs assessment, the most appropriate multiple criteria to measure success. The complexity of these criteria should be represented in those criteria chosen to judge the initial success of individuals in the training program and on the job. Of course, dependent on the level of expertise expected by the organization, there will be many instances in which the trainee will not be able to perform with the same skill as an experienced worker. The criteria must reflect these differences.

A system's perspective that regards training as one part of an organizational system suggests that there are probably other forms of deficiency. It is quite possible that the needs assessment indicates that particular KSAs are required for the job but that there is no intention for the material to be learned through training. For example, a salesperson could be hired with the understanding that the individual will already have all the necessary knowledge concerning the advantages and disadvantages of various advertising media. In this case, even though this knowledge component is identified as a critical item for job success, it is not to be learned in the training program. Thus, criteria developed for evaluation of the training program for the salesperson would not be deficient if criteria to measure this knowledge component were excluded. However, it should be represented in the selection system.

The issues related to deficient criteria are just as important to the measurement of organizational objectives. This adds a degree of complexity that some evaluators would prefer to avoid. It is one matter to specify all components that determine the success of an individual on required tasks, but it is another matter to insist that all components that determine the success of an entire training program also be specified in criteria that can be measured and evaluated. However, it should be clear that criteria representing organizational objectives provide information that is critical for the feedback and decision processes. It should not be avoided.

Criterion Contamination

Box C in Figure 5.2 and the lower circles in Figure 5.1 present a third construct—*criterion contamination.* This construct pertains to extraneous elements present in the criteria that result in the measure inaccurately representing the construct identified in the needs assessment. The existence of criterion contamination can lead to incorrect conclusions regarding the validity of training programs. For example, a supervisor may give better work assignments to those individuals who have participated in the new training program because they are "better equipped" to handle the assignment than those persons who have simply been placed on the job. In this case, the training program may demonstrate its validity in that the participants have better assignments, but it is just as easy to describe situations in which the opposite phenomenon occurs. Previous efforts describe some of the factors that contribute to criterion contamination mainly as related to selection systems (Bellows, 1941; Blum & Naylor, 1968). In the following presentation, this approach is adapted and the issues are related to training and instructional procedures.

Opportunity bias. This type of bias refers to situations in which individuals have differing opportunities for success, unrelated to the skills developed through their training program. The preceding example concerning work assignments is an illustration of opportunity bias. In other instances, educators may provide more or less opportunity for students who have previously been instructed through innovative media like computer-assisted instruction (CAI). Thus, data may indicate that students from a CAI program do not perform well in a second course using more traditional techniques because the educator does not provide the same opportunities for them as for the students educated traditionally. On the other hand, some educators have extraordinary faith in media like CAI and do not offer equal remedial help to more traditionally trained students. Any approach that treats individuals from various instructional conditions differentially will contaminate the criteria and lead to improper evaluation of the program. A study done by Dorcus in 1940 demonstrates that criteria-contamination problems were a serious concern even in the relatively simple job of door-to-door sales of bakery products. To reduce opportunity bias, Dorcus constructed economic maps of the city, based on rental values of homes, so that he could have an estimate of the effect of sales territory on sales volume. Another investigation by Ohmann (1941) underscores the large number of variables that could lead to opportunity bias. To establish territories with equal potential for each salesperson of construction materials, Ohmann considered the following factors:

1. Sales volume for 1937
2. Average number of calls per day
3. Number of years worked at Tremco
4. Salesman's net commission earnings for 1937
5. Average size of order
6. Average number of new accounts per month
7. Average sales volume per year for length of time employed
8. Sales volume for the first six months on the job
9. Trend of sales volume over a period of years
10. Amount of allowances to customers
11. Amount of returned merchandise
12. Classes of trade called on
13. Classes of products sold (p. 19)

Similar factors must be considered for any environment in which there is variability in the transfer setting.

Group-characteristic bias. Another type of bias can result from the characteristics of the group in the transfer setting. In some instances, trainees are not permitted to demonstrate the skills they have gained from the training program because informal or formal regulations do not permit them to work at capacity levels. Thus, experienced personnel often socially ostracize workers who produce at too rapid a rate, or regulations often restrict the use of particular equipment that might raise the level of production.

Knowledge of training performance. The contamination occurs here because the people responsible for judging the capabilities of the trainees allow their knowledge of the training performance of the individual to bias their judgment of the individual's capabilities in the transfer setting—that is, on the job or in the next class. Thus, individuals who performed well in the training setting would be evaluated correspondingly well on the job. This problem becomes particularly serious when more subjective measures of performance, like rating scales, are used to determine capabilities. It is important to be continually aware of the potential danger of criterion contamination because, in many instances, control is possible. For example, training designers should keep trainee scores confidential and should control for factors like trainee work assignments. There are other factors that interrelate with the criteria measures, including the experimental design used in the evaluation. These issues will be examined in Chapter 6.

Criterion Reliability

Criterion reliability refers to the consistency of the criteria measures. If the criteria are ratings of performance and little agreement exists between two raters, then there is low reliability. Correspondingly, consistently different performance scores by the same individual at different times also reflect low consistency and thus low reliability. Reliability is a necessary condition for stable criteria measures, but it is important to recognize that it will not replace the need for relevant criteria. Because reliability can be measured statistically, some evaluators emphasize it rather than relevance, but as mentioned earlier, there is no utility in carefully measuring the wrong indicant of success.

Nagle (1953) suggests that the instability of a given activity is the main limitation in achieving reliable criteria. He lists the following factors that affect the reliability of measures:

1. The size of the sample of performance
2. The range of ability among subjects
3. Ambiguity of instructions
4. Variation in conditions during measurement periods
5. The amount of aid provided by instruments (p. 277)

In addition, Nagle (1953) lists sources of unreliability that are peculiar to those situations in which ratings are used as criteria:

1. The competency of the judges
2. The simplicity of the behavior
3. The degree to which the behavior is overt
4. The opportunity to observe
5. The degree to which the rating task is defined (p. 277)

Issues regarding rater training will be covered later in this text. The point here is to note that many of the typical conditions under which ratings are collected will result in ratings that are not reliable. Many of these same conditions will result in ratings that are also not valid in the sense that they do not accurately describe the behavior of the individuals being assessed.

Other Considerations

Besides relevancy and reliability, there are several other considerations in the evaluation of criteria. These include acceptability to the organization, cost, and realistic measures. These factors cannot replace relevancy and reliability; they are of consequence only after the relevancy and reliability have been determined. If these latter factors have been established, the training analysts know that they are convincing the organization to accept criteria that may be costly but that are the most valid measures to judge the adequacy of the training program.

THE MANY DIMENSIONS OF CRITERIA

There are few, if any, single measures that can adequately reflect the complexity of most training programs and transfer performance. When all facets of human behavior are considered, including satisfaction, motivation, and achievement, it is clear that there is a series of ultimate criteria from which actual criteria that are relevant and reliable must be obtained. A study by O'Leary (1972) further illustrates the importance of considering the many different dimensions of the criteria. She used a program of role-playing and group problem-solving sessions with hard-core unemployed women. At the conclusion of the program, the trainees had developed positive changes in attitude toward themselves, but these were not accompanied by positive attitudes toward tedious, structured jobs. Rather, these trainees apparently raised their levels of aspiration and subsequently sought employment in a work setting consistent with their newly found expectations. In this instance, it was obvious that the trainees were leaving the job as well as experiencing positive changes in attitude. However, there are many other cases in which the collection of a variety of criteria related to the objectives is the only way to effectively evaluate the training program.

One treatment of criterion development argues that performance can best be approximated by a single measure or a group of measures combined into a single measure. This is known as the *composite view* of the criterion. The other side of the issue, known as the *multiple-criteria approach*, states that the various performance measures must be treated independently. Advocates of the multiple-criteria approach believe a single composite measure is invalid; criteria are multidimensional. Considering that training programs must be examined with a multitude of measures, including participant reactions, learning, performance, and organizational objectives, it is necessary for training evaluators to view the criteria as multidimensional. Training can best be evaluated by examining many independent performance dimensions. However, the relationship between measures of success should be closely scrutinized because the inconsistencies that occur often provide important insights into training procedures. The collection of different criteria reflecting the many objectives of an organization leads to a more difficult decision process than the collection of a single criterion of performance. However, judgment and feedback processes depend on the availability of all sources of information. For instance, a particular instructional program might lead to increased achievement but dissatisfied participants. It is important to find out why the program is not viewed favorably so changes that might improve the reactions of the trainees may be considered. If decision makers are more concerned with achievement than with reaction, they might not be willing to institute changes. However, decision makers do have the information available to make the choice and can consider the possible consequences.

An illustration of the thoughtful development of multiple criteria is offered by Freeberg's (1976) study of youth work-training programs. Freeberg investigated training projects of the Out-of-School Program of the Neighborhood Youth Corps in thirteen cities. Freeberg notes the importance of developing criteria based upon constructs chosen on a rational basis from the stated objectives of the program. In this case, the youth training programs had goals related to trainee social, community, and occupational adjustments and attitudinal perceptions. The author examined the original manpower legislation and the standards of the sponsoring federal agency. He also interviewed the professionals running the training programs and directly observed the operational practices. Based on this work, Freeberg established a number of measures for both short-term program criteria and more distal postprogram criteria. He had a number of measures for each of the following short-term and long-term criteria. The short-term criteria were

1. Vocational awareness and planning skills (importance of various job characteristics, knowledge of relevant ways to seek a first job, rated quality of short-term and long-term job plans, and so on).
2. Personal-social adjustment (with regard to family, police, people in the community, financial management).
3. Work motivation (based on willingness to train full time and part time and to accept jobs under specified adverse conditions).
4. Work-training program adjustment (for example, proficiency ratings by counselors, work-site supervisors, and peers; work-site absences).
5. Vocational confidence (as measured by a seven-item scale).

The long-term criteria were

1. Extent and level of employment (for example, employment status, hours worked per week, rated "quality" of the job, starting salary).
2. Job performance and adjustment (for example, salary raises, employer proficiency rating, number of jobs held).
3. Personal-social adjustment (with regard to family, police, community members, financial management, personal health).
4. Vocational motivation and planning (for example, time required to find the first job, number of sources used, level of short-term and long-term job plans).

The careful tracing-out process for each criterion listed above is made obvious by the measures chosen to reflect each criterion. For example, measures chosen for the construct of job motivation include the number of places interviewed, applications filed, sources used to find a first job, and visits to state employment service. In his study, Freeberg (1976) studied the relationship between his short- and long-term criteria and found a number of strong relationships. For example, trainees who assessed themselves higher on the necessity for keeping out of trouble tended to have higher ratings from their employer, fewer actual police contacts, and families that had more positive feelings about the trainee. Similar relationships were found for trainees who had positive self-perceptions of employment capability, high proficiency ratings by counselors and peers, and a positive attitude toward further training.

As is made obvious by Freeberg's study, there are many different dimensions by which criteria can vary, including the time the criteria are collected and the type of criterion data collected. These dimensions are not independent. For example, learning criteria and behavior on the job not only are different types of criteria but also vary according to the time of collection.

Some of the more important dimensions that should be considered are discussed in the following sections.

Levels of Criteria

Kirkpatrick (1959) suggests that evaluation procedures should consider four levels of criteria—reaction, learning, behavior, and results.

Reaction. Kirkpatrick defines *reaction* as what the trainees thought of the particular program. It does not include a measure of the learning that takes place. The following are suggested guidelines for determining participant reaction:

1. Design a questionnaire based on information obtained during the needs assessment phase. The questionnaire should be validated by carefully standardized procedures to ensure that the responses reflect the opinions of the participants.
2. Design the instrument so that the responses can be tabulated and quantified.
3. To obtain more honest opinions, provide for the anonymity of the participants. Often, it is best to provide for anonymity with a coding procedure that protects the individual participant but permits the data to be related to other criteria, like learning measures and performance on the job.
4. Provide space for opinions about items that are not covered in the questionnaire. This procedure often leads to the collection of important information that is useful in the redesign of the questionnaire.
5. Pretest the questionnaire on a sample of participants to determine its completeness, the time necessary for completion, and participant reactions.

Participant reaction is often a critical factor in the continuance of training programs. Responses on these types of questionnaires help ensure against decisions based on the comments of a few very satisfied or disgruntled participants. Most trainers believe that initial receptivity provides a good atmosphere for learning the material in the instructional program but does not necessarily cause high levels of learning. It is important to realize that reaction measures may not be related to learning and eventual performance on the job. It is entirely possible for participants to enjoy the training but not to produce the behavior that is the objective of the instruction. The study by Campion and Campion (1987) on interviewer training is such an example. In that instance, trainees not only had favorable reactions to the program but also demonstrated book knowledge of the principles on an essay exam. However, they could not demonstrate the required behaviors any better than a control group that had not been trained. The issue of the interrelationships of criterion measures is further discussed later. However, even if there is not a consistent relationship between trainee reactions and performance, few peo-

Table 5.1 University teaching-reaction measure

Use the rating scale below to respond to the remaining statements.

Strongly Agree	*Agree*	*Neither Agree nor Disagree*	*Disagree*	*Strongly Disagree*
A	B	C	D	E

Reactions and Attitudes of Students

As a result of this course I believe that I:
- developed specific skills or competencies that can be used later in life.
- gained a greater understanding of the subject.
- gained factual knowledge (terminology, classifications, methods, trends).
- learned fundamental principles, generalizations, or theories.
- would like to take another course from this instructor.
- would recommend this course and instructor to others.
- was encouraged to think.
- really learned a lot.
- learned to apply course material to improve rational thinking, problem solving and decision making.
- gained a greater interest in this subject.
- developed skill in expressing myself orally and/or in writing.

From scale developed by C. J. Bartlett for Division of Behavioral and Social Sciences, University of Maryland.

ple would argue that it makes sense to run a training program that results in participants having unfavorable reactions.

In one study of reaction measure, Bartlett (1982) met with academic university departments, interviewed individual faculty members, and used questionnaires to develop a teaching-evaluation instrument. Stemming from the needs assessment, one part of that instrument is a reaction and attitude measure, which students filled out, concerning the course. This part of the scale is shown in Table 5.1. Here, the students were not indicating how happy they were about the course, but rather their reactions to specific goals and objectives that stemmed from the needs assessment. Interestingly, a study using this scale with college students shows that favorable reactions were positively related to expected student grades and self-reported attendance in the course. Another example (Grove & Ostroff, 1991) of a trainee reaction measure, which is more specific to a training course, is shown in Table 5.2. Which specific items trainee-reaction forms include should stem from the needs assessment and should reflect the goals of the program.

Learning. The training analyst is concerned with measuring the learning of principles, facts, techniques, and attitudes that were specified as training objectives. The measures must be objective and quantifiable indicants of the learning that has taken place in the training program. They are *not* measures of performance on the job. There are many different measures of learning performance, including paper-and-pencil test, learning curves, and job com-

Table 5.2 Part of a form used to obtain trainee reactions

Instructions: For each statement below, circle the number that best describes the extent to which you agree or disagree with that statement using the following scale: (1) "Strongly Disagree;" (2) "Disagree;" (3) "Neither Agree Nor Disagree;" (4) "Agree;" and (5) "Strongly Agree." If you do not agree with a statement, please clarify this issue further in the "Other Comments" section at the end.

	Strongly Disagree	*Disagree*	*Neither Agree nor Disagree*	*Agree*	*Strongly Agree*
1. The objectives of this program were clear.	1	2	3	4	5
2. The instructor(s)/trainer(s) was/were helpful and contributed to the learning experience.	1	2	3	4	5
3. There was an appropriate balance between lecture, participant involvement, and exercises in the program.	1	2	3	4	5
4. The topics covered in this program were relevant to the things I do on my job.	1	2	3	4	5
5. I can see myself performing more effectively after attending this program.	1	2	3	4	5
6. The logistics for this program (e.g., arrangements, food/beverage, room equipment) were satisfactory.	1	2	3	4	5

7. The length of the program was (circle one):
   (1) Too long (2) Too short (3) Just right
8. Overall, how would you rate this program (circle one)?
   (1) Poor (2) Fair (3) Good (4) Very good (5) Excellent
9. What from this progam was *most* valuable for you?

Reprinted by permission from Chapter 5.6 "Progam Evaluation," by David A. Grove and Cheri Ostroff, Figure 2, page 5–211, from *Developing Human Resources,* edited by Kenneth N. Wexlery and John Hinrichs. Copyright © 1991 by The Bureau of National Affairs, Inc., Washington, D.C. 20037.

ponents. Again, the objectives determined from the needs assessment must be the most important determinants of the measure to be employed. The importance of developing good proficiency measures for training is illustrated in the work of Gordon and Isenberg (1975). These investigators note that the growing concern in a program for machinist training was this: A trainee's passing or failing had become a matter of how lucky one was in having a particular trainer as the grader. These researchers developed standardized exercises based on the goals of the training program. They developed a criterion based on the difficulty of the machine operation, tolerance requirements, and finish specifications. For example, they developed a point system

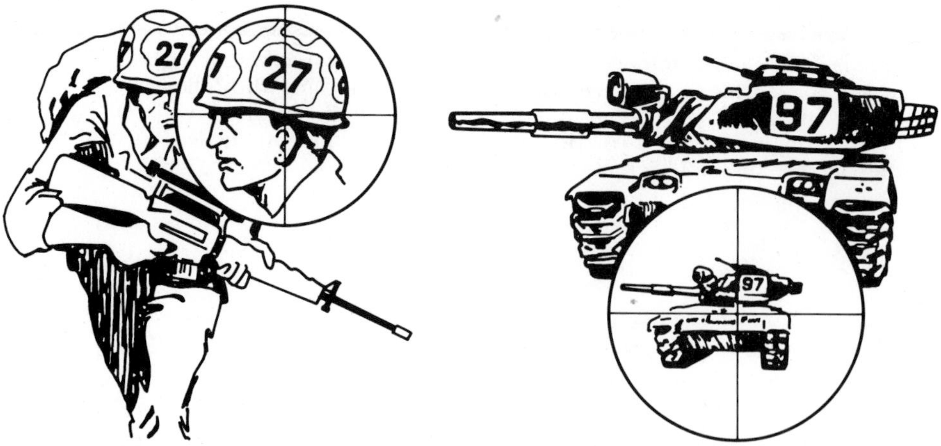

Figure 5.3 Realtrain simulation identification. From "Military Research on Performance Criteria: A Change of Emphasis," by J. E. Uhlaner and A. J. Drucker. In *Human Factors*, 1980, *22*, pp. 131–139. Copyright 1980 by the Human Factors Society, Inc. Reproduced by permission.

whereby the smoother the finish required for the part, the higher the points earned by the trainee for completing the work within the specified standards. As a result of this work, the investigators were able to develop a reliable system whereby judges strongly agreed on the scores earned by individual trainees.

There are many other imaginative examples of the development of relevant criteria. One example is the measure used by the army to assess the performance of trainees involved in a two-sided exercise under simulated battlefield conditions. As described by Uhlaner and Drucker, "Each soldier's weapon is equipped with a 6× telescope, and all participants wear black, three inch, two digit numbers on their helmets. Opponents try to read each other's numbers using the telescopes" (1980, p. 134). This system is depicted in Figure 5.3. When opponents can identify the number, they fire a blank shot and radio a report to the controller, which results in the person or equipment that has been observed being removed from the exercise.

Another illustration, involving peer evaluations of police trainees at the end of their eleven-week training program, is offered by Goldstein and Bartlett (1977). Trainees were to rate each other based on the following instructions:

RECRUIT BACKUP QUESTIONNAIRE

Again, assume that your recruit class has graduated, and that all of you are regular police officers in *X* city. If you were to find yourself in a crisis situation (such as an armed robbery, a high-speed chase, a domestic dispute, a drug raid, a multiple-car accident, or a riot), which five members of your recruit class would you *most like to have* as your backup?

On the following page is an alphabetical list of the members of your recruit class. *First,* find your own name and cross it off the list by drawing a line through it. *Second,* go through the remaining names and circle the five names you would most like to have as your backup in a crisis situation. Make sure you consider all names before choosing. *Then circle five and only five names.*

It was found that these paper nominations did not correlate with grades and other learning measures at the end of the eleven-week police academy training measures. However, the peer nominations did predict a later training performance measure. That is, the police trainees, after graduating from the academy, went into field training, with each trainee assigned to an individual field-training officer. The length of time that the trainee stayed in field training was determined by each trainee's performance as judged by the training officer. The peer nominations at the end of academy training correlated –.43 with the number of days that a trainee spent in field training. That is, the more positive the peer nominations, the fewer days were spent in field training. Evidently, the trainee's peers saw something in the performance of their fellow trainees that was not reflected in their grades in the police training academy.

Behavior. Kirkpatrick (1959) uses the term *behavior* in reference to the measurement of job performance. Just as favorable reaction does not necessarily mean that learning will occur in the training program, superior training performance does not always result in similar behavior in the transfer setting. A large number of measures can be employed to assess on-the-job performance. It is important to ensure that on-the-job measures are related to the objectives of the training program. Because training is not usually intended to relate to all job functions, using a job-performance measure that is unrelated to the objectives of the training program can be misleading.

On the other hand, measures employed during training frequently can be useful in measuring job performance. For example, the illustration offered by Gordon and Isenberg (1975) for machinist training, including finish specifications and tolerance requirements, is just as useful on the job as it is in training. In other cases, measures might be needed that reflect other skills expected to be developed on the job as a result of initial learning in training. Again, it is particularly important to make sure that the criteria fit the objectives of the training program as established by the needs assessment.

Latham and Wexley (1981) offer a large number of behavioral rating–item examples for a number of different jobs, based on careful needs assessment. For example, managers who had been trained in these areas could be rated from "almost never" to "almost always" on the following types of items based on job performance:

Establishes mechanisms for spotting trends/patterns in key departmental/functional areas.
Clearly defines the role responsibilities of key managers.

A mechanic in a bowling alley might be rated on the following items:

Asks the mechanic leaving the shift what machines need watching.
Checks the tension of chains weekly and keeps them oiled.

Table 5.3 Example of one performance dimension for evaluation of police officers

1. Ability to state factual information objectively without interjecting personal biases
   Please rate the behaviors listed below from

Almost Never 1	2	3	4	*Almost Always* 5

A. Clearly separates fact from personal opinion.
B. Uses neutral words and professional terminology in presenting situation.
C. Develops conclusions that flow logically from incident facts.
D. Does not attempt to hide or minimize rule violation even when directly questioned.
E. Does not attempt to omit discrepant informaton from presentation of facts.
F. Does not attempt to embellish or exaggerate facts.

In another example, a training program might be developed to teach individuals who are police officers to state factual information objectively when describing a crime incident. In that instance, some on-the-job behaviors that might be examined could include those presented in Table 5.3. As the reader might imagine, being able to perform such behaviors is just as important as being able to accurately fire a weapon.

Results. Kirkpatrick (1959) uses this category to relate the results of the training program to organizational objectives. Some results that could be examined include costs, turnover, absenteeism, grievances, and morale. In Chapter 3, we described the various components of organizational analysis, including goals and objectives, which in turn should suggest relevant organizational criteria. Again, it is important to emphasize the tracing-out process so that relevant criteria stemming from the needs assessment are developed. A criterion that has received increasing attention over the last several years is cost. Many organizations have designed instructional programs in the hope that it will reduce other costs. Thus, an entry-level sales-training course is used in the hope that the trainee, upon beginning the job, can produce at a higher rate than might otherwise be expected. Obviously, these kinds of analyses require very careful detailing of all the costs and gains associated with training.

Mirabal (1978) outlines the costs associated with the actual instructional program. Table 5.4 shows some of these costs as related to the trainee, the instructor, and the facilities. Other charts developed by Mirabal address items such as the development costs of training. An important addition to the concept of cost in evaluating training programs is the idea of utility. Most of the work involving utility has been applied to the usefulness of selection programs, but Cascio (1989) has applied the concepts to training programs. The basic idea is that the utility of a training program is the translation of validity information into cost figures that permit comparisons between different types of programs. The use of such concepts considerably increases the number of ways one would measure the success of a training program. For example, it is possible to ask what the training program will add to other interventions, such as a selection system, which itself has varying degrees of success. It is also possible to ask what the utility of a formal training program is, as compared to expecting employees to learn on the job from other, more experienced, people. Here, it becomes necessary to ask what differences in productivity for the new employee result from the two approaches, what is the loss in productivity from people on the job who have to teach the employee (compared to the cost of the formal training program), and what is the dollar payoff to the organization? If the cost of formal training is very great and the production return is very little and if the employee moves on to other jobs in a short time, a formal training program may not be worth it. Cascio (1989) demonstrates the use of such models. They will be explored further in Chapter 6.

The Interrelationship of Reactions, Learning Behavior, and Results

Although all these categories of criteria are important, and comparisons across the four types would be interesting, few studies have collected data across criteria. Also, as noted in a survey of over 600 firms, the most commonly collected criterion measure is the reaction of participants (Saari, Johnson, McLaughlin, & Zimmerle, 1988). In 1982 Clement reported being unable to find any literature that might clarify the relationships between these measures. In 1989 Alliger and Janek reported they found only twelve articles on training programs reporting twenty-six correlations between various criteria. Therefore, some of the reported interrelationships are based on a small number of correlations, making generalizations difficult. However, these investigators did find the following patterns:

1. The relationships among reaction measures and the other three criteria were very slight, and the only conclusion that could be reached at this time is that there is no established relationship.
2. On the other hand, the mean correlation between learning and behavior was .13; between learning and results, .40; and between behavior and results, .19.

It is hard to have great faith in the actual correlation estimates given the small number of samples, but the pattern of results for the criterion measures, excluding the reaction measure, does seem to suggest a relationship. One would hope that increased learning should result in increased behavior, which should also impact results. Yet, as discussed earlier, a study by Campion and Campion (1987) on interviewer training found that trainees had actually learned the principles but it did not translate into behavioral change. So, it is necessary to be careful in assuming that learning *always* translates into behavioral changes. On the other hand, reaction measures do not even necessar-

Table 5.4 Charts for specifying training costs

DATE:	CHART 1: Trainee Costs									
Course Title	Trainees and Hours				Salary		Travel and Per Diem	Materials and Supplies	Total Trainee Costs	
	No. of Trainees	*Level and Step*	*Curri-culum Hours*	*Trainees Hours*	*Hourly Salary Plus Benefits*	*Total Salary*	*Annual Travel and Per Diem*	*Annual Cost*	*Total Trainee Cost*	*Trainee Cost per Trainee Hour*
	1	2	3	4	5	6	7	8	9	10

Course Title	Chart II: Instructor Costs													
	Agency Instructors							Non-Organization Instructors			Travel and Per Diem		Total Instructor Costs	
	No. Instruc-tors and Level	*Salary per Hour*	*Over-head per Hour*	*Salary Plus Over-head*	*Hours per Year*	*Annual Salary Plus Over-head Cost*	*Annual Salary Plus Over-head Cost per Trainee Hour*	*No. Instruc-tors*	*Annual Salary or Fee*	*Annual Salary per Trainee Hour*	*Annual Travel and Per Diem*	*Annual Travel and Per Diem per Trainee Hour*	*Total Annual Instruc-tor Costs*	*Annual Instruc-tor Costs per Trainee Hour*
	1	2	3	4	5	6	7	8	9	10	11	12	13	14

Table 5.4 *continued*

Course Title	Chart III: Facilities Costs										
	Non-Organization Owned Space				Improvement to Space		Equipment and Furnishings			Total Facilities Costs	
	Annual Cost of Required Space	*% of Time Used for Course*	*Annual Cost of Space for Course*	*Cost per Trainee Hour*	*Cost per Year*	*Annual Cost per Trainee Hour*	*Total Cost of Items*	*Annual Cost of Items for Course*	*Annual Cost of Items per Trainee Hour*	*Total Annual Facilities Cost*	*Annual Facilities Cost per Trainee Hour*
	1	2	3	4	5	6	7	8	9	10	11

Adapted from "Forecasting Future Training Costs," by T. E. Mirabal. In *Training and Development Journal*, 1978, *32*, pp. 78–87. Copyright 1978 by the American Society for Training and Development, Inc. Adapted by permission.

ily reflect the same behavioral domains. In some cases, reaction measures are simply indicators of how much people enjoyed the course. Again, the point being that enjoyment does not necessarily result in learning but yet, training programs that make it miserable for trainees to learn will not in the long run enjoy a healthy existence. Sometimes, reaction measures are really trainee self-estimates of how much they think they have learned. In that case, the reaction measure is theoretically more closely related to the same domains as the learning and behavior measure. Here the difficulty is with trainees being able to estimate their own performance. In cases where that is possible or where feedback has been received, one might expect that reaction measures would have more of a relationship to the other criterion measures. Unfortunately, at this time, there are not enough data to fully understand these relationships.

Process and Outcome Measures

Outcome measures refer to criteria, like learning and performance, that represent various levels of achievement. Although these measures are critical in determining the viability of instructional programs, strict reliance on outcome measures often makes it difficult to determine why the criteria were achieved. Thus, I have stressed the importance of *process measures* that examine what happens during instruction (Goldstein, 1978b). This emphasis is illustrated in the training instructional model in Figure 2.1 (p. 21) by the arrow between "Training" and "Use of Evaluation Models."

It is not unusual for a training program to bear little relationship to the originally conceived format. One of my favorite examples occurred in a basic-learning laboratory, where the experimenter's ability to control the setting supposedly prevents these events. In this study, a pigeon was trained to peck at a key for food. Later in the experiment, the researcher noted that the response rate of the animal was surprisingly low. The researcher decided to observe the pigeon and discovered that it was not pecking the key to earn reinforcement. Instead, it was running across the cage and smashing into the wall that held the key, thereby setting off the mechanism and earning food! This example was used in the very first edition of this book, and it often prompted readers to ask me if the incident was true or made up for the sake of the book. Sadly, I have to inform them that it is true! Even in basic-research laboratories, complete reliance on outcome measures often misleads the investigator. Because this example has seemed to entertain so many students, I decided to again use it in this edition. In Chapter 6, it will be noted that even the use of rigorous experimental designs does not necessarily provide the investigator with the degree of understanding that is anticipated.

Evaluation designs and specification of outcome criteria have often been based on a product, or outcome, view of training validity. Thus, researchers collected pre-criterion and post-criterion measures, compared them with control groups, and discovered that they did not understand the results they had obtained. This problem became especially apparent when the collectors of these data were outside consultants who appeared only to collect pre-data and post-data but had no conception of the processes that had occurred in training between the premeasurement and postmeasurement. An experience of mine illustrates this issue. In a study of computer-assisted instruction in a school setting, two teachers agreed to instruct a geometry class by traditional methodology and by computer-assisted instruction (CAI) (Rosenberg, 1972). Each teacher taught one traditional and one CAI class. Further, the teachers agreed to work together to design an exam that would cover material presented in each of the classes. At the end of the first testing period, the traditional classes taught by each teacher significantly outperformed the CAI groups taught by the same teachers. However, at a later testing, one of the CAI groups improved to the extent that it was equivalent to the two traditional groups. The other CAI group performed significantly worse than the other three instructional groups. One reasonable conclusion for this series of events might be that one of the teachers learned how to instruct the CAI group so that it was now equivalent to the two traditional groups, but the other teacher had not been able to perform that task with the other CAI group. Indeed, if the investigators had only collected the outcome measures, this or other similar erroneous conclusions would probably have been offered as explanations for the data. In this case, the investigators also observed the instructional process to provide further information about the program. In this way, the evaluators learned that the instructor for the CAI group that eventually improved had become disturbed over the performance of his students. As a result, the teacher offered remedial tutoring and essentially turned the CAI class into a traditional group.

From an industrial psychology perspective, process measures might provide important insights for the analysis of instructional programs in organizations. As indicated, process measures can help determine the source of the effect. If it is found that the trainers' attitudes or the trainees' expectations account for a substantial portion of the variance in the outcomes, those variables must be considered in the design of instructional programs. The utilization of process measures may provide all sorts of unanticipated dividends. I will never forget the look of astonishment on the faces of a number of high-level executives who had just discovered that the reason entry-level grocery clerks could not operate the cash register was that the instructional sequence was no longer part of their carefully designed instructional program. Another perspective on these events is that there are both intended and unintended outcomes that result from our programs. This view stresses the concern for side effects, which is familiar to medical researchers but has been ignored by many training researchers. For example, criteria might be established to measure the side effects of a training program for hard-core unemployed workers. Because such a program would place more minority-group workers on the job, it might have the unintended and unwanted effect of increasing racial tensions by introducing workers with different sets of personal and social values. By carefully considering these possibilities, criteria could be established to measure these unintended outcomes so that informa-

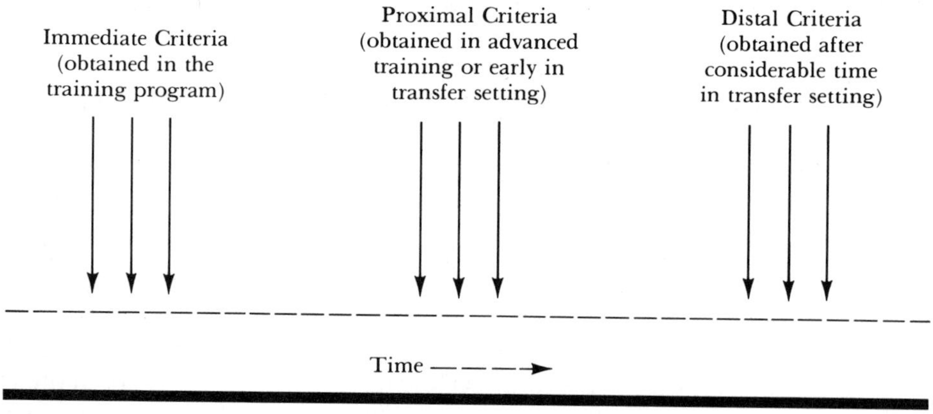

Figure 5.4 The time dimensions of criteria.

tion is available to determine side effects. In many cases, these criterion data become important elements in shaping policy and determining future objectives. Again, this view reinforces the belief that criterion development should be approached with thoughtful emphasis on broadly relevant criteria.

Time Dimension

Criteria also vary according to time of collection. Thus, learning-criterion measures are taken early in training, and behavior-criterion measures are taken after the individual has completed the training program and transferred to the new activity. Figure 5.4 depicts the time dimensions of criteria. In this diagram, *immediate criteria* refer to those measures that are available during the training program. *Proximal criteria* are measures that are available shortly after the initial training program. They might include performance in an advanced section of the training program or initial success on the job. *Distal criteria* are available after considerable time in the transfer setting. There are no exact rules that tell when to measure or when a proximal criterion becomes a distal criterion. Several previously mentioned examples in this chapter illustrate the time dimensions of criteria. Thus, Freeberg's (1976) study of youth work-training programs reports the relationship between measures collected at the end of training and other criteria collected six months after training. Similarly, Goldstein and Bartlett (1977) discuss the use of peer nominations collected at the end of a police academy training program and a later field-training measure consisting of the number of days required to complete field training.

Ghiselli (1956) originally introduced the concepts of static and dynamic dimensions to account for the changes in criteria that occur during the passage of time. The *static dimension* describes criteria that do not change over time. The *dynamic dimension* indicates that successful performance is affected by factors that change with time. Thus, organizational objectives might change, in which case new criteria become necessary. The initial objectives might be growth and acquisition of new clients, whereas the later objectives might be stability and cultivation of present clients. As is clearly indicated by Schneider and Bowen (in press), organizations are developing objectives related to managers being able to operate in a service-oriented environment. Some of the training implications of this approach will be discussed in Chapter 9. For now, suffice it to say that new criteria will have to be developed to measure these objectives. A further implication is that the relationship between training performance and transfer performance is dependent on the time of measurement.

TYPES OF CRITERIA

This section provides a few general criterion categories that are meaningful for training research but have not been emphasized in previous sections. These categories include criterion- and norm-referenced measures and objective and subjective measures.

Criterion- and Norm-Referenced Measures

Criterion-referenced measures are dependent on an absolute standard of quality, whereas norm-referenced measures are dependent on a relative standard. *Criterion-referenced measures* provide a standard of achievement for the individual as compared with specific behavioral objectives and therefore provide an indicant of the degree of competence attained by the trainee. *Norm-referenced measures* compare the capabilities of an individual to those of other trainees. Thus, schools administer nationally standardized exams that determine the individual's standing in comparison with a national sample. The norm-referenced measures tell us that one student is more proficient than another, but they do not provide much information about the degree of proficiency in relationship to the tasks involved. Unfortunately, many training evaluations have employed norm-referenced measures to the exclusion of other forms of measurement. To properly evaluate training programs, it is necessary to obtain criterion-referenced measures that provide information about the skill level of the trainee in relationship to the expected program-achievement levels. Data informing us that the student is equal to or above 60% of the population provide little information about his or her specific capabilities; thus, it is difficult to design modifications to improve the program.

Although there are not many examples of the use of criterion-referenced measures in training settings, it is obvious that many of the rules for the development of test items follow the philosophy of the critical importance of criterion relevancy espoused in this chapter. Readers interested in the procedures necessary to develop criterion-referenced measures should consult an excellent book by Swezey (1981). One example of the development of such

Table 5.5 Hits and misses in classification of trainees

Module	*% False Positives* [a]	*% False Negatives* [b]	*% Hits*
1	8	4	88
2	22	0	78
3	16	16	68
4	8	6	86
5	12	14	74
6	2	6	92
7	8	6	86
8	18	10	72
9	12	10	78
10	16	4	80
11	10	2	88
12	8	4	88
13	12	2	86
14	8	2	90

[a] A false positive is diagnosing a preinstruction group member as not needing training.
[b] A false negative is diagnosing a preinstruction group member as needing training.
From "Construction of a Criterion-Reference, Diagnostic Test for an Individualized Instruction Program," by R. C. Panell and G. J. Laabs. In *Journal of Applied Psychology*, 1979, *64*, pp. 255–261. Copyright 1979 by the American Psychological Association. Reprinted by permission.

measures in a training situation is offered in a study by Panell and Laabs (1979). These investigators were interested in using criterion-referenced measures for a training program for navy boiler technicians. They designed a set of 186 items by setting up hypothetical job situations that required the knowledge and skills contained in each of the training modules. They then had job experts check the items to determine the correspondence between the job situations and the knowledge and skills and to ensure adequate question representation for each module. The hypothetical job situations were also checked to determine that each situation was based on known job requirements and that each situation used job materials such as maintenance requirement cards, charts describing maintenance actions, and illustrations of tools and equipment.

Panell and Laabs (1979) followed these procedures with empirical methods to establish the reliability of the items and cutoff scores for passing and failing. This resulted in 127 usable items. The investigators then administered the test to seventy-five trainees who were about to enter the training course and another seventy-five trainees who had just completed the course. They then compared the results of the performance of the two groups on the test items. Those results are presented in Table 5.5. Using the cutoff scores established by these investigators, it is possible to see that in a large number of cases, the test items did differentiate between the two groups. For example, in module 1, 88 % of the individuals who were in either the group entering training or who had completed training were identified correctly by their test-score performance. That is, people who had completed training knew the test items stemming from the needs assessment, whereas people entering training did not know the test items. For that same module, 4 % of the preinstruction group did well enough on the test that they were identified as not needing training, and 8 % of the group that had completed training was still identified as needing training. Of course, there could be many reasons why some people were misidentified. It is possible that some trainees knew the materials before they entered and that others did not know the materials after they completed the course. If that happened with large numbers of people, it could also be possible that the test items were not very well constructed or that the training course was not doing its job. As Swezey (1981) points out, it is critical that the criteria be developed with an emphasis on criterion relevance. Otherwise, it is not possible to make any judgments about the training program or the level of knowledge of the trainees. As Swezey states it,

> First, it must be determined that objectives have been properly derived from adequate task analyses that prescribe clearly what an examinee must do or must know in order to perform the task under examination. Second, each item must be carefully evaluated against its associated objective to ensure that the performances, conditions, and standards specified in the item are the same as those required by the objective. (p. 151)

Objective and Subjective Measures

Measures that require the statement of opinions, beliefs, or judgments are considered subjective. For example, rating scales are subjective measures, whereas measures of absenteeism are more objective. (However, supervisors' ratings of the absenteeism level of employees could turn that measure into a subjective criterion.) Objective measures—for example, rate of production—are especially vulnerable to criterion contamination based on opportunity bias, whereas subjective measures are affected by the difficulties that one individual has in rating another without bias. For various reasons, rating scales have been the most commonly employed measures in applied settings. This appears to be the case partially because there are not many objective measures of the performance of individuals in complex jobs, such as that of manager. Unfortunately, another reason is that it is simple to throw together a rating scale with a few traits (such as honesty, interpersonal sensitivity), rate individuals, and delude yourself into believing that you have a useful measure of performance. Professionals who have developed relevant-criterion measures know that the steps in the process are very similar for objective and subjective measures and that shortcuts do not work in either case.

For any criterion, the issues discussed in this chapter, such as relevance, deficiency, contamination, and bias, are critical. The tracing-out process from the needs assessment in order to develop relevant criteria is the same for both objective and subjective measures. As discussed earlier, Freeberg (1976) examined manpower legislation, interviewed people running training programs, and directly observed the programs as input into the development of criteria. Some of the objective measures for job motivation for the trainees in youth work training include number of places interviewed, number of applications filed, number of sources used to find first job, and the like. Goldstein and Bartlett have developed an approach for linking behavioral rating scale items directly to the needs assessment. They run workshops where job-knowledge experts are trained to write rating scale items. As input, they are given task items and asked to write behavior items that reflect effective, ineffective, and average performance on the task. Thus, they tie the rating items directly to the needs assessment by using as input tasks identified in the needs assessment as critical tasks. The instructions they use for this procedure are presented in Table 5.6. After the development of these behavioral items, they still have to be edited, judged to be certain they are important behaviors (as described in Chapter 3), and checked for reliability. However, the starting point is that these behaviors are tied to important tasks for that job.

Some interesting research by Ostroff (1991) raises the possibility of using ratings more effectively in evaluating training research. Her analysis suggests that ratings, which are the most commonly used measures of behavior change, often do not show positive effects of training. On the other hand, the use of other measures such as work samples seems to produce more positive results. She suggests that might occur because the traditional rating scales are not designed in a way that allows raters who are judging the performance of trainees to easily and accurately recall and report observations of others. Ostroff notes that cognitive psychologists suggest that scripts specifying a sequence of events or behaviors leading up to an outcome can enhance performance. In a rating situation, it is possible to have a script that might enhance the performance of raters by making it easier for them to recall and remember specific behaviors. In this case, the script would contain sequences of interconnected behaviors, rather than the individual items usually found on a rating scale. An example of a script is found in Table 5.7.

In examining a two-day training program to improve the administrative and interpersonal skills of educators, Ostroff (1991) used both a traditional rating scale format and the script format. The traditional rating scale required rating a person on items such as "skill in recognizing when a decision is required to act quickly" on a five-point scale ranging from little to a great deal. It turned out that the script method was much more sensitive in showing differences between trained and untrained individuals and that, in many cases, the traditional rating format did not distinguish between people who had been trained and others in a control group. Clearly, further research on the script method might produce a more sensitive measure of training performance.

Unobtrusive Measures

As a final reminder about the importance of establishing relevant criteria, classical research has seriously questioned the reliance of social science work on interviews and questionnaires (Webb, Campbell, Schwartz, & Sechrest, 1966). In comments relevant to training research, Webb et al. suggest that

Table 5.6 Instructions for performance-measurement workshop

Industrial/Organizational Psychology Program
Department of Psychology
University of Maryland
College Park, Maryland 20742

The industrial/organizational psychology program at the University of Maryland has agreed to help develop rating scales for the use of the Police Department. This rating scale will be used as part of the appraisal system for police officers. During the past several weeks, the personnel department has conducted a job analysis in order to obtain a list of job tasks performed by officers in X city. For example, a few of the many tasks include:

Check bars for liquor law violation.
Engage in high speed pursuit driving to apprehend suspects.
Admininster first aid to injured persons.
Conduct bank security checks to determine level of protection.

The next step in obtaining relevant items for a rating scale is obtaining performance examples for each of these tasks. For example, consider the task of "conduct conflict resolution between members of the community." Performance examples for this task might be:

Effectively calms the emotions of others at the scene of an incident.
Demonstrates good self-control when harassed by the public.

Note that you would probably consider these performance examples to be illustrations of effective behavior. We would also like to have performance examples which might illustrate ineffective behavior. For example:

Makes insulting remarks to law violators.
Becomes belligerent when interacting with citizens.
Questions the sincerity of rape victims.

Finally, we would like to obtain some behavior statements which you would judge to be of average effectiveness. For example:

Discuss police actions with private citizens affected.
Explains court procedures to complainants.

Thus, we would like you to write out examples of behaviors according to the instructions that are given to you.

Instructions to job knowledge experts:
Please write out examples of effective behavior* for item ___ through ___ on the enclosed sheet. An example of effective behavior should be a sign of good performance in the sense that it contributes to the goals of good police functioning. The behavior should also have the following characteristics:

(a) The behavior should be realistic in the sense that this type of behavior has occurred in the police department.
(b) The behavior should be relevant to the jobs of police officers.
(c) The behavior should consist of specific behavioral examples that tell us what happened.

For example, saying the officer "showed good judgment" does not tell us what the person did (or did not do) that made you feel it was effective. An effective example here might be "did not fire at an escaping criminal when it would endanger innocent bystanders."

*Similar instructions are used to obtain examples of ineffective and average performance.
Adapted from instructions developed by I. L. Goldstein and C. J. Bartlett.

Table 5.7 Example of situational item

The administrator receives a letter from a parent objecting to the content of the science section. The section topic is reproduction. The parent objects to his daughter having exposure to such materials and demands that something be done. The administrator would most likely (check one):

____ Ask the teacher to provide handouts, materials and curriculum content for review.

____ Check the science curriculum for the board approved approach to reproduction and compare board guidelines to course content.

____ Ask the head of science department for his/her own opinion about the teacher's lesson plan.

____ Check to see if the parent has made similar complaints in the past.

From "Training Effectiveness Measures and Scoring Schemes: A Comparison" by C. Ostroff. In *Personnel Psychology*, 1991, *44*, pp. 353–374.

these techniques create and measure attitudes and that they are chosen solely on the basis of accessibility and availability. Although these authors agree that any method is subject to serious flaws, they are especially concerned because these methods are the only techniques being employed. Thus, they suggest that some measures not requiring the cooperation of a respondent and not themselves contaminating the response should be examined. They offer two examples:

1. The floor tiles around the hatching chick exhibit at the Museum of Science and Industry must be replaced every six weeks. Tiles in other parts of the museum need not be replaced for years. The selective erosion of tiles, indexed by their replacement rate, is a measure of the relative popularity of exhibits.
2. Library withdrawals were used to demonstrate the effect of the introduction of television into a community. Fiction titles dropped; nonfiction titles were unaffected. (p. 2)

Although it is difficult to imagine the use of the first example's measure as a criterion for a training program, the second example does suggest an interesting way to examine the implications of educational and training programs offered through television. These methods are not without their own drawbacks and sources of bias. This is clearly indicated by D. T. Campbell's discussion of the use of archival methods:

> Those who advocate the use of archival measures of social indicators must face up not only to their high degree of chaotic error and systematic bias, but also to the politically motivated changes in record keeping that will follow upon their public use as social indicators. (1969, p. 415)

With that warning taken into consideration, it still appears that the solution to the criterion problem will depend on the effective use of the analyst's imagination and willingness to work to uncover relevant measures of success.

CONCLUSIONS

In summary, the following suggestions about the determination of criteria appear relevant.

1. Place the greatest degree of effort on the selection of relevant criteria. Relevance should be conceptualized as a relationship between the operational measures (criteria) and KSAs determined from the needs assessment. Thus, several suggestions can aid in the selection of relevant criteria. First, carefully examine the behavioral objectives established from the needs assessment procedures. Because the objectives are statements about terminal performance, they suggest potential criteria. Next, carefully examine all components suggested by the needs assessment so that the criteria are not deficient. For example, criteria that measure the performance of grocery cashiers include not only measures of register skills but also ratings of various aspects of customer service. Finally, carefully reduce the extraneous elements that often cause criterion contamination. As described earlier, two contaminating factors that can be effectively eliminated are opportunity bias and preknowledge of training performance.

2. After establishing relevant criteria, statistically determine the reliability or the consistency of the measure. If the criteria are not measured reliably, they are useless as indicants of success. Several factors that affect the reliability of the measure are listed on page 158. Because ratings are often used as measures of success, consider the difficulties in rating a bus driver on a trait like "being careful." Compare that to the following rating statements used by a bus company:

Slowing and Stopping

1. Stops and restarts without rolling back.
2. Tests brakes at tops of hills.
3. Uses mirrors to check traffic to rear.
4. Signals following traffic.
5. Stops before crossing sidewalk when coming out of driveway or alley.
6. Stops clear of pedestrian crosswalks.

Note that the behaviors are overt, easy to observe, and well defined. Certainly, more reliable measures could be expected by using these statements than by simply rating "being careful" or even "slowing and stopping" without further defining the behaviors.

3. Because of the complexity of most training programs and the corresponding evaluation efforts, criterion selection must reflect the breadth of the objectives. One especially useful paradigm is suggested by Kirkpatrick's (1959) measures of reaction, learning, behavior, and results. This particular analysis provides for measures of training performance, transfer performance, and organizational objectives. It is critical that the criteria chosen not

only be relevant but also reflect the breadth of the program. Thus, it makes little sense to have measures that reflect training performance but not job performance. Similarly, it makes no sense to have measures of various types of performance without considering cost or utility factors. The criteria must be chosen so that they reflect the breadth of the approach. Thus, it is not only important to have measures that reflect the outcomes but also equally important to collect data that provide information about why those outcomes occurred. Also, criteria must reflect the organizational objectives as determined by the organizational analysis. Otherwise, no matter how successful individual performance is, the organization might judge the training intervention as having failed.

Evaluation Procedures

6

CHAPTER

As previously stated, evaluation is the systematic collection of descriptive and judgmental information necessary to make effective training decisions related to the selection, adoption, value, and modification of various instructional activities. The objectives of instructional programs reflect numerous goals ranging from trainee progress to organizational goals. From this perspective, evaluation is an information-gathering technique. The necessary information will then be available to revise instructional programs to achieve multiple instructional objectives.

It is interesting to categorize the questions that are asked about training programs. I have indicated some of the kinds of concerns to which evaluators are asked to respond by trainees, trainers, and organizational executives (Goldstein, 1978a). A close examination of these complaints reveals certain underlying evaluation questions that have to be asked in order to respond to the complaints. The complaints are as follows:

1. *The trainee complaint.* There is a conspiracy. I just finished my training program. I even completed a pretest and a posttest. My posttest score was significantly better than the scores of my friends in the on-the-job control group. However, I just lost my job because I couldn't perform the work.
2. *The trainer complaint.* There is a conspiracy. Everyone praised our training program. They said it was the best program they ever attended. The trainees even had a chance to laugh a little. Now, the trainees tell me that management won't let them perform the job the way we trained them.

3. *The organization complaint.* There is a conspiracy. My competition used the training program, and it worked for them. They saved a million. I took it straight from their manuals, and my employees still can't do the job. (p. 131)

Most people concerned with training development and evaluation have heard these and other, similar statements a bewildering number of times. These complaints can be scaled on many dimensions, including who complains, the type of complaint, and the many potential sources of difficulty that resulted in the complaint. The dimensions that are of particular relevance for this chapter are the evaluation questions that must be asked and answered in order to respond to these complaints. Rational decisions related to the selection, adoption, support, and worth of various training activities require some basis for determining that the instructional program is responsible for whatever changes occurred. Instructional analysts should be able to respond to the following questions:

1. Does an examination of the various criteria indicate that a change has occurred?
2. Can the changes be attributed to the instructional program?
3. Is it likely that similar changes will occur for new participants in the same program?
4. Is it likely that similar changes will occur for new participants in the same program in a different organization?

These questions could be asked about measures at each criterion level (reaction, learning, behavior, results). Thus, evaluations of training programs are not likely to produce dichotomous answers. However, training analysts who expect results to lead to a yes or no value judgment are unrealistically imposing a simplistic structure and are raising false expectations among the recipients and sponsors of training programs. Although the answers to these questions provide information about the accomplishments of training programs and the revisions that may be required, investigators may be interested in asking other types of questions. In some cases, they are interested in the relative accomplishments of two different training approaches. It is also possible to ask which training approach works best with what type of training participant or in what type of organization. Researchers may also be interested in testing various theoretical hypotheses that provide the foundation for the design of a new training approach. In this latter instance, researchers will still want to know if a change has occurred and whether it can be attributed to the training program. However, they may also ask questions concerning the effects of the training program on trainees with varying characteristics (for example, high and low verbal ability). Before discussing particular methodologies for training evaluation that help answer these types of questions, it is important to recognize that there are many different viewpoints about the desirability of evaluation, the approach to evaluation, and the effects of evaluation. In the following sections, we discuss the most prominent of these viewpoints.

VIEWS OF THE EVALUATION PROCESS

Phases of Evaluation

In the opening section of Chapter 4, I described some of the reasons why evaluation is avoided and what advantages can be gained from a thoughtful evaluation. In a real sense, evaluation has evolved through a series of phases (Goldstein, 1980). In the most primitive phase, appropriate methodology is ignored, and decisions are at best based on anecdotal trainee–trainer relations. Randall (1960) describes people with these kinds of views as *negativists*. These individuals feel that evaluation of training is either impossible or unnecessary. Some negativists feel that the value of formal training programs cannot be demonstrated by quantitative analysis, whereas others feel that the positive effects of the training program will be so obvious that evaluation is unnecessary. In this text, I argue that many developing methodologies now permit the investigator to gain valuable information about the instructional program.

In part, the reason that people originally believed programs could not be evaluated is that many methodologies were relevant to studies conducted in basic laboratory settings but did not consider the demand characteristics of research conducted in work organizations. However, as the reader will see, many researchers are now developing appropriate methodologies. Also, of course, the idea that the value of programs will be obvious without evaluation certainly fails to consider the complexity of the organizational environment and all the interacting forces that are acted out in training and on the job. A consideration of the difficulties associated with criterion contamination alone makes it clear that casual observations are not likely to provide much more than the observer's biased opinion. Also, the negativist's view that trainee improvements in the transfer setting will be obvious treats evaluation of programs in extremes—the program is either good or bad. Instead, training programs should be considered dynamic entities that slowly accomplish their purpose in meeting predesigned objectives. Without systematic evaluation, there is no feedback to provide the information necessary to improve programs or quality information to make decisions. At this time, it is possible to state that the number of negativists appears to be diminishing although Saari, Johnson, McLaughlin, and Zimmerle's survey (1988) certainly makes it clear that reaction measures are still the favorite tool of evaluators.

A second phase in evaluation is represented by those people who believe that only rigorous scientific evaluation of training is a worthwhile approach. Randall (1960) names these people *positivists*. These individuals feel that anything less than an experimental study using scientifically established control groups is not worth the effort or resources. Interestingly, this phase, which is dependent upon strict adherence to the basic experimental methodologies of academic laboratories, can also be very unproductive in providing relevant information. This phase is characterized by designs that do not recognize constraints imposed by the environment or the influences of the multitude of organizational variables. Researchers discover that these types of studies come to a screeching halt because of organizational constraints or because a technology has been applied that does not answer the questions being asked. Even worse, advocates of this approach would have the researcher avoid studying a situation where the sample size is too small for traditional designs. This view, if carried to extremes, could result in research only in academic laboratories where systematic control of the environment can be maintained. Although the data collected in these settings are important, the approach could have the undesirable effect of reducing our understanding of training programs in real settings.

Fortunately, fewer researchers are feeling constrained by the views of positivists. Instead, evaluation research is evolving into a third phase. People who have reached this phase recognize that training programs must be evaluated but are concerned with the methodology necessary to perform the evaluation. This group recognizes that all programs will be evaluated, either formally or informally; thus, it is concerned with the quality of the evaluation rather than with the question of whether to evaluate. Randall (1960) names this group *frustrates* in recognition of their continuing battle to work out designs appropriate for that environment, but I am renaming this group the *activists.* My support goes to the activists. It is important to use the most systematic procedures available that fit the particular setting being investigated, to control as many of the extraneous variables as possible, and to recognize the limitations of the design being used. Thus, the better experimental procedures control more variables, permitting a greater degree of confidence in specifying program effects. Although the constraints of the environment may make a perfect evaluation impossible, an awareness of the important factors in experimental design makes it possible to avoid a useless evaluation. The job of the training analyst is to choose the most rigorous design possible and to be aware of its limitations. These limitations should be taken into account in data interpretation and in reports to the program sponsors.

Values and the Evaluation Process

Before beginning a discussion of evaluation models and strategies, considering the context in which evaluation occurs is important. There are a whole set of values and attitudes that belong to the evaluator, the trainees, the decision makers in the organization, the trainers, and so on. It would be naive to suggest that these values and attitudes do not affect many of the decisions involving both the evaluation and the resulting data interpretations. Some of the more obvious factors can be controlled by some of the evaluation designs. Thus, medical researchers use designs so that the investigator does not know which subjects were given the experimental drug and which subjects were given a placebo. However, it is useless to pretend that all values and attitudes that affect our research are controlled, much less that the factors are even recognized. Researchers are now beginning to acknowledge these variables and are designing research to study the outcomes that occur when these variables are manipulated. Thus, Campbell (1978) warns us that the choice of criteria is a value judgment that all concerned parties should examine and discuss; otherwise, when the results are in, there will be widespread disagreement about the outcome. In this regard, Weiss (1975) notes that decision maker values often determine how data are interpreted. For example, if the decision maker is concerned about trainees holding on to skilled jobs, then negative evaluations about the impact of instructions are treated with alarm. However, if the evaluator is interested in keeping the ghetto quiet, negative training evaluations might be treated as irrelevant and be ignored. That is, training is provided as a way of appeasing the community, not because management cares whether or not the training works. At the very least, the organizational analysis part of the needs assessment should provide the opportunity for these value systems to be made public so that their potential interaction with the evaluation is explored.

Ball and Anderson (1975) have made up a chart of some of the predispositions and preferences of evaluators and how they might affect decisions about the design and interpretation of evaluation studies. As an illustration of this concept, a few of these dimensions are presented in Table 6.1. My view is that it is often quite useful to consider both sides of some of these dimensions. Thus, in the first dimension, well-done case-study and process measures are as useful in providing information as experimental-design and objective-measurement methods. However, that is a statement about my value system, and there is no doubt that other evaluators espouse different values. Understanding the value system of all parties and its effects on evaluation choices before the investigation begins is important. It is also important to warn the reader that the categories represent extreme points on a continuum and that many investigators fall somewhere between these dimensions. However, the table is still useful in pointing out some of the ways that the predispositions of evaluators affect some very important choices.

Besides realizing that values affect evaluation efforts, there is a growing recognition that all our decisions in conducting research have an effect on the study itself. This point of view is often described as the *philosophy of intervention.* It recognizes that even the decision to evaluate affects the data collected. Cochran makes this point with the following tale about Grandma Moses:

> It is reported that Grandma Moses told an art dealer who purchased one of her early paintings from a gallery exhibit that there were 15 more like it at home. He bought them sight unseen and paid the same price for each as he paid for the one on display. Arriving at her home the next day to pick them *up,* the dealer found Grandma Moses with a saw, cutting one of her paintings in half. It seems that when she got home she found she had only 14 paintings and, not wanting to fall back [*sic*] on her agreement, she was correcting the discrepancy. (1978, p. 366)

Table 6.1 Predispositions and preferences of evaluators

	PHENOMENOLOGICAL	BEHAVIORISTIC
Design	Clinical or case study	Experimental or quasi-experimental design
Measurement	Subjective measurement methods, content analyses, self-reports	Objective measurement methods, tests, systematic observations
Interpretation	Judgmental, value-laden	Nonjudgmental
	ABSOLUTIST	COMPARATIVE
Design	One-group design	Experimental or quasi-experimental design with comparison group(s)
Interpretation	Standard-referenced	Comparison-group-referenced
	PRAGMATIC	THEORETICAL
Design	Widely varying	Experimental or quasi-experimental design (hypothesis testing)
Measurement	Ad hoc measures, records	Established measures, construct validity emphasized
Interpretation	Program-specific conclusions, little generalization (ideographic)	Hypothesis confirmation, generalization (nomothetic)
	NARROW SCOPE	BROAD SCOPE
Measurement	Few and specific measures	Many and global measures
Interpretation	Oriented toward component functioning	Oriented toward system functioning

From *Professional Issues in the Evaluation of Education/Training Programs*, by S. Ball and S. B. Anderson. Office of Naval Research, Arlington, VA. 1975.

In an example that may be more relevant to work organizations, Cochran also points out that changes in the use of criterion data occur when organizations discover that these data are being used in an evaluation study. For example, when there are programs to lower crime, the criterion data often consist of the number of larcenies of $50 or more, which are counted in the Uniform Crime Act. One result is that statistics give the appearance of a decrease in crime when none actually exists. In some cases, this comes about because of outright falsification of data. In other cases, it is more subtle. Larceny figures are based on stolen goods, which are used items. Thus, there is some value judgment in setting the actual dollar value of a stolen item. Many psychological studies indicate that the criteria used in making these judgments are often altered by the context and purposes of the study. A dramatic illustration of this is described by Rosenthal (1978), who examined over 140,000 observations in various psychological studies. He discovered that 1 percent of the observations were in error. Two-thirds of all errors favored the hypotheses of the observer.

An early but still very important warning statement about the consequences of conducting research is provided by Argyris (1968) in an article with the very descriptive title "Some Unintended Consequences of Rigorous Research." Argyris makes the point that our empirical-appearing research tends to treat research subjects in an authoritarian manner as passive, predictable creatures. He thinks that subjects do not simply accept deception research and less-than-meaningful control procedures. Instead, they try to second-guess the research design or, in some cases, to circumvent the study in some other fashion. Thus, the result of these well-controlled studies may be behavior that is not representative of what happens in that organizational situation. Support for Argyris's concerns is offered by Hand and Slocum's (1972) study, which speculates that decrements in control-group performance occur as a consequence of their being upset over more favorable treatment being given to the training group.

In another study (Pfister, 1975), the researchers' procedure of assigning twenty-four of seventy-eight police officer volunteers to a control condition resulted in officers becoming angry and withdrawn and making unpublishable comments regarding the research investigators. Argyris (1968) suggests that the meaningful inclusion of research subjects in the design and evaluation of programs that will ultimately affect their lives is one important way to avoid such problems. One way of doing this is to set up representative steering committees in the organizational analysis phase of the needs assessment. Some researchers have resolved some problems of the control group by eliciting the cooperation of the trainees based on an understanding that the control subjects will be trained after the experimental group has completed their training. The most important aspect of the issue is the understanding that trainees are cognitive and emotional human beings with concerns about their relationship to the organization for which they work. The development or the evaluation of a training program is an intervention in their lives. Researchers who ignore these concerns are likely to suffer the consequences. Many evaluation models discussed in this chapter reflect these types of issues.

Formative and Summative Evaluation

As originally conceived by Scriven (1967), *formative evaluation* is used to determine if the program is operating as originally planned or if improvements are necessary before the program is implemented. The major concern of *summative evaluation* is the evaluation of the final product with the major emphasis being program appraisal. Thus, formative evaluation stresses tryout and revision processes, primarily using process criteria, whereas summative evaluation uses outcome criteria to appraise the instructional program. However, process criteria (such as daily logs) are also important in summative evaluation because they supply the information necessary to interpret the data. Of course, both formative and summative evaluations can lead to feedback and program improvements. Design changes based on summative evaluations are determined by the degree to which program objectives are achieved. Campbell (1988) discriminates between two types of summative evaluations. The first type, simply labeled *summative evaluation,* refers to the question of whether a particular training program produces the expected outcomes. The comparison is between a trained and untrained group. When evaluation is accomplished, that is the traditional design. Campbell notes that a more powerful question is the *comparative summative evaluation* where the question is which of two or more training methods produces the greatest benefits. Unfortunately, there have been much fewer of these types of efforts. One instance where there has been such comparisons is in programmed instruction versus a conventional method, usually a straight classroom lecture procedure. In those comparisons, the usual outcome has been that programmed instruction produces quicker learning to mastery of the subject, but the eventual level of retention is the same with either technique.

Improvements based on formative evaluations are related more to how close to the original design the program is operating. The formative evaluation should be completed and judged adequate before summative evaluations are begun. Many research problems result from one-shot evaluation studies that attempt to combine formative and summative evaluations. Thus, the program is often appraised as if it is a completed product when it has not been implemented as originally designed.

A false concern with formative evaluations is that methodological difficulties might be caused by the continual changes adopted from collected data. But that constant modification is exactly the purpose of the formative period, and experimental-design considerations should not prevent the necessary changes. Once the formative evaluation is completed, experimental design provides the foundation for the summative evaluation. On the other hand, satisfactory formative data indicating that the program is operating as designed do not mean that summative evaluations are unnecessary, just as the satisfaction of the personnel responsible for the implementation of the program does not mean that the program is meeting the stated objectives.

Practical, Statistical, and Scientific Significance

Analysts often emphasize the importance of statistically significant changes. The achievement of practical significant changes assumes that the differences are indeed reliable and will recur when the next instructional group is exposed to the treatment. Interacting with both ideas is the concept of scientific significance—that is, the establishment of meaningful results that permit generalizations about training procedures beyond the immediate setting being investigated. As Campbell, Dunnette, Lawler, and Weick suggest for managerial training, "Once the effects of such a program are mapped out for different kinds of trainees and for different types of criterion problems under various organizational situations, the general body of knowledge concerning management training has been enriched" (1970, p. 284). If the instructional program is well designed, it should contribute to the solution of organizational goals and add to the body of instructional knowledge.

In one way, statistics serve as the gatekeeper for social scientists. Cook,

D. T. Campbell, and Peracchio put in this way: "Though statistics function as gatekeepers, they are fallible even when properly used, sometimes failing to detect true patterns of co-variation and sometimes indicating there is co-variation when it does not exist" (1990, pp. 493–494). Thus, if statistical power is low because the sample size is small or the reliability of the criterion measure is low or because a statistical test is not powerful, then relationships that exist would not be found. On the other hand, when large numbers of comparisons are made, some will be statistically significant by chance. In addition, with very large sample sizes, statistical differences might be found that are not especially meaningful in the sense that they are too small to have practical value. This text does not attempt to treat the large number of statistical considerations in instructional evaluation analyses except to warn the reader that statistical expertise is necessary to properly evaluate programs.

METHODOLOGICAL CONSIDERATIONS IN THE USE OF EXPERIMENTAL DESIGNS

Each research design has different assets and liabilities in controlling extraneous factors that might threaten the evaluator's ability to determine (1) if a real change has occurred, (2) whether the change is attributable to the instructional program, and (3) whether the change is likely to occur again with a new sample of subjects. Specific research designs will be discussed in a later section, but several general design concepts, including control groups and pretesting/posttesting, are mentioned here as background for the presentation of the sources of error that can affect the validity of the experimental design.

Pretesting/Posttesting

The first question is whether the participants, after exposure to the instructional program, change their performance in a significant way. A design to answer this question would use a pretest administered before the instructional program begins and a posttest given after exposure to the instructional program. The timing of the posttest for the evaluation is not easily specified. A posttest at the conclusion of the training program provides a measure of the changes that have occurred during instruction, but it does not give any indication of later transfer performance. Thus, other measures should be employed after the participant has been in the transfer situation for a reasonable time period. Comparisons can then be made between (1) the pretest and the first posttest, (2) the pretest and the second posttest, and (3) the first and second posttests. For convenience, only pretests and posttests are referred to in this section, but it is important to remember that one posttest immediately after training ordinarily will not suffice. An additional factor in the analysis of pretest and posttest scores is how scores on the pretest affect the degree of success on the posttest. One possibility is that the participant who initially scored highest on the pretest will perform best on the posttest. To examine this effect, it is necessary that the pretest scores be partialed out of the posttest.

The variables measured in the pretests and posttests must be associated with the objectives of the training program. The expected changes associated with the instructional program should be specified so that statistically reliable differences between the pretests and posttests can confirm the degree to which the objectives have been achieved.

Control Groups

The specification of changes indicated by premeasurement and postmeasurement is only one consideration. It must be determined that these changes occurred because of the instructional treatment. To eliminate the possibility of other explanations for the changes between pretest and posttest, a control group is used (treated like the experimental group on all variables that might contribute to predifferences and postdifferences, except for the actual instructional program). With control procedures, it is possible to specify whether the changes in the experimental group were due to instructional treatment or to other factors, like the passage of time, maturation factors, or events in the outside world. The kinds of errors that can occur will be specified in the next section, but, as an example of the necessity for control groups, we can consider the placebo effect. As mentioned earlier, the placebo is an inert substance administered to the control group by medical research so that subjects cannot distinguish whether they are members of the experimental group or the control group. This allows the researcher to separate the effects of the actual drug from the reactions induced by the subjects' expectations and suggestibility. In instructional research, similar cautions must be taken to separate the background effects sometimes employed in the experimental setting and the actual treatment.

As discussed earlier, it is also becoming increasingly obvious that the use of experimental design, including the assignment of persons to control groups, sometimes produces profound changes in the behavior of participants, with consequences that can include the sabotaging of outcomes of programs. Obviously, if these effects are not detected by investigators, misinterpretations of the results of the study are very likely. Before discussing specific research designs, it is necessary to consider those factors that contribute sources of error. D. T. Campbell and Stanley (1963) originally organized and specified these threats to experimental design. Cook and D. T. Campbell (1976, 1979) and most recently Cook, Campbell, and Peracchio (1990) have updated these findings and include discussions of many of the intervention threats stemming from a growing appreciation of the values of trainees, trainers, evaluators, and organizational sponsors. For the most part, these writers' labels and organization are used in this text.

INTERNAL AND EXTERNAL VALIDITY

Internal validity asks the basic question, Did the treatment make a difference in this particular situation? Unless internal validity has been established, interpreting the effects of any experiment, training or otherwise, is not possible. *External validity* refers to the generalizability, or representativeness, of the data. The evaluator is concerned with generalizability of results to other populations, settings, and treatment variables. External validity is always a matter of inference and thus can never be specified with complete confidence. However, the designs that control the most threats to internal and external validity are, of course, the most useful.

Threats to Internal Validity

These threats are variables, other than the instructional program itself, that can affect its results. The solution to this difficulty is to control these variables so that they may be cast aside as competing explanations for the experimental effect. Threats to internal validity include the following.

History. History refers to specific events, other than the experimental treatment, occurring between the first and second measurements that could provide alternative explanations for results. When tests are given on different days, as is almost always the case in instructional programs, events occurring between testing periods can contaminate the effects. For instance, an instructional program designed to produce positive attitudes toward safe practices in coal mines may produce significant differences that have no relationship to the material presented in the instructional program because a coal mine disaster occurred between the pretest and posttest.

Maturation. Maturation includes all biological or psychological effects that systematically vary with the passage of time, independent of specific events like history. Participants become older, fatigued, or more or less interested in the program between the time of the pretest and the time of the posttest. Thus, performance can change for reasons unrelated to the instructional material.

Testing. Testing refers to the influence of the pretest on the scores of the posttest. This is an especially serious problem for instructional programs in which the pretest can sensitize the participant to search for material or to ask friends for information that provides correct answers on the posttest. Thus, improved performance would occur simply by taking the pretests and posttests, without an intervening instructional program.

Instrumentation. Instrumentation results from changes in the instruments that might result in differences between pretest and posttest scores. For example, fluctuations in mechanical instruments or changes in grading standards can lead to differences, regardless of the instructional program. Because rating scales are a commonly employed criterion in training research, it is important to be sensitive to differences related to changes in the rater (for example, additional expertise in the second rating, bias, or carelessness) that can cause error effects.

Statistical regression. Participants for instructional research are often chosen on the basis of extreme scores. Thus, students with extremely low and extremely high intelligence-test scores may be chosen for participation in a course using programmed instruction. In these cases, a phenomenon known as statistical regression often occurs. On the second testing, the scores for both groups regress toward the middle of the distribution. Thus, students with extremely high scores would tend toward lower scores, and those with extremely low scores would tend toward higher scores. This regression occurs because tests are not perfect measures; there will always be some change in scores from the first to the second testing simply because of measurement error. Because the first scores are at the extreme ends, the variability must move toward the center (the mean of the entire group). Students with extremely high scores might have had unusually good luck the day of the first testing, or students with extremely low scores may have been upset or careless that day. On the second administration, however, each group is likely to regress toward the mean.

Differential selection of participants. This effect stems from biases in choosing comparison groups. If volunteers are used in the instruction group and randomly chosen participants are used in the control group, differences could occur between the two groups simply because each was different before the program began. This variable is best controlled by random selection of all participants, with appropriate numbers of participants (as determined by statistical considerations) for each group. Random selection is a particular problem in educational settings where one class is chosen as the control group and another class as the experimental group. Establishing experimental and control groups by placing individuals with matched characteristics (for example, intelligence, age, gender) in each group is still not the best alternative. Often, the critical parameters that should be used to match the participants are not known, and thus selection biases can again affect the design. One alternative is a combination of matching and randomization in which participants are matched on important parameters; then, one member of each pair is assigned randomly to the treatment or control group.

Experimental mortality. This variable refers to the differential loss of participants from the treatment or control group. In a control group of volunteers, those persons who scored poorly on the pretest may drop out because they are discouraged. Thus, the group in the experimental program may appear to score higher than the control group because the low-scoring performers have dropped out.

Interactions. Many of the preceding factors—for example, selection and maturation—can interact to produce threats to internal validity. When younger students are compared with older students over a period of a year, differences in initial selection and differences in maturation changes could occur at varying rates for each of the different groups. The following threats to internal validity can be labeled intervention threats because they stem mainly from the decision to evaluate a program. Interestingly, many of the internal threats to validity can be constrained by the use of experimental-design procedures. For example, the internal threat of history effects can often be constrained by having an experimental and a control group so that whatever the historical occurrence, it affects both groups. However, most of the next set of threats cannot be constrained by experimental methodology. Rather, as discussed in the section on values and evaluation, it will take other approaches—for example, working with the participants as part of the evaluation model so that they do not feel threatened by events such as being assigned to a control group. Many people in organizations are interested in achieving success. Therefore, it should not surprise anyone that a mysterious announcement from a training analyst that assigns only certain individuals to a training program might be viewed by the control subjects as a message that they are not in favor with the organization. Also, as described below, some organizations tend to interfere with the assignment of treatment effects because they are certain that training will work and they want the control group to have the benefit of the effect even while evaluation is proceeding. Some of these types of threats to validity (adapted from Cook & D. T. Campbell, 1976, 1979; Cook, D. T. Campbell, & Peracchio, 1990) include the following.

Diffusion or imitation of treatments. In organizations where members of the experimental and control treatments know each other, information passed on to the controls by members of the group being trained can diffuse the effects of training. Thus, members of the training group tell control individuals how to use this wonderful new procedure. As a result, differences between the two groups based on the training treatment disappear, and the evaluator does not learn whether the program accomplished its goals. Basically, what has happened is that the functional differences between the control and experimental group have to some extent disappeared. Cook, D. T. Campbell, and Peracchio (1990) use the term *treatment crossovers* to describe this phenomena.

Compensatory equalization of treatments. When the training treatment is perceived to produce positive benefits, there is often a reluctance to permit perceived inequalities to exist. Thus, administrators or trainers provide control subjects with similar or other benefits that wipe out any measured differences between the control and experimental groups in the evaluation. Cook, D. T. Campbell, and Peracchio (1990) note that in several national educational experiments, so-called control schools tended to be given other federal funds by well-meaning administrators. This resulted in these control schools actually being another form of experimental condition. Unfortunately, as later analyses indicate, it also wiped out the differences between the experimental and control treatments, leaving many confused individuals wondering why their training treatments had no effect. The powerful effect of this category is supported by the large number of lawsuits being brought by minorities, women, and other protected classes because they believe they are not being permitted on an equal basis to enter training programs that are required as stepping stones for promotion opportunities. In this instance, the question is not how the evaluation data should be evaluated but rather the large impact of the perceived positive benefits of training programs. Again, this is a clear indication of the importance of understanding value issues and how they effect interventions.

Compensatory rivalry between respondents receiving less desirable treatments. In some situations, competition between the training group and the control group may be generated. This is more likely to occur when the assignments are made public or when intact units (like a whole department or work crew) are assigned to a particular condition. The problem is that this special effort may wipe out the differences between the two groups but not be a reflection of how control subjects would ordinarily perform. This kind of effect is also possible where the control condition is the old training procedure. Here again, the controls might work extra hard so that their performance would be equivalent to the persons assigned to the new treatment condition. Saretsky (1972) labels this type of effort the "John Henry effect." As memorialized in the folk song, John Henry competed against a steam drill. He worked so hard that he outperformed the drill and died of overexertion. In several firefighter jurisdictions, women have worked together outside the organization to set up special training programs to help them build the upper-body strength necessary to qualify for the job of firefighter. If these women had been assigned to the control group in large numbers, data comparing the "control" to a more traditional program would not be meaningful. On the other hand, as will be discussed in Chapter 9, such training efforts are having an important impact on the entry of women into so-called nontraditional jobs.

Resentful demoralization of respondents receiving less desirable treatments. In some instances, people selected for a control condition can become resentful or demoralized. This is especially possible when control subjects believe that the assignment might be a message that they are not as highly valued by management. This can result in the person not performing as capably as possible. In this instance, the control subjects' drop in performance could result in differences between the treatment and control that lead to the incorrect conclusion that the training program has been successful.

Threats to External Validity

External validity refers to the generalizability of the study to other groups and situations. Internal validity is a prerequisite for external validity because the results for the study must be valid for the group being examined before there can be concern over the validity for other groups. As noted by Cook, D. T. Campbell, and Peracchio (1990), the concern in external validity is generalizing to or across times, settings, and people. In that sense, the issues become the "available samples or instances, the populations or categories they represent, and the populations or categories to which potential research users want to generalize" (p. 509). In general terms, the representativeness of all aspects of the investigation to the categories the investigator wishes to extrapolate determines the degree of generalizability. For example, when the data are initially collected in a low-socioeconomic setting, claiming that the instructional program will work equally well in a high-socioeconomic area may be difficult. In that sense, threats to external validity are those threats that limit the generalizations. The following are examples of threats that are potentially relevant to external validity generalizations.

Reactive effect of pretesting. The effects of pretests often lead to increased sensitivity to the instructional procedure. Thus, the participants' responses to the training program might be different from the responses of individuals who are exposed to an established program without the pretest; the pretested participants might pay attention to certain material in the training program only because they know it is covered in test items. Usually, it is speculated that pretest exposure will improve performance. However, Bunker and Cohen (1977) discovered that the posttest scores of individuals low in numerical ability were hindered by exposure to the pretest. They offer two possible reasons for this development: (1) Trainees may mistakenly have attended to only the limited sample of material appearing on the pretest; (2) trainees who were low in numerical ability may have become quite anxious because of the pretest and that might have interfered with later learning. Further research will be needed to explore that possibility. However, generalizations to later training populations that would not be exposed to a pretest would be in error. Interestingly, however, the problem occurred only for low ability students. Thus, the external validity threat of pretesting interacted with the selection of the participating group. That type of threat is discussed next.

Interaction of selection and experimental treatment. In this case, the characteristics of the group selected for experimental treatment determine the generalizability of the findings. The characteristics of employees from one division of the firm may result in the treatment's being more or less effective for them, as compared with employees from another division with different characteristics. Similarly, characteristics, such as the low numerical ability example, may make trainees more or less receptive to particular instructional programs.

Reactive effects of experimental settings. The procedures employed in the experimental setting may limit the generalizability of the study. Observers and experimental equipment often make the participants aware of their participation in an experiment. This can lead to changes in behavior that cannot be generalized to those individuals who will participate in the instructional treatment when it is not the focus of a research study. The Hawthorne studies have become the standard illustration for the "I'm a guinea pig" effect. This research showed that a group of employees continued to increase production regardless of the changes in working conditions designed to produce both increases and decreases in production. Interpreters believe that the experimental conditions resulted in the workers' behaving differently. Explanations for the Hawthorne effect include novelty; awareness of being a participant in an experiment; changes in the environment due to observers, enthusiasm of the instructor; recording conditions; social interaction; and daily feedback on production figures. The important point is that, because the factors that affect the treatment group will not be present in future training sessions, the performance obtained is not representative of that of future participants. The potency of these types of variables was demonstrated by Eden and Shani (1982) in their "Pygmalion effect" study of military combat training for the Israeli Defense Forces. As described in Chapter 5, instructors had been led to expect that some of these trainees were better students than others, although actually there were no greater ability differences for the persons chosen. The individuals for whom trainers had high expectancies scored significantly higher on objective achievement tests, exhibited more positive attitudes toward the course, and had more positive perceptions of instructor leadership. These types of variables become an external validity threat because there is often more enthusiasm when courses are first being offered (and evaluated). However, that enthusiasm sometimes disappears when the course becomes more routine. To the extent that the training effect was due to enthusiasm, it will disappear with the more routine course. On the other hand, if organizations can learn to use and maintain variables underlying factors such as enthusiasm, there are indications that training performance will improve. It is hoped that the positive attitudes and performance generated in the Eden and Shani study will continue on the job. However, further studies will be needed to make that determination.

Multiple-treatment interference. The effects of previous treatments are not erasable; therefore, threats to external validity occur whenever there is an attempt to establish the effects of a single treatment from studies that actually examined multiple treatments. Thus, trainees exposed to role playing, films, and lectures may perform best during the lectures, but that does not mean that they would perform in a similar manner were they exposed to lectures only.

EXPERIMENTAL DESIGN

Some of the many designs that examine the effects of experimental treatments are presented in this section. In the sections on internal and external validity, some of the factors that make it difficult to determine whether the treatment produced the hypothesized results were discussed. As will become apparent, these threats are differentially controlled by the various designs. Given a particular setting, the researcher should employ the design that has the greatest degree of control over threats to validity. Certainly, it is possible to avoid choosing a useless design. In many cases, the main difficulty has been the failure to plan for evaluation before the program was implemented. In these instances, the utilization of a few procedures—for example, pretesting/posttesting and control groups—could dramatically improve the quality of information.

For convenience in presenting the experimental designs, T_1 will represent the pretest, T_2 the posttest, X the treatment or instructional program, and R the random selection of subjects. Cook and D. T. Campbell (1979) and Cook, D. T. Campbell, and Peracchio (1990) have organized a detailed examination of the variables that should be considered when choosing a research design. The designs in this text, organized into several different categories, provide examples of the numerous approaches available. The first category includes preexperimental designs that do not have control procedures and are more difficult to use in analyzing cause-and-effect relationships. Experimental designs, the second category, have varying degrees of power that permit some control of threats to validity. The third category includes quasi-experimental designs that are useful in many social science settings where investigators lack the opportunity to exert full control over the environment.

Preexperimental Designs

1. The one-group posttest-only design:

$$X \qquad T_2$$

In this method, the one-group posttest-only design, the subjects are exposed to the instructional treatment (without a pretest) and then are tested once at the completion of training. Without the pretest, ascertaining any change as a result of the training treatment from before to after training is not possible. Also, without the control group, it is difficult to infer that the cause of the change is the training treatment rather than an internal threat to validity, such as history. Thus, the limitations include the lack of hypothesis testing and problems in generalizability. However, valuable information can be obtained from this method. Very rich descriptions can stem from this type of design. For example, case-study approaches used in the social sciences often employ a posttest-only design that provides considerable information based on the collection of a large number of measures at the posttest time. This information can provide very important hunches and hypotheses, which can be used as input for another study. Replication with more controlled conditions, which are based on hypotheses stimulated by the case-study method and previous theory development, is a powerful methodology. However, interpretations of causality and generalizability in a single posttest-only design are precarious at best.

2. The one-group pretest/posttest design:

$T_1 \qquad X \qquad T_2$

When this design is employed, the participants are given a pretest, presented with the instructional program, and then given a posttest. This design is widely used in the examination of instructional settings because it provides a measure of comparison between the same group of subjects before and after treatment. Unfortunately, without a control group, it is difficult to establish whether the experimental treatment is the prime factor determining any differences that occur between the testing periods. Thus, the many threats to internal validity, including changes in history and maturation, testing effects, changes in instrumentation, and statistical regression, are not controlled. This design does, however, control biases due to subject mortality.

Research Example of Preexperimental Designs

Golembiewski and Carrigan (1970) carried out a training program that used a predesign and postdesign without a control group in one of a series of investigations designed to change the style of a sales unit in a business organization. They had a series of goals including the integration of a new management team, an increase in congruence between the behaviors required by the organization and those preferred by the men, and a greater congruence of individual needs and organizational demands. The training program consisted of a laboratory approach using sensitivity training to encourage the exploration of the participant's feelings and reactions to the organization. The program also included confrontation in which management of various levels were given an opportunity to discuss their ideas and feelings. The instrument used to measure preexperimental and postexperimental changes was Likert's profile of organizational characteristics, which includes items related to leadership, character of motivational forces, communication, interaction influence, decision making, goal setting, and control.

After statistical analyses, Golembiewski and Carrigan (1970) conclude that the learning design had the intended effect in terms of the measured attitudes. The authors indicate that they had included all managers in the treatment and so did not have a control group. Thus, their design did not permit them to be certain that the effects were a result of the training program rather than of random factors or the passage of time. This design uncertainty is expressed by Becker in an article entitled "The Parable of the

Pill," which expresses complex design issues with a simplicity that most writers, like myself, would love to achieve:

> There once was a land in which wisdom was revered. Thus, there was great excitement in the land when one of its inhabitants announced that he had invented a pill which made people wiser. His claim was based on an experiment he conducted. The report of the experiment explained (l) that the experimenter secured a volunteer; (2) the volunteer was first given an IQ test; (3) then he swallowed a pill which he was told would make him more intelligent; (4) finally he was given another IQ test. The score on the second IQ test was higher than on the first, so the report concluded that the pill increased wisdom. Alas, there were two skeptics in the land. One secured a volunteer; gave him an IQ test; waited an appropriate length of time; then gave him another IQ test. The volunteer's score on the second test exceeded that of the first. Skeptic One reported his experiment and concluded that taking the first test was an experience for the subject and that the time between the tests allowed the subject to assimilate and adjust to that experience so that when he encountered the situation again he responded more efficiently. Time alone, the skeptic argued, was sufficient to produce the increase in test score. The skeptic also pointed out that time alone could have produced the change in test score reported in the experiment on the Wisdom Pill.
>
> Skeptic Two conducted a different experiment. He held the opinion that most people were to some extent suggestible or gullible and that they readily would accept a suggestion that they possessed a desired attribute. He further believed that people who accept such a suggestion might even behave in a way such as to make it appear, for a time at least, that they indeed did possess the suggested ability. Therefore, the skeptic secured a volunteer; gave him an IQ test; had him ingest a pill composed of inert ingredients; told him the pill would increase his intelligence; then gave him another IQ test. Skeptic Two dutifully reported his subject achieved a higher score on the second test and, based on his hypothesis, explained how the disparity arose. He also pointed out that the increase in test score in the Wisdom Pill experiment could have been due to the taking of the pill and expectations associated with taking the pill rather than to the ingredients in the pill.
>
> The inventor of the wisdom pill drafted a reply to the two skeptics. He wrote that, although he did not employ a control group or a placebo group, he is confident that the pill's ingredients caused the observed change because that change is consistent with the theory from which he deduced the formula for his pill. (1970, p. 94)[1]

The point in the parable is that Skeptic One, Skeptic Two, or the inventor of the pill may be right. There is no way of being certain, given the present design, what was responsible for the effect. The next group of designs shows how easily many of the preexperimental designs can be improved. Design 1 can be strengthened by adding a pretest, and both design 1 and design 2 can be improved by adding a control group. Even where the environment makes a

[1]From "Parable of the Pill" by S. W. Becker. In *Administrative Sciences Quarterly*, 1970, *15*, pp. 94–96. Copyright 1970 by Administrative Sciences Quarterly. Reprinted by permission.

control group impractical, these designs can be improved by using the approaches described in the section on quasi-experimental designs.

Experimental Designs

3. Pretest/posttest control-group design:

Experimental group (*R*)	T_1	X	T
Control group (*R*)	T_1		T_2

In this design, the subjects are chosen at random from the population and assigned randomly to the experimental group or control group. Each group is given a pretest and posttest, but only the experimental group is exposed to the instructional treatment. If there is more than one instructional treatment, it is possible to add additional experimental groups. This design represents a considerable improvement over designs 1 and 2 because many of the threats to internal validity are controlled. The differential selection of subjects is controlled by the random selection. Variables like history, maturation, and pretesting should affect the experimental group and the control group equally. Statistical regression based on extreme scores (if subjects are chosen that way) is not eliminated but should be equal for the two groups because of the random-selection procedures. However, any effects not part of the instructional procedure that are due to differential treatment of subjects in the control and experimental groups must still be controlled by the experimenter. This includes the problems of intervention threats such as compensatory rivalry or resentful demoralization of control groups.

This design is affected by external threats to validity, which are not as easily specified as the threats to internal validity. The design does not control the effects of pretesting; thus, T_1 could have sensitized the participants to the experimental treatment in a way that makes generalizations to future participants difficult. Generalizations would also be hampered because subjects in the experiment might be different from those who will participate at later times and because the guinea pig effect could lead to differences between the experimental and control groups. This latter concern is dependent on the ingenuity of the experimenter in reducing the differences between groups by treating the control group in the same manner as the experimental group (except for the specific instructional treatment).

The difficulties associated with external validity should not freeze the researcher into inactivity. Although most threats to internal validity are reasonably well handled by experimental designs, generalizations, which are the core of external validity, are always precarious. As D. T. Campbell and Stanley (1963) originally pointed out, experimenters try to generalize by scientifically guessing at laws and by trying out generalizations in other specific cases. Slowly, and somewhat painfully, they gain knowledge about factors that affect generalizations. (For example, there is now ample evidence that pretesting does sensitize and affect participants.) As shown in the following design, a control for pretest sensitization is relatively easy to achieve by adding a group to design 3 that is exposed to the treatment without first being presented with the pretest.

4. Solomon four-group design:

Group		
1 (R)	T_1	XT_2
2 (R)	T_1	T_2
3 (R)		XT_2
4 (R)		T_2

The Solomon four-group design represents the first specific procedure designed to consider external validity factors. This design adds two groups that are not pretested. If the participants are randomly assigned to the four groups, this design makes it possible to compare the effects of pretesting. (Group 4 provides a control for pretesting without the instructional treatment.) It also permits the evaluator to determine the effects of some internal validity factors. For example, a comparison of the posttest performance for group 4, which was not exposed to pretesting or instructional treatments, to the pretest scores for groups 1 and 2 permits the analysis of the combined effects of maturation and history.

Research Example of Experimental Designs

A number of carefully carried out empirical research efforts have been reported, and a study by Latham and Saari (1979) sets an excellent standard for the conduct of training research. In their study, they randomly selected 40 supervisors from a total group of 100, and then randomly assigned 20 of them to a training condition and the other 20 to a control group. The control group was informed that they would be trained at a later date. They were trained at a later time, but in the interim they served as a control condition for the study. In Chapter 8 in "Behavioral Role Modeling," I will describe the procedures used in the training sessions in some detail. Basically, the program consisted of viewing a film modeling the behavior, which also presented the points to be learned, group discussion, practice in role playing, and feedback from the class.

At the end of each session, the trainees were sent back to their jobs with instructions to use the supervisory skills they had gained. The purpose here was to facilitate transfer of the learned skills back to the job. At the next session, the trainees reported their experiences, and for situations where they had experienced difficulties, they repracticed the desired behavior.

Besides carefully designing a training program, Latham and Saari (1979) also evaluated the results using reaction measures, learning measures, behavioral measures, and job-performance measures and found strong evidence supporting the training program. For example, they used job-performance indicators consisting of ratings made by supervisors of the trainees; the rating scales were based on a job analysis that produced critical incidents depicting effective and ineffective supervisory behavior. The investigators found no difference between pretest measures of the training and control group. Posttest measures indicated that the training group performed significantly better than the control group.

As a final step, Latham and Saari (1979) trained the control group. After their training was complete, all differences on all four measures between the control group, which was now trained, and the original training group disappeared. This kind of careful implementation and evaluation in a real-work environment should serve as a model for what can be accomplished with some thoughtful effort. For the interested reader, Frayne and Latham (1987) employed a similarly powerful design in examining self-management training programs as a tool in reducing absenteeism. That research will be also discussed further in Chapter 8, which emphasizes training techniques for managers and interpersonal skills.

Quasi-Experimental Designs

5. The time-series design:

$T_1 \quad T_2 \quad T_3 \quad T_4 \quad X \quad T_5 \quad T_6 \quad T_7 \quad T_8$

This design is similar to design 1, except that a series of measurements are taken before and after the instructional treatment. This particular approach illustrates the possibilities of using quasi-experimental designs in situations in which it is not possible to gain the full control required by experimental designs. An examination of internal validity threats shows that this design provides more control than design 1. If there are no appreciable changes from pretests 1 to 4, it is unlikely that any effects will occur due to maturation, testing, or regression. The major internal validity difficulty with this design is the history variable; that is, events that may happen between T_4 and T_5 (such as environmental changes and historical occurrences) are not controlled by this procedure.

The use of the time-series design does not control most of the external validity threats. Thus, it is necessary to be sensitive to any relationships between the treatment and particular subject groups (like volunteers) that might make results difficult to generalize to other groups; it is also necessary to be aware that subjects might be sensitized to particular aspects of the instructional program through the use of pretests.

6. The nonequivalent control-group design:

Experimental Group	T_1	X	T
Control Group	T_1		T_2

The nonequivalent control-group design is the same as design 3, except that the participants are not assigned to the groups at random. (The choice of the group to receive the instructional treatment is made randomly.) This design is often used in educational settings where there are naturally assembled groups such as classes. If there is no alternative, this design is well worth using and is certainly preferable to designs that do not include control groups (such as design 2). The more similar the two groups and their scores on the pretest, the more effective the control becomes in accounting for extraneous influences—for instance, internal validity factors like history, pretesting, maturation, and instrumentation. However, the investigator must be especially careful because this design is vulnerable to interactions between selection factors and maturation, history, and testing.

Because the participants were not chosen randomly, there is always the possibility that critical differences exist that were not revealed by the pretests. For example, some studies use volunteers who might react differently to the treatment because of motivational factors. Thus, the investigator must be sensitive to potential sources of differences between the groups. The dangers of instrumentation changes and of differential treatment of each group (unrelated to the treatment) remain a concern for this design as well as for design 3. Although the external validity issues are similar to those for design 3, the nonequivalent control-group design does have some advantages in the control of the reactive effects of experimental settings. The utilization of intact groups makes it easier to design the experiment as part of the normal routine, thus reducing some of the problems associated with the guinea pig effect. Because this design is not as disruptive, it is also possible in some settings (for example, educational systems), to have a larger subject population, thus increasing generalizability.

Research Example of Quasi-Experimental Designs

An ingenious example of the use of quasi-experimental design is offered by the research of Komaki, Heinzmann, and Lawson (1980). This study was described briefly in Chapter 4 in the section on feedback of results. Because it is a good illustration of quasi-experimental designs, it will be described here in more detail. These investigators were studying safety problems in the vehicle-maintenance division of a city's department of public works. The department being studied had one of the highest accident rates in the city. Komaki and her colleagues performed a needs assessment including an analysis of the factors that led to unsafe practices and hindered safe acts. They examined safety logs for the previous five years to determine what type of accidents occurred and then wrote safety behavioral items that would have prevented that accident. Throughout this procedure, they interacted with supervisors and workers on the specification and development of safety procedures. Some examples of safety items generated for the vehicle maintenance department are:

1. *Proper use of equipment and tools.* When reaching upward for an item more than 30 cm (1 ft.) away from extended arms, use steps, stepladder, or solid part of vehicle. Do not stand on jacks or jack stands.
2. *Use of safety equipment.* When using brake machine, wear full face shield or goggles. When arcing brake shoes, respirator should also be worn.

3. *Housekeeping*. Any oil/grease spill larger than 8 × 8 cm (3 × 3 in.) in an interior walking area (defined as any area at least 30 cm [1 ft.] from a wall or a solid standing object) or an exterior walking area (designated by outer white lines parallel to the wall and at least 30 cm [1 ft.] from the wall) should be soaked up with rice hull or grease compound.

4. *General safety procedures*. When any type of jack other than an air jack is in use (i.e., vehicle is supported by jack or off the ground), at least one jack stand should also be used. (pp. 262–263)

Komaki and her colleagues (1980) designed a training program that used slides to depict the unsafe practices employed in the department, examined the trainees on their knowledge of appropriate safe behaviors, discussed correct safety behaviors, and then showed the same slides but this time demonstrated safe practices. Also, employees were given copies of the appropriate safety rules to take with them. This procedure was designated the Training Program. Another procedure used later in the program was called Training and Feedback. In this procedure, besides the training given earlier, employees were informed about realistic safety goals that were set on the basis of their previous performance. Then, randomly timed, daily safety observations were made, and the results were posted on a graph so that employees could see how they were progressing toward their goals. The design of this study was a time series with at least four or five observations for each of the first three phases of the study and an average of three observations per phase for the last two phases.

The phases are depicted in Figure 6.1. The first phase, referred to as baseline, consisted of the collection of data before any training or feedback. It essentially consisted of multiple pretests. The second phase was the training program, and the third phase added feedback to the already-trained employees. The fourth phase went back to training only with no feedback being given, and the final phase reinstituted feedback to the already-trained employees. Note that all trainees proceed through the entire sequence of five phases and that there are multiple data-collection points in each phase. The data collected consisted of the number of incidents performed safely. Data were collected by trained observers, and there was high-level agreement between the observers. In the data shown in the graph for two departments (preventive maintenance and light-equipment repair), performance improved from baseline to after training and then improved more when feedback was added. When feedback was taken away, performance went down, but performance improved again when feedback was put back in the last phase of the study. Komaki's point is that, besides training, feedback on employee performance is a critical component of the program. In two other departments, Komaki obtained similar data for the first four phases, but improvement did not occur again as a result of the fifth phase. The investigators in this study considered the various threats to validity and how their quasi-experimental design accounted for these factors. They noted,

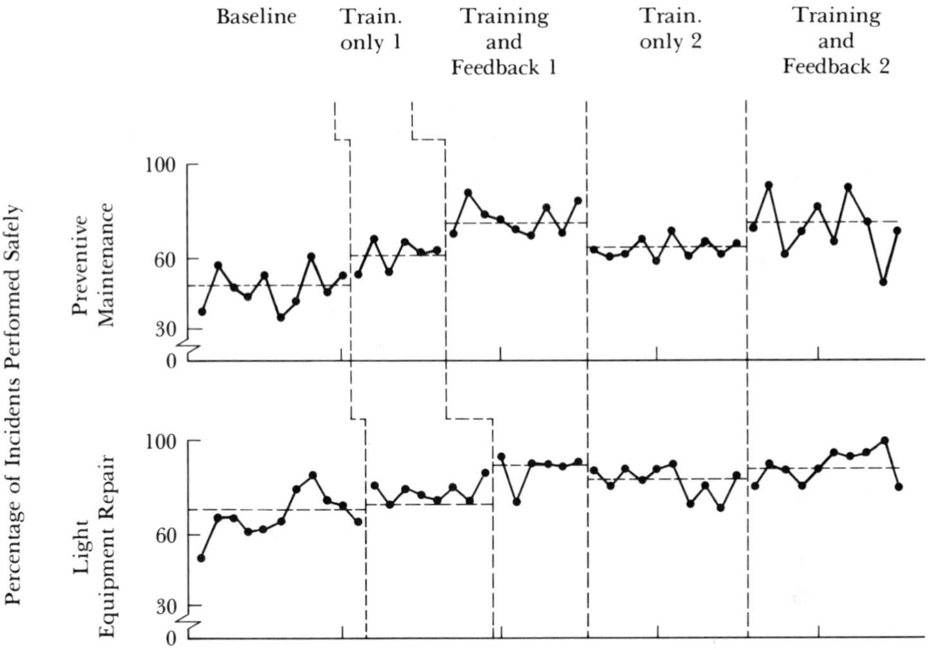

Figure 6.1 Percentage of incidents performed safely by employees in vehicle-maintenance departments under five experimental conditions. From "Effect of Training and Feedback: Component Analysis of a Behavioral Safety Program," by J. Komaki, A. T. Heinzmann, and L. Lawson. In *Journal of Applied Psychology,* 1980, *65,* pp. 261–270. Copyright 1980 by the American Psychology Association. Reprinted by permission.

Plausible alternative hypotheses (history, maturation, statistical regression) were ruled out because the two phases were introduced to the sections at different points in time and improvements occurred after, and not prior to, the introduction of these phases. History was ruled out as a source of internal invalidity because it is not likely that an extraneous event would have the same impact in separate sections at different times. If maturations were responsible, performance would be expected to improve as a function of the passage of time; however, improvements occurred, with few exceptions, after the introduction of Phase 3. The effects of statistical regression were ruled out because regression effects would be seen in any series of repeated measurements and not just after the introduction of the two phases.

Reactivity of measurement was also not likely to be a plausible explanation for the improvements obtained because the observers were present during all phases. Therefore, improvements in performance during any one phase could not be due to the reactivity of the measure per se. Questions concerning reactivity and external validity, however, were not so straightforward. Although the issue of the generality of improvements was not addressed directly in the present study, support was provided by accident records, which showed that injuries were reduced by a factor of seven from the preceding year. Since the observers were present during a relatively small percentage of working hours, it is unlikely that improvements were confined to these times. (Komaki, Heinzmann, & Lawson, 1980, p. 267)

Komaki's wonderfully detailed explanation of the threats to validity and how they can be controlled by quasi-experimental designs serves as a wonderful teaching tool and reminds us that these type of designs can be extremely effective in field settings.

UTILITY CONSIDERATIONS

As mentioned in Chapter 5, an important consideration in the evaluation of training programs is the concept of utility. As noted by Schneider and Schmitt (1986) in their discussion of utility and selection procedures, psychologists act as if a significant validity coefficient relating a test and criterion measure was proof of the test's usefulness. However, meaningful terms for management usually involve monetary considerations. They note that when a production manager requests a new piece of machinery, it is usually supported by projected increases in productivity and resultant decreases in unit cost of production. Maintenance managers support hiring requests with figures showing decreases in downtime due to equipment problems and the resulting savings. As Schneider and Schmitt note, this means translating our validity coefficients into dollar values even if the translations are crude. These kinds of translations are called *utility analysis.* The analysis not only enables researchers to have information about the costs of their programs but also permits comparisons between the costs of different programs—for example, a formal training program versus on-the-job training or a training program versus a selection program.

Again, this is an area where there have been important developments. Cascio (1989) has developed methodology for the application of utility analysis to the assessment of training outcomes. His considerations involve several steps. First, Cascio introduces the use of capital budget methodology to analyze the minimum annual benefits in dollars required from any program. This phase of the analysis requires specifying the cost of the program, the increased benefits expected for any given period, the duration of the benefits, and a determination of the discount rate to specify the firm's minimum expected return on investment. The acceptance ratio that Cascio specifies for a training program based on these figures is that the net present value of the program must be greater than zero. Second, Cascio details the use of a break-even analysis originally introduced by Boudreau (1984) to estimate the minimum effect size for a program to produce the required benefits. Basically, this operates on the premise that if the training program has any effect, the mean of the job performance of the trained group should exceed the untrained group. The degree to which there is a difference between the trained and untrained group, expressed in standard deviation units, represents the effect size. Once the effect size is corrected for unreliability of the criterion, it is an estimate of the true differences between the trained and untrained group.

As a third step, Cascio (1989) uses data across multiple studies to estimate the expected actual payoff from the program. Further, Cascio also provides information on the effects of the outcome when other factors are considered, such as an enhancement or decay of the size of the training effect. As a result of Cascio's work, it is now possible to express the gains resulting from effective training in terms of a number of outcomes such as dollar, percentage increases in output, or reductions in the size of the work force required to accomplish the same work. It is likely that Cascio's work will have ramifications for many years to come as managers attempt to assess the utility of their interventions.

An important point raised by Cascio (1989) is that these analyses depend on a careful tracing out of the costs of training. An examination of such costs and issues in the examination of structured training versus unstructured training for a production worker is presented in Cullen, Sawzin, Sisson, and Swanson's (1978) work, illustrated in Figure 6.2. Training costs would include training development, training materials, training time, and production losses. The analysis requires that measures be developed for each of the categories (training costs, training returns, and analysis). This involves all criterion issues (relevancy, reliability, and so on) discussed in Chapter 5. The final stage of assessing the cost effectiveness (as shown in the figure) is evaluation. Here, the structured and unstructured training methods are compared on all variables in the diagram. Each variable must be translated into monetary terms. Thus, each factor in the analysis would be specified and translated. For example, raw-material usage would be specified as the "weight of the raw material supplied to the machine versus weight of scrap and amount of quality product produced" (Cullen et al., 1977, p. 27). The translation of these measures into monetary figures includes the conversion of variables such as worker attitudes. As Cascio (1989) notes, this is difficult to accomplish, but the failure to analyze our programs in dollars ensures that training will continue to be viewed as a cost rather than as a benefit to the organization. It is clear that utility analyses will become an increasingly important part of evaluation analyses. Mathieu and Leonard (1987) applied utility analysis to examine a behavioral role-modeling training program to teach supervisory skills for bank head tellers, branch managers, and operations managers. Their analyses indicate that the training program was effective and the future utility to the organization for training a group of fifteen supervisors in each of the three job classes was over $13,000 for the first year and over $100,000 by year 3. The increase over a period of years results from the increased effectiveness of supervisors already trained who remain in the organization plus training other new supervisors. In addition, these researchers provide utility estimates showing that there is more to be gained financially from emphasizing training for branch managers as compared to operations

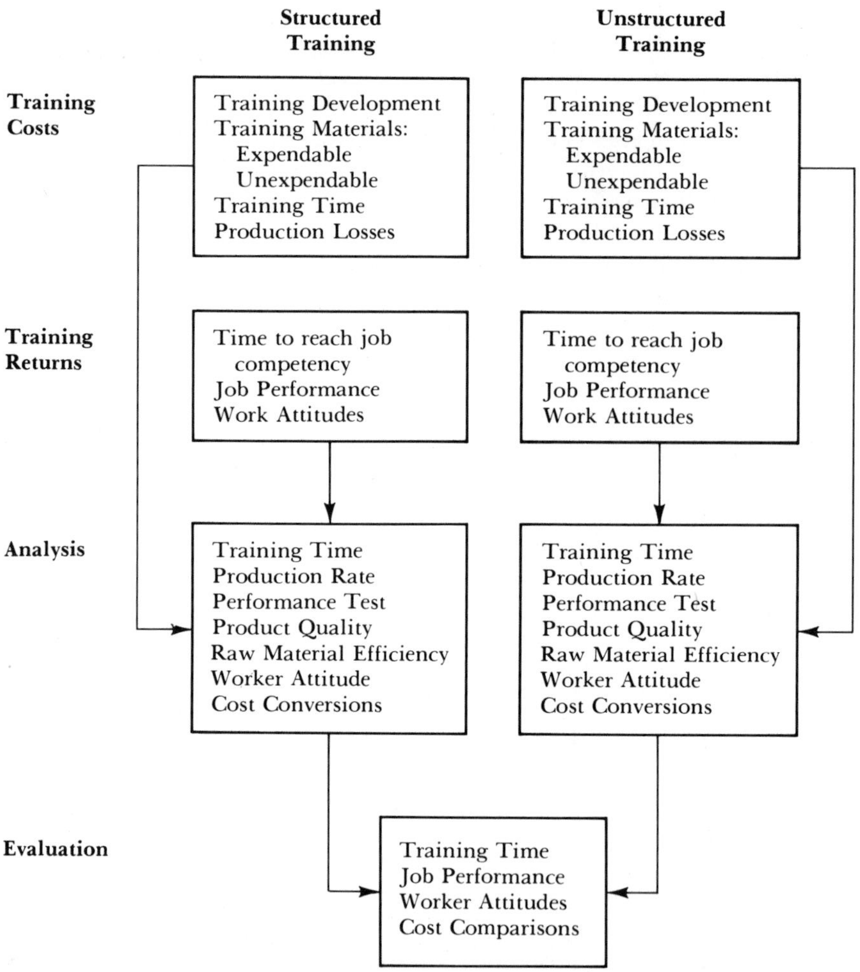

Figure 6.2 Industrial training cost-effectiveness model. From "Cost Effectiveness: A Model for Assessing the Training Investment," by J. G. Cullen, S. A. Sawzin, G. R. Sisson, and R. A. Swanson. In *Training and Development Journal,* 1978, *32,* pp. 24–29. Copyright 1978 by the American Society for Training and Development, Inc. Reprinted by permission.

managers or as compared to head tellers. Thus, the organization can receive information from utility analysis that not only permits decisions on the effectiveness of the program but also permits important comparisons related to a large number of factors, such as the effects of training people in different jobs, the effects of different rates of turnover of trained individuals, or even estimates of what would occur if the training program decreased in efficiency over several years.

OTHER METHODS OF EVALUATION

The experimental models of evaluation that center on pretests and posttests, control groups, threats to validity, and so on represent the traditional models used to assess the effects of training programs. However, there are a large number of other evaluation models. For example, there is the adversarial model, which stems from a criticism of the classical experimental model (Levine, 1974). This point of view maintains that the traditional point of view is not well suited to decision making and does not focus well on questions of the value or worth of the program being evaluated. The adversarial model is developed around a system similar to a court of law. The model takes the point of view that all researchers are biased and the best way to counteract this problem and determine the value of the program is to have two sets of researchers. Each group gathers its own data to support its viewpoint and advocates a point of view to a judge or jury, who then renders a decision about the value of the program. Many of the rules of data gathering, analysis, and so on are similar to the experimental model. However, the final decision is based on a judge's or jury's determination of worth based on the evidence presented by the advocates.

There are many other evaluation models, but unfortunately it is not possible to discuss them all in this book. However, a few other models are particularly relevant to the evaluation of training programs. They are individual-differences models and content-validity models.

Individual-Differences Models

Many industrial psychologists have emphasized the use of training scores as a way to predict the future success of potential employees. The use of trainability scores (discussed in Chapter 4 in the section on trainee readiness) is an example of the use of a pretraining measure to predict training performance. It is also possible to use performance in training to predict either later training performance or actual job performance. Figure 6.3 presents a hypothetical set of scores on a sales-training test and a criteria consisting of sales volume at the end of one year on the job. One way of characterizing the relationships between these two variables is by the statistical determination of the correlational coefficient. The value of the correlational coefficient ranges from +1.00 for a perfect positive relationship to − 1.00 for a perfect negative correlation. A .00 correlation indicates that there is no evidence that the two variables are associated. In this example, people with higher scores on the training test also tended to perform better on the job in terms of sales volume. Thus, the better performers in training were better performers on the job, and the poorer performers in training were poorer performers on the job.

A number of these types of studies show meaningful relationships between training performance and on-the-job performance. For example,

Figure 6.3 Hypothetical scores on a sales test at the end of training and sales volume after one year on the job.

Kraut (1975) found that peer ratings obtained from managers attending a month-long training course predicted several criteria including future promotion and performance-appraisal ratings of job performance. Bartlett and Goldstein (1974) found that a road test, which was part of a bus driver–training program, predicted accidents on the job for those same trainees. Other investigators have used early training performance to predict performance in more advanced training. An example of this approach is offered by Gordon and Cohen (1973), whose study involved a welding program that was part of a larger manpower development project aimed at training unemployed and underemployed individuals from the eastern Tennessee area. The program consisted of fourteen different tasks that fell into four categories and ranged in difficulty from simple to complex. Advancement from one task to the next was dependent on successful completion of all previous tasks. Thus, trainees progressed at a rate commensurate with their ability to master the material to be learned. For each trainee, data were collected on the amount of time spent on each task. The correlations between the completion times for the four categories of tasks and total time to complete the plate-welding course are given in Table 6.2.

Gordon and Cohen indicate that the results show

> that early performance in the lab generally is an excellent predictor of final performance. Furthermore, the greater the number of tasks included in our predictor, the better our prediction will become. It is possible, therefore, to identify those trainees who will take longer than average to complete the plate welding course by simply examining their performance on the first few tasks. (1973, p. 268)

Table 6.2 Correlations between the time to completion for various segments of the course and total time required to complete the plate-welding course

	Correlation of Task			
	1 with Finish	*1 and 2 with Finish*	*1–3 with Finish*	*1–4 with Finish*
1 (N = 21)	0.55	0.76	0.81	0.84
II (N = 19)	0.70	0.83	0.94	0.96
III (N = 18)[1]	0.09	0.18	0.77	0.78
Total (N = 58)	0.69	0.79	0.87	0.87

Note: Groups I, II, and III differed in their starting dates.
[1]A word of explanation is due regarding the poor predictability of tasks 1 and 2 in Group III. Discussion with the training supervisor of the welding program indicated that illness had caused two of his three instructors to be absent for most of the period during which Group III was learning tasks 1 and 2. Consequently, the amount of supervision and guidance provided was necessarily below normal. It is probable that this temporary understaffed situation changed the usual conditions of learning, and caused the correlations observed in Group III to be unlike those recorded for Groups I and II.

These investigators understood that they were predicting the performance of individuals on a later task—for example, on the job or later in training—based on performance in the training program. As a matter of fact, once these relationships have been established in an appropriately designed study, it is possible to select individuals for a job or for later training based on these training scores. In other words, the training score serves as a validated predictor of future performance.

However, caution should be used when this technique is considered as an evaluation of the training program. The relationship between training performance and on-the-job performance simply means that individuals who perform best on the training test also perform well on the job. This does not necessarily mean that the training program is properly designed or that individuals learned enough in training to perform well on the job. It is entirely possible that the training program did not teach anything or that the trainees did not learn anything. In those cases, there would still be individual differences on the training test. Even if the training program did not teach the relevant material for the job, there would still be a strong relationship if the people who performed well on the test also performed well on the job and the people who performed poorly on the test performed poorly on the job. That is, the training program might not have achieved anything except to maintain the individual differences between trainees that might have existed before they entered training.

At least several suggestions could be helpful in this instance. First, the use of appropriate pretests and control groups will establish whether learning has occurred and whether it is likely to be a result of the training program. In other words, even when the purpose is to use the training scores as a predictive device, it is useful to use experimental-methodology evaluation to ensure that the training program has actually accomplished its learning objectives.

Another procedure that lends some credence to individual-difference methodology is to demonstrate that the training program and the criteria used to evaluate training are based on a thorough needs assessment so that the training program really does reflect the required knowledge, skills, and abilities (KSAs). This latter procedure introduces another evaluation methodology—content validity.

Content-Validity Models

If the needs assessment is appropriately carried out and the training program is designed to reflect KSAs, then the program will be judged as having content validity. That is, the training program should reflect the domain of KSAs represented on the job that the analyst has determined should be learned in the training program. An interesting question is whether it is possible after the design of the training program to determine if indeed it has content validity. Another question is whether it is possible to determine if a training program designed several years ago is content-valid in the sense that it reflects the content established by a recently completed needs assessment.

One way of conceptualizing the content validity of a training program is presented in Figure 6.4. In this figure, the horizontal axis across the top of the figure represents the dimension of importance, or criticality, of the KSAs as determined by the needs assessment. Although the diagram only presents KSAs as being important or not important, it is vital to realize that this is an oversimplification of a dimension with many points. The vertical dimension represents the degree of emphasis for the KSAs in training. Again, to simplify the presentation, the dimension indicates that the KSA is or is not emphasized in the training program.

This results in the fourfold table presented in Figure 6.4. Using this approach, both boxes A and D provide support for the content validity of the training program. KSAs that fall into box D are judged as being important for the job and are emphasized in training. Items in box A are judged as not important for the job and are not emphasized in training. Conceptually, to the degree to which KSAs fall into categories A and D, it is possible to think about the training program as being content-valid. Of course, this is an oversimplification. There will be KSAs that are judged as moderately important for the job or KSAs that are moderately emphasized in training. However, it is possible to conceive of this type of relationship and to actually measure the degree to which those KSAs judged as important are emphasized (and hopefully learned) in training. Very few people would be unhappy with a training program that tends to emphasize the objectives associated with KSAs that are judged critical or important for job performance.

Box B represents a potential error and could affect the degree to which a program is judged content-valid. KSAs falling into the B category are judged as important for the job but are not emphasized in training. From a systems perspective, these items must be analyzed to determine whether the organization intends for these KSAs to be gained as a result of training. If that is the

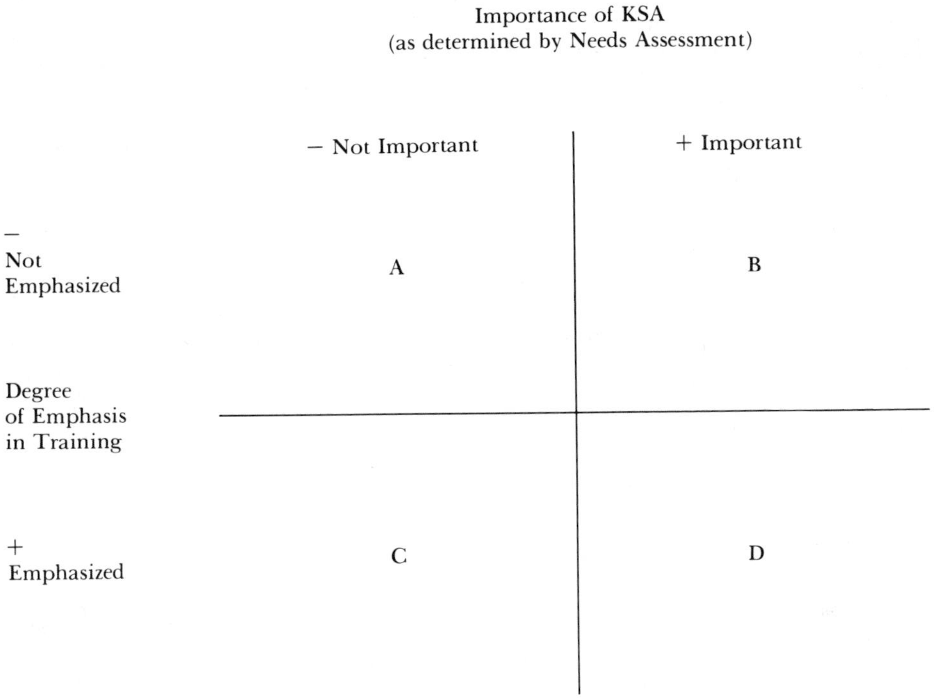

Figure 6.4 A conceptual diagram of content validity of training programs.

case, then there is a problem. However, it is also possible that individuals are expected to be selected with that particular KSA or that individuals are expected to learn the material related to that KSA on the job. To that extent, the training program should not be expected to emphasize the item, and its content validity would not be questioned. However, it would still be important to determine that KSAs judged as important or critical are covered in another system, such as the selection of employees. If the item is not represented, then the organization must decide whether revision of the training program is necessary or if some other system must be designed to cover that material.

Box C represents KSAs that are emphasized in training but are judged as not being important for the job. This is often a criticism of training programs. That is, they tend to spend time emphasizing material that is not job-related. Most analysts agree that the use of needs assessment procedures and examination of training content results in a decrease in the amount of training time necessary to complete the training program. This usually occurs because of a reduction in the program based on an elimination of the types of items present in box C. Interestingly, a systems view of this process might even suggest a reduction of items that would appear in box D. Selection experts like Bartlett (1982) might suggest that sometimes KSAs included in box D are unnecessary because they have already been used as a basis for selection.

Thus, if such materials are included in the training program, trainees are again subjected to materials on KSAs that are already in their repertoire. As noted earlier, there are very few analyses in the research literature based on these types of content-validity strategies.

Ford and Wroten (1984) explored some of these strategies in an examination of police officer training programs. On the basis of needs assessment procedures, these investigators identified 383 KSAOs (the *O* stands for other personal characteristics—for example, attitudes—determined in the needs assessment in addition to KSAs used to define the content-training domain). They then had 114 experts independently rate the importance of each item for job performance. Basically, these investigators chose items that would be identified as emphasized and determined whether the item fell into category C (not important for job performance) or category D (important for job performance). They discovered that 237, or 62 percent, of the KSAOs met the criteria they specified as being important for job performance. In another analysis, these investigators also found 57 items that were rated as important for job performance but that were not included in the training program. A few of those items were judged to be KSAs that were trainable and important, and they were thus added to the program.

As part of a research program involving our attempts to develop content-validity models to understand training, Newman (1985) conducted research examining the implications of the diagram in Figure 6.4. His study was conducted on the job of cook supervisor for the Federal Bureau of Prisons. First, a needs assessment was conducted to determine the KSAs needed for the job. In addition, because the training program was already in existence, another, separate needs assessment was conducted to determine the KSAs taught in the training program. The training program was a two-week course covering the basics of institutional cooking and baking for cook supervisors who oversee inmates in the preparation of meals in the federal prisons. Trainees came from forty-five institutions across the country. A KSA analysis was done for the training program, as well as the job, to include the possibility that KSAs not important on the job (box C in Figure 6.4) might be emphasized in training. Both sets of KSAs were combined in an inventory. Newman then had eighty-seven job subject-matter experts (SMEs) rate the KSAs in terms of importance on the job, difficulty of learning, and where best acquired. The same KSAs were also rated by two training SMEs (the training director and the course instructor) on importance on the job, difficulty to learn, and time spent in the program teaching the KSAs. As an indicator of content validity, Newman correlated the KSA job-importance ratings and the training-emphasis ratings (as reflected by time spent). For the cooking and baking KSAs, the correlation was .52. For another set of KSAs related to supervision and administration, the correlation was .55. These data provide some evidence that KSAs judged higher in job importance were KSAs most emphasized in training. Interestingly, the trainer SMEs and the job SMEs also agreed on what was important with a correlation of .59 for cooking and baking KSAs and .76 for supervision and administration KSAs. As a result of this study, it was also possible to do an analysis of where KSAs should be learned and which KSAs fell into the four boxes diagramed in Figure 6.4.

Newman (1985) also collected other quantitative and qualitative data about the program. For example, he found improvement from pretraining to posttraining based on test scores and found that trainees as compared to a control group received higher performance ratings on training-relevant dimensions. A final word of caution should be added to any conclusion about the use of content validity of training programs. Obviously, content validity is very important, and all training programs should be content-valid. It makes no sense to have training programs that do not cover the KSAs necessary for the job. The whole purpose of performing a needs assessment and then tracing out the training program objectives based on the needs assessment is to have a content-valid program. If the reader reexamines Chapter 5 (see Figures 5.1 and 5.2), the concept of criterion relevance is based on exactly the same idea. Also, if both the criterion and the training program are based on the needs assessment, then the criterion should form a good basis for the evaluation of the training program. However, the point is that the reason for concern about the development of criteria is the importance of having a measure of trainee performance both in the training program and on the job. That is why using only the concept of content validity in the evaluation of a training program is a problem. The program may very well be content-valid, but that does not provide information about whether trainees learned the material in the training program and whether trainees were able to transfer that knowledge to the job.

Some of the additional data that Newman (1985) collected about pre-differences and postdifferences allow stronger inferences about training program effects than content-validity information by itself could permit. Information concerning that issue requires the use of principles of experimental design and quasi-experimental design to ensure that learning occurs and that it transfers to the job. For these types of reasons, some researchers (for example, Guion, 1977) argue that the term *content validity* should not be used. Rather, they prefer a term that reflects the fact that the important domains are present in the instrument or program but that assumptions about validity are weak. That view makes sense, and it should be clear from the preceding discussion that various things can be done to strengthen or weaken the inferences that can be made. However, for want of a better term, I have chosen to continue to use *content validity*. People who prefer a different term might consider *content relevance*. In any case, the important point is not the terminology but an understanding of the strength of the inference that can be made based on the procedures used.

The same point might be made about the use of individual-difference methodology. As described previously, a correlation between scores in training and on the job does not guarantee that the program is doing the job. It does mean that individuals who perform well on the test in training also perform well in job performance and those individuals who perform poorly on the training test perform poorly on the job. These same relationships may exist regardless of whether the training program accomplished anything. If the training program was also shown to be content-valid, then there is reason to be more optimistic. It is also possible to consider training evaluation as a succession of steps that provides information of better and better quality. Thus, as a next step, adding a pretest and posttest on relevant criteria is possible. More certainty is then possible because there will be information on changes in trainee performance from before to after training. If, in addition, it is possible to add a control group, there will be more information about ruling out other reasons for the changes from pretest to posttest.

In summary, establishing the validity of training programs involves building a network that gives more and more information with better and better controls so that the evaluator has more faith in the information. In some cases, it may be possible only to start with an individual-difference methodology. On that basis, the investigator will know whether people who perform well on training test measures also perform well on the job. Then, it might be possible to obtain a pretest, then content validity, and so on. As I have stated previously,

> In order to gain an appreciation for the degree to which training programs achieve their objectives, it is necessary to consider the creative development of evaluation models. The models should permit the extraction of the greatest amount of information within the constraints of the environment. . . . Researchers cannot afford to be frozen into inactivity by the spectre of threats to validity. (Goldstein, 1980, p. 262)

Statistical Considerations in the Choice of Designs

Some of these measurement considerations are beyond the scope of this chapter, and thus I have placed this material at the end of the sections on evaluations for students who have the background expertise. Earlier in this chapter, I indicated that statistical considerations and the choice of design interact. This has been made even more obvious by a very important article by Arvey and Cole (1989). One factor these authors explore is the likelihood of detecting a difference when it is really there (otherwise known as *statistical power*). They note that when they compared different designs, they were not all comparable in detecting differences that really existed. The designs compared were a posttest-only design that ignored pretest information completely, a gain-score design that analyzed the differences between pretest and posttest, and an analysis of covariance (ANCOVA) design that statistically treated the pretest as a covariate in a between-group design. In general, they found that the ANCOVA was more powerful. However, the extent of these power differences between designs was dramatically affected by a host of other factors including the sample sizes and the degree of correlation between the pretests and posttests. For example, in the gain-score and ANCOVA design, power always increased as the correlation between pretest and posttest increased.

Alternatively, when the correlation was very small, the advantage of

ANCOVA over the gain-score approach was substantial, and any advantages for the posttest-only design became nonexistent. Also, the effect of greater score reliability increases the power of all three designs but the benefits are more substantial in the gain-score and ANCOVA design than in the posttest-only design. Most important, in all the work described in this article, the assumption is made that the pretest scores are equivalent. The effect of nonequivalent groups at the pretest phase is crushing on the power of all of these designs. It is clear that evaluators should pay careful attention to these types of considerations before choosing experimental designs and procedures.

FROM NEEDS ASSESSMENT TO TRAINING VALIDITY: SOME CONCLUDING WORDS

This chapter began with a number of complaints concerning training made by trainees, trainers, and organizations. Answers to these complaints require the analyst to examine various components of the training systems approach, including needs assessment, criterion development, and evaluation models. One way of conceptualizing responses to these complaints is to ask, What is the actual purpose of the instructional system? Is there interest in having a program where trainees perform better at the end of the training program? Or is there interest in trainees who perform better at both the end of the training program and on the job? Goals might include all these considerations, but an additional goal might be knowledge about how another group of trainees (after the program has been developed and evaluated) are going to perform. Then again, someone might be interested in how the program might work in another organization with other trainees. The answers to these questions require the analyst to consider what systems-training issues must be addressed. It is possible to characterize instructional design as an attempt to achieve one of the following types of validity (Goldstein, 1978a):

1. *Training validity*. This particular stage refers only to the validity of the training program. Validity is determined by the performance of trainees on criteria established for the training program.

2. *Transfer validity*. This stage of analysis refers to the validity of the training program as measured by performance in the transfer or on-the-job setting. Ordinarily, training and transfer validity are both considered indicators of internal validity. That is, they indicate whether the treatment made a difference in a very specific situation. Here, performance validity is considered an external validity concept because training programs are typically developed in a particular environment that is different from the organizational settings in which the trainee will eventually be expected to perform.

3. *Intraorganizational validity*. This concept refers to the performance of a new group of trainees within the organization that developed the original training program. In this instance, the analyst is attempting to predict the

performance of new trainees based on the evaluated performance of a previous group.

4. *Interorganizational validity.* In this instance, the analyst is attempting to determine whether a training program validated in one organization can be used in another organization.

The first two stages, training validity and transfer validity, have been the topics of the first five chapters of this book. Thus, *training validity* begins with the needs assessment process and continues with criterion development, evaluation, and the feedback necessary to revise the program. *Transfer validity* requires attention to all aspects of training validity but must include the idea that the trainee must perform on the job. Considering the needs assessment procedures and evaluation procedures necessary to establish training validity, it would seem that there is little to add to a section on transfer validity. Unfortunately, this is not the case. In a sense, this is now a discussion of external validity operations, which involve the transfer of performance in one environment (training) to another environment (on the job). As noted in Chapter 5, the tracing-out process from needs assessment to criterion development must now be concerned with relevant on-the-job criteria while avoiding deficiency and contamination. Also, transfer validity is affected by the fact that the trainee will enter a new environment and will be affected by all the interacting components that make up organizations today. Certainly, some aspects of the environment contribute to the success or failure of training programs beyond the attributes the trainee must gain as a result of attending the instructional program. For example, as described in Chapter 3 in "Organizational Analysis," the training program and the organization often specify different performance objectives, and trainees are caught in a conflict which sometimes results in failure. Thus, the trainee and the training program are declared inadequate because the training analyst never considered the relevant variables that determine success or failure at each of the four stages of validity. I have become convinced that many training programs are judged failures because of organizational systems' constraints. Transfer validity thus requires the use of organizational analysis as a critical component of program development. Most of these concepts have been discussed in the preceding chapters in this book. However, the concepts of intraorganizational and interorganizational validity prompt several new considerations. These are discussed next.

Intraorganizational Validity

Intraorganizational validity presupposes that the trainer has established training and performance validity and is concerned now with the performance of a new group of trainees. Just as performance validity presupposes the consideration of the points established for training validity, intraorganizational validity presupposes that the points discussed for training and transfer validity have been established. It should be noted that the previously expressed view concerning evaluation stated that evaluation is considered an information-gathering process that provides feedback about the multiple objectives of most training programs. Thus, it becomes apparent that evaluation should be a continual process that provides data as a basis for revisions of the program. New data should be collected based on the performance of a new group of trainees. The new data provide further understanding about the achievement of objectives or about the variables that affect the achievement of objectives. That does not mean that each effort must start from the very beginning. However, collecting further new information about the effects of revisions should be possible. Also, it should be possible to collect data that can be checked against previously collected information to ensure that the instructional program is having the same effect.

Given the above philosophy, it is still possible to ask how dangerous it is to generalize results from the previous training program to a new group of trainees in the same organization. The answer to that question stems from a consideration of many of the factors already discussed. First, it is necessary to consider the components of the needs assessment process, including task, person, and organizational aspects. If the job tasks and resulting KSAs have been revised or if their frequency, importance, or degree of difficulty have changed, then the training program requires revisions. In these cases, generalizations based on the old program are speculative at best. These kinds of task changes can occur for a variety of reasons, including technological developments or revisions in jobs being performed at various levels in the organization. Similarly, if the kinds of people entering the organization are different, then it is difficult to generalize from the old program. These kinds of changes also occur for a variety of reasons, including moving the organization from an urban to suburban environment or market and career shifts that result in differences in the KSAs of individuals desiring particular types of employment. Also, of course, modifications in the organization or constraints that affect the organization affect the degree to which generalizations are safe. Although time itself is not ordinarily considered a variable, these types of changes eventually occur in all organizations, rendering long-term generalizations of training results to new populations increasingly suspect. A good procedure might be to recheck the needs assessment for applicability before attempting to generalize to new trainee populations. If needs assessment procedures are not carried out, the original program is questionable, and generalizations are treacherous.

A second factor to consider before generalizing is how well the evaluation was performed in the first place. If the data on which the generalizations will be based are only the reactions of the trainees to the instructional program, then the original evaluation and any future generalizations are suspect. In the same sense, properly evaluated instructional programs will provide a variety of information about the achievement of multiple goals. It is necessary to consider what has been achieved and what remains questionable before deciding whether to generalize to new trainees.

A third consideration is whether the training program will be the same.

This factor is misleadingly simplistic. Almost everyone would agree that it is dangerous to generalize to new trainee populations when they are not being instructed in the same training program. However, most training analysts fail to realize how different established training programs tend to be from the original training program from which evaluation data were collected. Some of these difficulties generally can be labeled problems of reactivity. Observations, experimental equipment, and questions being asked often result in changes in behavior that are not a result of the actual training program. To the extent that these variables are a source of training results and to the extent that these variables are not present the next time training is offered, it is difficult to generalize. There is a certain aura of excitement surrounding new instructional treatments or training programs that simply disappears over time.

In some studies, researchers have specified how the expectations of the experimenters (or trainers or teachers) themselves have an effect on the performances of individuals (Rosenthal, 1978). To the extent that these factors change over time, the training program has changed, and it is difficult to generalize. Also, programs tend to change over time as trainers and managers add to and delete from the originally designed program. Sometimes changes in carefully designed programs radically alter the training system. One of the most compelling reasons for the use of process criteria is to attempt to specify these variables and their effects. When the process criteria indicate that the training programs have not changed, then it is obviously safer to generalize. From a consideration of the needs assessment component, the quality of the evaluation, and the similarity of the training program, the decision of whether to generalize becomes easier. It should also be clear that the more the confidence in training and transfer validity, the easier it is to generalize. Even so, my personal choice will always be to collect some evaluative information to ensure that the program continues to work.

Interorganizational Validity

In *interorganizational validity*, the analyst attempts to determine whether a training program validated in one organization can be used in another organization. All factors discussed in training validity, performance validity, and intraorganizational validity affect this decision. As indicated in the previous section, when the needs assessment shows differences (that is, the task, person, or organizational components), or the evaluation is questionable, or the training program will differ, then generalization is dangerous. In this instance, the needs assessment and evaluation have not been performed for the organization that desires to use the training program. Clearly, the more similar the organizations, as shown by a needs assessment, the more likely similar results will occur. Still, considering the incredible number of ways organizations differ, attempting to generalize the training results in one organization to trainees in another organization is dangerous. On the other hand, borrowing needs assessment methodologies, evaluation strategies, and training techniques to try out in different organizations is entirely appropriate. Through these procedures, organizations can establish techniques that work, and perhaps it will be possible to begin to understand what variables affect the success of programs across organizations. However, given the present state of knowledge, simply borrowing results from another organization as a shortcut in the training process is asking for trouble.

Instructional Approaches

3

PART

A Variety of Instructional Techniques

7

CHAPTER

A complete, systematic needs assessment procedure includes a set of learning objectives that determines the type of learning necessary to achieve the goals. The instructional designer can then examine the media and techniques available and choose the method most appropriate for the behaviors being considered. This procedure should be appropriate for all different types of objectives, from motor skill specifications in pilot training to styles of managerial behavior in various organizations. At a molar level, basic knowledge helps specify the appropriate technique for particular behaviors. For example, machine simulators are used for the development of motor skills, whereas role playing is designed to acquaint managerial trainees with a variety of interpersonal situations. Unfortunately, there has been no advancement beyond molar generalities. In part, this is due to the difficulties encountered in the development of a comprehensive set of categories to describe the type of learning underlying the behavioral objectives. Another dilemma is the determination of the behaviors that are likely to be modified by the various techniques. Campbell (1971) originally expressed this dilemma by noting that it is impossible to organize empirical research around dependent variables. Campbell and his colleagues (Campbell, McCloy, Oppler, & Sager, in press) further lament the lack of conceptual understanding about the dependent variable or performance. These authors note that

> People can get goose-bumps over a new treatment (e.g., empowered work groups), or a new ability variable (e.g., tacit knowledge), but spending a lot of time or resources to understand performance itself seems not to be very exciting or fundable.

Although these authors are referring to any type of treatment, the remarks also apply to training treatments. Campbell argues for examining which kinds of experiences produce particular outcomes and which variables affect the relationship between treatments and outcomes. However, for a variety of reasons, instructional designers have not arrived at that state of knowledge. First (as stated many times before), the empirical research necessary to establish these relationships has been insufficient. Second, most research efforts have emphasized reactions and learning in the training setting rather than performance in the transfer setting. Third, empirical studies have tended to cluster around demonstrations of the value of the technique rather than the nature of the learning activities for which the method is useful. Thus, the material in this chapter is organized around instructional approaches, with the hope that future texts on instructional procedures might be able to choose a different format.

Part 3 is titled "Instructional Approaches" (rather than media or techniques) because some topics are clearly not dependent on a particular method. Some topics focus on particular groups of trainees, like managers, police, the hard-core unemployed, or individuals searching for second careers, rather than on particular methods. Also included in this multitreatment category are studies of individual differences in which investigators have attempted to match the abilities of the learner to a variety of different instructional approaches. Part 3 also includes material devoted to particular methods such as programmed instruction, computer-assisted instruction, business games, behavioral role modeling, role playing, and behavior modification. Examining every training technique or the many variations of each technique is not possible. The criteria for inclusion are almost as complex and difficult to express as the criteria for most training programs. I have selected techniques that have aroused the interest of the training community and that appear likely to be used in the 1990s. I have also favored approaches that elucidate the topics presented in the first six chapters. For example, behavioral role modeling represents a technique that is a direct development of cognitive and social learning approaches.

Other approaches are included because they represent attempts to deal with today's serious social problems. Thus, there are sections devoted to training and fair employment practices, training the hard-core unemployed, and training for second careers. In some instances (notably, training for second careers), not much information is available to offer the reader, but the seriousness of the problem demands its exploration. The tremendous variety of approaches requires a flexible format for the presentation of techniques. In those cases in which the technique consists of well-defined approaches, such as programmed instruction, descriptive background material and specific research examples are included. In those approaches that do not have well-defined characteristics, such as on-the-job instruction, only general descriptions can be included. Where enough empirical information is available, there is a general discussion of the evaluation data, with particular emphasis on the problem areas that must be faced by the researcher and the practitioner. Finally, there is a summary of the advantages and limitations of the approach, based on evaluation studies whenever possible. The grouping and ordering of techniques was another judgment call. This chapter consists of a variety of techniques, including programmed instruction, machine simulators, behavior modification, audiovisual, and so on. Most of the techniques described are related to knowledge (for example, learning math) and skills (for example, flying an airplane) training. Of course, many of the techniques can be used for a variety of situations. Thus, programmed instruction can teach interpersonal skills to managers, and audiovisual techniques are often used in role playing as a basis for examining interpersonal behavior. However, granting that there are many exceptions, most of the techniques in this chapter are designed to teach skills and provide knowledge. The training programs discussed in Chapter 8, including techniques such as role playing and sensitivity training, are more often related to such interpersonal interaction situations as responding to a complaining employee or customer or teaching managers how to supervise employees. As a matter of fact, many of these techniques are employed in management or supervisory training programs.

Chapter 9 presents special issues, including training for those looking for second careers, training for the hard-core unemployed, training and fair employment practice issues, and training and socialization issues.

CONTROL PROCEDURES—ON-THE-JOB TRAINING AND THE LECTURE METHOD

Before beginning a discussion of the more specific instructional approaches, it is important to consider the two most frequently used general procedures—on-the-job training and the lecture method. Valid information about the utility of these two procedures is not readily available. Everyone uses these methods, but they are rarely investigated except when they are employed as a control procedure for research exploring another technique. Even in those cases, the discussion of results centers on the "new" technique. This is especially shortsighted because many research investigations have not found any differences in achievement between control techniques and other methods such as films. The "no differences" results have led many investigators to believe that films and television are at least as good as the more traditional lecture method. Thus, they suggest focusing attention on those situations that are particularly appropriate for films. However, the question could be reversed to determine what lectures and on-the-job training can offer the learner. For example, it could be asked whether there are particular learning behaviors that are especially well taught by on-the-job training. As indicated in Table 1.3, both the lecture method and one-on-one instruction are used often and are relatively inexpensive compared to methods like computer-assisted instruction. Burke and Day (1986) employed a technique called meta-analysis, which is statistical procedure that permits comparisons across studies to examine various managerial-training techniques. They found that the lecture method fared well as a training method. They note that these results were encouraging especially because criticisms of its use often arise.

On-the-Job Training

Almost all trainees are exposed to some form of on-the-job training. This form of instruction might follow a carefully designed off-the-job instructional program, or it might be the sole source of instruction. There are very few, if any, instructional programs that can provide all the required training in a setting away from the job. At the very least, provisions for transfer to the job setting must be part of the initial learning experience of the actual job environment. Unfortunately, an on-the-job instructional program is usually an informal procedure in which the trainee is expected to learn by watching an experienced worker. This informal approach reflects the main argument against the use of on-the-job training as the fundamental instructional system. Although there is no reason why a carefully designed on-the-job instructional system should not be as successful as any other approach, the success of the program still demands that the objectives and the training environment be carefully prepared for instructional purposes. Given the proper conditions, there are certain advantages to on-the-job training. For example, the transfer problem becomes less difficult because the individual is being trained in the exact physical and social environment in which he or she is expected to perform. There is also an opportunity to practice the exact required behaviors. As far as evaluation is concerned, on-the-job instruction could result in the collection of more job-relevant criteria.

Sullivan and Miklas (1985) present a useful example of an on-the-job training program that was carefully planned for assistant office managers in a bank. They had a series of steps in the program, which included the following:

1. The objectives of the program were first presented to the executive leadership who in turn worked with their managers to ensure that there would be support for the program.
2. They worked to identify the specific areas of training that assistant managers needed, such as customer credit.
3. The areas were then analyzed through a needs assessment process to determine the skills and knowledges required for each specific area of training.
4. The training staff worked with experts in the organization to design a training schedule that would permit the trainee to learn the identified skills for each area.
5. Before each trainee arrived, the training department worked with the organization to have mentors for each trainee for each specific area. The mentor was a person who volunteered and was interested in working with

the trainers to ensure that the trainee was guided through all course objectives.

6. A manual was developed describing all specific areas, the mentor for each area, the schedule, the training specifications, and trainee-reporting forms on accomplishments.
7. The final step was an assessment by the mentor of the trainee's performance on completion of the specific area.

Another example of the potential positive results of on-the-job training is described by Lefkowitz (1970), who studied the effects of a training program on the productivity and tenure of sewing-machine operators. He demonstrated that on-the-job training programs can produce direct benefits. The experimental program integrated off-site simulation training, which was instituted in a room off the assembly line, with on-site training. Some training groups were exposed only to varying lengths of off-site simulation. The group experiencing both off- and on-site training achieved the best balance of productivity and employee retention. Employee retention had been a serious problem before the study, with turnover as high as 68 percent in one year. Lefkowitz notes that the on-the job phase of the training program provided for job-oriented discussion following the first exposure to the factory. Thus, trainees were able to discuss various difficulties, like scheduling and job-related tension, and to reach solutions to the problems that led to the high turnover of previous employees. Lefkowitz also noticed that first-line supervisors paid greater attention to these trainees during their first days of integrated training. He suggests that this occurred because the trainees would be returning to the off-site simulation and reporting their experiences to the trainer.

It is clear that these programs were not being used as a way of avoiding planning for an appropriate training effort. Unfortunately, most on-the-job training programs are not planned and thus do not work well. Too often, practicality is the main reason that this form of training is chosen; it is cheap and easy to implement with no planning at all. The simple instruction "help John learn the job," to *any* employee, fully implements the training program. The entire instructional process is placed in the hands of an individual who may or may not be capable of performing the job and who probably considers the entire procedure an imposition on his or her time. Under these conditions, training takes second place to the performance of the job. Even if the "instructor" is capable, it may not be possible to slow the pace, appraise the responses, and supply feedback to the trainee in a job setting where performance is the criterion for success. In these cases, the job environment may not be a good learning environment. Although this point is obvious when very complex behaviors must be learned (for example, flying an airplane), it is too often neglected for other behaviors that appear easy enough to learn on the job. Thus, although on-the-job training can work, as demonstrated by the above studies, it is not usually successful when used to avoid the necessity of designing a training program. As long as programs are designed solely for that purpose, they will face difficulties of incompetent instructors, priority production schedules, and a generally poor learning environment. On-site training must be treated like any other method; the technique should be chosen because it is the most effective way of implementing certain behaviors. Once the training analyst ascertains that on-site training is the most effective technique to teach the pertinent skills, the environment must be designed as carefully as any other instructional environment. A few examples of on-the-job training approaches are presented next.

Embedded training. As the workplace becomes technically more sophisticated, organizations will likely need to take advantage of all possible job-training opportunities. Also, the same technology that characterizes the workplace will have to be developed for appropriate use in on-the-job training systems. *Embedded training* is an example of this combination of on-the-job use of equipment and on-the-job training. This type of training is instruction that is an integral part of the equipment itself. An example of embedded training is an office machine with graphic displays that show where a problem has occurred and then lists the steps (thus training the worker) needed to remedy it. Many word processing systems have extremely effective instructional systems with vivid graphics describing new procedures that are being added or old procedures where the worker may be having difficulty. This type of training has several advantages. It is available at the workplace whenever the trainee needs it, and it focuses on the immediate need. Also, it permits co-workers to discuss it and immediately try out the system. On the other hand, effectively designing these systems is not easy. The designer must focus on which problems the user is likely to have and anticipate how to answer the questions. This is another example where the experiences of cognitive and instructional theorists in working with novices and experts to ensure the effective design of instruction should be very useful.

Apprenticeship training. Apprenticeship systems provide another good example of the complex relationship between classroom-type training and on-the-job experiences. It also makes it clear that the distinctions between training on and off the job are not always a good distinction. These formal programs have most often been used to teach various skilled trades. Typically, the trainee receives both classroom instruction and supervision from experienced employees on the job. At the end of a specified period of training, the apprentice becomes a journeyman. This system is employed in a wide variety of skilled trades, such as bricklayers, electricians, and plumbers, and is commonly accepted as a valid mode of instruction for large numbers of trainees.

The original purposes of the apprenticeship-training programs were formulated in 1937 by the National Apprenticeship Act, which created the Federal Bureau of Apprenticeship and Training (BAT) as part of the Department of Labor. These purposes, which are largely unchanged, were to formulate labor standards to safeguard the welfare of apprentices and to extend the application of those standards. In addition, another mission was to bring together employers and labor to develop programs and to cooperate with state agencies in developing standards for apprenticeships. In the past two decades, the apprenticeship system declined. Between 1980 and 1987, the number of apprentices in federal programs declined from .3 percent of the U.S. civilian workplace to .16 percent (Office of Technology Assessment, 1990). Now, there is widespread interest in revitalizing the system because of the concerns about the shrinking supply of young workers and the rising skill requirements in many occupations.

In addition, there is now interest in using apprenticeship systems for work organizations in occupations other than traditional trades. For example, the Service Employees International Union (SEIU) represents about 875,000 service workers, most of whom work in public or private health care (Office of Technology Assessment, 1990). As a result of support from BAT, the union has developed joint training programs called Career Ladders. The program specifies exactly what a worker needs to do to be promoted in jobs, ranging from housekeepers to pharmacists. One program that has been particularly successful is for phlebotomists, people trained to draw blood from patients. This program has been helpful for a hospital in the Cape Cod, Massachusetts, area where phlebotomists have been in great demand, especially during the summer months. At this point, the hospital does not even have to provide its own training program. All nonmanagement training is done through the Career Ladders program. This effort has also been significantly important in providing training opportunities for minorities and women. In previous years, a number of commentators have been critical of apprenticeship-training efforts because some unions controlled the training programs and restricted entry to women and minority-group members. Our discussion of these issues in Chapter 9 will indicate that employment discrimination is not a problem that has been resolved. However, the effort described above demonstrates that it is possible for apprenticeship programs to be a positive force in the workplace.

Lecture Method

Although on-the-job training is the most extensively used procedure in industrial settings, the lecture method enjoys that status in educational environments, from primary school to evening-division programs for employed workers. In addition, the lecture method is the most frequently employed control procedure in the analysis of recently developed techniques such as films, television, and programmed instruction.

Originally, many authors (McGehee & Thayer, 1961; Bass & Vaughan, 1966) questioned the usefulness of the lecture method as an instructional technique. Their criticisms focus on its one-way communication aspects. Too often, the lecture method results in passive learners who do not have the opportunity to clarify material. In addition, the lecturer may have difficulty presenting material that is equally cogent to individuals who have wide differences in ability, attitude, and interest. By the time a criterion test is employed, some individuals may be hopelessly behind. Many of these difficulties can be overcome by competent lecturers who make the material meaningful and remain aware of their students' reactions by effectively promoting discussion and clarification of material.

However, many studies have compared programmed instruction or televised instruction to the lecture technique. The results indicate that these newer techniques do not necessarily lead to superior student achievement, although there is some evidence that the student completes the material faster. Thus, there appears to be little empirical reason for the bias against the lecture procedure. As shown in Table 1.3, classroom lecture methods are a frequently used technique. Interestingly, the authors also found that the research does not support the poor opinions of the lecture technique as an instrument in the acquisition of knowledge. Certainly, the lecture method has shortcomings. It is insensitive to individual differences, and it is limited in providing immediate feedback to the learner. However, considering the low cost of the lecture method, it is important to determine empirically when and how it can be used. Evidence indicates that the technique is not appropriate when complex responses (for example, motor skills) are required but may be quite applicable when acquisition of knowledge is the goal. There is general uncertainty about the benefits of the lecture method for other behaviors, such as attitude change. Most authors and training directors think that the lecture method is not useful in promoting attitude change, but, again, little empirical evidence supports their view. Actually, several studies conducted by Miner (1961, 1963) suggest that the lecture was appropriate as an attitude-change technique. One study examined seventy-two supervisors in the research-and-development department of a large corporation. These employees had been neglecting their supervisory activities in favor of their scientific interests. Miner developed a course that placed considerable emphasis on scientific theory and research findings relevant to supervisory practices. He found that the experimental group developed more favorable attitudes toward supervisory training as compared to a control group that did not participate in the lecture program. Interestingly, the control group developed negative feelings during the training period because of the threat of department reorganization.

Unfortunately, few studies have examined lecture courses that are specifically designed as part of a training program. Usually, when the lecture method is employed as a control procedure, most of the effort is devoted to the development of the experimental technique. Almost all other techniques have many proponents who excitedly proclaim the validity of their procedure with little, if any, empirical evidence. On the other hand, the lecture technique is viewed with disdain without much empirical evidence. The lecture is still used, however, in a wide variety of settings. It would be interesting to learn which conditions help determine the usefulness of this technique. Is the method of instruction important? Is discussion necessary? What determines

Table 7.1 Classroom trainng at NUMMI

New United Motor Manufacturing International (NUMMI), a joint venture between General Motors and Toyota in Fremont, California, cross-trains maintenance mechanics who are responsible for all plant maintenance plus special projects such as building robots. Trainees spend 5 years studying five trades (plumbing, pipefitting, welding, electrical, and machinist). The program includes about 20 percent lecture (theory) and 80 percent lab (troubleshooting small equipment, making projects), supplemented with on-the-job training. It is much less intensive in any one trade than registered apprenticeship programs, however. Graduate trainees receive a United Auto Workers electrical journeyman card and a State of California multi-craft journeyman card, neither of which would be recognized by other unions.

Before entering the program, candidates take placement tests in both basic skills and their individual crafts. Basic skills deficiencies are remediated in class contexts (e.g., math skills in blueprint reading). Classes are 2 hours a day, at the end of each shift; during the most intensive training, classes meet 4 days per week (for this period, a trainee is in the workplace 48 hours per week). The lab component of each course includes 10–15 projects that the trainee has to complete satisfactorily. Each project has three basic steps: describe the process, make a materials list, then return the finished product for review of quality/quantity. The projects range in difficulty from troubleshooting small electrical devices to machining parts to welding. Trainees have to pass each class with a score of at least 80 percent or repeat it. Training continues on the shop floor as those mechanics most skilled in one field assist their co-workers in maintenance tasks.

Training aids in the laboratory include basic electrical units (e.g., volt-ohm-meters, circuits, switches, small motors), machine tools, welding booths and equipment, and other equipment and tools common to the factory (most were scrounged rather than purchased).

The maintenance mechanics feel their productivity has improved as a result of cross-training (e.g., one cross-trained worker often can complete repairs that previously required two or three specialized maintenance workers). However, in some crafts—particularly electrical—the mechanics do not feel they have had sufficient training to tackle complicated repairs without assistance from a union-certified journeyman.

From "Worker Training: Competing In The New International Economy" by Office of Technology Assessment, U.S. Congress, 1990, OTA-ITE-457, Washington, D.C.: U.S. Government Printing Office.

the quality of the instructor? A few of the answers to these questions are discussed in "The Training Environment" in Chapter 4.

Lectures are unlikely to disappear. If anything is likely to vanish, it is probably the distinctions between off-the-job classroom training and on-the-job training. Rather, as training becomes more sophisticated, many different techniques will likely merge, including classroom, embedded training, on-the-job training, and so on. This is made particularly clear by the example presented in Table 7.1. This effort describes a program that cross trains mechanics who are responsible for plant maintenance and special projects like building robots. It consists of 20 percent lecture and 80 percent lab and is supplemented by on-the-job training. The on-the-job portion includes *job aids.* These are instructional devices that aid learning by serving as reminders in recalling training information. One interesting application of job aids is employed by Domino's Pizza (Feur, 1987). They place large, glossy illustrations of exactly what a pizza is supposed to look like at each stage of preparation. Domino's does this even though it expects employees to produce pizzas at high speed and to memorize thoroughly the production procedures. One display shows a different type of cutting error for each slice presented in the picture, and the other shows a perfect pizza. These types of learning aids have been a common feature of military-training programs and are now making their appearance in a large variety of civilian on-the-job situations. Again, this blurs the distinction between formal training and informal training in a very healthy way.

Programmed Instruction

Since the mid-1950s, a large number of devices, such as self-instructional materials, automated teaching machines, and programmed texts, have been developed. These programmed materials systematically present information to the learner while using the principles of reinforcement (Silverman, 1960). Programmed instruction (PI) is dependent not on the physical characteristics of the display (for example, a book, a computer, or a mechanical apparatus) but on the quality of the program.

In 1962 Bass and Vaughan (1966) found that 165 commercial programs were available. More recent estimates from educational, industrial, and government sources signal an astounding increase in the number and kinds of programs available. Any survey of educational institutions would reveal that few students graduating today have not been exposed to programmed devices as teaching aids. Surveys in work organizations would also indicate that PI is being used in an ever-increasing number of activities. For example, the Life Insurance Marketing and Research Association has a variety of texts to train new agents in areas such as the purpose of life insurance, use of mortality tables, types of policies, and so on. This company also has PI texts on sales skills, including the use of the telephone, prospecting for clients, and the like. Wexley and Latham (1981) report on a gift-shop retail chain that uses PI to train their Christmas-rush sales force. The material consists of self-paced texts and diagnostic pretests that permit trainees to skip material that they know. This is especially valuable for this organization because many of their Christmas employees return year-after-year. These employees can skip over material that they remember from their last tour of work. The PI material covers many work-related topics, ranging from customer relations to operating the cash register, handling refunds, and cashing checks. Why have these programs been adopted by many institutions? What is expected from programmed learning that is not available from other techniques? To answer these questions, it is necessary to examine the historical development and objectives of PI.

Approaches to Programmed Instruction

Autoinstructional method. In the early 1900s, Thorndike introduced the *law of effect.* This law states that stimulus–response associations that are followed by a satisfying state of affairs are learned, whereas those that are followed by unsatisfying states of affairs are weakened and eliminated. In the 1920s, Pressey (1950) applied Thorndike's principles of learning to the classroom environment by using the feedback from examinations. He argues that immediately scored exams can provide the feedback necessary to help students determine their strengths and weaknesses; thus, he developed *autoinstructional* programs to supply immediate feedback. In this system, students read a question and choose the appropriate response from a series of multiple-choice answers. If students are correct, they are immediately reinforced by a light or a buzzer, which "stamps in" the correct associations. If the response is incorrect, learners are not reinforced, thus weakening the incorrect association. Students then must respond with one of the remaining alternatives. This process continues until students pick the correct answer, at which time they are reinforced and proceed to the next question.

Although a number of studies conducted by Pressey indicate that the technique was promising, a movement favoring the use of PI never developed. A variety of reasons have been offered for this lack of interest. Some commentators suggest that the onset of the Great Depression created an unfavorable social climate for an "industrial revolution" in the schools (Lysaught & Williams, 1963). Other educators believe that Pressey's autoinstructional system was really a testing device that did not provide for systematic programming of materials. Thus, they contend that the method had little new to offer.

Linear programming. Opinions about PI changed radically when B. F. Skinner (1954) published his article "The Science of Learning and the Art of Teaching," which applies his models of operant conditioning to the educational process. Skinner argues that a program could successively shape the learner by reinforcing the achievement of small steps in the same way that the pigeon is conditioned by the reinforcement of successive approximations to peck a key. Because Skinner believes that positive reinforcement of correct responses is the most efficient way to produce learning, he designed his programs to condition the learner through a series of small steps so that few errors occur. Thus, the learner is expected to continually earn positive reinforcement. If errors are made at a particular point in the program, there is a problem with the program, not the student. The only variability that is permitted among learners is the speed with which they complete the program. Because a student proceeds through each successive step, the technique became known as *linear programming.* Its essential parameters include the following characteristics (Fry, 1963; Bass & Vaughan, 1966):

1. All material is presented in small units called frames. Each frame varies in size from one sentence to several paragraphs, depending on the amount of material necessary to guide the learner.
2. Each frame requires an overt response from the learner. The student reads the frame and then constructs a response by filling in the blank. Thus, the learner is actively involved in the learning process.
3. The learner immediately receives feedback indicating the correctness of the response. Because the program is constructed for a minimum number of errors, the learner usually receives immediate positive reinforcement.
4. The program is predesigned to provide proper learning sequences. Because the units must be presented in small steps to achieve low error rates, the programmer must carefully analyze both the material and the learner's characteristics in order to obtain the most appropriate step size and sequence. This process requires pretesting of the program and revisions based on student responses. If a criterion of approximately 90 percent correct by all trainees is not met, the material must be rewritten.
5. Each trainee proceeds independently through the program at a pace commensurate with his or her own abilities. A sample of a program that discusses two of the principles of linear programming, self-pacing and small steps, can be found in Table 7.2.

Intrinsic or branching programming. In branching programs, correct responses by the learner lead directly to the next step of the program, whereas incorrect answers lead to a branch designed to correct the mistake. The branches can vary in complexity from a few short frames to an elaborate subprogram. Intrinsic programs have had the greatest impact on the development of branching techniques (Crowder, 1960). These programs have relatively long frames followed by a series of multiple-choice answers. If the program is in text form, learners turn to the page number associated with their answer choice. There, trainees are presented with another series of frames based on their previous answers. If the chosen answer is correct, the response is simply confirmed, and learners are directed to the next frame. If the answer is incorrect, learners proceed to a remedial set of frames designed to correct the previous response.

Table 7.3 presents an example of an intrinsic branching program. Branching programs cannot eliminate all errors; however, students do not proceed until they can demonstrate by their performance on the branching step that they understand the concept previously missed. Crowder (1960) designed his steps so that they are larger than those that appear in linear programming. The superior student can then proceed through larger steps, whereas the student experiencing difficulty is directed into branching programs with smaller steps. Crowder believes that this procedure permits the designer to consider the individual differences and backgrounds of students. The superior student can progress through the program without becoming bored, and the slower student is given special attention. Of course, most branching programs have limited flexibility. Only a certain number of

Table 7.2 Sample of a linear program

	1. You are now beginning a lesson on programmed instruction. The principle of *self-pacing* as used in programmed instructions allows each trainee to work as slowly or as fast as he chooses. Since you can control the amount of time you spend on this lesson, this program is using the principle of self- __________ .
Pacing	2. People naturally learn at different rates. A program that allows each trainee to control his own rate of learning is using the principle of __________ .
Self-Pacing	3. If a self-pacing program is to be successful, the information step size must be small. A program that is self-pacing would also apply the principle of small __________ .
Steps	4. The average trainee will usually make correct responses if the correct-size step of information is given. This is utilizing the principle of small __________ .
Steps	5. A program that provides information in a step size that allows the trainee to be successful is applying the principle of __________ .
Small Steps	6. A trainee knows the material being taught but has to wait for the remainder of the class. What programming principle is being violated? __________ .
Self-Pacing	7. Two principles of programmed learning are: (1) __________ . (2) __________ .
1. *Self-pacing* 2. *Small steps*	

Note: For practical reasons, the frames are arranged on one page rather than on succeeding pages. The answers should be covered until the preceding frame has been answered. Adapted from U.S. Civil Service Commission. *Programed Instruction: A Brief of Its Development and Current Status.* Washington, D.C.: U.S. Government Printing Office, 1970.

branches can be designed for the individual student without the whole project becoming cumbersome. However, computer-assisted instruction (discussed later) does offer increased flexibility for branching. Most educators agree that there is little empirical justification for a choice between linear or branching techniques (DeCecco, 1968). Using both techniques within the same program has become increasingly popular. The particular instructional objectives, entering behavior of the students, and material to be learned should determine the most appropriate procedure at any point in the program.

Table 7.3 Sample of an intrinsic branching program

Definition of the term "teaching machine"

Page 8: In 1924, Dr. Sidney L. Pressey invented a small machine that would score a multiple-choice examination automatically at the time the answer-button was pushed.

Although he designed it as a testing machine, he perceived that by a simple expedient he could use the machine as a teaching device. All he had to do was design it so that, for each question, the correct answer-button had to be pushed before a subsequent question would appear in the window.

From this simple beginning, the concept of *teaching machines* has grown until now the educator is faced with many types and styles, from the simplest cardboard device costing pennies to incredibly complex electronic wonders costing thousands of dollars.

But don't despair. All teaching machines have three characteristics in common:

1. They present information and require frequent responses by the student.
2. They provide immediate feedback to the student, informing them whether their response is appropriate or not.
3. They allow the student to work individually and to adjust their rate of progress to their own needs and capabilities.

Now, based on the three criteria listed above, is the educational motion picture, as it is normally used, a teaching machine?

YES *(Turn to page 6.)*
NO *(Turn to page 4.)*

Page 6: The educational motion picture, as it is normally used, *does* present factual information but does *not* satisfy any of the other conditions set down for a teaching machine; no response is called for, no feedback is given, and the student has no control over his rate of progress.

The standard educational motion picture, then, is similar to a well-prepared lecture but is not a teaching machine.

Please read the conditions on page 8 again, and then select the other alternative.

Page 4: Right! The educational motion picture, as it is normally used, is not a teaching machine.

1. Although the motion picture presents information, it does not require periodic responses from the student in the form of answers, selections, or motor responses.
2. Since it does not ask for responses, it does not indicate whether the responses are appropriate or not.
3. It does not allow the individual class member to adjust their rate of progress to their own needs and capabilities.

Adapted from *Explaining Teaching Machines and Programming* by D. Cram.

Evaluation of Programmed Instruction

A large number of programs remain unevaluated; however, as compared with research on most other training methods, the evaluation data available on PI represent a storehouse of knowledge. Holt's studies (Holt, 1963; Shoemaker & Holt, 1965) provide good early examples of and illuminating commentary about the utility of PI as a training technique. In one investigation, he compared the standard lecture–discussion method to a pretested linear PI course in basic electricity for telephone electricians. The main criteria were tests examining facts and concepts given at the completion of training and six months later. The assignment of trainees to treatment conditions was based on when the employees reported for training. The first set of trainees to arrive completed the course using the standard lecture procedure, consisting of ten days of class work. The next group of trainees was assigned to a PI group that attended only for as many days as were necessary to complete the program. Although this procedure does not use random assignments, good sampling is achieved if the variation for individuals assigned to training is not biased across time periods. This assumption is reasonable, but, as a further check, Holt compared the experimental and control groups on a number of factors including intelligence, knowledge of basic electricity, years of experience, and course work in electricity and math. No pretraining differences existed between groups on these measures. This method provides a good illustration of the procedures that can be employed even when strict randomization cannot be achieved. Holt's study also attempted to control for the Hawthorne effect by treating both groups as part of the experiment. This treatment included informing all trainees of the nature of the experiment as well as instituting similar procedures for both groups regarding pretesting, questionnaires, interviews, and other parameters that were not strictly part of the treatment procedure.

The data analyses indicate that the PI groups achieved superior performance on the immediate posttest and on the six-month retention test. However, on the six-month test, both groups' scores decreased substantially. This study represents one of the few efforts that examined performance at later time intervals, but the retention loss raised some question about the relevance of the training program to job performance. Holt examined the use of PI in a situation in which there was an already existing lecture course. Thus, the needs assessment procedure did not directly precede the development of the PI program. An analysis indicates that the retention loss for both groups occurred because the course itself was not relevant to the technician's job, and thus, the knowledge gained was not used in the transfer setting. A good needs assessment could avoid this difficulty by implementing courses that are job-relevant and by helping in the development of job-performance criteria that could establish the utility of the procedure. Although there is ample reason to believe that the course was not relevant, there is also the possibility that the criteria were not relevant. There may be many instances in which the six-month retention tests would show a decrease in performance, whereas more job-oriented criteria would not.

Holt's investigations also explore some questions about the time needed to complete the course. In his study, there were no differences between the two groups, but the common finding is that PI groups complete the program more quickly than do traditional groups that are locked into set time intervals. However, Holt notes that the traditional group in his study had materials available for home study, whereas the PI group did not. Most other investigations do not comment on the availability of opportunities outside the training setting that can contribute to time differences or changes in achievement scores. So that the outcomes of experiments can be understood, the data must be related to process-oriented criteria that provide information about the procedures employed during training. Otherwise, the interpretation of data remains tenuous.

A study involving cultural training for nurses being trained for work with Aborigines in Australia presents another fascinating example of some of the principles of PI (O'Brien & Plooij, 1977). Much of this work was based on a program known as the cultural assimilator (Fiedler, Mitchell, & Triandis, 1971). The principle is that individuals who work in a culture different from their own need information about the differences that will help facilitate cooperation with the host country. The main characteristic of the cultural assimilator training program is the presentation of cultural knowledge through specific situational contexts preceding the use of a programmed format for self-instruction. The main aspects of the O'Brien and Plooij study were the following:

1. The investigators interviewed people who had worked in these communities and asked them to describe positive and negative incidents. An incident was considered positive if it facilitated job performance and cooperation with the Aboriginals. The interviewers obtained information about the place of the incident, tasks being performed, the exact behavioral outcomes, and so on. This is, of course, a needs assessment technique, which is called the critical-incident technique.
2. The incidents were grouped and selected on the basis of frequency of occurrence and agreement about the interpretation of the event. They were also selected on the basis of their relevance to the role of medical workers, and they were checked by medical authorities and anthropologists for interpretation difficulties.
3. A programmed manual was written containing forty-one incidents that began with the simplest ones and proceeded to the more complex. The manual and feedback about the incidents were also checked by experts for potential problems.

Based on the development of the manual, studies were designed that tested retention of material, generalization of appropriate responses to other cultural incidents not in the manual, and attitudes and motivation to work with Aboriginals. One study involved seventy-four qualified nurses attending postgraduate studies at the Australian College of Nursing. The study used a pretest/posttest design with subjects being assigned to either the programmed condition, no training, or an essay condition. The essay condition consisted of the nurses reading a series of essays that were comparable in content to the manual in terms of the topics and cultural principles. Basically, the results show that the programmed manual had a stronger effect than essay training or no training on both retention and generalization of cultural knowledge.

Table 7.4 Comparisons of programmed instruction versus conventional methods for each criterion in studies that include two or more criteria

	Conventional Method Superior	*No Significant Difference Between Methods*	*Programed Instruction Superior*
Training time	1	2	29
Immediate learning	3	20	9
Retention[1]	5	16	5

[1]Of the 32 studies that included measures of both training time and immediate learning, only 26 also had a measure of retention. From "The Relative Practical Effectiveness of Programmed Instruction," by A. N. Nash, J. P. Muczyk, and F. L. Vettori. In *Personnel Psychology,* 1971, *24,* pp. 397–418. Copyright 1971 by Personnel Psychology, Inc. Reprinted by permission.

Interestingly, the programmed-manual group became much more cautious about wanting to work with Aboriginals. Previous work on the cultural assimilator had identified a similar effect. The authors think that in part this was due to the sobering effect of the realistic job preview provided by the programmed manual, which was based on the needs assessment.

Some researchers maintain that one advantage of well-designed training programs is that they will provide a realistic job preview and thus prepare the individual for entry into the work organization. Others maintain that such realistic previews might even dissuade individuals who are not interested in that job situation. The use of training techniques as socialization to the workplace will be examined further in Chapter 9. Because O'Brien and Plooij's (1977) study did not examine actual job performance, it is not possible to determine whether these effects would generalize to the work setting. However, it does give a fascinating example of the use of needs assessment and a training program based on the principles of PI.

Because a number of studies have investigated PI, it is possible to ask what generalizations can be gained from this research. Early analyses of the literature that compared student achievement in PI and in more traditional methods (for example, the lecture method) found that the majority of studies showed no significant differences between methods (Briggs & Angell, 1964; Schramm, 1964). Of the remaining studies, most favored PI. These analyses also tend to indicate that PI groups require less learning time. A review by Nash, Muczyk, and Vettori (1971) examined the relative effectiveness of PI in both academic and industrial settings. The largest proportion of these studies had been performed in academic settings, although there was no evidence of differential data due to location. Table 7.4 presents the Nash et al. data for three different criteria including training time, immediate learning, and retention. These authors include an important additional criterion in their review: For the technique to be judged the more effective, the statistical test had to be significant—the differences between the techniques had to exceed 10 percent. Nash et al. argue that the development of PI is an expensive endeavor; thus, they think that new techniques with differences in overall effectiveness of only a few percentage would not be worth considering for institutions that have less expensive techniques available.

Their analyses of the statistical data (excluding the practicality criterion) support earlier reviews stating that most studies examining achievement (immediate learning and retention) show no significant differences, and the remaining studies favor PI. However, when the authors examined those studies in which the statistical differences were significant but the practical effectiveness was not above 10 percent, the trend toward no differences between techniques was even stronger. The analysis of learning-time data supports the established trend, indicating that PI students learn faster (the average reductions often approaching one-third). A later review supports the Nash et al. data indicating that training time is reduced and that levels of retention are the same with programmed versus conventional methods (Hall & Freda, 1982). Although the data concerning learning time have been consistent, they must be interpreted cautiously. The PI group is self-paced, and learners may leave the program whenever they have completed the material. However, the more traditional programs have a fixed time limit, and superior learners cannot leave even if they have learned enough material to achieve the objectives. Of course, that is one of the advantages of programmed learning, but it might be interesting to discover what would happen if learners in the control condition could take their achievement tests when they have completed the program to their own satisfaction.

The thoroughness with which Nash et al. (1971) performed their review raises one other serious question about the effects of PI on achievement level. These authors divided the studies into effectively and less effectively controlled studies. Effectively controlled studies include the investigations that had (l) experimental and control groups selected by random assignment or a pretest measure used for adjustments when the groups varied on significant variables and (2) a sample average of twenty subjects, with a minimum of fifteen in each group. These, of course, are minimum standards and do not go so far as to require controls for pretest sensitization or a consideration of Hawthorne effects. However, many of the studies that did find that PI resulted in superior achievement levels were less effectively controlled studies.

Advantages and Limitations of Programmed Instruction

Advantages

1. Properly designed PI follows the basic steps necessary for an effective training program. It is more difficult to build frames, provide feedback, and design sequences without analyzing the instructional content. The procedure also includes objectives with built-in checks to ensure that learners understand the material.

2. The evidence indicating that trainees learn more using PI techniques is mixed, but they appear to learn at least as much as trainees in control procedures such as lecture groups. Sufficient evidence concludes that training time is effectively reduced for PI groups.

3. Programmed materials are easily packaged and can be sent to widely dispersed training centers. In addition, individual students may take the course when it is deemed most appropriate.

4. Many trainers believe that the reinforcement provided by programmed learning leads to a more highly motivated learner.

5. The individualization of instruction is an important aspect of PI. The self-pacing procedure permits learners to proceed at the rate most comfortable for their ability level and even permits them to take pretests and skip material that they have already learned. Thus, the training program for Christmas sales employees described previously allowed trainees to concentrate on materials they still needed to learn. In the Nash et al. (1971) review, the authors found a number of studies that show that higher low-ability trainees, who might be expected to benefit most from self-pacing, perform in a superior manner on immediate-learning criteria. Individual modes of instruction will be treated more fully in the next section on computer-assisted instruction.

Limitations

1. The major limitation of PI is the expense and preparation necessary. An examination of the requirements necessary to develop a linear or branching program clearly indicates that it is a time-consuming task involving considerable analysis and pretesting.

2. One limitation noted early in the history of PI is that, even with the increasing variety of programs, the emphasis of PI is on factual materials. Basically, that is still true because PI cannot as easily simulate the interactions between employees and managers that can be performed in role-playing training. On the other hand, materials regarding principles related to personal interactions can be presented. An example of this is described previously in the programmed material for training nurses to learn cultural material related to working with Australian Aboriginals.

3. Early student-reaction data indicate that PI by itself may not be an acceptable mode of instruction. Several early studies indicate that the learner is more satisfied with a combined technique, such as a conference or discussion along with programmed instruction (Patten & Stermer, 1969). More recently, similar comments have been made about other technologically based programs such as computer-assisted instruction. School systems often state that PI permits their instructors to spend more time with individual students or small groups of students. It may be equally important for the adult in industry to have similar human interaction. Actually, at this time, most learners and trainees are growing up with sophisticated, technological equipment, and comments about concerns involving human interaction are infrequent because the techniques are not used in isolation.

COMPUTER-ASSISTED INSTRUCTION

One of the more recent innovations in instructional technology is computer-assisted instruction (CAI). With the advent of microcomputers, a revolution is clearly occurring, exemplified by the number of primary schools teaching computer programming and the move toward office automation systems. This revolution is also affecting CAI. It is not unusual to use CAI to educate students on the use of the computer and employees on the use of office automation systems. In CAI systems, the student interacts directly with the computer, which has stored, within its systems, information and instructional materials necessary for the program. The degree of computer interaction with the student varies with the individual system. In 1969 Cooley and Glaser developed a general model that describes the processes in the design of CAI systems:

1. The goals of learning are specified in terms of observable student behavior and the conditions under which this behavior is to be manifested.
2. When the learner begins a particular course of instruction, the initial capabilities—those relevant to the forthcoming instruction—are assessed.
3. Educational alternatives suited to the student's initial capabilities are presented to him. The student selects or is assigned one of these alternatives.
4. The students' performance is monitored and continuously assessed as they learn.
5. Instruction proceeds as a function of the relationship between measures of student performance, available instructional alternatives, and criteria of competence.
6. As instruction proceeds, data are generated for monitoring and improving the instructional system. (pp. 574–575)

At that time, this description was more of a hope of things to come. Now it appears to be a rapidly developing reality. It is also interesting to note that many of these steps parallel the instructional model in Chapter 2.

State of the Art

The excitement about the development of CAI is based on the storage and memory capabilities of the computer, which in turn provide the potential for true interaction with the individual student. The proponents of this system believe that this potential provides the ultimate in branching programs. The computer records the individual's previous response, analyzes its characteristics, and determines the next presentation to the student on the basis of the learner's needs. Developments are beginning to occur. However, relatively few systems actually use CAI technology. Most of the large number of press releases, research articles, and institutional reports present vague speculations and still dwell on hardware development. For example, there are typewriters tied to computer devices, pens that draw curves on cathode-ray tubes, and devices that present auditory material and score student answers. Sometimes the sophisticated instrument is simply a PI device that uses electronic presentation instead of textbooks. Also, an examination of the use of these devices rarely presents validation data or cost estimates. These misguided efforts should not detract from the tremendous possibilities of computer technology in instructional systems and the fact that there are a number of actual programs being used. In 1968 Atkinson participated in a carefully developed system at Stanford University. He suggests that "the problem for someone trying to evaluate developments in the field is to distinguish between those reports that are based on fact and those that are disguised forms of science fiction" (p. 225). In 1984 Galagan wrote the following in an editorial for the *Training and Development Journal:*

> Personal computers will soon be a mass market appliance. They are tools that training cannot afford to ignore. When a technology appears, it will be used, and the time is ripe for trainers to influence the potential of this powerful medium to monitor, promote, encourage and reward not just learning but human development.
>
> Then, for instance, my computer/teller could train me to manage my cash flow or to understand its record-keeping system, rather than leaving me broke without warning or explanation. But I guess one can't expect money from a machine and training too. (p. 4)

Those who are concerned with the development of useful instructional techniques must be concerned with the distinction between fact and fiction. Eberts and Brock (1987) again warn us that computers will not automatically improve training. As with any other technique, success depends on the needs assessment and instructional design. Thus, we should not be fooled because CAI has more than the usual number of bells and whistles. On the other hand, CAI has tremendous potential. An example of a system for which extensive research and development is taking place is known as PLATO (Programmed Logic for Automated Teaching Operations). Its system includes capabilities for displays of all kinds, modifiable graphics, and touch-panel inputs. For example, the touch-panel graphics were used in one study of a pilot trainer where sets of push-buttons were graphically simulated. The system provides control and monitoring of student progress and has the capabilities to maintain student and evaluation data. The system can also handle large numbers of students. For example, PLATO IV at the University of Illinois has capabilities for handling 950 terminals for students as nearby as the university and as far away as San Diego. Training programs on topics as diverse as remedial math, oscilloscope preparation, and recipe preparation have been designed and evaluated (Hurlock & Slough, 1976). The researchers found the system to be highly effective for training, especially for performance involving sequencing and procedural learning. The next section provides further information about a few examples of these systems, which are likely to affect us all in the future. The Federal Aviation Administration has used PLATO for over a decade to train flight inspectors and maintenance specialists, and they have just introduced it for air traffic controllers (Office of Technology Assessment, 1990). The heavy training load, which was difficult to meet with only classroom instruction, is what initially led to the choice of the PLATO system.

Examples of CAI Systems

The preceding discussion implies that CAI is not a single method. It can involve drill and practice, tutorial programs, simulations, and so on. Two of the most well-developed systems are drill and practice and tutorial.

Drill and practice. The simplest of the two systems is drill and practice, which is ordinarily used as a supplement to conventional instruction (Suppes & Jerman, 1970). The program is usually controlled by a teacher, who first introduces the material in class and then specifies the topics that are to be practiced by the students individually at instructional terminals. This CAI system permits the teacher to present creative material in the classroom but also provides immediate feedback to large numbers of students on various sets of problems. The computer can present individualized material to a number of students simultaneously, as well as provide feedback to the individual student and records of progress to the teacher. One of the earliest drill-and-practice programs was developed at Stanford. The Stanford drill-and-practice program in mathematics has twenty to twenty-seven concept blocks for each grade level (Suppes & Morningstar, 1969). Each concept block contains a pretest, five days of drill, a posttest, and review drills. This system has provisions for administering the following program: (l) a pretest, which determines the student's entering ability for that concept block; (2) the assignment of a series of lessons (which vary in difficulty) according to the student's ability; (3) a compilation of records on the student's performance on each lesson; (4) the determination of the appropriate lesson as a function of the student's progress on the previous material; (5) a posttest, which assesses the student's progress.

Suppes and Morningstar (1969) reported on a series of research investigations that analyzed the effectiveness of the mathematics program. The data from these studies, which included primary-school students from California and Mississippi, generally favored the CAI group, although there were some criteria on which the traditionally educated students performed better than the CAI students. More interesting was the relative superiority of the experimental group in Mississippi as compared with its control group. An analysis of these data indicates that the differences occurred because the control group in Mississippi was not improving at the same rate as the one in California. This result led the authors to speculate that these programs will have striking benefits in environments that are not socially and educationally affluent. It is in these situations that the student benefits most from the opportunity to learn from effectively designed programs. Considering the difficulties that many industrial institutions have in designing basic instructional material, the opportunity for their employees to work at a terminal that is coordinated with a central instructional system must certainly be appealing. The Stanford project used a central computer in California for primary-school students in California, Kentucky, and Mississippi. The usefulness of drill-and-practice programs has also been established at the college level. In another Stanford project, Suppes and Morningstar (1969) also found that CAI students were superior to a traditional class in the first-year Russian program. There were also fewer dropouts in the CAI group, and a greater percentage of the CAI group enrolled in the second year of Russian.

The military has also developed a drill-and-practice program to teach remedial math (McCann, 1975). This program uses the PLATO system and teaches basic math for trainees in the Basic Electricity/Electronics School. The research here investigated different types of feedback systems as a way of reinforcing learning. The reinforcement system was the opportunity to make play movements in a game after correct performance on practice problems. Receiving game moves did not change student test performance or training time. As one might suspect, however, students indicated strong and favorable preference for practice having feedback with games.

Tutorial. The tutorial program, as compared to drill and practice, assumes the responsibility for most, if not all, of the information incorporated into the program. Most CAI programs are tutorial in nature and may be complete course sequences or special supplementary units. If they are supplementary units, the teacher incorporates the material into the course program. Such programs are especially useful when expertise for a particular unit of subject matter is not readily available. These programs have the capability for real-time decisions, with branching contingent on the student's previous responses or set of responses. The numerous branching patterns often result in students following diverse paths. The most creative work involving CAI stems from researchers investigating the possibilities of tutorial instruction. Collins (1977) has been exploring the Socratic method of teaching as a way of understanding the dialogue that occurs between teachers and students in a learning situation. Collins and his colleagues have analyzed dialogues between tutors teaching different subjects including medicine and geography. The strategies involve entrapping the students into different kinds of mistakes and then confronting them with examples that show the error. In this system, students are required to derive general principles from specific cases and then learn to use these principles to make predictions about new cases. These analyses have led to the development of a set of rules. For example, one rule used to point out irrelevant factors is as follows:

1. The student asks about the value of an irrelevant factor in trying to make a prediction, then (2) point out the factor is irrelevant, or (3) ask whether the irrelevant factor affects the dependent variable.
   Example: If the student asks whether Denver or Salt Lake City is further west in trying to decide which has the colder temperature, then point out that longitude does not matter, or ask whether longitude affects temperature.
   Reason for use: This forces the student to learn what is irrelevant, as well as what *is* relevant, in making any decision. (Collins, 1977, p. 348)

Table 7.5 An annotated excerpt of the dialogue between tutorial mode of SCHOLAR and a student (The student's inputs are between asterisks.)

Dialogue	*Annotated Comments*
WHAT IS CHILE? *COUNTRY IN SOUTH AMERICA* VERY GOOD.	This is the most important property of Chile. (A tutor would suppress it on the assumption that the student knows the answer.) In evaluating the answer, it looks for "country," ignores the rest.
CORRECT OR INCORRECT? CHILE IS IN NORTHERN SOUTH AMERICA. *INCORRECT*	Location is the next most important attribute under Chile.
YOU ARE CORRECT. CHILE IS IN SOUTHWESTERN SOUTH AMERICA.	The student answers correctly, so SCHOLAR will go deeper into Location.
THE EASTERN BORDERING COUNTRY OF CHILE IS— *I DON'T KNOW* THE ANSWER IS: ARGENTINA.	This is the most important Bordering-Country of Chile.
THE BOUNDARY OF THE EASTERN BORDERING COUNTRIES OF CHILE IS THE ANDES. THE NORTHERN BORDERING COUNTRY OF CHILE IS PERU. THE NORTHEASTERN BORDERING COUNTRY IS BOLIVIA.	Since the student has missed the question, SCHOLAR presents some related Bordering-Countries.

From "Comparison of Two Teaching Strategies in Computer-Assisted Instruction," by A. Collins and M. J. Adams. In *Contemporary Educational Psychology*, 1977, 2, pp. 133–148.

Collins and Adams (1977) have used these rules to develop tutorial strategies for CAI. One such system is known as SCHOLAR and, as noted in Chapter 4, is a good indication of some of the outcomes of the cognitive-instructional emphasis. This system is capable of carrying out a tutorial dialogue with a student. Various procedures present information to the student, ask questions, assess the answers, correct mistakes, and answer student questions. The idea here is that the system is not confined to the more rigid modes of interaction typical of PI. Rather, it is based on the type of interaction that is more typical of human tutors. Some dialogue generally representative of the interactions using this system is presented in Table 7.5. The annotated comments refer to comments about the interaction provided by Collins and Adams for the reader's benefit.

The flexibility of such programs is demonstrated by the work of Collins, Adams, and Pew (1978) in a program called Map-SCHOLAR. In the program, the system was further developed to permit the integration of graphic information with verbal information. The graphic information consists of map capability; the display can be referred to by the student by either inputting names of geographical areas or by pointing to the area. Figure 7.1 shows one of the displays and the dialogue between the stu-

Now let's see what you remember about the cities of Brazil. Please name the principal cities of Brazil now blinking on the display screen.

Manaos, Sao Paulo, and Lima.

Manaos and Sao Paulo are correct. Lima is in Peru, not in Brazil. The principal cities of Brazil are blinking on the screen.

Rio de Janeiro is in Southeastern Brazil. It is on Guanabara Bay and the Atlantic.

Brasilia is in Central Brazil. It is far from the ocean.

Figure 7.1 Interactions with Map-SCHOLAR showing answer evaluation and error correction. (From "Effectiveness of an Interactive Map Display in Tutoring Geography," by A. Collins, M. J. Adams, and R. W. Pew. In *Journal of Educational Psychology,* 1978, *70,* pp. 1–7. Copyright 1978 by the Journal of Educational Psychology. Reprinted by permission.)

dent and the system. The authors describe the activity of the dialogue as follows:

> Figure 1 illustrates how Map-SCHOLAR asks map-related questions, evaluates the student's answers, and corrects any mistakes. First, the dots indicating the location of the cities appear unlabeled on the map of Brazil and start blinking. Then SCHOLAR asks the student to name the blinking cities. When the student responds, it indicates which answers were correct and prints their

names on the map. Because Lima was given erroneously as an answer (see Figure 7.1), Map-SCHOLAR pointed out that Lima is in Peru and showed where Lima is on the map. Thus, Map-SCHOLAR gives both verbal and visual feedback to help the student learn the material. (1978, p. 2)

These investigators have combined their development work in CAI with a program of research to help determine the effectiveness of the systems they are designing. Thus, Collins and Adams (1977) examined the effectiveness of the program illustrated in Figure 7.1 when compared to a linear method derived from PI in systems. These authors generally found the SCHOLAR program to be more effective in promoting student learning. Besides studying the effectiveness of the technique, the investigators designed studies to help them understand the characteristics of the system and its effects on learning performance. Thus, an investigation of the system displayed in Figure 7.1 was designed to study the effects of the Map-SCHOLAR program with its interactive-map display when compared to static labeled maps or unlabeled maps (Collins, Adams, & Pew, 1978). They found that the interactive map was more effective. They believe that the reason for this is that the map changes with relevant information. It also permits questions to be posed in a visual form not possible with static-map displays. A final general comment about tutorial systems is that it is still possible to cite easily most of the operational systems in a very short summary chapter. However, it is also obvious that if CAI will really effect the development of training programs in work organizations, it will occur because of the potential power of tutorial programs.

Evaluation of Computer-Assisted Instruction

CAI research began in the mid-1960s but initially was hampered by hardware and software difficulties. Although recent efforts have resolved many of those problems, every new system development seems to underestimate these difficulties and the time necessary to resolve them. Analyses indicate that it can take up to 300 hours to produce one hour of computer-based instruction as compared to about thirty hours for one hour of classroom instruction (Office of Technology Assessment, 1990). Actually, all this depends on the complexity of the materials. Many of the studies reported above reflect well-designed and creatively conceived research investigations. Nonetheless, most CAI investigations have been little more than demonstrations of technology with an occasional posttest after the treatment. Thus, in the following section, we discuss trends and generalizations based on a still limited number of well-conceived studies. The following tentative statements are offered:

1. From the beginning of its development, a substantial number of studies have indicated that CAI requires less time than more traditional methods to teach the same amount of material. For example, studies by the U.S. Army Signal Center and School found that the CAI course took 11 percent less time than instructor-controlled methods (U.S. Civil Service Commission, 1971). A

revision of this program resulted in further time savings, raising the average savings of all groups to 20 percent. Davis (1977–1978) describes a number of efforts in the navy training systems that cited savings time ranging from 27 percent to 50 percent, and Dossett and Hulvershorn (1983) cite similar savings for the air force in electronics training. The latter investigators also describe research where air force trainees were assigned in pairs to CAI training. They refer to this as a peer-training system and compare it with an individually trained CAI group and a traditional training group. They found no differences in achievement level between the three groups, but both CAI groups took less training time. They also found that the peer group took less time than the individual CAI group. The authors note that, if the peer results hold up in future studies, training time will be even further reduced because two trainees receive instruction at one terminal. Clearly, more research is needed on that effect, but even so, research data consistently point to decreased training time when using CAI techniques.

2. The achievement data appear to parallel PI analyses. A number of studies indicate that CAI students perform better than traditionally educated students, and very few studies have shown CAI students perform more poorly. The largest number of investigations, however, found no significant difference between the two groups.

Most of the studies that were used as a basis for the preceding statements would be included in the Nash et al. (1971) category of effectively controlled studies. Yet, the authors of this research describe a variety of difficulties that hindered the interpretation of their data. One source of difficulty was criterion contamination. The criteria used for many of the studies conducted in school settings were originally designed for traditional-instruction classes. Often, they were nationally standardized exams constructed years before CAI existed. Some investigators state that the behavioral objectives specified in the design process of CAI systems are not appropriately measured by these standardized exams. They believe that the CAI method has unique features that should lead to the specification of new behavioral objectives. For example, CAI tutorial programs might permit students to learn certain concepts that could not be taught by a group lecture; the test of these programs should therefore include measures that adequately reflect the new objectives.

Many of the studies described above, especially those in work organizations, use measures that reflect the objectives of CAI instruction. Unfortunately, some administrators are unwilling to accept innovations unless students perform adequately on the traditional normative measures, which may not be a good indicant of course objectives. One apparent solution to this problem is careful needs assessment procedures that establish the objectives and the criterion measurements before the instructional program begins. A related concern is the appropriate timing of the criterion measurements. Students in traditional methods are given their exams when they complete all their course material. In many studies, CAI students are also required to take the examination at one specified time, although they may have completed the course material days earlier or may not even have finished it. Thus, the self-pacing procedures of CAI place the student at a disadvantage. The solution to this problem depends on effective testing procedures that are used when the trainee finishes the required material. There is little sense in a system in which students are permitted to pace themselves through the entire program only to await mass testing at one designated time.

Threats to external validity resulting from the Hawthorne effect are also a problem in CAI research. Whereas control students remain in their traditional school setting, CAI students are placed in a unique situation with new equipment, observers, and a generally experimental atmosphere. Seltzer (1971) notes that the superior performance of the Mississippi group in the Stanford study occurred in a poor socioeconomic environment where the students tend to be deprived of learning materials. Thus, it is necessary to speculate on the Hawthorne effect generated by the computer terminals and experimental environment. As mentioned earlier, some researchers (such as Atkinson, 1968) have attempted to partially overcome this problem by having the control group in one study participate as CAI students in another subject. Another concern is the interactive effects of program and teacher quality (Rosenberg, 1972). In most studies, little attention is paid to the quality of the traditional instructors or to the quality of the program. The interactive effects are especially apparent in the Suppes and Morningstar (1969) Mississippi study. The authors suggest that the superior effect of CAI may have been related not to the program but to poorer teacher preparation or training that adversely affected the traditional group. To assess the results of any particular instructional program, it is necessary to examine the quality of the traditional and innovative methods.

Advantages and Limitations of Computer-Assisted Instruction

Advantages

1. The major advantage of CAI is the individualization of instruction. PI can adapt to the gross characteristics of a specific individual, but CAI has the potential for responding to detailed characteristics of trainees and their needs at a precise moment. An illustration of this is apparent in the studies that used the Map-SCHOLAR system. CAI programs can attend to individual attributes—that is, demographic information, previous performance, most recent response, and any other variable that can be programmed for and stored in the computer.

2. The reinforcement provisions of CAI systems are a real benefit to the learner. As Singer originally notes, "The program has infinite patience. It does not have preconceived notions about a student. . . . Mistakes are not penalized by scorn or sarcasm, successes are marked by positive reinforcement" (1968, p. 3).

3. CAI systems present teachers with a new role. The role keeping is performed by machine, and complete analyses of student performance are readily available. This gives the instructor time to spend with individuals or

small groups of students. Dossett and Hulvershorn (1983) note that the required student–instructor contact time in their CAI electronics course was less than 2 percent of the total training time in the study. They think that permits the following activities:

a. An instructor can provide individual student help when required
b. the instructor's role may include the management of individualized instruction and
c. more training can be conducted with a smaller staff. (p. 558)

4. Due to the data-collection provisions, CAI offers the researcher a good opportunity to gain knowledge about techniques and the instructional variables that can support their systems.

Limitations

1. At the present time, a restraining factor in the use of CAI is the limited state of knowledge. The small number of empirical studies makes generalizations about the utility of CAI extremely hazardous. In 1968 DeCecco expressed the fear described below about the emphasis on technology leading instructional efforts astray:

> All these facilities and equipment, I must remind you, are much more sophisticated than any theory of teaching we presently have. The temptation in a technological society is to allow our fantastic machines to determine our research problems and our educational practice. It is far more important that we subordinate the machines to the theoretical and practical instructional problems which, undoubtedly, the machines can help us solve. (p. 539)

In 1985 his fears were well founded.

2. The cost of CAI systems remains a serious obstacle. It is true that the cost of hardware is decreasing significantly, but there are still large costs related to development, communications, and maintenance.

3. One remaining question concerns the effects of a machine-oriented learning environment on satisfaction, motivation, and development. As noted in the discussion of PI, several studies suggest that adult learners do not prefer to be taught exclusively by machine. At the present time, students still spend very little of their time in a CAI environment, and most students like CAI instruction. However, if the technique becomes widespread, it will become necessary to ask if a rich enough stimulus environment is being provided. Systems like CAI cannot be evaluated just in terms of learner achievement. CAI leads to new environments that must be investigated in relation to attitudes and the socialization process.

AUDIOVISUAL TECHNIQUES

Both television and films extend the range of stimuli that are normally brought into the training environment; they display events and sequences of events rather than simply present objects. The implementation of this instructional technique is extensive in scope with a variety of topics covered and studies performed. Topics include such subjects as automobile dealer-training sessions, customer engineering, dentistry, driver education, literacy training, and a variety of other topics. For example, Wexley and Latham (1981) report that the Weyerhaeuser Company uses entertainment films such as the *Bridge on the River Kwai* and *Twelve O'Clock High* as a basis for discussing interpersonal and social relationships in their management school. Many professional societies such as the American Bar Association offer videotape self-study courses as a way of meeting continuing education requirements (Office of Technology Assessment, 1990). With the increasing technology and size of organizations, many are finding that the live-lecture method is inadequate to handle the number of people who need to be trained. Also, organizations are finding that bringing people from very diverse locations to live training programs is extremely expensive. The use of audiovisual techniques is considered by some organizations as a partial solution to this problem.

Originally, audiovisual techniques were criticized because it was not possible to be responsive to the needs of individual students in diverse locations. However, developing technology has begun to resolve many of those problems. For example, a basic audiovisual system now uses standard telephone transmissions, allowing students and instructors to share the same basic materials, including questions, written materials, voice communications, and so on. Many systems have electronic blackboards and slide-projection equipment at each site. One major organization expects to cut its travel budget by 50 percent for its technical training by the use of audiovisual systems (Bove, 1984). The use of techniques combining audiovisual systems such as closed-circuit television and telephone communications has spawned a new term for this type of training—*teletraining*. The following examples are chosen from a number of diverse settings to illustrate the considerable variety of approaches to audiovisual techniques.

CIGNA, a large insurance company, faced the problem of delivering training to members of their property and causality group, which consists of 20,000 employees at more than 200 locations (Kung & Rado, 1984). Their training sessions were based on a job analysis that was used to develop the knowledge and skill requirements for employees. The purpose of the training session was to teach managers how to use the knowledge-and-skill guide with their subordinates by comparing actual knowledge-and-skill profiles with job requirements. The teletraining system used permitted active participation. Lectures were minimal, and a number of other activities such as exercises were used to keep participation active. The system also used local facilitators who were also trained using teletraining.

One of my favorite examples of this technique comes from the television program *Sesame Street* (Ball & Bogatz, 1970). The reason I enjoy this example is that many readers of this book learned basic concepts from *Sesame Street,* and very few people realize that this entertainment show was really a carefully designed training program. Basically, research on this program shows that (l) children who watched the program learned more than those who did not;

(2) those skills that were emphasized on the program were learned best; and (3) disadvantaged children, as compared with middle-class children, began the program with lower achievement scores on the topics being emphasized, but their performance surpassed middle-class children who watched the program infrequently. Viewers who were not part of the experimental design often did not realize that this creative and entertaining program was an experiment designed to achieve specific behavioral objectives. These objectives were carefully determined in a series of workshops attended by representatives of all pertinent fields, including psychologists, sociologists, teachers, film makers, writers, advertising personnel, and evaluators. They established objectives related to symbolic representation, cognitive processes, and physical and social environments. For example, behavioral objectives for symbolic representation might include: "given a set of symbols, either all letters or all numbers, the child knows whether those symbols are used in reading or counting," or "given a series of words presented orally, all beginning with the same letter, the child can make up another word or pick another word starting with the same letter" (Ball & Bogatz, 1970).

The evaluation design and criteria for *Sesame Street* were developed as part of the entire instructional program. The measures included outcome criteria, such as degree of learning, as well as process measures, which assessed what occurred during instruction. The process measures included the number of hours that the child viewed the program and the child's reactions while viewing. These measures also permitted the investigator to relate the number of hours of viewing to other criteria like learning. The pretests indicated that older children performed better than younger children. However, after viewing the program, the younger children who watched regularly often scored higher than older children who were infrequent viewers. This program is a fine example of the information that can be gained by the utilization of a variety of criteria developed from carefully defined goals and objectives.

Evaluation of Audiovisual Techniques

Most of the evaluation work on audiovisual techniques were conducted many years ago. However, the results of those studies were consistent. Many evaluation studies compare audiovisual techniques to conventional lecture-type instruction. However, a surprising number of studies compare techniques to control groups that receive no instruction at all. The investigators are asking whether the student or trainee learns anything from media like television and films. As reported by Chu and Schramm (1967), these studies show that the audiovisual groups systematically improved their performance over that of control groups. Several of these studies compared the experimental groups' scores to national scores on standardized tests, with the audiovisual groups again performing in a superior manner.

The results of the studies that compare audiovisual to other techniques are consistent. Two major reviews that analyzed 393 comparisons (Schramm,

1962) and 421 comparisons (Chu & Schramm, 1967) show few significant differences in achievement, with those differences present favoring audiovisuals. From another perspective, Schramm (1962) notes that in well over 80 percent of the cases, the audiovisual technique was as good as or better than the conventional technique. Thus, the majority of "no significant difference" cases should not lead to a rejection of the technique but rather to a determination of where and how it can be used effectively. For example, audiovisuals are extremely useful when good teaching is not immediately available or where courses or materials cannot be presented in the traditional instructional mode. The identification of other effective ways to use audiovisuals will undoubtedly contribute to the implementation of the technique. As will be discussed in the next section, videodisc technology is likely to be one of the next major steps. In summary, most studies indicate that the effective use of television is dependent on the basic qualities of good teaching. Chu and Schramm think that the important qualities are "simplicity, good organization, motivation, practice, knowledge of results, rest pauses at appropriate points, cues that direct the pupil to the essential things he is to learn . . ." (1967, p. 100).

One interesting factor should be mentioned because of its implications for all training procedures. Chu and Schramm (1967) discovered that almost all investigations compared instructional groups taught completely by television to those taught completely by conventional methods. However, Chu and Schramm contend that this is not a realistic comparison "because almost nowhere in the world is television being used in classrooms without being built into a learning context managed by the teacher" (p. 6). Thus, the technique should be examined in the context of how it can fit into the total learning environment as part of the instructional process. In the previous discussion of external threats to validity, it was indicated that it is difficult to generalize from multiple-treatment environments to environments where a single treatment is used in isolation. The opposite problem is present in this discussion. It is difficult to generalize from the application of a single treatment to situations in which the media are combined with other treatments. The only solution is to begin investigations that examine combinations of treatments.

Advantages and Limitations of Audiovisual Techniques

Advantages

1. The results of a large number of experiments indicate that audiovisual techniques can be effectively used for a wide variety of subjects.

2. Audiovisual techniques are especially useful for those situations in which competent instructors are not immediately available or in which travel costs make instruction prohibitive. It is reported that U.S. companies spend $35 billion a year on training and that more than 25 percent of that is spent on airfare, lodging, and meals for trainees. Obviously, this makes the use

of audiovisual-training programs very appealing to organizations (Bove, 1984).

3. Audiovisuals are uniquely appropriate for presenting dynamic events that unfold over time. Thus, it is possible to demonstrate the terminal performance expected in a complex motor sequence (Gagńe, 1970). Pictures used in learning sequences can also provide effective feedback to the participant. This medium can be used to control time by speeding or slowing particularly important aspects of behavior and by instant replay. Good editing can highlight crucial aspects of performance.

4. This particular medium is useful for presenting events that cannot be re-created in the traditional classroom. For example, films of simulated accidents can vividly demonstrate what happens to individuals who are not wearing a seat belt.

Limitations

1. Previously, the technique used to be only a one-way communication device. Although many of the new uses, including teletraining, make the technique into a two-way communication system, most audiovisual systems in use today are still one-way communication systems. Thus, it is often necessary to use individual facilitators at the site to overcome this problem. Also, not much research exists on the effectiveness of two-way communication systems or their effects on learning. Finally, audiovisuals are not easily adaptable to those situations in which there are great differences in the ability levels or interests of the participants. PI or CAI is more effective in such cases.

2. Audiovisuals often involve complex arrangements. For example, the CIGNA teletraining program involves distribution of a national implementation schedule, arrangements with operators to initiate all phone communications, training of facilitators, and so on. Clearly, scheduling and preparation become very important factors in these types of systems. Also, although many firms are finding these systems to be cost-effective because of the large number of trainees in diverse locations, it is also true that audiovisuals are expensive and may not be cost-effective in all situations.

VIDEODISC TECHNOLOGY

One interesting innovation in this area is the development of interactive videodiscs. As described by Pursell and Russell (1990), the hardware components of videodisc systems consist of computers, videodisc players, monitors, and connecting equipment. These instruments present information in many different forms including motion pictures, stills, text, and graphics along with sound tracks. Pursell and Russell note that there are several different levels of presentation options. The simplest presents information in a preset sequence with no options for changes (similar to linear programming). The second presents information but has various options linked with multiple-choice menus (similar to branching). The most sophisticated and the system typically thought of when using the term *interactive videodisc* has the student and system interacting to produce an individual learning experience. It also involves software that has a vast array of options ranging from tapping the user's history, employing multiple branching systems, and using touch screens and light pens. Interestingly, this technology has also been used as on-the-job training. Both Apple Computer and Martin-Marietta provide employees with workstations that have the capability to display brief videodiscs about manufacturing processes. They essentially provide what is called "just-in-time" training as manufacturing systems also driven by computer systems shift from one operation to another (Office of Technology Assessment, 1990). It is estimated that each station replaces hundreds of pages of written materials.

Another example of the interactive use of videodiscs explores the possibilities of using it to promote interpersonal skills training. Table 7.6 presents a description of that system. These types of systems have produced a great deal of excitement because it combines the audiovisual power of television with individual interaction. On the other hand, careful evaluation is still a necessity. Perhaps that is made clear by the following description of a vignette that clearly was not achieving its purpose:

> One vignette, showing what probably would not happen, depicts a supervisor terminating an employee who leaps up and profusely thanks the supervisor, claiming enthusiastically that this is just what she wanted. The humor is so overbearing that it defeats its aim. Viewers were laughing so loudly at some of the situations that information was lost. (Smith, 1990, p. 410)

Many advantages of audiovisual systems are also true for videodisc technology, except more so. The more sophisticated versions permit a variety of interactive experience ranging from diagnosis to remedial coaching. The primary obstacle to the development of these systems is the tremendous costs. Pursell and Russell (1990) quote costs of microcomputer-driven systems between \$6000 and \$12,000 plus one master videodisc for each application ranging from \$1700 to \$5000. Another disadvantage noted by these writers is that master videodiscs need to be redone when the video sequence is changed. Thus, the applications are either limited to relatively stable programs or to organizations that can afford the costs. However, there is no question that videodisc technology has become increasingly popular with a growing number of organizations. In addition, a review by Fletcher (1990) of forty-seven studies being conducted in the military, industry, and higher education shows promising results. It indicates that the studies were in very diverse areas of instruction ranging from equipment maintenance, medical procedures, military operations, and science education. Videodisc was generally found to be more effective than other forms of instruction (lecture, on the job). However, Fletcher notes that at this time it was difficult to determine which features of the technology contributed most. Videodisc systems are clearly going to be an emerging new technology, but there are also many questions that need to be addressed.

Table 7.6 Automating interpersonal skills training

Training effective interpersonal skills, such as selling, remains one of the biggest challenges in training today. In many of the top insurance companies, for example, at least 75 percent of the new sales personnel leave after 3 years, largely because they are unable to develop sufficient sales skills to make an adequate income from their commissions.

A combination of automated audio/video feedback and interactive videodisc (IVD) or computer-based training (CBT) is now being used to teach sales skills (or to aid in early recognition that one is not suited to sales). One IVD system uses a laserdisc player, touchscreen monitor and a PC coupled with a videotape recorder, camera, and microphone. The IVD presents full-motion/audio demonstrations of skills such as presenting credentials, then provides review exercises with proper and improper examples of those skills. Trainees can interrupt the presentation of a skill when a mistake is made and offer a critique of the action. Feedback is given on the appropriateness of their critique.

The camera or audio recorder is then used to allow the students to demonstrate proper behavior. Trainees face a new customer (provided on the IVD) and practice the skill they just saw modeled.[1] Their performance is recorded on videotape along with the customer's conversation. Students can practice in privacy, then review their performance based on a set of criteria (from the IVD) and evaluate their own behavior. They can erase and repeat, practicing as many times as they wish. When they feel they have successfully transferred the training to their performance, trainees can show the tape to the supervisor, who provides advanced coaching.

In a pilot evaluation program, insurance agents using this training program had a 16 percent increase in calls, a 24 percent increase in kept appointments, and a 43 percent increase in approach interviews with clients. In addition, new hire training time was reduced 30 percent over traditional classroom methods, and the subsequent on-the-job learning curve decreased. For example, one agency that had been using the IVD system for over a year compared 10 agents who used the system with 17 trained by traditional methods. The 10 using the IVD program were at a level 18 months ahead of the control group after the completion of training. While it is difficult to separate the impact of the IVD training from other changes in the company, its revenues also have gone up since introduction of the system, and the agent retention rate has increased.

IBM also experimented with an IVD system coupled with a videotape camera for teaching sales skills. In a comparison with their traditional person-to-person role playing training, they found that trainees using the IVD system did much better in structuring their sales calls and developing sales skills.

A second, similar, program uses CD-ROM combined with audio feedback. Full-motion video will be available on CD-ROM within a couple of years. For some training situations, such as telephone sales, audio feedback is actually closer to the real job situation, and full-motion video is not needed. CD-ROM also costs approximately $2,000 less per training station than IVD, has larger storage capacity, and can be used more easily for non-training applications.

[1]Although the "customer" on the IVD cannot respond in all of the unexpected ways a real person might, this will change with advances in artificial intelligence.

Sources: William Ives, "Soft Skills in High Tech: Computerizing the Development of Interpersonal Skills," *Instruction Delivery Systems,* March/April 1990; and Beverly Geber, "Goodbye Classrooms (Redux)," *Training,* vol. 27, No. 1, January 1990.

From "Worker Training: Competing In the New International Economy: by Office of Technology Assessment, U.S. Congress, 1990, OTA-ITE-457, Washington, D.C.: U.S. Government Printing Office.

MACHINE SIMULATORS

Training simulators are designed to replicate the essential characteristics of the real world that are necessary to produce learning and transfer. These efforts can vary from flight simulators, which have a substantial degree of *physical fidelity* (that is, representation of the real world of operational equipment), to role-playing methods, in which the degree of physical simulation is minimal. In any case, the purpose of the simulation is to produce *psychological fidelity*—that is, to reproduce in the training tasks those behavioral processes that are necessary to perform the job. A variety of simulators have been designed for specific training purposes, including skills development, decision making, and problem solving. In this section, simulators designed for skills training will be discussed. Most of these types of devices are called machine simulators. They are more likely to be found in flight training, maintenance training, and the like. Simulations that are designed for training interpersonal skills or management skills, such as role playing, will be saved for Chapter 9, which focuses more on management and leadership training. However, before beginning a discussion of any type of simulation, it is important to discuss the reasons that simulation is considered a valuable method.

Reasons for Simulation

1. *Controlled reproducibility.* Simulations permit the environment to be reproduced under the control of the training analyst. They represent a training laboratory outside the real-world setting, where uncontrolled parameters make it difficult to produce the desired learning environment. By careful design and planning, environments can be created that supply variation in the essential characteristics of the real situation. In addition, simulation permits the trainer to expand, compress, or repeat time, depending on the needs of the trainees. A business game designed to simulate market-and-supply conditions can present six weeks of essential financial operations in six hours, and a flight simulator can provide months of aircraft-landing experience in several hours.

2. *Safety considerations.* In many cases, the required terminal behavior is too complex to be safely handled by a trainee. The simulator permits learners to be slowly introduced to the essential task characteristics, without any danger to themselves, their fellow workers, or the expensive equipment. Many observers recognize the validity of carefully planned introductions to complex tasks, like flying an airplane, but they fail to realize that many jobs, like assembly-line operations, also require considerable pretraining. Some industrial firms solve this problem by a vestibule-training program, which consists of a simulation, off the production line, of the equipment and materials used on the job. Simulations also permit the trainee to practice emergency techniques before being exposed to hazardous situations in real settings. The focus of safety should not be narrowed to skills development. It is also

Table 7.7 Terror at zero feet: A crew's simulated brush with disaster

In this accident, one can hear rain pelting the windshield. And there is thunder. "We would never take off in conditions like this," Carter said.

But true to the real event, Hill took the plane's controls while Carter spooled up the engines. They began racing down the runway.

"Eighty knots," Carter said. About 92 mph.

As the plane passed 127 knots—the speed that pilots call V_1, essentially the point of no return—the air speed indicator abruptly stopped moving.

"Wind shear!" shouted Carter as he slammed the throttles into the full "firewall" position—as much power as he could muster.

"Keep it on the runway," he told Hill, who eased the nose wheel back down onto the runway to gain as much speed as possible on the ground—a maneuver that amounts to "banking energy" for the ordeal ahead. Even with the increased ground speed, the air speed dropped 20 knots—about 23 mph.

As did the real aircraft in the real incident, the simulator began climbing steeply as it neared the end of the runway, pushing everyone back in his seat. Then came the bad news.

Decreasing air speed," Carter said.

"Sinking," he said: "200 feet . . . 160 feet . . . 140 feet . . . 80 feet."

"Bring your stick higher," he said. Hill, already fighting his control yoke as if it were a bull in a rodeo, pulled the nose higher into the air as the engines roared.

With that, pandemonium broke out in the cockpit. Lights began flashing and the control yoke began vibrating loudly like a giant rattlesnake—the "stick shaker" that warns of a stall.

An artificial voice boomed out in a deliberate but loud monotone, "Don't sink! Don't sink! Don't sink!" It was the ground proximity warning having its say.

As all appeared lost, the plane began emerging from the shear.

"Air speed recovery," said someone out of the din.

A later reading of the simulator tapes showed that the plane dropped within 20 feet of the ground before it recovered and took off.

A lot of people died on the real plane, in the days before pilots were trained to survive wind shear. This was just a simulator. But the cold sweat, fast heartbeat and weak knees were not simulated.

From "Terror at Zero Feet: A Crew's Simulated Brush with Disaster" by D. Phillips, in *The Washington Post*, January 1, 1991, p. A3.

reasonable to consider the psychological safety of a manager required to face the problems of racial strife on the job. Role playing several solutions to that situation in the comparative safety of the training environment could have some benefits. One of the most striking examples of a simulator designed to produce a dangerous safety event is the wind shear simulator. Wind shear is a sudden shift of wind that has killed thousands of air travel passengers, with over 500 in the last ten years. United Airlines training center produces all the effects of wind shear, including hydraulic stilts that mimic every bump and roll, aircraft sounds, rain pelting the windshield, and thunder. The material presented in Table 7.7 presents the conversations and happenings from a training session. After reading the material, I would guess that most observers would prefer to have pilots learn how to fly under those conditions in a simulator and would prefer not to be on board if there was a real practice try.

3. *Utilization of learning considerations.* Most simulations permit the effective utilization of learning principles. Because the environment is carefully controlled by the trainers, they can easily (1) introduce feedback, (2) arrange for practice, (3) use part or whole and massed or spaced methods, and (4) design the environment according to the best-known principles of transfer. Thus, careful design of simulations can produce an environment conducive to positive transfer.

Cost. The acquisition of skills requires practice, and if practice is not feasible in the real world, simulation provides a viable alternative. Although most simulation efforts are expensive, they are often an economical alternative to using high-priced, on-the-job equipment. For example, Americans being trained to assume vital roles in overseas environments are being exposed to simulated training settings because trial-and-error performance in foreign countries is too expensive. And, quite probably, the behavior of a beginning trainee handling a multimillion-dollar jet might quickly convince passengers to make donations to simulation-training programs. All the previously mentioned reasons for simulation have prompted the development of skill simulators. These simulators are used when the required skills are explicit and the behavior can be measured objectively. Frequently, these simulations have extensive physical fidelity and can represent a large number of potential environmental situations. Because flight simulators are becoming so complex, many airlines expect that *all* flight training soon will be done on a simulator. Simulators can be very expensive. However, after the nuclear power plant accident at Three Mile Island, there was no hesitation to design a $1 million control-room simulator to attempt to avoid such problems. Research flight simulators are built for many of the same reasons. For example, the navy's primary jet trainer is simulated for research purposes at the Naval Training Equipment Center in Orlando, Florida. This simulation includes all normal operations including carrier arrest landing and carrier simulation, which provides for ship pitch, roll, and heave, as well as variations in sea conditions, wind conditions, and turbulence. (I have flown the simulator and can attest to the complexities of landing a plane on an aircraft carrier. In my weaker moments, I might even mention that in numerous tries, I never even hit the carrier but rather managed to land in the ocean.) The description of the wind shear incident in Table 7.7 indicates just how complex a flight simulator can be.

The design of machine simulators need not be limited to expensive, large-scale operations. Many efforts are part-simulations, which replicate a critical or difficult portion of the task without attempting to provide a complete environment. Also, simulators are not just useful in large-scale system training such as that found in flight simulation. A good example of another use of simulation is provided in a study by Salvendy and Pilitsis (1980), who investigated its use in teaching medical students suturing techniques needed in operations. The traditional method consists of a lecture–slide presentation and videotape describing the technique. Included in the instructions were materials related to the general geometry of the suture path, descriptions of the instruments and their functions, and general guidelines. The student then used these instructions while practicing on pigs' feet until the instructor determined that the student was performing the task appropriately. One simulator used as an alternative to the above procedure is known as the "Inwound" procedure simulator. A description of this device and its characteristics is as follows:

> The "Inwound" procedure simulator . . . assists the student in acquiring the manipulative motor skills during the inwound procedure phase by puncturing a simulated tissue with an electrically activated needle holder. . . . The simulated tissue contains related wound path geometry such as "entry" and "exit" points. The overall unit is mounted on a revolving fixture located in a mannequin-type arm. The student is able to monitor his/her progress by gaining information as to correctness of motions through the student feedback console. This console consists of 11 clearly marked amber and red lights that correspond to correct and incorrect motions. Both audio and visual channels are activated by the suture needle as the needle is guided by the student through the "wound." If the various phases (entry, depth, exit) are performed correctly, the amber lights are activated. . . . An incorrect needle motion while the needle is in the wound causes a corresponding red light and tone generator to be activated momentarily. When the needle is corrected in its path, the related visual and auditory feedback is discontinued. Number of errors, time in the wound, and number of cycles performed for each of the procedure phases are recorded individually on the monitoring console. (pp. 155–156)

These investigators also designed a knot-tying simulator. Besides the simulators, another training condition in this study consisted of a perceptual training method where students observed filmed performance of experienced surgeons and inexperienced medical students in addition to traditional techniques.

Generally, the investigators found that simulation training and perceptual training improved the performance of the medical students beyond the traditional training methods. In addition, the investigators collected psychophysiological measures of stress such as heart-rate variance and muscle tension. The data also tend to confirm that students trained by simulation method showed less stress when they were required to perform new suturing tasks. Another interesting and more amusing study of part-simulators in a laboratory study is provided by Rubinsky and Smith (1973). They examined simulated-accident occurrence in the use of a grinding wheel. Traditionally, teaching the operation of power tools relies on written or verbal instructions, with an occasional demonstration. These authors devised a task that exposed operators (college students) to a simulated accident (a jet of water). The "accident" was designed to occur when the operator stood in front of the grinding wheel during the starting operation—that is, the time when there is the greatest danger of the wheel exploding. The investigators found that those subjects who experienced a simulated accident as part of their training program were less likely to repeat the hazardous behavior than those who were given written instructions or demonstrations of safe procedures. The results were maintained over a series of retention tests. The authors suggest that simulated accidents might be effective in reducing power-tool accidents. Certainly, this procedure provides an interesting form of feedback for incorrect responses.

Due to the large scale of many of these simulation efforts and investigator concerns about the adequacy of simulation, a number of topics are often discussed whenever simulators are being considered. These are discussed next.

Fidelity of simulation. Most researchers maintain that simulation efforts must have psychological fidelity (that is, the representation of the essential behavioral processes necessary to perform the job) as their chief objective. However, the question remains, How much physical representation is necessary to achieve psychological fidelity? The entire task is rarely produced in a simulation. In some cases, it is simply too expensive or dangerous; in other instances, certain factors are judged as not important to the learning of the task (for example, training the pilot in opening or closing the door to the aircraft). However, the choice is not always clear. For example, it is still not certain whether the simulation of motion is a necessary aspect of pilot training. Besides the question of whether such variables contribute to learning, this becomes an important question because of the extra cost involved.

It costs at least $250,000 extra to include motion as a part of flight simulation (Orlansky & String, 1977). However, little is gained in the production of expensive simulators in which tasks that are critical for positive transfer are being excluded. These issues reflect the same problems faced in the design of all training programs. Initially, the only solution is careful design based on needs assessment techniques. After accomplishing that part, questions about the relationship of certain components to training effectiveness can only be determined by a careful program of empirical research.

Transfer of training issues. It is important to remember that simulation efforts are directly related to transfer of training. Individuals are trained on a simulator so that they will perform better in the work situation. Many of the parameters involving transfer were considered in "The Conditions of Transfer" in Chapter 4. However, despite accomplishments in the literature and laboratories, the degree of understanding that might be expected has not been achieved. Researchers are attempting to design systems that permit predictions concerning whether a particular device will lead to positive transfer. For example, Swezey (1982–1983) applied a model of the transfer process developed by Wheaton (1976) to two different training devices in order to predict which one would lead to more transfer. Some of the parameters of the model include

1. *Task commonality:* whether the device permits the trainee to practice skills required for actual performance on the real task.

2. *Equipment similarity:* whether the equipment involves physically similar equipment and the same information requirements.
3. *Learning deficit analysis:* an examination of the task to determine its relationship to the input repertoire of trainees and the difficulty level of training the necessary skills and knowledges.
4. *Training technique analysis:* an estimate of the instructional effectiveness of the device based on the degree to which relevant principles of learning are used.

Research involving models like this one are an encouraging sign that it may soon be possible to understand what variables contribute to transfer of learning. Simulator training for complex skills, motor or otherwise, offers a real opportunity for research that will contribute to an understanding of the learning process. Most sponsors prefer to have their trainees learn skills on simulated instruments rather than on original equipment. Thus, the research opportunities are there; it is not necessary to sell anyone on the need for training. Rather, it is necessary to produce the carefully designed research that contributes to understanding and knowledge. The importance of gaining this understanding is further illustrated by a problem that up to now has received very little attention. That is, increasing evidence indicates that persons become ill in simulators. The term *simulator sickness* is now being used to describe this phenomenon. Symptoms include disorientation, dizziness, nausea, spinning sensations, and confusion. McCauley (1984) found that such disturbances can occur during simulation trials and often continue for hours afterward. He notes that the sickness can result in a number of serious problems including such posteffects as placing the individual at risk when in such real-life situations as driving a car. Again, noting the description of the wind shear-training session in Table 7.7 probably makes this problem salient for most readers.

TEAM TRAINING

To perform in many of the complex systems that exist in the world of work, there clearly needs to be coordinated activity by a group of individuals. This led early investigators to define a team as a group working together to achieve a common goal (Blum & Naylor, 1968). The activities of teams are especially apparent for groups that operate machine simulators such as those of airplane pilot crews, air traffic controllers, nuclear power plant operators, and the like. The reader can imagine that there is intense interest in how to train teams effectively to work together. Of course, the concern about *team training* could apply equally well to other work groups such as surgical teams in hospitals. Although it does not take much imagination to speculate about this, many activities in organizations likely involve the work of teams. At the time of the last edition of this book in 1986, virtually no research was being conducted on this important topic. Indeed, a more recent review of the literature (Salas, Dickinson, Tannenbaum, & Converse, 1991) could hardly find any empirical work on teams up through the mid-1980s. At that time, most training efforts had not even decided whether teams require special considerations beyond the principles used in the training of individuals. The state of research in this important area is well captured by the following quote:

> Relatively little research has been devoted to carefully examining such issues as how team members interact with each other; whether such interactions vary over time, with what situation, and/or with team experience; what meaning can be assigned to such terms such as teamwork, coordination, and cooperation; and what role is played by the leader in team behavior. (Dyer, 1984, p. 294)

In the past five years, a group of researchers has seriously increased effort to begin to understand team behavior and team training. One obstacle to understanding teams had been that no one seemed to understand what they actually do while performing. In addressing this concern, Glickman, Morgan, and their colleagues studied military command and control teams while they were being trained (Morgan, Glickman, Woodard, Blaiwes, & Salas, 1986; Glickman, Zimmer, Montero, Guerette, Campbell, Morgan, & Salas, 1987). Glickman et al. found that two different sets of behaviors evolved. One set, which was labeled *taskwork,* was the development of skills related to execution of tasks. The other set, *teamwork,* described behaviors necessary to perform effectively as a member of a team. Morgan et al. collected critical behaviors from instructors and team members and identified ninety behaviors describing crew development. The broad dimensions included effective communication, coordination, team spirit and morale, cooperation, adaptability, acceptance of suggestions or criticism, and giving suggestions. Morgan et al.'s analysis of naval gunnery crews reveals that these dimensions could be used to distinguish between effective and ineffective crews. Basically, the effective crews had a higher number of the critical behaviors in each dimension. Morgan et al. also hypothesize that "a substantial portion of the energies devoted to building better crews can be accounted for in terms of activities that are aimed at people (i.e., other team members) and relationships" (p. 17).

Later research began to examine the specific behaviors across training phases that distinguished between successful and unsuccessful teams (Oser, McCallum, Salas, & Morgan, 1989). Oser et al. also found that it was possible to identify sets of team behaviors that are observed to be associated with effective teams and that they could discriminate between more and less effective teams. Using naval gunnery teams, this investigation examined the relationship between the team behaviors and the performance of the gunnery team. Some of the specific behaviors that distinguished between effective and ineffective teams can be found in Table 7.8.

In another study of teams performing during a helicopter flight simulation, the investigators tape-recorded the preflight brief and the simulator performance (Franz, McCallum, Lewis, Prince, & Salas, 1990). Then raters

Table 7.8 T-test results for significantly correlated behaviors between more effective and less effective teams

Behaviors
Helped another member who was having difficulty with a task.
Made positive statements to motivate the team.
Assisted another member when the latter had a difficult task to perform.
Praised another member for doing well on a task.
Made negative comments about the team or training. *(I)*
Suggested to another that he recheck his work so that he could find his own mistake.
Raised his voice when correcting another member. *(I)*
Thanked another member for catching his mistake.
Coordinated gathering of information in an effective manner.
Provided suggestions on the best way to locate an error.

[1]$N = 6$
I = Ineffective behaviors, the remainder were effective behaviors.
From "Toward A Definition of Teamwork: An Analysis of Critical Behaviors" by R. Oser, G. A. McCallum, E. Salas, B. B. Morgan Jr., 1989, Technical Report 89-004, Human Factors Division, Naval Training Systems Center, Orlando, FL.

reviewed the transcripts and independently indicated which behaviors were displayed by the crew. A safety officer independently rated the crew on their safety performance. They found that behaviors in two broad dimensions, leadership and decision making, particularly distinguished between effective and ineffective crews. Some specific behaviors for leadership were behaviors that included determining clearly the tasks to be assigned and keeping the crew focused on the task at hand. The decision-making behaviors included gathering information before making a decision, crew members checking information, and members frequently identifying alternatives and contingencies available to them.

These important studies are beginning to provide information about the differences between effective and ineffective teams. As these differences are systematically determined, they will clearly lead to recommendations about how teams should be trained. Swezey and Salas (1991) have already begun to try to develop guidelines for team training. They have preliminarily identified a number of areas, but four seem particularly important:

1. Team training should encourage communication that supports the desire to work for the team and provides encouragement and respect for team members and their input.
2. Team training must emphasize interaction and the need for team members to depend on one another.
3. Team training must emphasize the team and member goals and

responsibilities. It must also provide for the opportunity to learn the responsibilities of team members and challenge the team to react to changes and unexpected events.

4. Training must emphasize teamwork skills. It must be organized to address the amount of teamwork needed and provide examples of both acceptable and unacceptable teamwork. In addition, it must stress interdependence and flexibility.

Another particularly interesting development, which has important implications, is the application of cognitive mental models to understanding teamwork. Cannon-Bowers, Salas, and Converse (1990) suggest that accurate mental models permit team members to predict the behavior of team members and anticipate information requirements of members even when there is no actual communication. Their analysis of team tasks suggests that members need to understand a number of facets. First, they must understand the equipment with which they are working. Second, they must understand the team task and how it is achieved in the sense of how information is processed and shared. Finally, members must understand their own roles and contributions—meaning how and when to interact or when to change their own behavior to meet the needs of the team. These points certainly raise the issue of the relationship between team and individual training. At the moment, there are no answers to questions such as whether individual training should be offered first or what should be included in individual training as compared with team-training efforts. These investigators further speculate that the extent of overlap between team members' mental models has an important impact on the team's effectiveness. For example, shared models would mean that there would be more successful use of implicit strategies because team members would anticipate each other's needs even in situations when they do not have time to communicate. This is a very intriguing idea, which fits in well with the thought that shared mental models permit the team to use more of their attention to deal with emergencies and anticipate each other's needs. Of course, the other implication of these ideas is that if shared mental models do increase the effectiveness of teams, then training team members in their use is perhaps possible. Research on this issue and other issues regarding team training are certain to continue to appear in the next decade, and it is a pleasure to see that the topic has been so nicely advanced in the last several years.

BEHAVIOR MODIFICATION

Behavior modification is a direct application of the principles of reinforcement developed by B. F. Skinner in his operant-conditioning studies. Originally, behavior modification was used in clinical settings as a change technique for maladaptive behavior. Some training analysts suggest that the principles of behavior modification might be effectively used in the design of training programs (Nord, 1970; Feeney, 1972). The basic procedures suggested by this approach can be summarized in the following way:

1. An assessment is performed to specify where problems exist and to help in the determination of precise behaviors that require elimination, modification, or development.
2. Reinforcers appropriate to the situation and to the individual are selected.
3. The implementation of the actual program consists of a variety of different procedures dependent on the behavior of the trainees.
4. Desired responses are immediately and continuously reinforced. Once the behavior is established, intermittent programs of reinforcement are instituted.
5. Evaluation procedures are employed to determine the degree of change.

The original efforts describing these techniques actually consisted of a reinterpretation of previous work into a reinforcement framework to demonstrate the potential value of the system. For example, Nord (1970) describes a program instituted by a retail firm to reduce tardiness and absenteeism. The absenteeism problem involved secretaries and sales and stock personnel at the firm's stores, warehouses, and offices. The firm instituted a program whereby monthly drawings were held for prizes, which were appliances worth approximately $25. There was one prize for each twenty-five employees. To be eligible, the employee had to have a perfect attendance and punctuality record for the preceding month. Similar drawings for a major prize (such as a color television) were based on performance over a six-month period. After one year, absenteeism and tardiness were reduced to about one-fourth the level prior to the program. Sick-leave payments were reduced approximately 62 percent. Nord concludes that the lottery system served as a stimulus to reinforce punctuality and attendance at work.

Feeney (1972) notes that particular responses and associate contingencies represent the core of the behavior modification system. Proponents of the system, like Feeney, criticize other training efforts for emphasizing the teaching of processes like general-management skills with the hope that the knowledge gained will solve a problem. Instead, Feeney suggests a performance audit to define a particular difficulty, followed by the reinforcement of the appropriate responses necessary to overcome the problem. Feeney demonstrated these principles in a widely publicized project conducted at Emery Air Freight, which drew attention to the possibilities of behavior modification as a training technique. A performance audit indicated that employees believed that, nine out of ten times, they were responding to customer inquiries within ninety minutes. Emery Air Freight was also committed to combining small packages into large containers. The employees believed that they were effectively using containerized shipments 90 percent of the time. Feeney's data show that the responses to customer inquiries were occurring within ninety minutes only 30 percent of the time and that the use rate on shipments was actually 45 percent. Focusing on these particular problems, Feeney instituted a program based on the principles of positive reinforcement. He talked with employees and found out their needs. Then, he used positive reinforcers to reward early approximations of the desired terminal responses. He focused on frequent reinforcement at the onset of the program and later switched to more intermittent programs. In all cases, the reinforcement was directly related to the performance. This emphasis on performance and feedback is illustrated by one aspect of the program, called the feedback system. The key elements are the following:

1. Find out what people think they should be doing.
2. Find out what they are doing—not by asking but by getting the raw data and comparing that with their perceptions.
3. Be sure feedback is measurable and that it gives comparisons to performance in previous similar periods.
4. Ensure that feedback gets to the proper unit in the organization—to the people who need it, as well as to their supervisors and intermediate management levels.
5. Make certain the feedback is timely—provided as soon after the performance as possible. The best procedure is to have the worker measure his own performance. That way, feedback is immediate; the employee is more likely to accept it and more likely to react favorably to it.
6. Design feedback in positive terms; even if there is no performance improvement, at least the employee can be complimented on his honesty in reporting accomplishments. (Feeney, 1972, p. 8)

Feeney estimates that Emery Air Freight saved several million dollars in a three-year period because of the changes in performance resulting from the application of reinforcement principles. Although Feeney's study received considerable publicity because of the estimates of savings produced by the technique, it is really only possible to suggest that this method has potential as a behavior-change technique. The demonstrations and reinterpretations of previous programs do not permit any powerful statements about the accomplishments of the program or about the important parameters of the technique. When a program like the one used at Emery Air Freight is introduced, many variations in the environment could be responsible for changes in behavior. Unfortunately, the lack of scientific procedures makes it difficult to ascertain why changes occurred. It has already been mentioned that on-the-job training is often employed to avoid the development of training programs and generally indicates a lack of commitment by the organization. Perhaps the use of any method, including behavior modification, with appropriate fanfare and commitment by management, could result in changes similar to those achieved by Emery Air Freight. Any real gains in understanding await the employment of procedures beyond anecdotal case studies without control procedures. Unfortunately, as noted by Wexley (1984), the actual implementation and evaluation of behavior modification techniques in work organizations remains limited.

However, a few examples of well-conceived and thoughtful studies do demonstrate the possibilities of behavior modification techniques. One set of these studies is demonstrated by the work of Komaki, Heinzmann, and Lawson (1980) in reducing accidents. That work is described in Chapter 6 (p. 208–210) as an example of quasi-experimental designs and in Chapter 4 in "feedback." The reader should reexamine those studies because they provide a fine illustration of the possibilities of behavior modification as well as a good illustration of the use of effective research designs.

Certain aspects of behavior modification promise that careful attention will be paid to some of the most important determinants of program success. First, the emphasis on program audits before and after the implementation of the technique suggests that the proponents of behavior modification will look at the accomplishments of their program rather than assume that success will follow automatically. Second, the concern with particular performance problems and associated behaviors requires careful needs assessment procedures before the design of the program. If this technique follows a path that includes needs assessment and evaluation, there is reason for an optimistic outlook. On the other hand, the identification of positive reinforcers in complex organizations represents a serious obstacle. In any particular job, it will be necessary to determine which stimuli serve as reinforcing agents. These reinforcers may be attention, status, privileges, promotion, and recognition, as well as the more obvious reinforcers such as bonuses, pay raises, and vacation time.

McIntire (1973) cautions us that the determination of reinforcers for adult behavior is a complex task. For example, he suggests that it is difficult to modify safety practices in certain high-accident industries (for example, coal mining) by having contests and awarding lapel pins because these stimuli are typically not viewed as positive reinforcers. More likely, peer approval and the social reinforcers controlled by experienced workers would be effective. These reinforcements can be established by having respected and experienced workers serve as models to demonstrate the safe approach or by pairing a new trainee with an individual who uses correct procedures, thereby providing peer approval of the safe approach. The various views on motivation and learning (see Chapter 4) suggest that the reinforcing stimuli will be viewed differently by different individuals. In these cases, the treatment of individual differences results in additional complications for behavior modification. If different reinforcers are needed for different responses for different learners, the implementation of this technique in an on-the-job setting or in a training environment will present a real challenge.

One criticism often made about behavior modification in clinical settings (and likely to be repeated in training environments) is related to the manipulation of human behavior by reward systems. Actually, any training technique is designed to modify human behavior, and it is unreasonable to single out behavior modification if the method succeeds in changing behavior. The key issue should be the careful determination of individual and organizational goals. Where conflict exists, the issues must be resolved before training begins. A sure way to fail, no matter what the technique, is to proceed with a training program when there is wide-scale disagreement about the goals and objectives. If behavior modification requires the organization to face these problems, it has a definite advantage.

Training Techniques Emphasizing Managerial and Interpersonal Skills

8

CHAPTER

This chapter deals with training techniques that are related to interpersonal skills. Some strategies emphasize self-awareness, whereas others focus on skills for establishing communication and relationships with others. As such, many of the techniques are used with people who supervise others, such as managers in work organizations. Of course, these types of techniques are also used in other settings where people interact, such as school principals and teachers, hospital administrators and staff, and teachers and students. In part, the grouping of techniques in this and the preceding chapters is arbitrary. Thus, as with most techniques, behavioral role modeling involves knowledge components as well as the practice of interpersonal skills. I chose to include it here because of the technique's emphasis on learning interpersonal strategies.

SIMULATIONS

In Chapter 7, simulations oriented toward skills training were presented as important components of simulation training. This presentation also applies to simulations involving interpersonal skills. It would therefore be useful for the reader to reexamine that material before continuing with this section.

The use of simulations in interpersonal skills training involves a variety of techniques and procedures. Sometimes the simulation forms the foundation for the entire training program, as in the technique called *business games.* In other cases, the simulation is one part of a much larger training exercise. In a technique called *behavioral role modeling,* particular situations are simulated; however, a variety of other procedures, including audiovisual presentations, role playing in simulations, obtaining group feedback on role-playing performances, and trying out behavior on the job, are also involved. In that sense, labeling sections "simulations" or "role playing" is a simplification for presentation purposes.

Business Games

A survey by Faria (1989) has found that business games are now a widely used technique. As Thornton and Cleveland (1990) note, the games are extremely diverse in terms of a large number of aspects including complexity of the issues addressed, the number of participants, and the complexity of the tasks. They range from simple situations for individuals to complex simulations. Business games are a direct outgrowth of war games used to train officers in combat techniques. One military war game developed in 1798 used a map with 3600 squares, each representing a distinctive topographical feature, on which pieces representing troops and cavalry were moved (Raser, 1969). After visiting the Naval War College in 1956, members of the American Management Association developed the first business game. It is estimated that over 30,000 executives participated in the large number of games that were developed in the following five years (Stewart, 1962). Dill, Jackson, and Sweeney give a general description of business games:

> A business game is a contrived situation which imbeds players in a simulated business environment where they must make management-type decisions from time to time, and their choices at one time generally affect the environmental conditions under which subsequent decisions must be made. Further, the interaction between decisions and environment is determined by a refereeing process which is not open to argument from the players. (1961, pp. 7–8)

Most business games include the following steps (Greenlaw, Herron, & Rawdon, 1962; Moore, 1967):

1. The participants are first oriented to the simulated game by instructions describing the business objectives, decisions required, and rules of the game.
2. The competing teams then organize themselves and become cognizant of background information on the operations of the business. Then, the first series of decisions are made. Depending on the simulation, the decision may be based on one day or several months of operations.
3. After the first period is completed, the decisions for the competing teams are given to the game administrators.
4. The results are tabulated, manually or by computer, and are returned to the team participants along with other information that describes changes in their operating environment.
5. The cycle is repeated a number of times. Usually, at the completion of the game, the results are analyzed in a critique session.

Although this description is appropriate for most business games, there are many variations. For example, the complexity of the games in terms of days played and variables implemented as part of the gaming process varies greatly.

The early business games were nearly all designed to teach basic business skills. For example, the following is a description of one of the more complex games, known as the Carnegie Tech Management Game:

> The packaged detergent industry has served as a general model for the industry of the game. The selection of this industry for our model was primarily one of convenience. Its advantages included the existence of a national market, a small number of firms, and a set of differentiated products. . . . There are three companies in the game. The players have the role of executives in the three competing companies. Each firm consists of one factory, located in one of the four geographical territories that comprise the total detergent market. At this factory, there are the following facilities: (1) a raw-materials warehouse, (2) production facilities that can be used to produce different mixes of product, (3) a factory warehouse for the storage of finished product, and (4) offices and facilities for new-product research and development. (Cohen, Cyert, Dill, Kuehn, Miller, Van Wormer, & Winters, 1962, pp. 105–106)

The players receive realistic and copious data in almost all areas of operations, including finance, sales, production, and marketing. They are expected to make realistic decisions based on this information. The computer processing of players' decisions, based on a programmed economic model, results in a new supply of data, and the cycle repeats.

Interestingly, whereas most of the early games involved skills similar to those necessary for the Carnegie Tech Management Game, some of the newer games are just as concerned with interpersonal skills such as the ability to communicate effectively. Some of these types of simulations are spin-offs from the concept of an assessment center. The term *assessment center* refers to a standardized set of simulated activities. The activities, which should be based on a careful needs assessment of the job, could include business games, leaderless group discussions, and so on. The original purpose of these activities was to assess individuals for management jobs under controlled testing conditions. Typically, candidates for these jobs would be assessed in groups of six or seven by a highly trained group of assessors. They might be assessed on anywhere from ten to fifteen dimensions, such as oral communication skill, organization and planning ability, and decision making. A small part of a description of an individual's performance in an assessment center is presented in Table 8.1. Even from the short summary provided of Mr. Smith's performance, it is clear that there are at least two types of organizational questions that can be asked as a result of such activities. There is an assessment question, which refers to who should be selected, and there is a development question, which refers to how people can be trained to perform better on these job-relevant activities. Bray (1976) notes that it is now common for organizations to spend several days in assessment activities. Several more days

Table 8.1 Sample of descriptions and strengths and weaknesses from a candidate in an assessment center

Smith's overall performance in the Management Development Centre (MDC) was average or below average on most exercises. He showed strengths in energy and initiative.

In the background interview, Smith was extremely open in discussing his problems and hopes in detail. He came across as a loyal, hard-working, highly motivated person who had a strong desire to do a good job, but he was weak in creativity, initiative, independence, and leadership skills. He appeared to be tenacious and have a high stress tolerance but to be weak in problem analysis. He struck the assessor as being overwhelmed by his job, where his efforts are not bearing the fruit he would like. He may well have feared for his job, given the division's performance. Delegation seemed weak, as was subordinate development. He felt the only way to train was to teach by example. Sensing poor morale, he did not know how to improve it.

Questioning in the 'research budget' fact-finding exercise was not well organized, but effective. He appeared to find decision making difficult, but once the decision was made, he stuck to his idea. Slightly nervous, he was not stressed by the resource person.

Writing seemed to be a weak area. Smith's financial presentation was hard to read and disorganized. Similar observations were made about his creative writing assignment, and his in-basket.

Strengths

Work standards: Tried hard in every exercise; worked very hard on job; did not want to settle, personally, for less than the best. Was disappointed by own performance, as indicated by his self-evaluation.

Intelligence: Fast reader, caught on fast.

Corporate thinking: A company man, very loyal.

Integrity: Will not compromise convictions, e.g., copy-machine discussion.

Energy: Active in all exercises.

Weaknesses

Use of delegation: Not effective on job, average in in-basket. He reported he did a lot of work that should be done by subordinates.

Financial analytical ability: Below average on financial problems, e.g., missed opportunity to change product mix.

Temper: When he did not get his way in discussion, he became obstructive to leader.

Impact: Good first impression—after that, would not stand out in a crowd.

Adapted from "The Use of Assessment Centres in Management Development," by W. C. Byham. In B. Taylor and G. L. Lipett (Eds.), *Management Development and Training Handbook.* Copyright 1975 by McGraw-Hill Book Company (UK) Limited. Adapted by permission.

are then spent in developmental activities, which include training sessions and feedback to participants. While the latter activity is more relevant to our purposes, the fact that assessment centers can be used for these multiple objectives again speaks to the complex systems' nature of most organizational activities. Unfortunately, as noted by Wexley and Latham (1981), there are no published evaluation studies of the developmental learning part of assessment centers. However, there has been increasing effort in the area of using simulations as a learning technique.

One of the most carefully developed simulation efforts is known as Looking Glass, Inc. (McCall & Lombardo, 1982). Its purpose is the development of management teams, which is most relevant to the questions of training addressed here. A brief description of Looking Glass follows:

> Looking Glass, Inc. is a hypothetical medium-sized glass manufacturing corporation. . . . For a simulation, Looking Glass is quite realistic. Complete with annual report, plausible financial data and a variety of glass products, the simulation creates the aura of an authentic organization. Participants are placed in an office-like setting, complete with telephones and an interoffice mail system. The positions actually filled in the simulation are the top management of the corporation, including four levels ranging from president to plant manager. . . . The company consists of three divisions whose environments vary according to the degree of change, with one division's environment being relatively placid, another turbulent, and the third a mixture of the two. Lasting six hours, the simulation is intended to be a typical day in the life of the company. It begins by placing each participant face-to-face with an in-basket full of memoranda. Together with background information common to all participants, this information, which differs somewhat from division to division, level to level, and position to position, constitutes the stimulus. Participants spend the rest of the day responding to these interlocking sets of stimuli, acting and interacting as they choose. Contained in the collective in-baskets of the 20 participants are more than 150 different problems that participating managers might attend to. The problems vary in importance, and they also vary, realistically, in how apparent or hidden they are to the one or more individuals who ought to be concerned about them. Also true to life, the number of problems far exceeds the time available to deal with them. (Kaplan, Lombardo, & Mazique, 1983, p. 29)

The purpose of this simulation is management development, both as individual members and as members of a team. It involves capturing communication and group dynamics in a way that permits managers to learn both by doing and by the feedback provided at the end of the exercises. Although what happens during this simulation varies somewhat with each group, there are several stages:

1. *Preparing for the simulation.* This stage starts with meeting the team and assessing both their willingness and readiness to participate in the simulation. During this period, the group also tries out experiential methods and begins with low- to moderate-risk situations. Because simulations involve public scrutiny, it is necessary to spend time understanding group functioning and building relationships between teams and staff. This also involves feedback to individuals and the team.
2. *The simulation.* During this stage, the group spends a complete day in the Looking Glass, Inc., simulation. The participants begin by reading a thick set of materials, including annual reports, job descriptions, and memos that they "wrote or received." The participants then spend the rest of the day reacting to the 150 or so problems and running the company. They

work in an officelike setting and can hold meetings, call each other on the phone, write memos, read, plan, and so on.

3. *Feedback.* Debriefing sessions involving participants and consultants are designed to provide both individual and group learning. Kaplan et al. (1983) describe the performance of one group of seventeen managers who came from the same organization. At the time of their attendance at the simulation, their organization, which was a public agency in a midwestern city, was besieged by problems. At the end of this group's participation, the members of the team and the consultants reached the following conclusions about themselves as a team:
   a. Most team members spent their time sitting alone at their desk doing paperwork in a cloud of cigarette smoke. This was contrasted with other groups who usually spent their time tracking down information and "fighting fires."
   b. The group wrote over 150 memos, which was about twice as many a group that size usually wrote.
   c. In general, the managers did not choose well between high- and low-priority items. As a result of these and other similar patterns, the team reached conclusions about how their individual behavior was hurting their performance as a team. They also discussed their simulated performance and its relation to their on-the-job performance.
4. *Application.* After the simulation and debriefing, the procedure calls for the application of what the team has learned. One way this is done is to resolve one problem identified by the team. This is known as a breakthrough project. The consultants try to help the group choose a project that is both important and resolvable. If the breakthrough occurs, the group will achieve both a tangible result and a real boost in self-confidence.

The advantages and disadvantages of business games such as these are similar to those expressed for other types of simulation efforts. Thus, experience is necessary to provide the opportunity to develop the capabilities to perform. Yet, most firms cannot afford the trial-and-error learning period necessary for the development of such skills. Simulations and business games are seen as the solution to this problem. The games provide practice in decision making, interaction among various components of the firm, and interaction among participants. Similar to machine simulations, business games permit control over time. Thus, numerous samples can be presented in a short period of time. Furthermore, most games place a premium on planning that requires the participants to consider objectives, long-term plans, and overall point of view. The feedback provisions and dynamic quality of the play are seen as being intrinsically motivating to the participant. Some early writers (Bass & Vaughan, 1966) warn us that the dynamic quality of the environment makes it difficult to use games effectively as a teaching tool. In some games, participants may become so involved in the excitement and in the competitive aspects of the game that they lose sight of the principles and evaluations of consequences that are its most important aspects. Instead, participants tend to become more concerned with beating the system and one another. Clearly, this is a serious danger unless the game involves careful feedback sessions.

Also, of course, the effectiveness depends on the design of the game, which should itself be based on careful needs assessment. If the purpose of the game based on the needs assessment is to provide a competitive atmosphere, then it should be designed that way. The Looking Glass, Inc., simulation obviously has goals related to team development, and thus the game is designed to foster cooperation. There is no reason for a business game to have competitiveness as an inherent aspect, unless that is its purpose. Another issue relates to the fidelity of the simulation. Most business games are not based on a real business enterprise but (ideally) on psychological fidelity principles. Of course, this is simply another way of saying that the design of the simulation must be based on the same careful needs assessment procedures as any other training technique. The problem here is that the simulation is designed to be relevant to the large number of organizations who send participants. Very complex needs assessments are required to prevent particular solutions rather than basic principles and concepts being carried away from the game and inappropriately applied in the real organizational setting. As a step in this direction, McCall and Lombardo (1979) have analyzed Looking Glass by directly observing the participants. The research tracked various activities, including amount of paperwork, telephone time, time in meetings, and the like, and found it to be very similar to the composition of tasks in managers' jobs. In a sense, that type of analysis provides information about physical fidelity. Of course, the most interesting questions are whether psychological fidelity is produced and whether learned behavior actually transfers to the job. The issue of evaluation has a long but not very productive history.

Shortly after business games first became popular, McGehee and Thayer (1961) stated that there was no research on the relative effectiveness of games as compared with other techniques. There also were no data on the utility of various approaches, like competition or no competition and complex or simple games. These authors conclude, "For all we know, at this time, there may be a negative or zero relationship between the kinds of behavior developed by business game training and the kinds of behavior required to operate a business successfully" (p. 223). Since these authors stated their opinion, other investigators have expressed concern about the cost of gaming (for example, Raia, 1966) and the continued lack of descriptive and statistical information. In 1971 Campbell concluded, "There have been almost no recent attempts to study the development of problem-solving and decision-making skills, even though a number of strategies exist for developing these skills" (p. 585).

At this time, the 1961 and 1971 comments of McGehee and Thayer and Campbell continue to provide an accurate description of the vast number of business games. In the most recent *Annual Review,* Tannenbaum and Yukl (1992) reach the general conclusion that there is little evidence to indicate that these kinds of simulations result in any long-term improvement in management effectiveness. A particular problem identified by Hsu (1989) relates to what the game is supposed to accomplish. He points out that most games are designed to achieve learning related to problem-solving and interpersonal skills, yet that is not typically what is evaluated. He eloquently notes, "A violin practice lesson should not be judged by its musical beauty but by how much effort need be invested in fingering, bowing, and expression before the piece can be played for the audience to enjoy" (p. 429). Thus, the heavy emphasis on who wins the game or makes the most money has become a distraction in uncovering the characteristics of games that might work in effecting changes in key behaviors. After all, it is the key behaviors that should be learned in order for anything to transfer into the work situation.

One hopeful sign is the careful developmental work involving Looking Glass, Inc. Kaplan et al. (1983) describe an evaluation effort involving the seventeen managers from the public agency described previously. In that case, the authors presented process data describing the qualitative changes the observers had noted during the simulation. They also collected questionnaire data from the managers, who self-reported their responses on a variety of issues including trust within management team, their own management effectiveness, and so on. Those data are presented in Table 8.2. As shown in the table, these data were collected before the simulation, three weeks after the simulation, and six months after the simulation. As can be seen, there were a large number of reported positive changes from before the simulation to the three-week period following the program. This was also supported by the qualitative reports. Six months afterward, the reports were still positive, as compared with before the program, but there was a falling-off of reported effects from the data collected at three weeks. The qualitative data also supported these findings and identified some of the issues.

Three months after the simulation, the company laid off one-third of its 180 employees, and the insecurity created among the managers (none of whom were actually laid off) was quite high. Also, there was no one in the organization responsible for making changes. One comment was "no one is carrying the ball for change, and old habits are returning" (Kaplan et al., 1983, p. 26). On the other hand, as shown in the data, improvements were still noted when six-months scores were compared with pre-simulation scores. Some comments supporting those differences were "the changes are very much alive" and "there's a lot more direct communication, a lot less memos, and a lot more interaction among staff at all levels. We're not as concerned about turf as we used to be" (p. 26). Clearly, other data could be collected to strengthen this type of evaluation, including on-the-job observations by other employees of the changes in the managers' behaviors. However, the efforts at examining the effects of this simulation should be praised and encouraged. Unfortunately, efforts to examine business games are few and far between, and efficacy of the technique is typically based on the proponents' hard-sell verbal approach. This has led some investigators to suggest that it was time to stop assuming that learning would occur automatically as a result of the use of business games (Keys & Wolfe, 1990). Investigations of other media, like

Table 8.2 Questionnaire results before, three weeks after, and six months after Looking Glass[1]

Variable	*Before*	*Three Weeks*	*Six Months*	*Significant Effect Before—Six Months*	*Significant Effect Three/Six Weeks/Months*
	(n = 15)	(n = 14)			
Management effectiveness	3.12	4.17	4.00	Yes	No
Trust (within the management team)	2.85	4.43	3.50	No	Yes
Cooperation (among different functions)	3.00	4.30	3.79	Yes	Yes
Agreement on goals	3.47	4.03	4.00	Yes	No
Belief that CES can improve	3.35	4.53	4.21	Yes	No
Competence of managers	3.47	4.53	4.11	Yes	No
Absence of stress	2.47	2.60	2.25	No	No
Agency held accountable	2.44	3.60	3.36	Yes	No

[1]The scale ranged from 1 (strongly disagree) to 6 (strongly agree).
Adapted from "A Mirror for Managers: Using Simulation to Develop Management Teams," by R. E. Kaplan, M. M. Lombardo, and M. S. Mazique. Copyright 1983 by the Center for Creative Leadership, Greensboro, N. C.

programmed instruction (PI) and audiovisuals, have not always produced definitive results. However, the empirical research already accomplished on PI, computer-assisted instruction (CAI), and audiovisuals has resulted in an appreciation for their advantages and limitations that does not exist for business games.

Case Study

The conditions of an organization are sometimes simulated by a case study. The trainee receives a written report that describes an organizational problem. He or she is then expected to analyze the problem and offer solutions based on a number of factors including people, environment, rules, and physical parameters. The trainee usually studies the case individually and prepares solutions. He or she then meets with a group that discusses the various solutions and tries to identify the basic principles underlining the case. The group procedure is designed to promote feedback and allow the individual to learn by observing others developing their respective solutions. It is generally recognized that there is no correct solution; the trainees are thus encouraged to be flexible.

Critics of this approach think that the method is not useful for learning general principles and that the lack of guided instruction generally characterizing the group process is detrimental. Proponents of this technique think that the self-discovery occurring during these sessions is likely to lead to longer retention of the principles. (For a discussion of these views, see Campbell, Dunnette, Lawler, & Weick, 1970.) As discussed earlier, Raia (1966) found that business games, as compared with the case-study method, led to superior performance on several criterion measures including standardized case studies and the final exam. Moore (1967) also examined business games and case studies. Essentially, he found no differences between the two groups on a series of criterion measures. However, he suggests that one disadvantage of business games is the participants' preoccupation with beating one another instead of learning the basic concepts. Thus, he suggests that the case study, with the more static setting, provides an atmosphere more conducive to the examination of general principles and issues.

The validity of Moore's point depends on the ability of the participants or the leaders (if they are included) to evaluate and reinforce one another. Participants in the case-study technique can become entangled in the large amount of information presented and never find the basic issue; the technique cannot work unless the group focuses on the issues. Also, the principles learned from the case study should be applied to everyday situations on the job. This avoids the danger of trainees becoming so engrossed in the case study that they never see the relevance of the principles to everyday life.

Argyris (1980) provides a more interesting criticism of the case-study method. He believes that there are two types of learning. First, there is the form that involves the detection and correction of error. An example of this type of learning, known as single-loop, is a thermostat, which detects when a room is too hot or cold and corrects that situation. Argyris describes the second form of learning as double-loop; this involves changes and corrections in underlying policies, assumptions, and goals. In this case, the thermostat would be a double-loop learner if it questioned why it was set at 65 degrees or even why it was measuring heat. Argyris's concern is that the case method may unintentionally undermine double-loop learning.

Specifically, this view about case studies stems from his observations and tape recordings of a three-week management-development program for a multibillion-dollar company, which used the case-study method as its major form of instruction. He observed that trainers dominated classroom activities, designed procedures to save face for trainers and participants, and generally designed the atmosphere to avoid confrontation and open discussion of new ideas. Argyris also notes that trainers espoused views such as "people should expose their ideas, maps, strategies for solving the problem; yet faculty members do not expose many of their ideas and strategies about the case" (1980, p. 295). He also thinks that there was little time or effort spent on ensuring that learning transferred back to the organizational environment, a criticism that is common to most training programs. Argyris argues that trainers should be taught to be less dominating, that open discussion should be encouraged, and that cases from their own organization should be used to enhance transfer. Argyris's view concerning transfer is a continual issue and is one of the reasons that evaluation is so important. His views concerning single- and double-loop learning remain controversial. He strongly believes in experiential learning and group confrontation as a way of unfreezing old values. Some of these issues will be discussed again in the section on sensitivity training. However, in part, the answer is very dependent on the needs assessment and the training objectives. There may be instances where single-loop learning is the goal. However, even if it is not, the training environment must still be designed to achieve the appropriate goals and must be analyzed to determine if the goals are realized. Actual studies demonstrating both the need for and the achievement of double-loop learning remain an important agenda item.

Role Playing

In this technique, trainees act out simulated roles. Role playing is used primarily for analyses of interpersonal problems and attitude change and development of human relations skills (Bass & Vaughan, 1966). This technique gives trainees an opportunity to experience and explore solutions to a variety of on-the-job problems. The success of the method depends on the participants' willingness to actually adopt the roles and to react as if they were really in the work environment (Campbell et al., 1970). There are many different role-playing techniques. In one variation, trainees who disagree are asked to *reverse roles* (Speroff, 1954). This procedure is intended to make a person more aware of the other's feelings and attitudes. In another variation, called *multiple role playing,* a large number of participants are actively involved in the role-playing process (Maier & Zerfoss, 1952). The entire group is divided into teams that role-play the situation. At the end of a specified period of time, participants reunite and discuss the results achieved by each group.

One of the more unique uses of role playing is called *self-confrontation.* In this procedure, the trainee is shown a videotape replay of his or her entire performance. While viewing the tape, the trainee is given a verbal critique of the performance by the trainer. One set of studies exploring this technique was prompted by the image of American advisers and officers overseas (King, 1966). Researchers believe that a lecture on how to behave in a foreign country is equivalent to a lecture on how to fly an airplane. With the self-confrontation technique, the trainee is first given information about the culture and the desired general behavior. Then, the learner plays the role of an adviser in a foreign country. Typically, the trainee interacts with a person from the foreign country who is a confederate of the trainer. After role playing, the trainee views the tape and is given a verbal critique of the performance by the trainer. Several studies have indicated that the videotape and feedback session does result in changes in behavior. In one study, the subjects played the role of a United States Air Force captain who was required to report to a foreign counterpart (King, 1966). They were required to reprimand the counterpart on one aspect of the behavior and to commend another aspect. This conversation was to take place in a highly prescribed way, consistent with the culture and containing fifty-seven different behaviors, ranging from gross motor movements to subtle voice cues.

The results of this study indicate that trainees who participated in self-confrontation performed consistently better than another group of subjects who had spent an equivalent amount of time studying the behavioral requirements outlined in the training manual. Retention tests given two weeks later indicate that the self-confrontation group maintained their skills. Although self-confrontation techniques can be applied as a feedback supplement for a variety of training techniques, a number of studies demonstrate that it is especially useful with interaction procedures like role playing (Haines & Eachus, 1965; Eachus & King, 1966). As already mentioned, the key to techniques like role playing and business games is the feedback and critique session. The self-confrontation method provides accurate and detailed feedback, and, when it is combined with sensitive analyses of performance, it appears to be a very useful procedure.

In a study that provides an important illustration of the unintended consequences of interventions, Teahan (1976) reports on a study that investigated role-playing effects on the attitudes of police officers. As part of their academy training, both white and black police officers role-played sensitive racial situations. Attitude-change scores indicate that black officers became more positive in their views of whites. However, white officers, while becoming more sensitized to the presence of black-white problems, became more prejudiced toward blacks. The author's interpretation of these results indicates that white officers had the perception that the program was intended for the benefit of blacks rather than whites. Independent of the interpretation, the results underscore the importance of examining the outcomes of our interventions rather than simply assuming that all is well.

Besides the few studies mentioned above, relatively few research efforts on role playing are available. Interestingly, one reason is that role playing by itself does not seem to be used very frequently. Rather, it has become part of other techniques such as behavioral role modeling, which will be discussed next. Early concerns about the technique were that participants might find the role playing childish (Liveright, 1951) and that they might have a tendency to put more emphasis on acting than on problem solving (Bass & Vaughan, 1966). If the emphasis is on the acting of roles, participants might behave in a manner that is socially acceptable to other members of the group but not reflective of their actual feelings. In this case, role playing may not lead to any behavioral changes outside the role-playing environment (Ingersoll, 1973). In the traditional format, the feedback is controlled by the participants in the role-playing setting. If the feedback focuses more on the acting ability of the participant than on the solution to problems, the entire learning process can be circumvented. Again, the leader becomes the key element to a successful training session. Later techniques such as behavioral role modeling have focused on specific problem situations in the work environment in order to avoid such difficulties.

Behavioral Role Modeling

For over a decade, the technique that has generated the most excitement has been behavioral role modeling. This approach is based on Bandura's (1969, 1977) social learning theory, which stresses the use of observing, modeling, and vicarious reinforcement as steps for modifying human behavior. This theory as an approach to learning is presented in Chapter 4 (pp. 94–96). Bandura's theory focuses on the acquisition of novel responses through observational learning. He notes that evidence for this form of imitative learning consists of persons exhibiting novel responses that have been demonstrated by observers and that are not likely to have occurred without such a demonstration. Also, the responses of the observers should be similar in form to the response of the model. Bandura obtained these types of effects in a number of studies, many of which focused on children demonstrating highly novel responses. As a result, Bandura (1969) suggests a number of subprocesses that are important parts of the observation learning process. They are

1. The attentional processes that relate to the ability of the observer to attend to and differentiate between cues. Bandura notes that some factors that can influence these attentional characteristics include variables like model characteristics and the ease with which modeling conditions can be discriminated. As noted by Wexley and Latham (1981), these factors include evidence that modeling increases when the model is perceived as relevant in terms of variables such as age and gender. If the observers see very little similarity between themselves and the model, they are less likely to imitate the behavior. Also, greater modeling will occur when the behavior is demonstrated in a clear and detailed manner.

2. The retentional processes that have been characterized as the capability required to remember the stimuli over a period of time. Bandura points out that this factor is likely to be affected positively by covert and overt rehearsal and negatively by factors like interference from previously learned material.

3. The motor reproduction processes that refer to the physical abilities needed to acquire and perform the behavior portrayed by the model. Most of the constraints related to this process refer to physical abilities. Thus, without

considerable amounts of practice and skill, an observer might not be able to imitate the behavior of a skilled craftsperson, such as a carpenter, even if the behavior had been modeled appropriately.

4. The incentive and motivational processes that have been defined as the reinforcement conditions existing at the time the observed behavior is performed. Bandura argues that reinforcement is not a necessary condition for the learning of models' responses, but he does note that it is important in getting persons to actually exhibit the behavior that has been learned. Evidence also indicates that observers are more likely to retain those modeling sequences seen as having some utility at a later time.

In 1974 A. Goldstein and Sorcher published a book called *Changing Supervisory Behavior,* which adapted many of the principles of Bandura's social learning theory into a training approach; their goal was to improve interpersonal and related supervisory skills. These authors criticize other approaches to training managers as focusing on attitudes and not on the behaviors necessary to carry out their work. Thus, they argue that training programs typically tell managers that it is important to be good communicators, with which almost everyone agrees (and probably knows before coming into the training program). However, the programs do not teach the manager *how* to become a good communicator, motivator, or whatever. Also, as described by Moses (1978), most training programs do not appear to have any usefulness for later job performance. Thus, the adult learner tends to be turned off by the artificial atmosphere of a training program that doesn't seem to be job-relevant. In contrast, the A. Goldstein and Sorcher approach consists of

> Providing the trainee with numerous, vivid, detailed displays (on film, videotape or live) of a manager-actor (the model) performing the specific behaviors and skills we wish the viewer to learn (i.e., modeling); giving the trainee considerable guidance in and opportunity and encouragement for behaviorally rehearsing or practicing the behaviors he has seen the model perform (i.e., role playing); providing him with positive feedback, approval or reward as his role playing enactments increasingly approximate the behavior of the model (i.e., social reinforcement). . . . (1974, p. 37)

A. Goldstein and Sorcher's approach stimulated the imaginations of a number of people and resulted in a symposium (Kraut, 1976) reporting on a number of preliminary studies that showed promise for the vitality of the approach. As often happens, practitioners were excited by the approach and started using the method, without much empirical evidence for evaluating the technique or for determining the important characteristics of the technique and under what conditions it is effective. As a result, McGehee and Tullar (1978) wrote an article criticizing the growing support for these new methods before further empirical developments had been reported. Since that time, a number of carefully carried-out empirical research efforts have been reported. Also, in a review of the training literature examining the effectiveness of managerial techniques, Burke and Day (1986) found that behavioral role modeling is one of the more effective training methods. This has not prevented debate in the literature about various aspects of this technique. Mayer and Russell (1987) express concern about two points: Little evidence shows that role modeling is more cost-effective than other methods, and too many of the studies only examined immediate learning. Although those points are well taken, in some sense the level of the debate is healthy and is different from discussions about some other techniques where virtually no data indicate support for the approach.

One of the best of the behavioral role-modeling studies was reported by Latham and Saari (1979). Their study involved 100 first-line supervisors who would receive training. Because it was not possible to train everyone at once, they randomly selected 40 supervisors and randomly assigned 20 of them to a training condition and the other 20 to a control group. The control group knew that they would be trained and were actually unaware of the fact that they were serving as a control. In this clever design, they simply assumed that for logistical reasons it was not possible to train everyone and thus they would be trained afterward. (As a matter of fact, they were trained at a later time, but in the interim they served as a control condition for the study.)

The training program was based on nine training modules developed by Sorcher on the basis of the work by A. Goldstein and Sorcher (1974). These modules were designed to increase the effectiveness of first-line supervisors in working with their employees. The topics included orienting a new employee, motivating a poor performer, correcting poor work habits, handling a complaining employee, overcoming resistance to change, and the like. Each of Latham and Saari's training sessions for the topics followed the same procedure:

> (a) Introduction of the topic by two trainers (attentional processes); (b) presentation of a film that depicts a supervisor model effectively handling a situation by following a set of 3 to 6 learning points that were shown in the film immediately before and after the model was presented (retention processes); (c) group discussion of the effectiveness of the model in demonstrating the desired behaviors (retention processes); (d) practice in role playing the desired behaviors in front of the entire class (retention processes; motor reproduction processes); and (e) feedback from the class on the effectiveness of each trainee in demonstrating the desired behaviors (motivational processes). (1979, p. 241)

During the practice sessions involving role playing, one trainee took the role of the supervisor, and another trainee had the role of the employee. The trainees did not use prepared scripts. Instead, they were asked to re-create an incident, which had occurred during the past year, that was relevant to the training topic for that week. During the session, the learning points emphasized in the film were posted so that the person playing the role of supervisor could make use of the principles. An example of the learning points for one program—handling a complaining employee—consisted of the following:

> (a) Avoid responding with hostility or defensiveness; (b) ask for and listen openly to the employee's complaint; (c) restate the complaint for thorough

understanding; (d) recognize and acknowledge his or her viewpoint; (e) if necessary, state your position nondefensively; and (f) set a specific date for a follow-up meeting. (Latham & Saari, 1979, p. 241)

Trainees playing the role of supervisor had no idea what the employee role player would do. The supervisor role player simply responded as best he or she could using the learning points and information gained from watching the role models in the film carry out the learning points. Two trainers were present at all sessions, with the first trainer supervising the role-playing practice. The second trainer worked with the group to teach them how to provide constructive feedback that would enhance the confidence and self-esteem of the person receiving feedback. At the end of each session, trainees received printed versions of the learning points and were sent back to their jobs with instructions to use the supervisory skills they had gained. The purpose here was to facilitate transfer of the learned skills back to the job. At the next session, trainees reported their experiences. In situations where the supervisors had difficulty, they were asked to report it to the class. Then they role-played the situation, with the class providing feedback on desired behaviors and the supervisor again practicing the appropriate behaviors. Latham and Saari (1979) also note that some of the learning points for some of the programs did not fit their specific situation, and so the points were revised by the trainees and the investigators. Latham and Saari also provided training for the supervisors of the trainees to ensure that the trainees would be rewarded for their on-the-job behavior.

Besides carefully designing a training program, Latham and Saari (1979) evaluated the results using reaction measures, learning measures, behavioral measures, and job-performance measures:

1. The reaction measures were collected immediately after training and consisted of information on items such as whether the training was helpful for performing the job better and for interacting more effectively with employees. These indicators showed positive results. A follow-up eight months after training had been completed also indicated that there was no difference in response immediately after training and eight months later.

2. The learning measure consisted of a situational test with eighty-five questions developed from critical incidents found in the job analysis. An example of one situational question is as follows:

> You have spoken with this worker several times about the fact that he doesn't keep his long hair confined under his hard hat. This constitutes a safety violation. You are walking through the plant and you just noticed that he again does not have his hair properly confined. What would you do? (Latham & Saari, 1979, p. 243)

Trainees were asked how they would handle each situation. A scoring response was developed based on the training program for each situation before the test was administered to the trainees. The test also contained items for behavioral situations that were not covered in the training program so that trainees had to generalize what they had learned to new situations. The data indicate that the mean score for the training group was significantly higher than the score for the control group.

3. The behavioral measure consisted of trainees rating the tape-recorded behaviors of supervisors resolving supervisor–employee problems. These were based on scripts that had been developed to reflect job situations and use of learning points as presented in the training programs. None of the situations presented had previously been described during training, nor had they been shown in the training films. The researchers again found that the performance of the trained group was superior to that of the control group even when some of the controls were given the learning points (but not the rest of training) to use in making their ratings.

4. The job-performance measure consisted of ratings by the supervisors of the trainees on rating scales based on a job analysis that produced critical incidents depicting effective and ineffective supervisory behavior. The investigators found no difference between premeasures of the training and control group. Posttest measures indicate that the training group performed significantly better than the control group.

As a final step, Latham and Saari (1979) trained the control group. After their training was complete, all differences on all four measures between the control group, which was now trained, and the original training group disappeared. This kind of careful implementation and evaluation in a real-work environment should serve as a model for what can be accomplished with some thoughtful effort. Since the Latham and Saari study, a number of studies (for example, Meyer & Raich, 1983) have produced similar positive results. However, the dangers of simply assuming a technique will work and skipping the evaluation step are made obvious by another study by Russell, Wexley, and Hunter (1984), which produced less favorable results. The results of this study indicate that although the modeling elicited favorable reactions and showed an increase in learning, it did not appear to produce changes on the job or improved performance results. The authors offer the possibility that the posttraining environment did not permit adequate reinforcement of the learned behaviors.

Besides the evaluation research, some recent research on behavioral role modeling has been concerned with issues exploring such questions as, What components of the program make it effective? A series of studies by Decker (1980; 1982; 1983; 1984) are particularly noteworthy in their efforts to explore various means of enhancing the behavioral rehearsal and social reinforcement components of behavioral modeling training. For example, Decker (1983) explored two issues affecting learning in a typical role-modeling workshop. His results indicate that small groups of observers (one or two) should be present during a behavioral rehearsal and that videotaped feedback presented with the trainer's critique is more effective than the trainer's critique without videotape. Other studies have focused on issues of symbolic coding. Thus, a field study by Hogan, Hakel, and Decker (1986) compared trainee-generated coding to trainer-provided coding for generalization purposes. The underlying rationale was that allowing individuals to generate their own codes would facilitate the integration of the information in each one's cognitive framework. Trainee-generated codes were found to result in significantly superior performance, although it is not clear that all trainees are capable of producing their own codes. An excellent book by Decker and Nathan (1985) provides a complete review of this research, as well as an extremely informative section on how to develop and implement behavioral model–training programs.

A more recent example of the use of these training models comes again from Latham and his colleagues (Frayne & Latham, 1987; Latham & Frayne, 1989) and relates to self-management skills. In their 1987 study, training in self-management was given to unionized government employees with the goal being to increase attendance at work. The training in self-regulatory skills was based upon F. H. Kanfer and Gaelick's (1986) work on self-management, which teaches individuals to assess their problems, set goals, monitor their behaviors, and identify and administer reinforcers for working toward goal attainment. The researchers administered the program to employees who had used more than 50 percent of their sick leave. Within the F. H. Kanfer framework, employees were taught how to manage personal and social obstacles to job attendance. Employing experimental and control groups, the data indicate that the trained groups did learn the self-management skills, which resulted in raising their perceived self-efficacy that they could influence their own behavior. Finally, employee attendance was significantly higher in the training group, and the higher the perceived self-efficacy, the better the attendance performance.

In their next study, Latham and Frayne (1989) conducted a follow-up at the six-month and nine-month mark. Their data reveal that the enhanced self-efficacy and improved job attendance was maintained and that the degree of self-efficacy still predicted the degree of subsequent job attendance. Also, in this study, the control group from the previous study was given the same self-management training by a different trainer. Three months following their training, this group showed the same positive improvement—increased self-efficacy and increased job attendance—as the original group. The studies provide another important example of the combination of thoughtful theory-driven training development followed by empirical research. The interesting possibilities for training researchers is further enhanced by Gist's (1989) research; she found that different training methods might be useful for persons with high and low self-efficacy. In her examination of a training program for teaching computer software, Gist found that people with low self-efficacy benefited most from a one-on-one tutorial, whereas modeling was most beneficial for people with self-efficacy in the higher ranges. Through research efforts such as those of Latham, Frayne, Saari, and Decker, it is possible that behavior role modeling will not only be used but will also actually be understood.

Laboratory (Sensitivity) Training

Laboratory (sensitivity) training refers to a variety of techniques such as T-group training, encounter groups, L- (for learning) groups, and action groups. This approach originated in an intergroup community-relations workshop held in Connecticut in 1946. The learning results of this group-interaction meeting stimulated the participants to organize the first formal sensitivity-training session in Bethel, Maine, during the summer of 1947. From this session, a group known as the National Training Laboratories (NTL) was formed to promote and investigate sensitivity training. This group is still active today, presenting programs (which vary in length from a few days to several weeks) on topics such as power in organizations, supervisory relationships, and personnel development for executives and managers. In addition to NTL, hundreds of other organizations sponsor similar laboratory training. The large number of laboratory techniques vary not only in length but also in focus (from personal growth to the building of teams), qualifications of the trainer (from individuals trained at NTL to self-designated leaders), and type of participants (strangers, members of the same firm, married couples) (Buchanan, 1971).

Characteristics and Objectives of Laboratory Training

Laboratory training is characterized by face-to-face interaction among individuals in a group. In addition, Blumberg and Golembiewski (1976) describe the elements of laboratory groups:

1. There is a concern for the here-and-now. The basis for this is this belief: The data that will most help people learn about themselves are those that are most available.
2. Feelings are both appropriate and important material for analysis. This is based on a belief that feelings must be part of the learning process.
3. There is frequent feedback and analysis, including self-disclosure involving here-and-now events that occur during group interactions. This is considered an important part of the development of self-awareness based on reality testing.
4. It is important to have a climate that permits individual choice. That is, it is the choice of the individuals who receive feedback whether they will do anything to change.

The setting is designed to foster psychological safety where members are away from their organizations and free to voice their opinions. Some of the remarks may cause hard feelings, but Argyris (1964) feels that any pain caused must be viewed from the perspective of personal growth. To be effective, the experience should be gut-level and emotional. Anxiety is viewed as useful in creating an atmosphere in which individuals examine interpersonal and group problems in order to gain a deeper understanding of their own reactions toward colleagues and supervisors (Burke & Bennis, 1961). As an example of the processes that occur during a laboratory session, let's examine Argyris's (1967) sample of a group experience. The president and nine vice presidents of a large corporation attended a week-long retreat to discuss their problems. The seminar leader defined the objectives of the educational experience and prompted the group to begin. There was a long period of silence that was eventually broken by individuals who asked what was going on and who was in charge of the meeting. Then one participant began:

> "You know, there's something funny going on here."
> "What's funny about it?"
> "Well, up until a few minutes ago we trusted this man enough that all of us were willing to leave the company for a week. Now we dislike him. Why? He hasn't done anything."
> "That's right. . . . He's the leader and he ought to lead."
> ". . . I honestly feel uncomfortable and somewhat fearful. . . ."
> "That's interesting that you mention fear, because I think that we run the company by fear."
> The president turned slightly red and became annoyed: "I don't think that we run this company by fear, and I don't think you should have said that." A loud silence followed.
> The vice-president thought . . . and said, "I still think we run this company by fear, and I agree with you. I should not have said it."
> The group laughed, and the tension was broken. (p. 66)

At this point, the president apologized for his remarks and indicated a desire to achieve an open and trusting relationship. He went on to say that he always had an open door and that it wasn't easy to hear his company described as being run by fear. The group members discussed how they judged the openness of a person and how they had all inhibited one another.

These types of educational experiences are designed to achieve a variety of different goals. The following, summarized by Campbell et al. (1970), lists most of the objectives:

1. To give the trainee an understanding of how and why he acts toward other people as he does and of the way in which he affects them.
2. To provide some insights into why other people act the way they do.
3. To teach the participants how to "listen"—that is, to actually hear what other people are saying rather than concentrating on a reply.
4. To provide insights concerning how groups operate and what processes groups go through under certain conditions.
5. To foster an increased tolerance and understanding of the behavior of others.

6. To provide a setting in which an individual can try out new ways of interacting with people and receive feedback as to how these new ways affect them. (p. 239)

The Controversy over Laboratory Training

Laboratory training often uses anxiety-provoking situations as stimulants for learning experience. Many observers (for example, Odiorne, 1963; House, 1967) think that these experiences are disruptive to the health of some participants. Critics also think that it is one matter to express true feelings in the psychological safety of the laboratory but quite another to face fellow participants back on the job. These views are buttressed by reports that some individuals are hurt by the emotional buffeting experienced during the session and that more than one person has left the group feeling disturbed. For example, Klaw (1965) reports that some people return from these sessions liking themselves less and feeling unsure what to do about it. His survey of 100 graduates from Western Training Laboratories revealed that one in ten graduates felt that way. Kirchner expresses the views of these critics:

> Do we really want to rip off the "executive mask," which hides from the individual his true feelings, desires, and knowledge of self? Most people have taken many years to build up this "mask" or to build up their psychological defenses. While it can be very enlightening to find out that nobody loves you and that some people think that you have undesirable traits, this can also be a very shocking experience to individuals and not necessarily a beneficial one. (1965, p. 212)

These early reports continue to appear, but they are being countered by a number of investigators who maintain that figures citing high rates of casualties are misleading. Cooper (1975) reports on a number of studies where the problem rates are low. Cooper also notes that few studies control for the possibility that reported problems may be reflecting increases in willingness to self-disclose rather than increases in disturbances. However, Cooper does agree that disturbances are more likely to occur when individuals are randomly assigned to groups without prescreening to assess an individual's capability for participating in the give and take of laboratory sessions. Also, some of Cooper's research (1977) indicates that both positive and negative effects in groups are strongly related to the trainer's behavior and personality; trainers who are relaxed, self-sufficient, and tranquil produce the most positive benefits. To avoid potential problems, Jaffe and Scherl (1969) make several very sensible suggestions:

1. Participation should be completely and truly voluntary.
2. Participation should be based on informed consent with complete information about purposes and goals provided for each person. For example, potential participants should be warned that these groups are not intended for therapy or for persons who feel a need for treatment.

3. Participants should be screened, preferably through an interview procedure.
4. Participants should be advised about what types of behavior are acceptable during the group session.
5. Follow-up help for all participants should be available to deal with any issues stemming from group termination.

It is important to note that these suggestions result in some evaluation difficulties. If the participants are all volunteers, there will be limited generalizability because of the threat to external validity resulting from possible interactions for the selection of subjects and the experimental treatment. However, until the effects of laboratory training are more certain, it is safer to accept limited generalizability. Also, studies, which compare the characteristics of people who do or do not volunteer to participate in laboratory-training exercises, are needed for understanding the volunteer effect in this situation. Some observers believe that controversies about the use of laboratory training are related to the lack of evaluative studies. At best, this is only partially true. Although there have been questions regarding methodology and doubts about what is transferred to the job, there are more studies of laboratory training than of any other managerial-development technique. Yet other training procedures have not suffered the criticism leveled at laboratory training. The controversy is really related to concerns about the psychological safety of individuals who participate in T-group experiences.

Evaluation of Laboratory Training

Early in the history of the application of laboratory training, Dunnette and Campbell (1968) criticized the work in this area for its failure to meet basic scientific standards. Due to concerns over both ethical issues and the welfare of individual participants, their comments attracted considerably more attention than most remarks about poor evaluation, although the standards they stressed were certainly reasonable. They included pre- and postmeasurement, a control group, and some procedures to control for interaction between the pretest and behavior in the training program. This latter point is often referred to as the *reactive effect* of pretesting and results from increased sensitivity to the training program caused by exposure to the pretest. This effect is a special concern in human relations–type training in which the participants' expected changes do not concern complex motor skills but rather attitudes and social skills. Several techniques can be used to provide some estimate of the presensitization effect. For example, a group can be given a pretest with feedback and then a posttest after an intervening period that does not include training. Any changes in the scores provide an estimate of the sensitization effect; however, possible contaminants can result from specific events that occur between pre- and posttesting. A second procedure can have one group undergo training and the posttest without even taking the pretest. Comparing those scores to scores of the group that participated in the pretest, training, and posttest is then possible. These control procedures are not especially demanding, but, as we have already noted in our discussion of other training techniques, they are not often adopted.

When Dunnette and Campbell (1968) presented their criticism, virtually no studies even employed pre- and postmeasurement and a control group. Although it is not possible to be sure why, a large number of studies were conducted in the years following the criticism. In a review in 1975, Smith found ninety-five studies that met reasonable standards such as the use of pre and postmeasurement and control groups. About three-quarters of the studies detected some changes immediately following training that were not found in the control group. Among studies that examined follow-up data at least one month after training, the effect rate dropped to about two-thirds of the studies. However, evaluating the changes that have been found is not always easy. For example, when observers are being used from the everyday setting, they tend to know who has and has not been trained; thus, they are not impartial observers. These are, of course, the problems of doing research in field settings.

Burke and Day (1986) in their review of management-training techniques used a technique called *meta-analysis* that permits the examination of statistical effects across studies. Their analysis did not find that the research strongly supported the effectiveness of sensitivity training, especially as it related to changes on the job. Further, they express some of the same concerns noted above about the criterion measures being used. They note that, in many cases, observers were simply asked to report changes in behavior without determining whether it actually affected job performance. In other cases, the measures were unconfirmed self-report measures.

Burke and Day's (1986) data reconfirm concerns expressed by Dunnette and Campbell (1968) that even if sensitivity training produces observable changes, the utility of these changes for the individual and the organization remains in question. As an example of this issue, Underwood (1965), describing changes found for his training groups, notes that fifteen incidents indicated increased supervisory effectiveness, while seven indicated decreased effectiveness. He points out that the decreased effectiveness changes revealed a heavy emotional loading. Underwood speculates that "these subjects were venting emotion to a greater degree than usual, and to the observers, operating in a culture which devalues such expression, this behavior yielded a negative evaluation" (p. 40). Whether such changes are acceptable depends on the organization's objectives. At the present stage of development, it appears that laboratory training has the potential to modify the behavior of at least some of the participants. It would be very interesting to learn if there are particular characteristics of individuals that make them more amenable to change, but that is a research issue that remains to be explored. In any case, each organization and individual must explore the potential changes. They must then decide whether to participate based on their own personal and organizational objectives. At least there is a growing research base to help in making those choices.

ACHIEVEMENT MOTIVATION TRAINING

A number of leadership-training approaches have been developed based on theoretical models of the leadership process. Most of these approaches are at best characterized by efforts concerning theory and conceptual development but include virtually no empirical research that would permit tests and modification of the theory. Two of these approaches have provided the basis for some empirical efforts. They are achievement motivation training, which is discussed in this section, and Leader Match training, which is discussed in the following section.

McClelland (1976) has been studying the idea of need for achievement as a construct for over twenty-five years. He has symbolized the term *nAch* and defines it as the urge to improve or a desire to excel. McClelland and his associates have identified individuals who have high nAch as those who have a drive to persist in attaining goals and who seek challenging tasks and responsibility (McClelland & Winter, 1971). However, these researchers also estimate that only 10 percent of the population is high in nAch. On the other hand, they have identified situations where high nAch is particularly important for success. One such situation is the small-business organization. As McClelland states,

> It was concluded on the basis of evidence, that entrepreneurs needed high n Achievement; therefore they were taught to think, talk and act like a person with high n Achievement as that behavior has been worked out by years of empirical research in the laboratory and in the field. (1978, p. 205)

The training program consists of a variety of training materials including business games, paper-and-pencil exercises, outside readings, and tests (McClelland & Winter, 1971). However, the researchers organize their description of the program under four main headings:

1. The achievement syndrome. The purpose of this part of the training program is to teach participants how to both recognize achievement fantasies and then produce those fantasies themselves. They start by taking the Thematic Apperception Test, which requires that they write imaginative stories about a series of pictures. Trainees are then taught how to code what they have written according to a standardized scoring system for identifying nAch. That is, they learn when a statement in their story refers to "doing better" or competing with a standard of excellence. They are taught the difference between the desire to accomplish something, the act required to accomplish it, and blocks to accomplishment, which can either be personal or in the environment. Then participants are taught to rewrite the stories so that they can achieve the maximum points for need achievement. The purpose of this part of the training program is to form the associative network so that they begin to know what achievement is and how to think along those lines.

During the next phase of the achievement-syndrome part of the training program, participants are taught to tie the new cognitions to action. In this phase, they are taught how high-nAch individuals behave. For example, they are taught that high-nAch individuals like to take personal responsibility for the performance necessary to achieve a goal. These various action patterns are taught partially through involvement in business games where they have the opportunity to both practice these actions and observe others performing the actions. The final part of this stage of training is the use of cases similar to those discussed earlier. The purpose of this part of the training program is to illustrate how nAch thoughts and actions can be displayed in everyday business life. After the cases have been discussed, participants are asked to bring in their own problems from their business environment for analysis in terms of the achievement syndrome.

2. Self-study. The authors note that up to this point the goal of the training program is to teach participants what nAch is and how it influences behavior. In this next section of training, participants are asked to confront the ways in which need achievement relates to their own lives, careers, goals, and values. All of this is explained through the use of outside readings, lectures, group discussions, and films. Participants now decide whether they want to become that type of person, what this all means to them in terms of their self-image, and how it will affect them in their job and life. In this part of the program, an analysis is conducted using children's stories, myths, and customs to identify conflicts and issues between value systems and the achievement syndrome.

3. Goal setting. The authors note that many participants arrive with rather vague hopes and expectations about what they will achieve in the course. The purpose of the training during this phase now shifts toward more precisely defining the goals for each participant and determining ways that each participant can measure his or her progress toward these goals. Toward the end of the course, each participant is asked to fill out a detailed achievement plan for the next two years. This consists of specifying what the participant wants to accomplish, the blocks each individual will have to overcome, and where he or she will seek help in accomplishing these goals. The plans are also reviewed in small-group discussions, where participants assist one another in formulating their goals. Participants are told to consider themselves in training for the next two years and that the ten- to fourteen-day course is too short to do more than present a new way of acting. Instructors help the participants during the next two-year period by contacting them every six months, obtaining reports on progress, and working with them in the specification and achievement of goals.

4. Interpersonal support. The authors note that many parts of the course could have been taken by correspondence. However, they point out that one distinguishing feature of the actual training program is the degree of warmth and interpersonal support that is provided to participants. Group leaders are there to help clarify what the person wants and provide information that will make the self-study more complete, while providing the warmth and respect that is needed when the participant goes through individual soul-searching.

McClelland and his colleagues have studied the effects of these programs in a variety of settings. McClelland and Winter (1971) report on the effects of achievement development courses in a number of small cities in India. In general, course participants showed improved performance as compared with their own pretest measures and with a number of matched control groups. The participants generally were more involved in development activities in the community, began more new businesses, and invested more in expanding their businesses. The results of a two-year follow-up period indicate they employed over twice as many new people as did the untrained businessmen.

Miron and McClelland (1979) report on other training programs similar to the one described above. The first was conducted through the business school at Southern Methodist University and another was conducted through the Small Business Administration in eight cities. A third program was designed to help mostly black business firms in Seattle that were experiencing business difficulties. The authors examined financial data for periods preceding training and for periods after training for all three programs. In general, all three programs resulted in increased profitability. For example, in the SMU training program, there were increases in sales, profits, and number of employees.

Before completing a discussion of this program, it is important to note that systematic evaluation efforts, including those for this program, are not easy to accomplish. These are large-scale programs where it is often difficult to obtain all of the pre-data and post-data, and many times control groups are also difficult to either obtain or find. Of course, random assignment to treatment and control conditions is often nonexistent. In many cases, investigators are forced to examine many factors and treat each finding as a piece of a puzzle. Often, researchers take a look at the consistency and direction of many different pieces of data to support their views on the value of their programs. There are many different strategies to consider in evaluating such efforts. One must ask the investigator to collect multiple criteria, including both process and outcome data, examine the relationships, and realize that no single study is going to provide extensive information about the value of the program. Also, it is important to recognize the limits of interpretation based on the threats to validity that result from the design utilized. It is also important to use the designs that control as many threats to validity as possible, given the constraints of the environment. Finally, researchers must share issues and problems in research so that the reader can make a reasoned judgment about the viability of the results and gain an understanding of the parameters that limit the interpretation of the data. Such analyses sometimes provide the most interesting and thought-provoking information about the entire study. In that regard, Miron and McClelland

(1979) frankly discuss some of the problems they have in interpreting their research data. Some of the problems include the following:

1. Interpreting the criterion data is sometimes difficult because it involves complex analyses that require finding matching groups or interpreting data across time periods. Thus, in the studies in India, overall business employment in the treatment group was compared to a city that was matched on a number of demographic and economic variables. Clearly, it is difficult to know whether you have matched on the right variables and whether the comparison city might have changed at different rates for other reasons. In some ways, this is similar to the problem of using a matched control group rather than random assignment. However, here it becomes increasingly complex because so many factors can affect the performance of both the control and experimental groups, especially when dealing with indicators like unemployment factors and profitability.

2. A particularly vexing problem in these studies is whether some of the results could be due to a selection rather than training effect. Maybe the businessmen who have higher nAch are the ones who tend to respond to recruitment efforts to participate in the training efforts. Thus, they would have performed better, anyway.

3. Another problem for the interpretation of results is that the opportunity for success is different for people who participate in training. Participants might become aware of consultant assistance or access to money resources because of the training program. Thus, success is not directly related to what they learn in training but rather to factors that result from their being in the training program.

For many of these factors, Miron and McClelland (1979) provide analyses and strategies that lead them to believe that these factors do not account for their data. However, by providing access to both the problems and their interpretations, it is possible for the outside observer to make his or her own judgment.

LEADER MATCH

Leader Match training is based on a contingency model of leadership, which has been developed by Fiedler and his associates (Fiedler, 1964, 1967; Fiedler, Mitchell, & Triandis, 1971). The theory states that effective leadership depends on a proper match between the leader's style and situational characteristics. That is, in certain situations, one kind of leader might be most effective, whereas other situations might require another kind of leader. Fiedler defines the leadership situation according to three major dimensions:

1. *Leader–member relations.* This dimension simply refers to whether the members of the group like or trust or have loyalty to the leader. Thus, leader–manager relations measure the managers' perceptions of the

amount of loyalty and support that the leader expects to receive from the group.
2. *Task structure.* This dimension measures how clearly such items as goals, procedures, and task requirements are specified for the manager.
3 *Position power.* This refers to how much authority the manager perceives the organization has, given in terms of control for dispensing rewards and punishments.

Fiedler dichotomizes each dimension so that leader–member relations could be considered good or bad, task structure could be high or low, and position power could be strong or weak. To the extent that a leader has good member relations, high task structure, and high position power, the situation is considered favorable. If there are poor member relations, the task is unstructured, and there is limited control or authority, the situation is considered unfavorable.

The second aspect of the match between a leader's style and situational characteristics refers to leader characteristics. This is measured on a scale known as the least preferred co-worker (LPC) scale. This index requires a leader to rate the very worst person he has ever worked with on a number of traits. The traits include dimensions on a scale such as pleasant versus unpleasant, sincere versus unsincere, nice versus nasty, cheerful versus gloomy, and so on. In Fiedler's terms, if you are a high-LPC leader, you will have values toward the positive end of the scale and will call your least preferred co-worker sincere, nice, cheerful. On the other hand, the low-LPC leader would describe the least preferred co-worker in terms such as insincere, uncooperative, and nasty.

On the basis of his research, Fiedler maintains that low-LPC leaders perform well in situations that are either highly favorable or highly unfavorable. The point is that low-LPC leaders, who are characterized as having a nonparticipative, direct, structured style, work best in extremely favorable or unfavorable conditions, whereas high-LPC leaders, who are characterized as participative, democratic, and relationship-oriented, tend to perform well in situations of moderate control. Because there are two aspects of the match, the leader's style and the situational characteristics, any attempt at change that is related to this model would have two options: Either change the leader's personality to more precisely match the situation or change the situation to more precisely match the leadership style. Fiedler and his co-workers maintain that changing the leader's basic style is a difficult and demanding chore. Essentially, he argues that organizational engineering that changes the nature of the situation to better match the style of the particular leader is the more fruitful approach.

Thus, Fiedler has designed a training program that shows prospective leaders how to increase or decrease the closeness of their interpersonal relations with their subordinates, how to structure the task, and how to change the various aspects of position power. This approach forms the foundation for his training program, known as Leader Match (Fiedler, Chemers, & Mahar,

1976). The training program itself consists of a self-administered programmed workbook, which trainees can complete on their own time and which can be augmented by lectures, discussions, or films. The program takes anywhere from four to twelve hours to complete, and it is recommended that this be done over several days to obtain maximum benefit. The first part of the workbook is designed to help trainees identify their own leadership style. Thus, they complete the LPC scale and interpret their own scores. The second part of the training program has the participants determine their own situational aspects. This is accomplished by filling out the scales and measuring their perceptions of leader–member relations, task structure, and position power. They are given information on how to change or modify situational factors in order to match the situation to their leadership styles. For example, depending on the situation judged most desirable, changes could consist of requests for more routine assignments or less structured assignments. It could also consist of the leader developing more or less formal relationships. The important point is that, depending on whether you are a high- or low-LPC leader, you will choose differently in modifying your situation to fit your leadership style. Each chapter of the workbook consists of a short presentation that explains the basic aspects of the contingency model and how it can be applied. Essays are followed by several short problems called probes, which consist of leadership episodes. Trainees are asked to select the best solution for each probe. Then they are given feedback on the correct response. If the participant makes an incorrect response, the trainee is required to review the material to make sure that the chapter is understood. Each chapter closes with a summary. There are several short tests throughout the program and a final exam.

The evaluation of the training program has mixed results. In part, there are difficulties, similar to those experienced by McClelland, that stem from conducting research in environments with many constraints and difficulties. It is possible to make the following points:

1. Fiedler and his associates have conducted more extensive research and evaluation studies than almost anyone else. Also, the studies tend to collect multiple criteria from different sources, and some of the studies have designs that include pre- and postmeasurement and control groups. Indeed, Fiedler correctly notes that many of his studies have employed rigorous procedures, including the random assignment of participants to training and control groups, which are not typical in complex environments.

2. The results of the studies are somewhat of a mixed bag. For example, Fiedler and Mahar (1979) reviewed twelve validation studies that they had conducted. Five of the studies examined participants in civilian occupations such as police sergeants and managers in county government, public service, and public health. In three studies, serious problems in attrition made the results difficult to interpret. For example, in the police study, only seven of the fifteen sergeants completed the training book. In most of the studies, rating scores were in the predicted direction but were often not statistically

significant. Thus, in the study of middle managers in county government, two superiors rated each manager on the organization's sixteen-item rating scale three months after training. Eleven of the sixteen items were in the predicted direction, but only two of the scales (cost consciousness and dependability/reliability) were statistically significant. In the study on public works supervisors, fourteen of sixteen were in the right direction, but only two were significant (makes decisions within the scope of the job and oral communication). The other studies were conducted in military settings involving either active-duty personnel, military-college students, or ROTC students. In those studies, there were fewer problems with the conduct of the studies, and the data were more consistent in supporting training program effects. Burke and Day's (1986) meta-analysis, which uses statistical techniques to examine results across studies, concludes that Leader Match is an effective technique. However, meta-analysis often accepts the statistical results of individual studies without necessarily examining alternative explanations for results, such as the threats to validity. Those issues are treated next.

3. Although Fiedler and Mahar (1979) strongly believe that these data support the vitality of their training program, they do share concerns about threats to validity that might lead some readers to be less certain. The first serious issue is the problem of subject attrition. Of course, one concern about attrition is that it is not random. Thus, it is possible that people who did not feel they were getting much from training were those subjects who managed not to continue participating. Also, in addition to subjects disappearing, data sometimes also disappeared. In one study of volunteer public health personnel in Central and South American villages, only eleven of twenty-five participants completed the program; in addition, some performance evaluations were lost in transit from Central America. Another issue of concern is rater bias. That is, raters tend to know who did and did not participate in training, and that can affect their ratings. Fiedler and Mahar (1979) point out that they tried to check that point in some of their studies. In one study involving six-month follow-ups, supervisors could not remember who did or did not complete training. Because training in these studies often consisted of reading the programmed manual on site, it is entirely possible that they had forgotten who had participated.

Another very interesting issue is the source of the effect. Is it Leader Match that makes the difference, or would any special treatment produce effects? Some people note that a positive benefit of this program is its cost effectiveness. Most programs require considerable amounts of time (consider McClelland's nAch program or the Looking Glass, Inc., simulation). However, all that is required here are four to twelve hours of reading. Others question how this minimum effort can achieve substantive benefits for such complex behavior. Fiedler argues that some of his studies do involve comparisons to other training. Further, he did an analysis that indicates the following: People who show on a test that they know more about the program tend to perform better. Also, those cadets who self-reported that they more often applied the principles also had higher performance ratings. On the other hand, Fiedler also reports that thirty-six cadets stated that they did not use the program on any occasion, but this group also performed significantly better than the control group. Reaching a final conclusion regarding the training program is difficult. The degree of effort must certainly be applauded. Also, as in the McClelland studies, the difficulties of the environment must be recognized. No investigator asks to be "blessed" by samples that disappear. Some data do support the efficacy of the training. Given the threats to validity, however, these data must be treated with caution. Certainly, more research that carefully specifies exactly how participants changed the environment to match their leadership styles would be extremely helpful. Because this technique is related to a theory of leadership, specific hypothesis concerning these situational changes and how leadership effectiveness is changed is important. Otherwise, questions remain about what happens in training to produce these effects.

RATER TRAINING

In Chapter 5, information was presented on various types of criteria used to measure the effectiveness of individuals in work environments. One type of criteria discussed was rating scales, which are used in many organizations by managers to rate their subordinates on various job-relevant performance dimensions. Table 5.6 (p. 177) presents an illustration of the procedures used in developing rating scale items and examples of behavioral items that make up rating scales. Although most textbooks recommend that raters be trained in the use of rating scales to appraise employees, until recently there has not been much systematic study of such programs. When the first edition of this book was written in 1974, not enough information was available to include a section on rater training. A number of studies have been published on the topic since then, and, more interesting, controversies have developed that mirror the issues involved in the design, analysis, and interpretation of most training programs.

Most of the first set of studies focused on issues related to reducing errors made by managers in the rating process. Some of the kinds of errors that research focused on include the following:

1. *Halo error:* is the tendency to rate a person high or low on all dimensions because of a global impression. In this instance, an impression that an employee is an effective performer tends to result in the individual being rated highly on all performance dimensions, including report-writing items, whether work is produced on time, whether work has quality defects. Similarly, a person considered an ineffective performer might be rated low on all dimensions, even though the employee might perform some aspects of the job well and others poorly.
2. *Leniency error:* in general, is the tendency to give everyone higher ratings

than are warranted. The opposite dimension is a *severity error,* where there is a tendency to give everyone lower ratings than are warranted.
3. *Central tendency:* is the tendency to give everyone scores in the middle of the scale and avoid extreme ratings. This can occur across dimensions for the single individual and/or across individuals for all dimensions.
4. *Contrast effect:* is a situation where a performance rating is given on two successive individuals. For example, a rater is asked to rate an individual who is an extremely effective (or extremely ineffective) performer and then to rate a second individual. If the rating of the second individual is affected by the rating of the first, the error is known as a contrast effect.

An illustration of the type of training program developed to reduce rating errors is provided in the work of Latham, Wexley, and Pursell (1975). These authors note that earlier work indicated that lectures on the problems of rating errors did not seem to have much of an effect on reducing the problem. They conclude that an intensive workshop that would give subjects a chance to practice observing and rating actual videotaped candidates, along with immediate feedback regarding the accuracy of their ratings, might be more effective. To study this problem, the authors randomly assigned sixty managers in a large corporation to one of three conditions: a workshop, a group discussion, or a control group that received no training. The workshop group viewed videotapes of hypothetical job candidates being appraised by a manager. Trainees then gave a rating indicating how they thought the manager would have rated the candidate and how they themselves would have rated the candidate.

Group discussion concerning the ratings followed. As the authors note, this gave trainees the opportunity to observe videotaped managers making observational errors, to find out how frequently they themselves made such errors, to receive feedback on their own behavioral observations, and to practice to reduce their own errors. The workshop group worked on a variety of rating errors, including contrast effects and halo errors, as well as errors such as first impressions where judgments are made based on initial observations rather than the behavior that follows. The group-discussion format consisted of trainers first defining the various types of errors and providing examples for each error being presented. They then generated personal examples involving the various kinds of rating errors. They also divided into subgroups so that they could share examples, discuss them, and generate solutions to each of the rating problems. The control group did not have any form of training.

The testing of the effects of the various forms of training was conducted six months later. Members of all three groups were given videotapes to observe. They also were given detailed job descriptions and lists of requirements for the job. They were then asked to rate the individuals in the videotapes in terms of the degree of job acceptability based on the job descriptions and requirements provided for them. Basically, the results showed that the workshop group was no longer prone to any of the types of rating errors examined in the study. The group-discussion trainees also performed well and exhibited only a tendency toward last-impression errors, which are errors that result from evaluating someone on previous behaviors based on the last impression of the person. The control group made a number of errors, including halo and contrast effects. The authors also collected data on trainee reactions to the training. They found that trainees reacted more favorably toward the workshop program than toward the group discussion. Trainees reported that the structured workshop format, including the videotapes, made them feel that their time away from the job was being used wisely. The only disadvantages that the authors note for the workshop procedure were that it is costly and time-consuming to develop. They also indicate that where these costs are important factors, the discussion-group technique could be used because it also worked well.

Interestingly, even though the study by Latham, Wexley, and Pursell (1975) was well done, a number of heated controversies surround the rater-training literature. In some cases, the controversy relates to the fact that most studies are not well done. Spool (1978), in a review of twenty-five years of research literature on training observers of behavior (of which rater training is one category), found a number of problems, including the designs of the studies, the criteria employed, and the fact that some interventions can be called training programs only by the most liberal of interpretations. However, even when obviously poor studies are eliminated from consideration, controversy continues. Speculation on why this might be the case will be saved for the conclusion of this section. Some issues that researchers are discussing include the following:

1. A number of design issues severely limits the interpretation of rater-training studies. These issues limit the external validity of the generalizations that can be made as a result of the research. One serious issue is raised by an analysis of twenty-two rater-training studies by Bernardin and Villanova (1986), which indicate that seventeen involved students doing the rating in an experimental context. Further, all but two of the studies involved ratings done in an experimental situation. In addition, Goldstein and Musicante's (1985) analysis of rater-training studies indicates that only three studies have investigated the effects of rater training over time and that two of these studies suggest that the positive effects associated with rater training may diminish over time.

2. There are serious questions about whether the criteria being chosen to analyze the results of rater-training studies really reflect what should be measured. In many ways, this issue is related to the concepts of criterion relevance discussed in Chapter 5. Spool argues that "accuracy in observation can be improved by training observers to minimize rating errors" (1978, pp. 866–867). However, as noted by Bernardin and Beatty (1984), researchers seem to have focused on minimizing rating errors (like halo error or leniency error) but have forgotten that the actual goal is accuracy in observing. These authors further argue that training programs that focus on reducing one set

of errors simply exchange one response set for another and thus may only substitute one set of errors for another without improving the accuracy of observations. They note that only three investigations have actually studied the accuracy of observations and that in those studies reducing errors did not actually result in more accurate observation. Bernardin and his colleagues think that more important issues should be addressed in rater training, including giving raters a common frame of reference for defining the importance of the behaviors being observed and training raters on techniques of information gathering. They also believe that systems such as formal diary keeping should be developed as another way of standardizing observations of behavior and improving the accuracy of ratings. Some examples of suggestions for writing descriptions of behaviors for diary keeping are presented in Table 8.3.

3. Some authors (Warmke & Billings, 1979; Bernardin & Beatty, 1984; Goldstein & Musicante, 1985) suggest that other variables, such as the context or boundary conditions surrounding the training situation, may have more influence on performance than originally thought. A consideration of organizational analysis questions such as those described in Chapter 3 would probably be helpful. Just as the transfer of training into the organization must consider items such as the willingness of supervisors to appropriately model the learned behaviors, the transfer of trained rating behavior may involve issues such as political and union pressure on raters, whether the raters trust that the ratings will be used appropriately, and to what ends the ratings will be used. If problems are discovered, they must be resolved before a training program will work. Of course, that principle is the same for all training programs.

It is interesting to note the amount of controversy surrounding rater-training studies. As is the case with sensitivity training, it is somewhat difficult to determine why so much heat has arisen over these particular training programs. The issues being discussed are clearly important, but they are issues that should be of concern in the analysis of any training program. Here, however, they are treated with a special degree of emotion. If forced to venture a guess about why this should be, I would speculate that it is necessary to understand the context of the use of rating scales in organizations. First, even though all criteria have problems related to relevance and contamination (discussed in Chapter 5), rating scales are called subjective, and there is the suspicion that somehow they are easier to manipulate than other so-called hard criteria. Also, the use of rating scales in measuring behavior in organizations has become more prevalent as our sophistication in designing rating scales has increased. In addition, there are many inadequate rating scales where attempts to make them job-relevant have not even been considered. This results in unsophisticated users concluding that rating scales are inherently poor devices.

Finally, in many fair employment practice lawsuits, performance differences between minorities and majorities as measured on rating scales have

Table 8.3 Suggestions for writing descriptions of behavior

1. Use specific examples of behavior, not *conclusions* about the "goodness" or "badness" of behavior.
   - *Use this:* Gwen told her secretary when the work was to be completed, whether it was to be a draft or a final copy, the amount of space in which it had to be typed, and the kind of paper necessary.
   - *Not this:* Liesa gives very good instructions to her secretary. Her instructions are clear and concise.
2. Avoid using *adjective qualifiers* in statements; use descriptions of behavior.
   - *Use this:* Aimee repeated an employee's communication and its intent to the employee. She talked in private, and I have never heard her repeat the conversation to others.
   - *Not this:* Kelly does a good job of understanding problems. She is kind and friendly.
3. Avoid using statements that make *assumptions* about an employee's *knowledge* of the job; use descriptions of behavior.
   - *Use this:* Sarah performed the disassembly procedure for rebuilding a carburetor by first removing the cap and then proceeding with the internal components. When she was in doubt about the procedure, she referred to the appropriate manual.
   - *Not this:* Sam knows how to disassemble a carburetor and does so in an efficient and effective manner.
4. Avoid using *frequencies* in statements; use descriptions of behavior.
   - *Use this:* Patrol Officer Garcia performed the search procedure by first informing the arrested of their rights, asking them to assume the search position, and then conducting the search by touching the arrested in the prescribed places. When the search was completed, Garcia informed the arrested. He then proceeded to the next step in the arrest procedure.
   - *Not this:* Patrol Officer Dzaidzo always does a good job in performing the search procedure.
5. Avoid using *quantitative values* (numbers); use descriptions of behavior.
   - *Use this:* Nancy submitted her reports on time. They contained no misinformation or mistakes. When discrepancies occurred on reports from the last period, she identified the cause by referring to the changes in accounting procedures and the impact they had had on this period.
   - *Not this:* Mr. Goebel met 90% of deadlines with 95% accuracy.
6. Provide sufficient detail so that an assessment can be made of the extent to which characteristics of the situation beyond the control of the ratee may have affected the behavior.
   - *Use this:* Mr. Dzaidzo's failure to hit the "target date" for the sky-hook quota was caused by the failure of Mr. Ressler's department to provide the ordered supply of linkage gaskets. Mr. Dzaidzo submitted four memos in anticipation of and in reference to the gasket shortage.
   - *Not this:* It wasn't Dzaidzo's fault that he didn't hit the deadline.

been a focal and volatile issue. Since training raters is considered a major way to improve the use of rating scales in organizations, training itself is right in the middle of these concerns. One can only hope that these pressures result in better needs assessment, better design, and better evaluation. The entire training field can then benefit regardless of the origins of all this activity. Actually, that is a good concluding statement for all the training techniques discussed in the last two chapters. It is a hopeful sign that much of the research describing these techniques has occurred in the last fifteen years. Many of the studies involve innovative designs in an attempt to study important learning and training phenomena. One can only applaud these efforts and hope they continue.

Special Training Issues

9

CHAPTER

This chapter focuses on issues where training often intersects with societal concerns. Many of these topics were introduced in Chapter 1 in "Implications of the Future Workplace for Training Systems." Now that the reader has completed reading about all the various aspects of training systems, it is possible to explore these issues in more depth. The first topic is on fair employment practice issues, including the importance of training in civil rights litigation and the 1991 Civil Rights Bill. The following section is about the training implications of the Americans with Disabilities Act, which extends issues of fair employment practices to people with disabilities. The next topic is instructional programs for the hard-core unemployed, where training in the traditional sense will not work because of diverse values and attitudes of individuals raised in different cultural environments. These programs must consider many aspects of a complex system, including the support services (for example, counseling and job placement) necessary for individuals who frequently have never been employed. It is also clear that training programs are only part of an answer to a complex problem. Next, retraining for second careers is discussed. Some individuals in this group have been placed out of work by technological changes, whereas others are no longer interested in their first career. As an additional barrier, these potential employees face the hurdle of age discrimination. The hard-core unemployed and the second-career groups present a complex social problem that cannot be resolved by narrowly examining specific techniques of training. Organizational entry, training, and socialization are considered next, thus returning to the entry of people into organizations; the issues of training as related to the increasing international emphasis in organizations are also discussed. The chapter concludes with a discussion of the implications of these societal issues for organizations who have the problem of training their future leaders.

TRAINING AND FAIR EMPLOYMENT PRACTICES

In 1964 President Lyndon Johnson signed the Civil Rights Act into law. One section of that act, Title VII, has had a dramatic effect on employers, employees, job applicants, labor unions, lawyers, and industrial-organizational psychologists. Title VII refers to employment and makes it illegal to discriminate on the basis of race, color, religion, sex, or national origin. The categories of the aged and handicapped were not included in this particular act but were added later on the basis of other legislative action. The 1964 act resulted in the establishment of the Equal Employment Opportunities Commission (EEOC) as an enforcement agency for fair employment practices. Since that time, numerous events have affected practices in this area. In 1972 an amendment to Title VII broadened its coverage from employers with fifteen employees to state and government agencies, as well as educational institutions. The amendment also extended the authority of the EEOC to bring court actions against organizations. The EEOC published a set of guidelines in 1970; the EEOC, the Civil Service Commission, the Department of Labor, and the Department of Justice published a new set of guidelines in 1978, all of which have had effects on personnel practices. Also, the Society for Industrial and Organizational Psychology published the *Principles for the Validation and Use of Personnel Selection Procedures* (1987) to help clarify and develop guidelines for the field. Various court actions ranging from district court decisions to those of the United States Supreme Court have added to the complexity. In 1991 a new civil rights bill was passed. In part, the bill was in response to a number of Court decisions that many persons felt were making it difficult to pursue fair employment practices. Thus, one Court decision (*Wards Cove Packing Co.* v. *Antonio,* 1989) had made it the responsibility of an employee, rather than employer, to show the organization used practices adversely affecting women and minorities without any "business necessity." In instances where it is shown that an organization's personnel practices adversely affect women and minorities, the 1991 Civil Rights Bill returns the burden of proof to employers to show that their practices are job-related and consistent with business necessity. There will probably be quite a bit of controversy about the definition of such terms as business necessity, but it is clear that the intent of the act is to ensure that businesses demonstrate the job-relatedness of personnel practices that have adversely affected minorities and women.

To understand the issues concerning training and fair employment practices, it is important to explore several basic ideas. First, there is the principle of discrimination. As noted by Arvey (1979), the basic object in selection is discrimination. That is, the employer uses a test instrument by which some employees will be selected and others rejected. Similarly, some people, on the basis of their training scores, might be selected for promotion to a new job. The problem occurs when unfair discrimination or bias enters into the situation. These terms are complex and subject to many interpretations, but Arvey's definition makes the point clear:

> Unfair discrimination or bias is said to exist when members of a minority class have lower probabilities of being selected for a job when, in fact, if they had been selected, their probabilities of performing successfully in a job would have been equal to those of nonminority group members. (p. 7)

These kinds of issues often translate into court actions when a lawsuit is filed by an individual (called a plaintiff) against an organization (known as the defendant). Plaintiffs attempt to establish that there has been adverse impact against an individual. The demonstration of adverse impact relates to unfair discrimination. It is necessary to show that a person from a protected class (such as race, as defined in Title VII of the U.S. Civil Rights Act) is treated unfavorably as compared with people in the majority group. Although the exact procedures are complicated, an example might be where 100 whites out of 100 applicants were hired, while only 5 of 50 blacks or females were hired. Once adverse impact has been demonstrated, the burden of proof shifts to the defendant. The organization must now show that the test or instrument being used, which results in adverse impact, is job-related or valid. Some additional complexities are that even if the instrument is job-related or valid, the defendant might be asked to show that other devices not having as much adverse impact have been considered and/or that the instrument is required for business necessity.

It should be clear from these examples that most of the original controversy involves questions concerning the selection of people into work organizations. Thus, it is possible to ask what this has to do with training issues. The answer is that fair employment practices and training issues are becoming increasingly important. The following points should be considered:

1. It is necessary to realize that in addressing the issue of testing in Title VII of the 1964 Civil Rights Act, the EEOC guidelines (1970) define a test ". . . as any paper-and-pencil or performance measure used as a basis for employment decision." This means that if adverse impact is established, it will be necessary to establish the job relatedness of any instrument used in the personnel decision. Almost all the original legal action decisions in the short history of fair employment practices involved people attempting to enter the job market. Thus, the cases concerned the job relatedness of selection tests such as paper and pencil, application blank, interviews, and so on.

More recently, as people from protected classes successfully enter the job market, the issues have shifted to concerns about opportunities to move up the organizational ladder. In addition, the 1991 Civil Rights Bill makes it clear that all phases of employment discrimination, not just tests involving entry into a job, are covered by the law. Unfortunately, the difficulties that individuals are having make employment discrimination a still very serious issue. For example, Gilliam (1988) reports on a training study designed to help individuals who could not find jobs. As we will see in the next section, there are many such individuals, and sometimes they are labeled as hard-core unemployed. The startling aspect of Gilliam's study is the group for which this training program was designed were all college graduates who were minorities and could not find employment. The scope of these difficulties is detailed in a Department of Labor report that examined the employment and promotion practices of nine Fortune 500 firms (Sugawara, 1991). The study found that invisible barriers, now called a "glass ceiling," block women and minorities from advancing in management. In addition, the study found that the barriers existed at a much lower level of management than was originally thought. The extent to which this type of problem affects training programs was made clear in a study by the General Accounting Office (Swoboda, 1991), which found that nearly one out of five federally sponsored training programs under the Job Training Partnership Act (JTPA) discriminates against women and blacks in the type of training opportunities made available. In these cases, minorities and women were more likely to be provided with training consistent with lower placement levels. The JPTA is the largest, single manpower-training program with a budget of billions of dollars. As will be seen, older people suffer the same problems. Given these developments, court cases concerning opportunities for promotions have become more frequent, and mixed-up right in the middle of these issues are training programs. For example, one target of litigation are programs that determine who is given the opportunity to attend a training program so they can be selected for promotion to a managerial job. Those personnel decisions are subject to the same laws as personnel decisions for entry into the job market.

Bartlett (1978), in an insightful analysis, lists some of the kinds of decisions involving training programs that are likely to be involved in litigation. His 1978 prognosis turned out to be extremely accurate. Some of the decisions he lists are presented below:

1. Use of training as a job prerequisite
2. Use of instruments to select people for training
3. Use of training performance, retention, or graduation as a criteria for another job or for entry into another training program
4. Use of training as basis for advancement or increased compensation

Russell (1984) has carefully detailed many of the court cases involving these type of training issues. For example, in cases involving a drug company and a bank company, the court ruled that the companies pay plan was inadequate because the training programs had a number of violations. For example, this included such factors as the training program excluded women and advancement from the training program to fully qualified employment was sporadic.

2. Readers of this book know that its author would insist on demonstrations of job relevancy even if there had not been an indication of

adverse impact. However, the courts would only be concerned if adverse impact had been established. In civil rights cases, if adverse impact is determined, the question becomes one of whether the program itself is job-relevant. In other words, what is the validity of the training program? In these cases, as described in Chapter 6, there are a number of evaluation methods, each permitting varying degrees of confidence about inferences of the validity process. Thus, experimental designs (assuming that threats to validity are controlled) permit the strongest inferences; quasi-experimental designs also permit inferences, assuming reasonable control of threats to validity. Also described in that chapter are content-validity models. Here, you can only show the content of training as matched with the important knowledge, skills, and abilities (KSAs) on the job. Thus, the model for inference is weaker because you cannot be sure that learning or transfer takes place. The point is that a variety of models can be used to make inferences about the job relevancy of the training program. The models can, in varying degrees, permit inferences to be made about validity. Also, of course, the procedures used in carrying out each of the evaluation models also affect the strength of the inferences. Thus, content validity with a poor needs assessment further weakens the inference.

3. Specifying the inferences you want to make is extremely important. Thus, if the goal is to make inferences about whether training programs provide the appropriate instruction to improve performance, then appropriate experimental design–evaluation models can provide that information. Even content-validity models can indicate whether the important KSAs from the job are represented in training, although they cannot specify whether trainees learn or transfer learning to the job. On the other hand, you might want to know if people who performed better in a training module also perform better on the job. Here the question is whether training performance can predict job performance. As described in Chapter 6 in "Individual-Differences Models," this evaluation technique asks whether people who perform better in training tend to perform better on the job. However, as noted in Chapter 6, this approach does not tell us anything about the quality of the training program. Of course, if the goal is to make inferences about the training program, "wrinkles" can be added. Thus, it is possible to add pretests and posttests in training or content-validate the training program. In the latter instance, you have at least established that the important KSAs are included in training and that people who do well in training do well on the job. A content-validation design may not permit as strong an inference as an experimental design, but it does permit a stronger inference than an individual-differences model without a content-validity component.

4. Another way that training scores are used in fair employment practice cases is as criteria. For example, a selection test or an interview score is used to predict training performance. Here again, the question becomes one of what inferences can be made. Clearly, this model is being used to predict which people, based on the selection test, will perform well in training. Again, this

model does not provide any information about the quality of the training program. As a matter of fact, it is extremely difficult to make any inferences about job performance from evidence relating selection measures and training performance. There is some confusion about this point. Some people assume that if a selection test predicts training performance, it should tell us something about job performance. Everything we have learned in this text about transfer should warn against making that assumption. Again, the question is one of strength of inferences. If there is a strong relationship between selection and training and the training program is content-valid, that relationship permits slightly stronger inferences.

In conclusion, it is important to note that training is now in the middle of fair employment practice issues, and many of these issues will be in front of the public over the next decade. Readers interested in an overall review of court cases involving training and fair employment practices up to this time should read an excellent review by Russell (1984). In addition, Goldstein and Gilliam (1990) have traced the problems of employment discrimination and issues involving training and fair employment practices for many affected classes, including the elderly, minorities, and women.

TRAINING AND THE AMERICANS WITH DISABILITIES ACT

It is important to note that another act, Americans with Disabilities Act of 1990 (ADA), has significant implications for the workplace. The act makes it unlawful to discriminate in employment against a qualified individual with a disability. Although this act is quite complex and the implications of its application to the workplace are relatively unknown, several important points seem apparent. The key provision is providing individuals with reasonable accommodation. This is defined in the following way:

> Reasonable accommodation is any change or adjustment to a job or work environment that permits a qualified applicant or employee with a disability to participate in the job application process, to perform the essential functions of the job, or to enjoy benefits and privileges of employment equal to those enjoyed by employees without disabilities. For example, reasonable accommodation may include:
>
> - acquiring or modifying equipment or devices,
> - job restructuring,
> - part-time or modified work schedules,
> - reassignment to a vacant position,
> - adjusting or modifying examinations, training materials, or policies,
> - providing readers and interpreters, and
> - making the workplace readily accessible to and usable by people with disabilities. (U.S. Equal Employment Opportunity Commission, 1991, p. 4).

The impact of these provisions remains to be determined, but it is clearly a violation of the ADA to fail to provide reasonable accommodation unless it would cause undue hardship to the operation of the business. *Undue hardship* means that the accommodation would require significant difficulty or expense. Factors used in making this judgment in each individual case would involve an assessment of the cost of the accommodation, the employer's size and financial resources, and the nature and structure of the operation. It is important to note that this act applies to individuals; thus, different individuals with different disabilities must be considered separately in terms of reasonable accommodation.

Training opportunities are clearly an important part of the act. Simply examining the list presented above makes it obvious that, to provide for reasonable accommodation for different people, training might need to be modified in many ways. For example, reasonable accommodation might mean ensuring that the trainee can physically enter the training classroom while using a wheelchair, providing a reader for a visually disabled trainee, or modifying the size of a desk so that an individual can reach a computer keyboard. Disabled individuals can be an important resource in meeting the organization's needs for the future. My guess is that training opportunities will be critical in determining whether individuals are given job opportunities. Thus, the implementation of the ADA will sharply focus on whether reasonable accommodation has been provided for the disabled in terms of training opportunities.

TRAINING FOR THE HARD-CORE UNEMPLOYED

The civil disorders of the 1960s prompted a reconsideration of our poverty-ridden communities. In the cities alone, there were 500,000 unemployed people (*Report of the National Advisory Commission on Civil Disorders,* 1968). Many of the members of these communities are hard-core unemployed (HCU); that is, they are not regular members of the work force, and, in many cases, they have been without employment for more than six months. The HCU are usually young, members of a minority group, and lacking a high school education. In addition, they are below the poverty level specified by the Department of Labor (Goodman, Salipante, & Paransky, 1973). Recent estimates support the fact that the HCU remain a serious problem. For the last decade, the jobless rate for black teenagers seeking employment has been two and three times the national unemployment rate.

The importance of this problem is likely to become magnified in coming years as a result of the declining number of individuals available for entry-level jobs. As discussed in Chapter 1, many of the people who will become available will lack many basic skills. This might result in the replacement of the term *hard-core unemployed youth* with the term *undereducated youth.* One of the most serious aspects of this difficulty is basic literacy skills. The U.S.

Department of Education estimates that 27 million Americans are functional illiterates who cannot read, write, or calculate at levels required to perform basic daily living tasks (Torrence & Torrence, 1987). In a report on the literacy gap, Gorman (1988) estimates that U.S. corporations as the educators of last resort are now spending more than $300 million a year. For example, Polaroid Corporation spent $700,000 offering courses in English and math for 1000 new and veteran employees. The possibilities for success are reinforced by reports from Sticht, Armstrong, Hickey, and Caylor (1987) on experiences in the military with "low-aptitude youth" training programs. These authors present data describing the success of their programs in terms of retention rates, numbers of people completing high school equivalency degrees, performance in the military, and other similar criteria. The training program is based on a functional literacy approach that focuses on the development of basic skills within the context of the job. In addition, the authors report on other training support schemes, including revision of training materials to match trainee aptitudes.

Besides the basic literacy issue, it is becoming clearer that the challenges facing us, because of the increase in workplace technology, are going to be even more serious. A U.S. Department of Labor (1991) report addressing what work requires of schools for the year 2000 makes that clear. The five competencies that will challenge schools and the workplace are presented in Table 9.1.

Thus, it is becoming apparent that basic literacy will not be enough. In addition, training systems must be examined from a broader perspective than just the trainee, the trainer, and necessary job skills. The need for sensitivity in designing programs is illustrated by the semantic differences that disrupt communication between trainees and employers: "Words that sound the same have different meanings. Sentence structure is different. Business and technical terms comprise another language. Thinking that they (minority-group trainees) understand, they often find that they really don't know what is wanted" (Van Brunt, 1971, p. 2). The seriousness of these issues is apparent from the research of Triandis, Feldman, Weldon, and Harvey (1975) on ecosystem distrust. This concept refers to distrust of people, things, and environment. The authors note that the environment for many persons in the ghetto is unpredictable and cannot be controlled. Ecosystem distrust is presumed to operate in an environment where negative reinforcements predominate, where parents have few financial resources, and where public authority figures are bureaucratic and tend to dispense few positive reinforcements.

These factors result in less trust for people, suspicion of motives, and a sense of individual powerlessness, as well as a feeling that if you are not careful you will get into trouble. This leads people from these environments to have different interpretations of events. Thus, the reactions of middle-class whites to items such as "to do your own thing" have to do with self-improvement and self-actualization. The responses of ghetto minorities to "doing your own thing" have to do with getting into trouble because that is the

Table 9.1 Five competencies

Resources: Identifies, organizes, plans, and allocates resources.
a. *Time:* Selects goal-relevant activities, ranks them, allocates time, and prepares and follows schedules.
b. *Money:* Uses or prepares budgets, makes forecasts, keeps records, and makes adjustments to meet objectives.
c. *Material and facilities:* Acquires, stores, allocates, and uses materials or space efficiently.
d. *Human resources:* Assesses skills and distributes work accordingly, evaluates performance and provides feedback.

Interpersonal: Works with others.
a. *Participates as member of a team:* Contributes to group effort.
b. *Teaches others new skills.*
c. *Serves clients/customers:* Works to satisfy customers' expectations.
d. *Exercises leadership:* Communicates ideas to justify position, persuades and convinces others, responsibly challenges existing procedures and policies.
e. *Negotiates:* Works toward agreements involving exchange of resources, resolves divergent interests.
f. *Works with diversity:* Works well with men and women from diverse backgrounds.

Information: Acquires and uses information.
a. *Acquires and evaluates information.*
b. *Organizes and maintains information.*
c. *Interprets and communicates information.*
d. *Uses computers to process information.*

Systems: Understands complex interrelationships.
a. *Understands systems:* Knows how social, organizational, and technological systems work and operates effectively with them.
b. *Monitors and corrects performance:* Distinguishes trends, predicts impacts on system operations, diagnoses deviations in systems' performance and corrects malfunctions.
c. *Improves or designs systems:* Suggests modifications to existing systems and develops new or alternative systems to improve performance.

Technology: Works with a variety of technologies.
a. *Selects technology:* Chooses procedures, tools or equipment including computers and related technologies.
b. *Applies technology to task:* Understands overall intenrt and proper procedures for setup and operation of equipment.
c. *Maintains and troubleshoots equipment:* Prevents, identifies, or solves problems with equipment, including computers and other technologies.

From "What Work Requires of Schools" by Secretary's Commission on Achieving Necessary Skills, U.S. Department of Labor, 1991, Washington, D.C.: U.S. Government Printing Office.

result of such behavior in the ghetto. The implications of many of these findings is that blacks from the ghetto are likely not to trust an authority figure and may misinterpret behavior that is intended to be friendly. Thus, a smile is interpreted as "he is trying to rip me off," and helpful behavior is perceived as being done only because the government forces it. Triandis et al. (1975) note that, unless supervisors and trainers are aware of ecosystem distrust, they will fail to modify their behavior so that it cannot be misinterpreted. Unfortunately, few HCU programs include motivational and attitudinal considerations; however, research indicates that programs that do not consider such factors are often doomed.

A vast number of techniques have been applied to the problems of the HCU. However, if we concentrate on studies that emphasize only remedial programs or job skills, few programs have any demonstrable utility. This is partially due to the now-familiar lament: There are many reports of programs but few reports of research studies focusing on results. However, another basic consideration is that programs that concentrate just on job skills, whether auto mechanics or retail selling, don't seem to work very well. This is evident in an early study that followed 418 trainees who had graduated from a training program for highway construction–machinery operators (Miller & Zeller, 1967). The authors obtained information from 279 graduates. Of these graduates, 61 percent were employed, and 39 percent were unemployed at the time of the interview. In addition, more than half of the total group said they were without jobs more than 60 percent of the time. Some reasons for the unemployment situation related to inadequacies in training, which included limited task practice and insufficient training time. One trainee noted that "the contractors laughed when I showed them my training diploma and said 'Come back after you get some schooling, buddy' " (pp. 32–33). However, the inadequacies of the training program were only one problem faced by the potential employees. Miller and Zeller state the problem this way: "It might have been helpful to have included, within the training experience itself, practice in job hunting, assistance in contacting employers before the end of training, follow-up counseling, and job-placement help" (p. 31). In case you might think that these kinds of issues have been resolved, examine Table 9.2 (p. 326) a real-life description of laid-off employees retraining for new jobs.

Research regarding these types of issues is not commonplace. An exception is an interesting study by Barbee and Keil (1973), who examined interview job training for the disadvantaged. They note that culturally disadvantaged people often present themselves passively in job interviews. Training was provided for people who were enrolled in HCU-training programs in interviewing skills. One training procedure, which was most successful, consisted of a combined videotape feedback and behavior modification program. In this procedure, trainees first participated in a simulated job interview, which included filling out an application and being interviewed by a researcher who previously had been a personnel interviewer. The initial interview was taped. Then subjects in the training program were asked to look at the tape and search for behaviors they might change. The trainer helped with this process. An example of a sample behavior item to change could be "clarify the exact kind of work you did on your last job" (p. 21). The trainer suggested ways of responding, indicating what kinds of behaviors interviewers sought. The trainer also helped the trainee rehearse and then reinforced behavior changes. The trainee then went through a second interview with the person simulating the role of personnel interviewer. That interview was also videotaped. All videotaped interviews were presented to a group of five judges who were responsible for entry-level hiring in government agencies and the business community. The judges were not told which tapes were pretraining and which were posttraining. Also, they were not told which tapes came from the training condition described above and which came from a control group that also had pre- and postinterviews but without any training. A second training condition, where participants had the opportunity to view the tape of their pretraining performance but did not receive any other instruction before the second interview, was also included as part of the study. Trainees had been randomly assigned to those conditions. The study found that the performances of groups that had received the combined treatment of watching interviews and receiving behavior modification treatment were more improved than those of the other groups (control condition or just viewing the tape) on several measures. These measures included assertiveness and initiative, asking about job tasks and conditions, and probability of hire. Unfortunately, the study did not provide data about the transfer of these skills to actual job-seeking behavior. Also, the study does not tell us whether the acquisition of these skills resulted in improved job performance once a job was obtained. Some might argue that teaching interview behaviors that might not be related to successful job-behavior characteristics is somehow not appropriate. On the other hand, others would argue that if one cannot obtain a job, successful job behavior is a moot point. Also, it seems to make sense that good communication skills should be useful both in the interview and on the job. However, given the problems in HCU programs, it is critical to conduct research on this issue so that trainees can avoid the problems exemplified in the Miller and Zeller study (1967).

Job placement and counseling are two indicants of a common theme in HCU research; that is, training systems must be examined from a much broader perspective than just the trainee, the trainer, and the necessary job skills. A program that considers job training as only one aspect of the instructional program was developed at the Pittsburgh Technical Institute (Nester, 1971). The lengths to which this program goes to gain the trust of trainees are extraordinary. Trainers not only call trainees if they do not report by 9:00 A.M. but also arrange for special tutoring, babysitters, and a variety of incentives to motivate trainees. Most interesting is the approach taken by the staff to ensure the success of trainees on the high school equivalency exam. Besides tutoring the students, trainers arrange for a special testing, pay for the exam, provide transportation, and have two staff members present so that students can see a familiar and friendly face. Another aspect of the total approach is a counseling program. Nester notes that some students have deep-rooted personal problems that make it difficult to learn or to keep a job. Therefore, to gain insights into the causes of the problems and to suggest effective ways of coping, counselors must be available from the beginning of the program. At the time of Nester's report, the training program in drafting had resulted in forty of fifty-two trainees being successfully placed, with eight possibilities pending. The commitment toward job placement is apparent from the 135 interviews that were arranged for the trainees. The same themes of job placement, counseling, and attention appear in most programs that have evidence of success. In some cases, the attention is manifested in health care for individuals who could not attend training previously because of their ills. In other cases, the attention is focused on careful transportation directions to aid trainees in finding their way to the training or job site. These factors make careful organizational analysis and needs assessment mandatory. For example, conflicts among government sponsors, employers, and training institutions can completely disrupt a program (Goodman, 1969). Many of these conflicts are based on differing goals and expectations. For example, the community training organizations are concerned with introducing people into the world of work, whereas the employer is concerned with obtaining and retraining people at a minimum cost. When these clashes remain unresolved, a situation with conflicting goals and objectives eventually undermines the potential success for the HCU.

Training analysts are still struggling with the factors that determine the success of HCU instructional programs, but the emerging emphasis on the nonskill variables suggests that the original analyses of the trainee population were not very astute. The important issue of motivation was rarely considered. One framework that can be used to examine this issue is the instrumentality theory of motivation (Goodman et al., 1973). This view states that the HCU expectancies about reward contingencies and attractiveness of these rewards determine whether the trainee will remain in the instructional program and on the job. From this framework, Goodman et al. have interpreted some of the results of HCU research. They note that older workers are more likely to be successful than younger workers. This suggests that younger workers are more distrustful of the system and therefore perceive lower expectancies, whereas older workers have higher expectancies and greater desires for rewards. This particular hypothesis receives additional support from data indicating that male HCUs who have family responsibilities are also less likely to drop out. Obviously, as discussed in Chapter 4, motivation issues, such as raising the level of self-efficacy, are also relevant here.

Regardless of the theoretical framework, a multitude of factors determine the success of the HCU, including the treatment they receive from other employees and supervisors. Thus, supportive behavior by the supervisor relates to more effective HCU performance: "An important inference is that programs geared primarily toward adapting the HCU's work attitudes to the predominant social structure in the organization are far less potent than those that also incorporate the adaptation of the organizational climate" (Friedlander & Greenberg, 1971, p. 287). The work on ecosystem distrust (Triandis et al., 1975) is consistent with these viewpoints. These authors point out that with appropriate training members of different cultures would be more understanding of their own behavior and the responses their behavior is likely to evoke. As part of their research, they describe a training approach called a *culture assimilator* (Triandis, Feldman, Weldon, & Harvey, 1974). It is a programmed-learning sequence where incidents of cultural conflict are described, and trainees are asked to judge which factors are likely to be the cause. Then answers are discussed with references to the norms and values of the group being discussed. This approach is also presented in Chapter 7 in "Programmed Instruction." In that study, the cultural assimilator involved nurses being trained to work with Australian Aboriginals. The approach described by Triandis et al. for work with the HCU is similar, although, of course, the types of incidents and references to cultural norms and values change as the cultures differ.

The work by researchers like Goodman, Friedlander, and Triandis makes it obvious that training programs must be considered in the context of the environments in which they operate. Some training analysts have concluded that training programs designed for remedial work or job skills do not work. They must realize that training programs need to include a number of factors like job placement, counseling, health needs, and the training of supervisors. Future gains in this area of training are dependent on the careful specification of these variables, including those motivational factors that are important to the younger trainee and to the person without family responsibilities.

CHANGING CAREERS AND TRAINING

A number of very interesting areas are related to training and changing careers. For example, many people, for one reason or another, are seeking retraining for new jobs or careers. The reasons for this are rather varied and complex. In some cases, individuals have lost jobs because of rapidly changing technologies. Thus, the rapid changes in automated and computerized systems have made some jobs obsolete. In other cases, individuals have reached a point in their careers where there is a formal or informal age limit (for example, athletes, airline pilots, or firefighters). In still other cases, the person recognizes that the first career offers little opportunity for advancement or wants to explore other interests.

These kinds of concerns involve a whole set of individual, organizational, and societal issues. One set of issues relates to the questions of the needs of the future labor force. Thus, as presented earlier, Vobejda describes the executives of the new Mazda plant in Michigan as having very clear future objectives for their work force:

> They want their new employees to be able to work in teams, to rotate through various jobs, to understand how their tasks fit into the entire process, to spot problems in production, to trouble shoot, articulate the problems to others, suggest improvements and write detail charts and memos that serve as a road map in the assembly of the car. (1987, p. A14)

Adding to this issue is rapid technical obsolescence of individuals who previously had very advanced training. Thus, the estimate is that the engineer's education has a half-life of five years. That is, half of what has been learned in school is obsolete five years after graduation. Some interesting research by Kaufman (1978) suggests that engineers who early in their careers are given extremely challenging assignments tend to relate positively to professional competence in later years. This suggests the possibility that early learning challenges result in the individual being stimulated for later efforts. It may also suggest that these particular people are continually being exposed to new learning challenges that result in their being continually brought up to date.

London and Bassman (1989) indicate that midcareer shifts will further complicate the training scene during the next several decades. These authors predict these shifts will occur more frequently because of changes in job requirements brought about in response to technological shifts. In addition, they note that health and economic factors beyond an individual's control will result in job shifts. Intriguingly, they also predict that as people live longer, individuals may discover forty years is a long time to devote to a single career and therefore may develop different careers for the later portion of their lives. I cannot help but wonder if individuals who have relatively secure retirement benefits may feel even freer to explore such alternatives than people have in the past.

These future kinds of issues present quite a menu of challenges for training. Some predict that the declining number of people in the population of a number of industrialized societies will make every worker a very valuable resource and training and retraining will become increasingly important. As discussed in Chapter 1, there is a strong belief that decreasing proportions of entry-level workers will eventually affect all sectors of the work economy. As we approach the year 2000, there will be increasing demand for workers especially in service industries. Some analysts (for example, Goldstein & Gilliam, 1990) believe that society will need to become concerned about keeping everyone in the work force. The effects of such views on employment of minorities, the elderly, and women should be dramatic.

Odiorne (1980) suggests that strategic planning should be an integral part of the jobs of industrial trainers. He thinks that trainers must assume part of the responsibility of determining the needs of future labor forces and start developing programs now to meet those needs. This type of planning is not just necessary for jobs that are being changed because of technology. Thus, Zenger (1981) points out career planning is an overlooked skill in the management-training area. In his view, one responsibility of the organization should be to ensure that employees have qualified people with whom to discuss their future career goals and how to attain them. One serious issue involved in the entire area of training and retraining is that people are often entering careers that at one time were not considered "traditional," such as women entering management. In other cases, individuals changing careers are older than people previously entering that particular career. As indicated above, both groups have been subjected to discrimination in employment situations, and the issues involved in these situations are emotional.

In the case of the older worker, most discrimination cases are based on the premise that older workers cannot perform as well on the job and cannot acquire new skills. It is important to note that these stereotypes persist despite research that does not provide support for such beliefs. A meta-analysis of ninety-six studies published in the last twenty-two years found that age and performance were generally unrelated across *all* types of performance measures (McEvoy & Cascio, 1989). It was only for young employees that age and performance were related in a modestly positive direction. A previous review of studies conducted over the last thirty years also does not support the stereotype (Rhodes, 1983). Basically, several studies found that relationships between age and performance disappeared when effects of experience were partialed out. In those instances where differences were found, they tended to be related to performance where there were high demands for speed and accuracy of movement. However, for the most part, the demands of most jobs were not extreme enough for ability differences to show up. Also, of course, in many jobs that were extremely physically demanding, the older workers who remained on the job were those who could perform. The complexity of these performance issues is illustrated by questions concerning the age limit of sixty years for airline pilots. The major concern here is sudden death or acute incapacitation while working. An Institute of Medicine report found that "usually no single age emerges as a point of sharp decline in function" (1981, p. 128). It was also noted that there was reason to believe that well-practiced skills showed little if any age decline, but about this the research was still scanty. Finally, they report that more thorough testing might be a better system than using age sixty as an age limit because it made no sense to retire able pilots at age sixty while less able, younger pilots continued to fly.

Of course, all this becomes more complicated when measures other than performance are examined. For example, Rhodes's (1983) analysis of turnover data in twenty-eight studies found strong evidence for a negative relationship—that is, the higher the age, the less the turnover. Similar studies have generally found that age is consistently and positively related to overall job satisfaction, job involvement, work motivation, and the like.

At the present time, even data that show a relationship between age and performance must be treated carefully. As noted by Rosen and Jerdee (1976), older workers are less likely to receive support for retraining as compared with younger, equally qualified workers. Fossum, Arvey, Paradise, and Robbins (1986) make the following point: When considering the obsolescence process, where a relationship exists between age and performance, it may result because management withholds developmental resources from older workers. An example of the problems that arise from such an approach are documented by the Office of Technology Assessment report (1990). They predict that as the senior lobby becomes more sophisticated, there will be an increasing number of lawsuits similar to those discussed in the earlier section on fair employment practices. As an example, the report describes a lawsuit against a television company that trained their newer, younger workers on the change in technology from film to videotape. The older workers sued when they were disproportionately affected by a layoff because they had not received the training. These factors plus poorly designed training interventions for older workers will need to be overcome if the older employees are going to be given opportunities in tomorrow's job market.

Unfortunately, the entire literature is marked by problems that were noted by Sheppard (1970) over twenty years ago. These include the following:

1. The literature fails to differentiate various aspects of the work situation, including physical, psychomotor, sensory, and social characteristics.
2. Most of the emphasis is on average performance, with little, if any, attention to the substantial number of individual differences.
3. There is a blind faith in straight-line trend extrapolations. If thirty- to forty-year-old workers have lower morale than twenty- to thirty-year-olds, it is simply assumed that forty- to fifty-year-olds will have even lower morale.

An additional problem is the lack of literature regarding analysis of training and retraining data to help us understand those issues. This is an area where the literature has been sparse. In this regard, Sterns and Doverspike's (1989) review of the training and retraining literature led them to suggest that many older trainees are highly motivated to learn but fear failure in competition with younger, more recently educated trainees. Training programs can address these issues through programs that enhance an individual's self-efficacy. Sterns and Doverspike's suggestions for achieving this are as follows:

1. Training should be organized so that the material is job-relevant, gives positive feedback, and encourages the self-confidence of the trainee.
2. Training must ensure complete task mastery of previous components before moving on to the next step.
3. Where possible, training should build on elements that are familiar to the trainees from past learning and jobs.
4. Systems should be designed to organize information systems so memory requirements are limited.
5. Paced or time-pressured situations should be eliminated.

Of course, it should be noted that most of these training principles would be beneficial in any training program, including those for young entry-level HCUs. However, they appear to be particularly pertinent for training older workers.

Another question is whether older workers perform differently in training programs as compared with younger workers. The answer to this question is not yet clear. A few studies indicate that older workers take a longer period of time to learn. For example, Hartley, Hartley, and Johnson (1984) found that older workers took longer and required more assistance than younger workers in word processing training. It is not obvious whether this will be a consistent finding and whether given enough time and support, older workers will continue to perform as well at the end of training and on the job. Clearly, considerable research is needed on these issues.

There are also a number of training issues concerning individuals entering careers that at one time were not considered traditional for those people. Women entering work organizations as managers is one example where there has been considerable controversy. White, Crino, and DeSanctis (1981) discuss many of these issues, including the problem of barriers to women entering such careers. One serious issue is whether people entering nontraditional fields require some sort of special training program. That is a very complicated question. For example, concerning the job of a manager, I have not seen any evidence from needs assessment that indicates that the job of a manager for a woman is different from the job of manager for a man. Also, there is no clear-cut evidence from person analyses that women need special training on particular KSAs that are not needed by men. Thus, at this time, it is difficult to support the need for special training programs for women, except perhaps training in helping them to overcome the barriers they may encounter. As noted by White et al., that has not prevented the development of a large number of special training programs for women. However, also as noted by White et al., data supporting any accomplishments by these programs are virtually nonexistent. At this time, my conclusion about these efforts is that it makes more sense to train people in the organization to understand how to be accepting and work with individuals who might have different ethnic and cultural values.

On the other hand, person analyses of women applying for firefighter jobs usually show that many women do not have the required upper-body strength and muscular endurance to pass job-relevant tests. In a fascinating study, Hogan, Quigley, and Stark (1991) designed a training program based on a needs assessment that determined which physical skills were needed to perform the job of firefighter. Their training program was designed to use minimal space and no commercial equipment and could be done at work or home. Thus, the program could be completed using a self-administered workbook, although Hogan organized the participants for a six-week program. The participants worked out six days a week for about thirty minutes a day. The study showed that upper-body strength and muscular endurance of nonathlete women were enhanced by the calisthenic training, with average gains between 30 percent to 50 percent. In another study, these authors found that women who attended the program more regularly (at least 75 percent of the time) were more likely to actually pass the physical ability test for admission into the firefighter job. Seventy-six percent of the high-attendance group passed, whereas only 25 percent of the low-attendance group passed. Hogan's work clearly shows how a training program can be helpful to individuals who wish to enter a nontraditional job.

Finally, it is also critical to remember the importance of the many attitudinal and motivational variables besides job skills and remedial training. Perhaps an editorial from the *Washington Post* reprinted in Table 9.2 says it best. The editorial combines more of the best thoughts available on the problems inherent in training both the HCU and people seeking second careers.

Table 9.2 How not to retrain workers

When General Motors laid off 3,800 assembly line workers in Southgate, Calif., a federal "trade-adjustment" grant enabled 30 of them to enroll in a specially created electronics training course. Washington Post reporter Jay Mathews spent eight months following the experience of the first enrollees. His observations—set forth in a four-part series in this newspaper last week—provide a handy guide for anyone who wants to run an unsuccessful training program.

The first requirement is to make sure the workers are unsuited to the training. You can administer a placement test just to make sure that you're on the wrong track, but be sure that the trainees are already enrolled and enthusiastic about their prospects so that there is no chance to replace them with a more suitable group. The Southgate program accomplished this mismatching so deftly that only two members of the class were able to pass a basic math test. Many couldn't use a simple calculator.

Run the class at breakneck speed. Many of the students will be highly motivated and will try to keep up by studying through the night even while holding evening jobs. But if you go fast enough—the Southgate course crammed a year of instruction into 20 weeks—you can quickly build up the frustration level so that even the best-prepared will fall behind. But don't flunk anyone. String the trainees along with inflated grades or they might drop out and cost you your training fee.

Of course, a little basic review could refresh the memories of the average trainee, who has, typically, been out of school for some years. And a few months of remedial education might help others to prepare for more suitable employment or training. But given the pace that you have set for the class, you won't have to worry that your trainees will be able to do any catch-up preparation.

You'll probably have to order some training equipment for appearance's sake. But make sure that it doesn't arrive on time and that certain key items are missing.

Create unrealistic expectations. You're dealing with longtime assembly line workers who have been earning as much as $12 an hour for what is basically unskilled work. They don't yet realize that most job openings for which they are qualified—including those in the electronics field—pay much less. Or that the higher-paying jobs in electronics—which are relatively few in number compared with the old-line manufacturing jobs—require substantially more training and experience than they are likely to get in your course. Tell them they are almost sure to find lucrative employment if they stick with the course so that they'll be especially embittered when they end up sweeping floors.

It's helpful to add to the stresses that the trainees and their families are already undergoing as a result of their prolonged—in this case more than six months—unemployment. That was accomplished by a two-month delay in paying continued unemployment benefits so that some of the trainees had to work at night in addition to their 12 hours of course work. (The administration's new job-training program has improved upon this technique by eliminating training stipends entirely.) General Motors also helped out in mid-course by ordering half the class to report to an assembly line in Oklahoma and terminating unemployment benefits for those who refused.

You can count on the fact that, once they have graduated, few of your trainees will have the foggiest idea how to find a job. Most of them went right from school to the assembly line, and they can't even write a resume much less sell themselves to an employer. Keep them away from "job clubs" and other successful placement programs. If you want to look as if you're doing something to help, offer employers special bonuses to hire and retrain your graduates—that's usually a sure-fire turn-off.

These lessons aren't new—ineffective training programs have flourished for years. But successful job programs keep cropping up, and their example poses a threat to training industry standards. That's why reporter Mathews' careful documentation of the necessary ingredients for failure is must reading for anyone concerned about the future of this country's training establishment.

From Washington Post (Editorial). "How Not to Retrain Workers." November 12, 1983, p. A18.

ORGANIZATIONAL ENTRY, TRAINING, AND SOCIALIZATION

It seems fitting in nearing the conclusion of this book on training to go back to the beginning. That is, the whole process of training often begins with a person entering the organization. Even when the person is already in the organization, entering training often occurs when a person is moving up to a new job or being given new responsibilities. It is even possible to say that people being trained are often in an uncertain position. That is, they are often moving from one organization to another; this certainly occurs when a person is seeking a new job in a new environment. Even when participating in a training program in the same organization, the trainee is frequently being prepared for a new job or new responsibilities with all the uncertainties of that new situation.

Wanous (1980) notes that one of the central themes in the entry process is the idea that people become socialized by the organization. Van Maanan defines *organizational socialization* as a "process by which a person learns the values, norms and required behaviors which permit him to participate as a member of the organization" (1976, p. 67). Feldman (1989) suggests that there are "multiple socialization processes," which include interactions between learning the actual work tasks and all other types of learning that new employees go through in understanding their organization. Wanous indicates that one of the first ways that people become socialized is through the training program. He points out that you can consider a newcomer's effectiveness according to three factors:

1. Having accurate knowledge of what is expected and clarity of the person's role in the organization
2. Having the KSAs necessary to perform the job
3. Being motivated to perform the job

Most of the time, training programs are considered in relationship to point 2—the KSAs necessary to perform the job. Recently, however, the relationship between training and socialization issues has become a topic of interest. Table 9.3 illustrates Wanous's view of the stages in the socialization process. An examination of those stages makes it clear that many of the learning processes involved in stage 1 through 3 begin with a training program as a person enters the organization. The interactive themes and their relationship to the importance of early experiences is well expressed by Hughes:

> The period of initiation into the role appears to be one wherein the two cultures (i.e., professional and organizational) interact within the individual. Such interaction undoubtedly goes on all through life, but it seems to be more lively, more exciting and uncomfortable, more self-conscious and yet perhaps more deeply unconscious—in the period of learning and initiation. (1958, pp. 119–120)

Table 9.3 Stages in the socialization process

Stage 1: Confronting and accepting organizational reality
- a. Confirmation/disconfirmation of expectations
- b. Conflicts between personal values and needs, and the organizational climates
- c. Discovering which aspects of oneself that are reinforced, not reinforced, and which that are punished by the organization

Stage 2: Achieving role clarity
- a. Being initiated to the tasks in the new job
- b. Defining one's interpersonal roles
  - (i) with respect to peers
  - (ii) with respect to one's boss
- c. Learning to cope with resistance to change
- d. Congruence between one's own evaluation of performance and the organization's evaluation of performance
- e. Learning how to work within the given degree of structure and ambiguity

Stage 3: Locating oneself in the organizational context
- a. Learning which modes of one's own behavior are congruent with those of the organization
- b. Resolution of conflicts at work, and between outside interests and work
- c. Commitment to work and to the organization stimulated by first-year job challenge
- d. The establishment of an altered self-image, new interpersonal relationships, and the adoption of new values

Stage 4: Detecting signposts of successful socialization
- a. Achievement of organizational dependability and commitment
- b. High satisfaction in general
- c. Feelings of mutual acceptance
- d. Job involvement and internal work motivation
- e. The sending of "signals" between newcomers and the organization to indicate mutual acceptance

From J. P. Wanous, *Organizational Entry*, © 1980, by Addison-Wesley Publishing Company, Inc. Reprinted with permission of the publisher.

Research involving these questions is still not very extensive. However, there have been a number of interesting efforts. One such study was conducted by Buxton (1979). She examined the perceptions of experienced police officers and new trainees concerning various aspects of the organization, such as personnel practice effectiveness, reward orientation, status and image, and inflexibility. First, she discovered that in general the experienced officers had a more negative view concerning these variables than did new trainees. However, she also found that as the trainees moved through the twelve-week academy training program and into on-the-job training, their perceptions become more negative, moving in the direction of the views of the experienced police officers. Buxton also predicted that the people who had more realistic expectations after academy training would obtain higher performance ratings from their field-training officers. She did not find such a relationship. However, a few other studies have found such effects.

Research conducted by Hoiberg and Berry (1978) examined the effects of expectations and perceptions along ten dimensions of performance within navy environments of recruit training, six training schools, and subsequent fleet-duty assignment. Within the first forty-eight hours of attendance, subjects enrolled in recruit training and the six navy schools were administered questionnaires regarding their expectations of the recruit or school training. At the midpoint in the various training programs, a questionnaire on perceptions was given. Upon graduation, students were given expectation questionnaires about fleet duty, and at the end of one year all subjects still on active duty were given a perceptions questionnaire and asked to describe their present duty stations.

Performance effectiveness was measured in different ways. For recruit training, effectiveness was defined as graduation from training. For the other six training schools and for the two-year survival period, effectiveness was defined as people who graduated from school and remained on active duty for at least two years. The results indicated that, in recruit training, expectations were significantly related to graduation. Recruits with expectations for innovative training methods and minimal emphasis on efficiency and control were met with a situation incongruent to these expectations. Ultimately, these unrealistic expectations were related to failure to graduate. The findings relative to the technical schools indicate that those schools emphasizing less pressure to complete work tasks and more opportunities for personal growth, support from instructors, and innovative teaching methods had greater percentages of effective students.

These findings reemphasize the concept that the greater the congruency between actual and expected conditions, the greater the performance effectiveness. Based on such results, a case can be made for attending to the context of training and organizational settings. As Hoiberg and Berry point out in their discussion,

> Another recommendation would be to more accurately prepare and train individuals for the work that they will actually perform in the school and work setting. A coordinated effect to align recruiting and training materials with actual work environments and job requirements would be expected to reduce discrepancies between expectations and perceptions. (1978, p. 15)

A study by Lefkowitz (1970) supports this view. He studied turnover problems among sewing-machine operators and found that an important determinant of turnover was encountering a job that was contradictory to the expectations developed through training.

Assuming that enrollment in training is a point of entry into an organization, then the organization has the opportunity at that point to provide the incoming trainee with a realistic view of what to expect from the organization. If the training program provides all the necessary and accurate information required for the trainee to perform effectively in the new position, then it is possible that some of the later "reality shock" of entering the new organization may be eliminated. Many of these issues have become particularly pertinent for individuals entering occupations that were not "open" to them. A good example of this is women entering management careers. An analysis by White et al. (1981) suggests that training for women should focus on a number of areas that clearly fall into the realistic expectations domain. These include programs designed to educate women in the perceptions, strategies, and skills needed in the corporate arena and the identification and removal of the in-place stereotyped behavior that results in blocks to the careers of women. Analyses and evaluations of such programs do not provide clear-cut conclusions; however, as obvious from work with the HCU, the success of women will be as dependent on organizations' willingness to change as it is on women's realistic expectations.

If the training program is designed to provide not only the necessary skills and knowledge but also realistic expectations, then the probability of future job success may be enhanced. In addition, the use of training as a method for providing realistic expectations may help obviate some of the negative consequences of unrealistic expectations of new jobholders. As Wanous (1977) points out, one of the most common consequences of jobholders with unrealistic expectations is turnover. An employee who has exaggerated beliefs about what the new job holds is likely to be disappointed and seek employment elsewhere. Unrealistic expectations may also result in poor transfer of training to the job, poor attitudes, and poor performance on the job.

In an early study, Gomersall and Myers (1966) investigated the effect of a realistic job preview given in the training program for technical operators who manufactured integrated circuits for Texas Instruments. They had determined that many of their turnover problems were related to the anxiety of new employees. Thus, they provided realistic expectations concerning the job and their supervisor. For example, one part of the training was related to disregarding "hall talk":

> Trainees were told of the hazing game that old employees played—scaring newcomers with exaggerated allegations about work rules, standards, disciplinary actions, and other job factors—to make the job as frightening to the newcomers as it had been for them. To prevent these distortions by peers, the trainees were given facts about both the good and the bad aspects of the job and exactly what was expected of them. (p. 167)

The preview resulted in improvements in a number of areas, including reduction in absenteeism and tardiness.

These views of organizational entry and the processes associated with it have considerably broadened the way researchers look at individuals and training programs. For example, Mobley, Hand, Baker, and Meglino (1979) studied the trainee-attrition process in military-training programs. They considered such turnover from the perspective of the choice that a trainee makes in deciding to affiliate with an organization. Their study found a number of variables that predict whether a person will complete the military-training program. For example, they discovered that dropouts, as compared with graduates, felt they had a significantly greater chance of being able to secure a civilian work role.

The discussions about the use of training scores as a predictor of job performance and the information in this section on realistic expectations suggest some interesting research interactions between the two approaches. For example, it is possible to consider miniature job training not only as providing prediction data to the organization but also as providing realistic information to the potential jobholder. Thus, miniature job training provides the individual with the opportunity to see what abilities are required and what the new job situation will be like. In this way, the person may be able to make a more valid organizational choice. Although these sections on prediction and realistic expectations are based on a limited number of research findings, future support for such efforts may expand our conception of the usefulness of training programs. This conception again emphasizes the systems nature of training programs and the organizational environment in which they exist. If there is only one lesson to be learned from this book, it should be that training programs do not exist in isolation. They appear in organizations and interact with all other complex components in the work environment. An understanding of the technical nature of the design of training programs must also include an appreciation of the complex environments in which they exist. This appreciation can produce positive efforts for both the individual, the organization, and the training designer.

It probably also makes sense to help people entering organizations by making the socialization process a part of training and entry. Wanous (1980) notes that one of the most important aspects of entry into organizations is the socialization process and that one of the first ways a person is socialized is through the training process. Although the evidence is limited, inaccurate or limited socialization in training may very well create unrealistic expectations about the work environment, which in turn makes the adjustment to work more difficult. Feldman (1989) explores the idea of "multiple socialization processes," which suggests that it is necessary to explain the interactions among learning work tasks and other types of learning during socialization. In that paper, Feldman explores in-depth issues integrating socialization and training research and sets a research agenda for years to come. Perhaps, in closing this section, it makes sense to again offer the idea that success depends on both the trainee and the organization. Thus, it is just as important for organizations to remove the in-place stereotyped behavior that results in blocks to the careers of the elderly, minorities, and women as it is for the trainee to have realistic expectations about the world of work.

INTERNATIONAL TRAINING ISSUES

Expectations are that more and more organizations will continue to cross international lines where training issues are likely to be serious concerns. Interestingly, Wexley (1984) describes a survey of 105 U.S. companies with overseas branches in which 68 percent have no training programs to prepare individuals for work abroad. The absence of such programs has been discussed as one possible reason for the high failure rate of U.S. companies abroad. One major issue in this work concerns where and how training should be conducted. Eden (1989) describes a study by the International Labour Office. This study concluded that, in the host countries, most multinational enterprises created training programs that were modeled after the training programs of the parent organization, a practice that may be dysfunctional. Mitchell (1981) points out that many U.S. organizations often automatically use their domestic training programs overseas without consideration of the appropriateness to the needs of the international setting. Eden (1989) suggests that whereas technology can be imported, training cannot. It certainly seems that needs assessment techniques focusing on organizational analysis should be useful here. One cannot help but feel that many of the lessons of working with the HCU may apply. In addition, many of the issues of fair employment practices are relevant here. Previous court decisions had made it unclear whether U.S. citizens are protected by civil rights legislation when working for U.S. companies abroad. The 1991 Civil Rights Bill made it clear that such workers are protected.

Ronen (1989) has done a masterful job of examining the theoretical and available research literature concerning training and the international assignee. Based on his review, he offers the following propositions:

1. Often international assignees (IAs) have good track records in their assignments before being sent overseas. This proposition implies that the cause of failure may not be technical knowledge but rather factors such as difficulty in adjusting for either the IA or the family members of the IA.
2. Reports appear to indicate that a manager's relational abilities (for example, interpersonal skills) account for the difference between success and failure.
3. IAs with previous overseas experience were more likely to succeed. This appears to be the case even when the previous experience was in a country different from their present assignment. Ronen suggests that perhaps the socialization experiences help create a better adaptation process.

Ronen (1989) also offers a list of the attributes (Table 9.4) that his analysis of the literature suggests makes a difference between success and failure. Many of these attributes could be the subject of training efforts, but it will be a challenge. In discussing the enormous training implications, Ronen notes

Table 9.4 Attributes of success in overseas assignment

Perseverance	Managerial ability	Resourcefulness
Empathy	Organizational ability	Creativity
Courtesy and tact	Administrative skills	Responsibility
Respect	High motivation	Alertness
Interest in nationals	Overseas experience	Desire to go abroad
Flexibility	Display of respect	Interest in foreign cultures
Adaptability	Listening skills	Intellectual curiosity
Patience	Confidence	Belief in mission and job
Tolerance	Frankness	Willingness to change
Initiative and energy	Kindness	Spouse's positive opinion
Openness	Communication skills	Adaptability of spouse and family
Nonjudgmentalness	Ability to deal with stress	Willingness of spouse to live abroad
Sincerity and integrity	Tolerance for ambiguity	Stable marriage
Emotional stability	Political sensitivity	
Nonethnocentrism	Integrity	
Positive self-image	Dependability	
Independence	Industriousness	
Outgoingness and extraversion	Variety of outside interests	
Experience in company	Youthfulness	
Technical skills and knowledge	Imagination	

From "Training the International Assignee" by S. Ronen. In *Training and Development in Organizations,* by I. L. Goldstein and Associates, 1989, pp. 417–453.

that the manager given an assignment in a foreign country must possess the "patience of a diplomat, the zeal of a missionary, and the linguistic skill of a U.N. interpreter" (p. 418). He sets out an agenda for interested trainers and researchers, which should keep everyone busy for sometime to come.

TRAINING ORGANIZATIONAL LEADERS FOR A COMPLEX WORLD

It seems appropriate to conclude by suggesting that the material presented in this chapter and Chapter 1 have important implications for organizations in training their future leaders. First, future managers will need to be very skilled individuals. They will have to provide on-the-job training to integrate unskilled youth into the work force, while also working with job incumbents and other managers who may not be a "traditional" part of the work force. Supervisors will need to perform these activities at a time when jobs become increasingly complex and national and international competition increasingly intense. In addition, the increase in service-sector jobs will require managers to work more with people rather than objects and things from the assembly line. All of this will make training in such areas as interpersonal skills even more important in the future workplace. As noted in Chapter 1, perhaps

Ronen's quote relevant to the international manager fits for managers assigned to their own country.

The complexities of all of this are made clear in a revealing needs assessment of manager jobs by Kraut, Pedigo, McKenna, and Dunnette (1989). The authors examined the differences in the jobs of first-level managers, middle managers, and executives. They found that first-level managers are heavily involved in managing individual performance, which includes providing feedback, keeping track of subordinates' training and skills, resolving performance problems, resolving conflicts, and so on. These authors also note that this is where most of our training programs have been focused. However, they found that the job of middle managers appears to be more related to linking groups. Thus, middle managers plan and allocate resources between groups, coordinate independent groups, and manage group performance. The authors suggest that training for these individuals should focus on implementing effective group and intergroup work and information systems. This is an area that has not, up to now, been a strong focus of training systems. The main functions for an executive manager are having an eye for the outside, which essentially means that the individual is a monitor of the outside business environment. They gather information about market trends, consult on companywide problems, attend outside meetings as representatives, and the like. Again, training efforts for this function remains to be explored in a systematic fashion.

Another effort to learn about the complexities of the job of a manager is represented by the work of McCauley, Lombardo, and Usher (1989). These authors based their framework on what managers have actually learned in their careers. In this process, they conducted extensive interviews with executives. For example, in one part of the development process, they interviewed nineteen top executives at three corporations and asked them to describe two people they knew very well: One was an executive who succeeded, and the other was an executive who had been demoted, fired, or held at a level below an expected achievement. As a result, these authors explored dimensions that ordinarily never appear in typical management-appraisal instruments. They have titled their system "Benchmarks." A sample of some of their scales, descriptions, and sample items appears in Table 9.5. The development of the scales was based on responses from 336 managers from eight Fortune 500 corporations who were rated by the supervisors. Those sample items represent training goals for managers in our complex society. It will be an interesting challenge to see what kind of career development combined with training efforts will be necessary to achieve those objectives.

Another indication of these complexities is shown in the work of Schneider and Bowen (in press), who are examining the implications of what being a service organization actually means. They note that service-organization employees are unique in the sense that they have frequent contact with consumers and the organization. This duality of function places great stress on the individual to have skills that fit both functions. This had led one organization, Selin Company (1984), to suggest that training needs to focus on the following functions:

Create understanding of the employee's role.
Learn techniques of communicating positively with customers.
Learn methods of solving customer complaints.
Learn techniques for dealing with difficult customers.
Learn procedures that support quality customer service.

Those of us who have stood in lines at banks and other organizations know how difficult it is to find people who have these skills. Again, the future training agenda is enormous.

Finally, it should be clear that these organizations will not be able to afford formal training programs to deal with all the complexities of these issues. Despite the investment of huge sums of money, analyses indicate that as many as 40 percent of job-holders have received no job-relevant training and only 10 percent of private-sector employees receive training from their own organization (Carnevale, Gainer, & Villet, 1990). As Campbell (1991) notes, even if these estimates are an overestimate of the problem, there still is a very serious situation. This is especially the case given the problems we will face over the next twenty years. If we do not find a way for individuals to take increased responsibility for their own training and development, we are in for a very difficult time.

One developing approach to these issues is the idea of the self-directed learner (Manz & Manz, 1991). The *self-directed learner* refers to learning that takes place outside a formal training program without the guidance of an actual trainer. As these writers note, this type of learning occurs because, in our work life, we cannot possibly gain all we need from formal programs. Manz and Manz propose that increases in self-directed learning occur with increases in self-efficacy and self-leadership skills. They also propose a number of strategies that are likely to enhance self-directed learning:

1. Give the learner the opportunity to gain success on relevant and important tasks.
2. Provide appropriate credible and constructive models to demonstrate the self-leadership skills.
3. Make sure there is a nonthreatening environment and encourage the taking of risks.
4. Ensure that the instructor model is open to other viewpoints for the sake of learning and make it clear that his or her viewpoint is open to challenge.

Manz and Sims (1989) also describe how leaders can facilitate this process and define a "superleader" as "one who leads others to lead themselves" (p. 3). Campbell (1991), while noting the importance of this enterprise, also suggests that considerable work needs to be done to explicate what and how this is

Table 9.5 Benchmarks: Scale names, descriptions, and sample items

Section 1 Scales	*Description of Scale*	*Sample Items*
1a. Resourcefulness	Can think strategically, engage in flexible problem-solving behavior, and work effectively with higher management.	— Makes good decisions under pressure with incomplete information. — Links his/her responsibilities with the mission of the whole organization.
1b. Doing Whatever It Takes	Has perseverance and focus in the face of obstacles.	— Faces difficult situations with guts and tenacity. — Controls his/her own career; does not sit and wait for the company to plan a course to follow.
1c. Being a Quick Study	Quickly masters new technical and business knowledge.	— Learns a new skill quickly. — Quickly masters new vocabulary and operating rules needed to understand how the business works.
2a. Building and Mending Relationships	Knows how to build and maintain working relationships with co-workers and external parties.	— When working with a group over whom he/she has no control, gets things done by finding common ground. — Relates to all kinds of individuals tactfully, from shop floor to top executives.
2b. Leading Subordinates	Delegates to subordinates effectively, broadens their opportunities, and acts with fairness towards them.	— Is willing to delegate important tasks, not just things he/she doesn't want to do. — Relies on persuasion or expertise first; uses the power of the position as a last resort.
2c. Compassion and Sensitivity	Shows genuine interest in others and sensitivity to subordinates' needs.	— Is willing to help an employee with personal problems. — Is sensitive to signs of overwork in others.
3. Straightforwardness and Composure	Is honorable and steadfast.	— Relies on style more than substance in dealings with top management. — Becomes hostile or moody when things are not going his/her way.
4. Setting a Developmental Climate	Provides a challenging climate to encourage subordinates' development.	— Is willing to pitch in and lead subordinates by example. — Develops subordinates by providing challenge and opportunity.
5. Confronting Problem Subordinates	Acts decisively and with fairness when dealing with problem subordinates.	— Is able to fire loyal but incompetent people without procrastinating. — Can deal effectively with resistant subordinates.

6. Team Orientation	Accomplishes tasks through managing others.	— Acts as if his/her managerial success is built by a team of strong subordinates.
7. Balance between Personal Life and Work	Balances work priorities with personal life so that neither is neglected.	— Acts as if there is more to life than just having a career. — Lets job demands cause family problems.
8. Decisiveness	Prefers quick and approximate actions to slow and precise ones in many management situations.	— Displays a real bias for action, calculated risks, and quick decisions. — Does not hesitate when making decisions.
9. Self-Awareness	Has an accurate picture of strengths and weaknesses and is willing to improve.	— Sorts out his/her strengths and weaknesses fairly accurately.
10. Hiring Talented Staff	Hires talented people for his/her team.	— Hires people who are not afraid of responsibility or risks.
11. Putting People at Ease	Displays warmth and a good sense of humor.	— Has a warm personality that puts people at ease.
12. Acting with Flexibility	Can behave in ways that are often seen as opposites.	— Is tough and at the same time compassionate. — Can lead and let others lead.
Section 2 Scales:		
1. Problems with Interpersonal Relationships	Difficulties in developing comfortable working relationships with others.	— Adopts a bullying style under stress. — Isolates him/herself from others.
2. Difficulty in Molding a Staff	Difficulties in selecting and building a team.	— Chooses an overly narrow subordinate group. — Is not good at building a team.
3. Difficulty in Making Strategic Transitions	Difficulties in moving from the technical/tactical level to the general/strategic level.	— Cannot handle a job requiring the formulation of complex organizational strategies. — Can't make the mental transition from technical manager to general manager.
4. Lack of Follow-Through	Difficulties in following up on promises, really completing a job, and attention to detail.	— Makes a splash and moves on without really completing a job. — Has left a trail of little problems.
5. Overdependence	Relies too much on a boss, powerful advocate, or one's own natural talent.	— Has chosen to stay with the same boss too long. — Might burn out, run out of steam.
6. Strategic Differences with Management	Disagrees with higher management about business strategy.	— Disagrees with higher management about how the business should be run.

From "Diagnosing Management Development Needs: An Instrument Based on How Managers Develop" by C. McCauley, M. M. Lombardo, C. J. Usher. In *Journal of Management,* 1989, *15,* pp. 389–403.

done. For example, is this actually a training strategy and, if so, how will it be done? One concern is similar to the same issues that exist with all training programs—that is, finding out the conditions that make it work. Obviously, this effort is at an early stage of development, but the fact that it exists probably is a reflection of the critical training issues that we will be facing now and in the next century.

Epilog

For the individual, training opportunities are very important because they are instrumental in earning entry and enjoying the satisfactions and rewards that are associated with the world of work. Thus, training represents a positive hope both for people first entering the world of work and for individuals changing their work environment. Individuals expect that training will give them the opportunities to enter the job market with needed skills, to perform in new functions, and to be promoted into new situations. This emphasis on training opportunities is consistent with the concept of work and the value of it as an activity in the daily lives of those within society.

At this time, employees, managers, and organizations are more frequently turning to training as a solution to work issues. This increased emphasis is reflected in a variety of ways. For example, as noted in the beginning of this text, labor unions are insisting that new contracts must include opportunities for training to meet technological changes in the workplace, and training programs are frequently offered as a court-imposed solution to give individuals who have been victims of discrimination an opportunity for equal employment. Also, organizations are turning to training as a solution to the complexities of customer service environments and international environments. Well-designed training programs are more likely to accomplish these goals, but the point here is that there are positive expectations that training can accomplish these purposes. One goal of this book is to present the knowledge base stemming from the research literature available that, if used, makes it more likely that training will have positive outcomes. Thus, to the degree that training is based on careful needs assessment, well-designed instructional strategies and a research strategy that permits the collection of data that provides feedback on where revisions are necessary, training is more likely to meet everyone's expectations.

One characteristic of training research is that although many of these same expectations concerning the positive value of training existed many years ago, theory and research lagged far behind. It has only been since the 1980s that there has been considerable research and theory development in these areas. For example, the material in Chapter 4 on the cognitive and motivational constructs reflects considerable research that has been accomplished in the past five years. This book arrives at a time when even more researchers are refocusing their attention on training issues. Thus, another goal of this book is to help stimulate a future research and practice agenda. There are many challenges facing us in the next several decades. As discussed in the text, demographic trends make it clear that the rate of growth in the work force will seriously decline during the next decade. This will make it increasingly important for each individual to have the opportunity to reach his or her maximum potential and will result in increased emphasis on the use of training programs for both entry-level and experienced workers. In addition, jobs are likely to become more technologically complex, resulting in increased cognitive demands on the individual worker. This situation is likely to result in demands for further emphasis on the use of training programs as a way of preparing the individual for jobs in the workplace.

For people involved in training research and design, these events present both a great opportunity and challenge. Although it is clear that there is a growing knowledge base, many issues still remain unresolved. For example, we are just at the beginning of understanding the factors involved in establishing a positive training–transfer climate and in attempting to determine the cognitive components of instructional-program design.

The demands of society and the emerging number of researchers interested in training make for exciting possibilities. It should keep researchers interested in exploring training issues busy for decades to come. I hope this book provides a little of the stimulation for those efforts.

References

Ackerman, P. L. (1987). Individual differences in skill learning. An integration of psychometric and information processing perspectives. *Psychological Bulletin, 102,* 3–27.

Adams, J. S. (1965). Injustice in social exchange. In L. Berkowitz (Ed.), *Advances in experimental social psychology.* Vol. 2. New York: Academic Press.

Alliger, G. M., & Janek, E. A. (1989). Kirkpatrick's levels of training criteria: Thirty years later. *Personnel Psychology, 42,* 331–342.

Ammerman, H. L., & Pratzner, F. C. (1977). *Performance content for job training.* R & D Ser. 121–125. Vols. 1–5. Columbus, OH: Center for Vocational Education.

Anderson, J. R. (1987). Skill acquisition: Compilation of weak-method problem solutions. *Psychological Review, 94,* 192–210.

Anderson, J. R., Farrell, R., & Sauers, R. (1984). Learning to program in LISP. *Cognitive Science, 8,* 87–129.

Argyris, C. (1964). T-groups for organizational effectiveness. *Harvard Business Review, 42,* 60–74.

Argyris, C. (1967). We must make work worthwhile. *Life, 62*(18), 56–68.

Argyris, C. (1968). Some unintended consequences of rigorous research. *Psychological Bulletin, 70,* 185–197.

Argyris, C. (1980). Some limitations of the case method: Experiences in a management development program. *Academy of Management Review, 5,* 291–298.

Arvey, R. D. (1979). *Fairness in selecting employees.* Reading, MA: Addison-Wesley.

Arvey, R. D., & Cole, D. A. (1989). Evaluating change due to training. In I. L Goldstein (Ed.), *Training and development in organizations.* San Francisco: Jossey-Bass.

Atkinson, J. W., & Feather, N. T. (1966). *A theory of achievement motivation.* New York: Wiley.

Atkinson, R. C. (1968). Computerized instruction and the learning process. *American Psychologist, 23,* 225–239.

Baldwin, T. T., & Ford, J. K. (1988). Transfer of training: A review and directions for future research. *Personnel Psychology, 41,* 63–105.

Baldwin, T. T., Magjuka, R. J., & Loher, B. T. (1991). The perils of participation: Effects of choice of training on trainee motivation and learning. *Personnel Psychology, 44,* 51–65.

Ball, S., & Anderson, S. B. (1975). *Professional issues in the evaluation of education/training programs.* Arlington, VA: Office of Naval Research.

Ball, S., & Bogatz, G. A. (1970). *The first year of Sesame Street: An evaluation.* Princeton, NJ: Educational Testing Service.

Bandura, A. (1969). *Principles of behavior modification.* New York: Holt, Rinehart & Winston.

Bandura, A. (1977). *Social learning theory.* Englewood Cliffs, NJ: Prentice-Hall.

Bandura, A. (1986). *Social foundations of thought and action: A social cognitive theory.* Englewood Cliffs, N.J.: Prentice-Hall.

Barbee, J. R., & Keil, E. C. (1973). Experimental techniques of job interview training for the disadvantaged: Videotape feedback, behavior modification, and microcounseling. *Journal of Applied Psychology, 58,* 209–213.

Barkin, S. (1970). Retraining and job redesign: Positive approaches to the continued employment of older persons. In H. L. Sheppard (Ed.), *Towards an industrial gerontology.* Cambridge, MA: Schenkman.

Bartlett, C. J. (1978). Equal employment opportunity issues in training. *Human Factors, 20,* 179–188.

Bartlett, C. J. (1982). *Teaching scale developed for Division of Behavioral and Social Sciences.* College Park: University of Maryland.

Bartlett, C. J., & Goldstein, I. L. (1974). A validity analysis of employment tests for bus drivers. *Training Educational Resource Programs Technological Report.* College Park: University of Maryland.

Bass, B. M., & Vaughan, J. A. (1966). *Training in industry: The management of learning.* Belmont, CA: Wadsworth.

Becker, S. W. (1970). The parable of the pill. *Administrative Science Quarterly, 15,* 94–96.

Bellows, R. M. (1941). Procedures for evaluating vocational criteria. *Journal of Applied Psychology, 25,* 499–513.

Bennett, H. L. (1983). Remembering drink orders: The memory skills of cocktail waitresses. *Human Learning: Journal of Practical Research and Applications, 2,* 157–169.

Bennis, W. (1969). *Organization development: Its nature, origins and prospects.* Reading, MA: Addison-Wesley.

Bernardin, H. J., & Beatty, R. W. (1984). *Performance appraisal: Assessing human behavior at work.* Boston: Kent.

Bernardin, H. J., & Villanova, P. J. (1986). Performance appraisal. In E. A. Locke (Ed.), *The generalizability of laboratory experiments: An inductive survey.* Lexington, MA: Heath.

Blum, M. L., & Naylor, J. C. (1968). *Industrial psychology: Its theoretical and social foundations.* New York: Harper & Row.

Blumberg, A., & Golembiewski, R. (1976). *Learning and change in groups.* Clinton, MA: Colonial Press.

Boudreau, J. W. (1984). Decision theory contributions to HRM theory and practice. *Industrial Relations, 23,* 198–217.

Bourne, L. E., & Ekstrand, B. R. (1973). *Psychology: Its principles and meanings.* Hinsdale, IL: Dryden.

Bove, R. (1984). Reach out and train someone. *Training and Development Journal, 38,* 26.

Bower, G. H., & Hilgard, E. R. (1981). *Theories of learning* (5th ed.). Englewood Cliffs, NJ: Prentice-Hall.

Bracht, G. H. (1970). Experimental factors related to aptitude-treatment interactions. *Review of Educational Research, 40,* 627–645.

Bray, D. W. (1976). The assessment center method. In R. L. Craig (Ed.), *Training and development handbook.* New York: McGraw-Hill.

Briggs, L. J., & Angell, D. (1964). Programmed instruction in science and mathematics. *Review of Educational Research, 34,* 354–373.

Briggs, L. J., Campeau, P. L., Gagné, R. M., & May, M. A. (1967). *Instructional media: A procedure for the design of multi-media instruction, a critical review of research, and suggestions for future research.* Palo Alto, CA: American Institutes for Research.

Brown, A. L., & Palincsar, A. M. (1984). Reciprocal teaching of comprehension-fostering and monitoring activities. *Cognition and Instruction, 1,* 175–177.

Brown, A. L., & Palincsar, A. M. (1989). Guided, cooperative learning and individual knowledge acquisition. In L. B. Resnick (Ed.), *Knowing and learning: Essays in honor of Robert Glaser.* Hillsdale, NJ: Erlbaum.

Bruner, J. S. (1963). Needed: A theory of instruction. *Educational Leadership, 20,* 523–532.

Buchanan, P. C. (1971). Sensitivity, or laboratory, training in industry. *Sociological Inquiry, 41,* 217–225.

Buchwald, A. (1970). Training on the train. *Washington Post.*

Bunker, K. A., & Cohen, S. L. (1977). The rigors of training evaluation: A discussion and field demonstration. *Personnel Psychology, 30*(4), 525–541.

Burke, H. L., & Bennis, W. G. (1961). Changes in perception of self and others during human relations training. *Human Relations, 14,* 165–182.

Burke, M. J., & Day, R. R. (1986). A cumulative study of the effectiveness of managerial training. *Journal of Applied Psychology, 71,* 232–245.

Buxton, V. M. (1979). *The evaluation of a police training program: Changes in learning, expectations and behavior.* Unpublished doctoral dissertation, University of Maryland.

Byham, W. C. (1975). The use of assessment centres in management development. In B. Taylor & G. L. Lipett (Eds.), *Management development and training handbook.* London: McGraw-Hill.

Campbell, D. T. (1969). Reforms as experiments. *American Psychologist, 24,* 409–429.

Campbell, D. T., & Stanley, J. C. (1963). *Experimental and quasi-experimental designs for research.* Chicago: Rand McNally.

Campbell, J. P. (1971). Personnel training and development. In *Annual Review of Psychology.* Palo Alto, CA: Annual Reviews.

Campbell, J. P. (1978). *What we are about: An inquiry into the self concept of industrial and organizational psychology.* Presidential address to Division of Industrial and Organizational Psychology, 86th Annual Meeting of the American Psychological Association, Toronto.

Campbell, J. P. (1988). Training design for performance improvement. In J. P. Campbell & R. J. Campbell (Eds.), *Productivity in organizations.* San Francisco: Jossey-Bass.

Campbell, J. P. (1991). Invited reaction: The compleat self-learner. *Human Resource Development Quarterly, 2,* 13–20.

Campbell, J. P., Dunnette, M. D., Lawler, III, E. E., & Weick, Jr., K. E. (1970). *Managerial behavior, performance, and effectiveness.* New York: McGraw-Hill.

Campbell, J. P., McCloy, R. A., Oppler, S. H., & Sager, C. E. (In press). A theory of performance. In N. Schmitt & W. C. Borman (Eds.), *Personnel selection.* San Francisco: Jossey-Bass.

Campion, M. A., & Campion, J. E. (1987). Evaluation of an interview skills training program in a natural field setting. *Personnel Psychology, 40,* 675–691.

Cannon-Bowers, J. A., Salas, E., & Converse, S. A. (1990) Cognitive psychology and team training: Training shared mental models of complex systems. *Human Factors Society Bulletin, 33*(12), 1–4.

Carnevale, A. P., Gainer, L. J., & Villet, J. (1990). *Training in America: The organization and strategic role of training.* San Francisco: Jossey-Bass.

Caro, P. (1984). ISD-CAI technology applications to pilot training. *Training Technical Group Newsletter of the Human Factors Society, 10,* 3–4.

Cascio, W. F. (1989). Using utility analysis to assess training outcomes. In I. L. Goldstein (Ed.), *Training and development in organizations.* San Francisco: Jossey-Bass.

Cascio, W. F., & Zammuto, R. F. (1987). *Societal trends and staffing policies.* Denver: University of Colorado Press.

Chapanis, A., Garner, W. R., & Morgan, C. T. (1949). *Applied experimental psychology: Human factors in engineering design.* New York: Wiley.

Chu, G. C., & Schramm, W. (1967). *Learning from television: What the research says.* Washington, D.C.: National Association of Educational Broadcasters.

Cicero, J. P. (1973). Behavioral objectives for technical training systems. *Training and Development Journal, 28,* 14–17.

Clancy, W. J. (1986). From GUIDON to NEOMYCIN and HERCULES in twenty short lessons: ONR final report 1979–1985. *AI Magazine, 7,* 40–60.

Clement, R. W. (1982). Testing the hierarchy theory of training evaluation: An expanded role for trainee reactions. *Public Personnel Management Journal, 11,* 176–184.

Cochran, N. (1978). Grandma Moses and the corruption of data. *Evaluation Quarterly, 2,* 363–375.

Cohen, K. J., Cyert, R. M., Dill, W. R., Kuehn, A. A., Miller, M. H., Van Wormer, T. A., & Winters, P. R. (1962). The Carnegie Tech management game. In H. Guetzkow (Ed.), *Simulation in social science: Readings.* Englewood Cliffs, NJ: Prentice-Hall.

Cohen, S. L. (1991). The challange of training in the nineties. *Training and Development, 45,* 30–35.

Collins, A. M. (1977). Processes in acquiring knowledge. In R. C. Anderson, R. J. Spiro, & W. E. Montague (Eds.), *Schooling and the acquisition of knowledge.* Hillsdale, NJ: Erlbaum.

Collins, A., & Adams, M. J. (1977). Comparison of two teaching strategies in computer-assisted instruction. *Contemporary Educational Psychology, 2,* 133–148.

Collins, A., Adams, M. J., & Pew, R. W. (1978). Effectiveness of an interactive map display in tutoring geography. *Journal of Educational Psychology, 70,* 1–7.

Cook, T. D., & Campbell, D. T. (1976). The design and conduct of quasi-experiments and true experiments in field settings. In M. D. Dunnette (Ed.), *Handbook of industrial and organizational psychology.* Chicago: Rand McNally.

Cook, T. D., & Campbell, D. T. (1979). *Quasi-experimentation: Design and analysis issues for field settings.* Chicago: Rand McNally.

Cook, T. D., Campbell, D. T., & Peracchio, L. (1990). Quasi-experimentation. In M. D. Dunnette & L. M. Hough (Eds.), *Handbook of industrial and organizational psychology.* Palo Alto, CA: Consulting Psychologists Press.

Cooke, N. M., & Schvaneveldt, R. W. (1988). Effects of computer programming experience on network representations of abstract programming concepts. *International Journal of Man-Machine Studies, 29,* 533–550.

Cooley, W. W., & Glaser, R. (1969). The computer and individualized instruction. *Science, 166,* 574–582.

Cooper, C. L. (1975). How psychologically dangerous are T-groups and encounter groups? *Human Relations, 28,* 249–260.

Cooper, C. L. (1977). Adverse and growthful effects of experiential learning groups: The role of trainer, participant, and group characteristics. *Human Relations, 3,* 1103–1129.

Craig, R. L. (1976). *Training and Development Handbook.* New York: McGraw-Hill.

Cram, D. (1961). *Explaining teaching machines and programming.* San Francisco: Fearon.

Cranny, C. J., & Doherty, M. E. (1988). Importance ratings in job analysis: Notes on the misinterpretation of factor analysis. *Journal of Applied Psychology, 73,* 320–322.

Cronbach, L. J. (1957). The two disciplines of scientific psychology. *American Psychologist, 12,* 671–684.

Cronbach, L. J. (1967). How can instruction be adapted to individual differences? In R. M. Gagné (Ed.), *Learning and individual differences.* Columbus, OH: Merrill.

Cronbach, L. J., & Snow, R. E. (1969). *Individual differences in learning ability as a function of instructional variables.* Final report, School of Education, Stanford University (Contract No. OEC-4-6061269-1217), U.S. Office of Education.

Cronbach, L. J., & Snow, R. E. (1977). *Aptitudes and instructional methods.* New York: Irvington.

Cross, T. (1986). *The black power imperative: Racial inequality and the politics of nonviolence.* New York: Faulkner.

Crowder, N. A. (1960). Automatic tutoring by means of intrinsic programming. In A. A. Lumsdaine & R. Glaser (Eds.), *Teaching machines and programmed learning.* Washington, D.C.: National Education Association.

Cullen, J. G., Sawzin, S. A., Sisson, G. R., & Swanson, R. A. (1978). Cost effectiveness: A model for assessing the training investment. *Training and Development Journal, 32,* 24–29.

Dachler, H. P. Personal communication, 1974.

Davis, J. D. (1977-1978). The Navy CMI system: A brief overview. *Journal of Educational Technology Systems, 6,* 143–150.

DeCecco, J. P. (1968). *The psychology of learning and instruction: Educational psychology.* Englewood Cliffs, N.J.: Prentice-Hall.

Decker, P. J. (1980). Effects of symbolic coding and rehearsal in behavior-modeling training. *Journal of Applied Psychology, 65,* 627–634.

Decker, P. J. (1982). The enhancement of behavior modeling training of supervisory skills by the inclusion of retention processes. *Personnel Psychology, 35,* 323–332.

Decker, P. J. (1983). The effects of rehearsal group size and video feedback in behavior modeling training. *Personnel Psychology, 36,* 763–773.

Decker, P. J. (1984). Effects of different symbolic coding stimuli in behavior modeling training. *Personnel Psychology, 37,* 711–720.

Decker, P. J., & Nathan, B. R. (1985). *Behavior modeling training: Principles and applications.* New York: Praeger.

Dill, W. R., Jackson, J. R., & Sweeney, J. W.

(Eds.) (1961). *Proceedings of the conference on business games as teaching devices.* School of Business Administration, Tulane University, April 26–28.

Dorcus, R. M. (1940). Methods of evaluating the efficiency of door-to-door salesmen of bakery products. *Journal of Applied Psychology, 24,* 587–594.

Dossett, D. L., & Hulvershorn, P. (1983). Increasing technical training efficiency: Peer training via computer-assisted instruction. *Journal of Applied Psychology, 68,* 552–558.

Downs, S. (1985). Retraining for new skills. *Ergonomics, 28,* 1205–1211.

Dunnette, M. D., & Campbell, J. P. (1968). Laboratory education: Impact on people and organizations. *Industrial Relations, 8,* 1–27, 41–44.

Dyer, J. C. (1984). Team research and team training: State-of-the-art review. In F. A. Muckler (Ed.), *Human Factors Review* (pp. 285–323). Santa Monica, CA: Human Factors Society, Inc.

Eachus, H. T., & King, P. H. (1966). *Acquisition and retention of cross-cultural interaction skills through self-confrontation.* (AMRL-TR-66-8). Wright–Patterson Air Force Base, OH: Aerospace Medical Research Laboratories.

Eberts, R. E., & Brock, J. F. (1987). Computer-assisted and computer-managed instruction. In G. Salvendy (Ed.), *Handbook of human factors.* New York: Wiley.

Eden, D. (1989). Training. In B. Bass., P. Drenth, & P. Weissenberg (Eds.), *Advances in organizational psychology: An international review.* Beverly Hills, CA: Sage.

Eden, D. (1990). *Pygmalion in management.* Lexington, MA: Lexington Books.

Eden, D., & Ravid, G. (1982). Pygmalion versus self-expectancy: Effects of instructor and self-expectancy on trainee performance. *Organizational Behavior and Human Performance, 30,* 351–364.

Eden, D., & Shani, A. B. (1982). Pygmalion goes to boot camp: Expectancy leadership and trainee performance. *Journal of Applied Psychology, 67,* 194–199.

Edgerton, H. A. (1958). *The relationship of method of instruction to trainee aptitude pattern.* (Technical Report, Contract Nornr 1042 [00]). New York: Richardson, Bellows, Henry.

Ellis, H. C. (1965). *The transfer of learning.* New York: Macmillan.

Ellis, J. A., & Wulfeck, II, W. H. (1978). *The instructional quality inventory: IV. Job performance aid.* (NPRDC SR 79-5). San Diego: Navy Personnel Research and Development Center.

Faria, A. J. (1989). Business gaming: Current usage levels. *Journal of Management Development, 8,* 59–65.

Feeney, E. J. (1972). Performance audit, feedback, and positive reinforcement. *Training and Development Journal, 26,* 8–13 .

Feifer, I. (1970). Training on the train: By Art Buchwald. *Training and Development Journal, 25,* 43.

Feldman, D. C. (1989). Socialization, resocialization, and training: Reframing the research agenda. In I. L. Goldstein (Ed.), *Training and development in organizations.* San Francisco: Jossey-Bass.

Feur, D. (1987). Domino's Pizza: Training for fast times. *Training, 24,* 25–30.

Fiedler, F. E. (1964). A contingency model of leadership effectiveness. In L. Berkowitz (Ed.), *Advances in experimental social psychology.* New York: Academic Press.

Fiedler, F. E. (1967). *A theory of leadership effectiveness.* New York: McGraw-Hill.

Fiedler, F. E., Chemers, M. M., & Mahar, L. (1976). *Improving leadership effectiveness: The Leader Match concept.* New York: Wiley.

Fiedler, F. E., & Mahar, L. (1979). The effectiveness of contingency model training: A review of the validation of LEADER MATCH. *Personnel Psychology, 32,* 45–62.

Fiedler, F. E., Mitchell, R. T., & Triandis, H. C. (1971). The culture assimilator: An approach to cross-cultural training. *Journal of Applied Psychology, 55,* 95–102.

Fine, S. A. (1978). Contribution of the job element and functional job analysis approaches to content validity. Paper presented at the International Personnel Management Assessment Council Annual Conference, Atlanta.

Fisk, A. D., & Schneider, W. (1981). Controlled and automatic processing during tasks requiring sustained attention: A new approach to vigilance. *Human Factors, 23,* 737–750.

Fleishman, E. A. (1972). On the relationship between abilities, learning, and human performance. *American Psychologist, 27,* 1017–1032.

Fleishman, E. A., Harris, E. F., & Burtt, H. E. (1955). Leadership and supervision in industry. *Bureau of Educational Research, Report No. 33.* Ohio State University.

Fleishman, E. A., & Mumford, M. D. (1989). Individual attributes and training performance. In I. L. Goldstein (Ed.), *Training and development in organizations.* San Francisco: Jossey-Bass.

Fletcher, J. D. (1990). *Effectiveness and cost of interactive videodiscs in defense training and education.* Alexandria, VA: Institute for Defense Analysis.

Ford, J. K., & Wroten, S. P. (1984). Introducing new methods for conducting training evaluation and for linking training evaluation to program redesign. *Personnel Psychology, 37,* 651–665.

Fossum, J. A., Arvey, R. D., Paradise, C. A., & Robbins, N. E. (1986). Modeling the skills obsolescence process. *Academy of Management Review, 11,* 362–374.

Franz, T. M., McCallum, G. A., Lewis, M. D., Prince, C., & Salas, E. (1990). *Pilot briefings and aircrew coordination evaluation: Empirical Results.* Paper presented at the 12th Annual Department of Defense Symposium, Colorado Springs, Colorado.

Frayne, C. A., & Latham, G. P. (1987). The application of social learning theory to employee self management of attendance. *Journal of Applied Psychology, 72,* 387–392.

Freeberg, N. E. (1976). Criterion measures for youth-work training programs: The development of relevant performance dimensions. *Journal of Applied Psychology, 61*(5), 537–545.

French, S. H. (1953). Measuring progress toward industrial relations objectives. *Personnel, 30,* 338–347.

Friedlander, F., & Greenberg, S. (1971). Effect of job attitudes, training and organizational climate on performance of the hard-core unemployed. *Journal of Applied Psychology, 55,* 287–295.

Fry, E. B. (1963). *Teaching machines and programmed instruction.* New York: McGraw-Hill.

Fullerton, Jr., H. N. (1985). The 1995 labor force: BLS' latest projections. *Monthly Labor Review, 117,* 17–25.

Gagné, R. M. (1962). Military training and principles of learning. *American Psychologist, 17,* 83–91.

Gagné, R. M. (1970). *The conditions for learning* (2nd ed.). New York: Holt, Rinehart & Winston.

Gagné, R. M. (1984). Learning outcomes and their effects: Useful categories of human performance. *American Psychologist, 39,* 377–385.

Gagné, R. M. (1985). Instructional psychology. In *Annual Review of Psychology.* Palo Alto, CA: Annual Reviews.

Gagné, R. M., & Briggs, L. J. (1979). *Principles of instructional design.* New York: Holt, Rinehart & Winston.

Gagné, R. M., & Dick, W. (1983). Instructional psychology. In *Annual Review of Psychology.* Palo Alto, CA: Annual Reviews.

Galagan, P. (1984). The trainer in the machine. *Training and Development Journal, 38,* 4.

Ghiselli, E. E. (1956). The placement of workers: Concepts and problems. *Personnel Psychology, 9,* 1–16.

Gilbert, T. F. (1960). On the relevance of laboratory investigation of learning to self-instructional programming. In A. A. Lumsdaine & R. Glaser (Eds.), *Teaching machines and programmed instruction.* Washington, D.C.: National Education Association.

Gilbert, T. F. (1982). A question of performance—Part I—The probe model. *Training and Development Journal, 36,* 20–30.

Gilliam, R. (1988). *The effects of a job acquisition training program on the attitudes, behaviors and knowledge of educated black adults.* Unpublished doctoral dissertation, University of Maryland, College Park.

Gist, N, E. (1989). The influence of training method on self-efficacy and idea generation among managers. *Personnel Psychology, 42,* 787–805.

Gist, M. E., Schwoerer, C., & Rosen, B. (1989). Effects of alternative training methods on self-efficacy and performance in computer software training. *Journal of Applied Psychology, 74,* 884–891.

Gitomer, D. H. (1988). Individual differences in technical trouble shooting. *Human Performance, 1,* 111–131.

Glaser, E. M., & Taylor, S. H. (1973). Factors influencing the success of applied research. *American Psychologist, 28*(2), 140–460.

Glaser, R. (1982). Instructional psychology: Past, present and future. *American Psychologist, 37,* 292–306.

Glaser, R. (1990). The reemergence of learning theory within instructional research. *American Psychologist, 45,* 29–39.

Glickman, A. S., Zimmer, S., Montero, R. C., Guerette, P. J., Campbell, W. J., Morgan B. B., & Salas, E. (1987). The evolution of teamwork skills: An empirical assessment with implications for training. Technical Report NTSC 87-016. Arlington, VA: Office of Naval Research.

Goldstein, A. P., & Sorcher, M. (1974). *Changing supervisor behavior.* New York: Pergamon Press.

Goldstein, I. L. (1978a). The pursuit of validity in the evaluation of training programs. *Human Factors, 20,* 131–144.

Goldstein, I. L. (1978b). *Understanding research in organizational environments: Can process measures help?* Paper presented at Annual Meeting of the Eastern Psychological Association, Washington, D.C.

Goldstein, I. L. (1980). Training in work organizations. In *Annual Review of Psychology.* Palo Alto, CA: Annual Reviews.

Goldstein, I. L., & Bartlett, C. J. (1977). *Validation of a training program for police officers.* Unpublished data, College Park: University of Maryland.

Goldstein, I. L., Braverman, E. P., & Goldstein, H. W. (1991). Needs assessment. In K. Wexley (Ed.), *Developing human resources.* Washington, D.C.: BNA Books.

Goldstein, I. L., & Gilliam, P. (1990). Training system issues in the year 2000. *American Psychologist, 45,* 134–143.

Goldstein, I. L. & Goldstein, H. W. (1990). Training as an approach for organizations to the challenge of human resource issues in the year 2000. *Journal of Occupational Change Management, 3,* 30–43.

Goldstein, I. L., Macey, W. H., & Prien, E. P. (1981). Needs assessment approaches for training development. In H. Meltzer & W. R. Nord (Eds.), *Making organizations humane and productive.* New York: Wiley.

Goldstein, I. L., & Musicante, G. R. (1985). From the laboratory to the field: An examination of training models. In E. A. Locke (Ed.), *The generalizability of laboratory experiments: An inductive survey.* Lexington, MA: Heath.

Goldstein, I. L., & Thayer, P. W. (1987). Panel discussion on facilitators and inhibitors of the training transfer process. Presented at the Society for Industrial and Organizational Psychology, Atlanta.

Goldstein, I. L., Tuttle, T. C., Wood, G. D., & Grether, C. B. (1975). *Behavioral action intervention strategies: Training.* Columbia, MD: Westinghouse Behavioral Sciences Center.

Golembiewski, R. T., & Carrigan, S. B. (1970). Planned change in organization style based on the laboratory approach. *Administrative Science Quarterly, 15,* 79–93.

Gomersall, E. R., & Myers, M. S. (1966). Breakthrough in on-the-job training. *Harvard Business Review, 44,* 66–72.

Goodman, P. S. (1969). Hiring and training the hard-core unemployed: A problem in system definition. *Human Organization, 28,* 259–269.

Goodman, P. S., Salipante, P., & Paransky, H. (1973). Hiring, training, and retraining the hard-core unemployed: A selected review. *Journal of Applied Psychology, 58,* 23–33.

Gordon, J. (October 1988). Who is being trained to do what? *Training, 25,* 51–60.

Gordon M. E., & Cohen, S. L. (1973). Training behavior as a predictor of trainability. *Personnel Psychology, 26,* 261–272.

Gordon, M. E., & Isenberg, J. F. (1975). Validation of an experimental training criterion for machinists. *Journal of Industrial Teacher Education, 12,* 72–78.

Gorman, C. (1988). The literacy gap. *Time,* December 19, 56–57.

Gray, L. E. (1983). *Aptitude constructs, learning processes and achievement.* Unpublished doctoral dissertation, Stanford University.

Greenlaw, P. S., Herron, L. W., & Rawdon, R. H. (1962). *Business simulation in industrial and university education.* Englewood Cliffs, NJ: Prentice-Hall.

Grove, D. A., & Ostroff, C. (1990). Program evaluation. In K. Wexley & J. Hinrichs (Eds.), *Developing human resources.* Washington, D.C.: BNA Books.

Guion, R. M. (1961). Criterion measurement and personnel judgments. *Personnel Psychology, 14,* 141–149.

Guion, R. M. (1977). Content validity—The source of my discontent. *Applied Psychological Measurement, 1,* 1–10.

Hagman, J. D., & Rose, A. M. (1983). Retention of military tasks: A review. *Human Factors, 25,* 199–214.

Haines, D. B., & Eachus, H. T. (1965). *A preliminary study of acquiring cross-cultural interaction skills through self-confrontation.* (AMRL-TR-65-137). Wright-Patterson Air

Force Base, OH: Aerospace Medical Research Laboratories.

Hall, D. T. (1986). Dilemmas in linking succession planning to individual executive learning. *Human Resources Management, 25,* 235–265.

Hall, E. M., Gott, S. P., & Pokorny, R. A. (1990). A procedural guide to cognitive task analysis: The PARI methodology. Working paper. AFHRL Laboratories, San Antonio, TX.

Hall, E. R., & Freda, J. S. (1982). A comparison of individualized and conventional instruction in navy technical training. Technical Report No. 117. Orlando, FL: Training Analysis and Evaluation Group.

Hand, H. H., & Slocum, Jr., J. W. (1972). A longitudinal study of the effects of a human relations training program on managerial effectiveness. *Journal of Applied Psychology, 56,* 412–417.

Hartley, A. A., Hartley, J. T., & Johnson, S. A. (1984). The older adult as computer user. In P. K. Robinson, J. Livingston, & J. E. Birren (Eds.), *Aging and technological advances.* New York: Plenum.

Hendrickson, G., & Schroeder, W. (1941). Transfer of training in learning to hit a submerged target. *Journal of Educational Psychology, 32,* 206–213.

Hicks, W. D., & Klimoski, R. J. (1987). Entry into training programs and its effects on training outcomes: A field experiment. *Academy of Management Journal, 30,* 542–552.

Hogan, J. C. (1978). Training of abilities: A review of nonspecific transfer issues relevant to ability training. *ARRO Technological Report 3010-TRI.* Washington, D.C.

Hogan, J., Quigley, A., & Stark, D. (1991). Effects of preparing for physical ability tests. Working paper, 1991. University of Tulsa, Department of Psychology.

Hogan, P. H., Hakel, M. D., & Decker, P. J. (1986). Effects of trainee-generated versus trainer-provided rule codes on generalization in behavior modeling training. *Journal of Applied Psychology, 71,* 469–473.

Hoiberg, A., & Berry, N. W. (1978). Expectations and perceptions of navy life. *Organizations of Behavioral Human Performance, 21,* 130–145.

Holding, D. H. (1965). *Principles of training.* London: Pergamon Press.

Holt, H. O. (Spring 1963). Programmed instruction. *Bell Telephone Magazine.*

House, R. J. (1967). T-group education and leadership effectiveness: A review of the empiric literature and a critical evaluation. *Personnel Psychology, 20,* 132.

Howard, A. (1971). Training for individuals and individual differences. Unpublished paper, University of Maryland.

Howell, W. C., & Cooke, N. J. (1989). Training the human information processor: A review of cognitive models. In I. L. Goldstein (Ed.), *Training in development and organizations.* San Francisco: Jossey-Bass.

Hsu, E. (1989). Role-event gaming simulation in management education. *Simulation and Games, 20,* 409–438.

Hughes, E. C. (1958). *Men and their work.* Glencoe, IL: Free Press.

Hughes, G. L., & Prien, E. P. (1989). Evaluation of task and job skill linkage judgments used to develop test specifications. *Personnel Psychology, 42,* 283–292.

Hurlock, R. E., & Slough, D. A. (1976). Experimental evaluation of Plato IV technology: Final report. *NPRDC Technological Report 76TQ-44.* San Diego.

Ilgen, D. R., Fisher, C. D., & Taylor, M. S. (1979). Consequences of individual feedback on behavior in organizations. *Journal of Applied Psychology, 64,* 349–371.

Ilgen, D. R., & Klein, H. W. (1989). Individual motivation and performance: Cognitive influences on effort and choice. In J. P. Campbell & R. J. Campbell (Eds.), *Productivity in organizations.* San Francisco: Jossey-Bass.

Ingersoll, V. H. (1973). Role playing, attitude change, and behavior. *Organizational Behavior and Human Performance, 10,* 157–174.

Institute of Medicine. (1981). *Airline pilot age, health, and performance.* Washington, D.C.: National Academy Press.

Jaffe, S. L., & Scherl, D. J. (1969). Acute psychosis precipitated by T-group experiences. *Archives of General Psychiatry, 21,* 443–448.

Kanfer, R. (1991). The role of motivation theory in industrial and organizational psychology. In M. D. Dunnette & L. M. Hough (Eds.), *Handbook of industrial and organizational psychology.* Palo Alto, CA: Consulting Psychologists Press.

Kanfer, R., & Ackerman, P. L. (1989). Motivation and cognitive abilities: An integrative/aptitude-treatment interaction approach to skill acquisition. *Journal of Applied Psychology, 74,* 657–690.

Kanfer, F. H., & Gaelick, L. (1986). Self-management methods. In F. H. Kanfer & A. P. Goldstein (Eds.), *Helping people change: A textbook on methods* (3rd ed.). Elmsford, NY: Pergamon Press.

Kaplan, R. E., Lombardo, M. M., & Mazique, M. S. (1983). A mirror for managers: Using simulation to develop management teams. Technical Report No 13. Greensboro, NC: Center for Creative Leadership.

Kaufman, H. G. (1978). Continuing education and job performance: A longitudinal study. *Journal of Applied Psychology, 63,* 248–251.

Kavanagh, M. J., Gueutal, H. G., & Tannenbaum, S. I. (1990). *Human resource information systems: Application and development.* Boston: PWS-Kent.

Keys, B., & Wolfe, J. (1990). The role of management games and simulation in education and research. *Journal of Management, 16,* 307–336.

Kim, J. S. (1984). Effect of behavior versus outcome goal-setting and feedback on employee satisfaction and behavior. *Academy of Management Journal, 27,* 139–149.

King, P. H. (1966). *A summary of research in training for advisory roles in other cultures by the behavioral sciences laboratory.* (AMRL-TR-66-131). Wright-Patterson Air Force Base, OH: Aerospace Medical Research Laboratories.

Kirchner, W. K. (1965). Review of A. J. Marrow's "Behind the executive mask." *Personnel Psychology, 18,* 211–212.

Kirkpatrick, D. L. (1959, 1960). Techniques for evaluating training programs. *Journal of the American Society of Training Directors, 13,* 3–9, 21–26; *14,* 13–18, 28–32.

Klaw, S. (1965). Inside a T-group. *Think, 31,* 26–30.

Klein, K. J., & Hall, R. J. (1988). Innovations in human resource management: Strategies for the future. In J. Hage (Ed.), *Future of organizations.* Lexington, MA: Lexington Books.

Komaki, J. (1977). Alternative evaluation strategies in work settings. *Journal of Organizational Behavioral Management, 1*(1), 53–77.

Komaki, J., Heinzmann, A. T., & Lawson, L. (1980). Effect of training and feedback: Component analysis of a behavioral safety program. *Journal of Applied Psychology, 65,* 261–270.

Kraut, A. I. (1975). Prediction of managerial success by peer and training-staff ratings. *Journal of Applied Psychology, 60,* 14–19.

Kraut, A. I., Pedigo, P. R., McKenna, D. D., & Dunnette, M. D. (1989). The role of manager: What's really important in different management jobs. *Academy of Management Executive, 3,* 286–293.

Kung, E. Y., & Rado, R. N. (1984). Teletraining applied. *Training and Development Journal, 38,* 27–28.

Landy, F. J., & Vasey, J. (1991). Job analysis: The composition of SME samples. *Personnel Psychology, 44,* 27–50.

Latham, G. P., & Frayne, C. A. (1989). Self-management training for increased job attendance: A follow-up and replication. *Journal of Applied Psychology, 74,* 411–416.

Latham, G. P., & Locke, E. A. (1979). Goal setting: A motivational technique that works. *Organizational Dynamics, 8,* 68–80.

Latham, G. P., & Saari, L. M. (1979). The application of social learning theory to training supervisors through behavioral modeling. *Journal of Applied Psychology, 64,* 239–246.

Latham, G. P., & Wexley K. N. (1981). *Increasing productivity through performance appraisal.* Reading, MA: Addison-Wesley.

Latham, G. P., Wexley, K. N., & Pursell, E. D. (1975). Training managers to minimize rating errors in the observation of behavior. *Journal of Applied Psychology, 60,* 550–555.

Ledvinka, J., & Scarpello, V. G. (1991). *Federal regulation of personnel and human resource management.* Boston: PWS-Kent.

Lefkowitz, J. (1970). Effect of training on the productivity and tenure of sewing machine operators. *Journal of Applied Psychology, 54,* 81–86.

Levine, M. (1974). Scientific method and the adversary model: Some preliminary thoughts. *American Psychologist, 29,* 661–667.

Liveright, A. A. (1951). Role playing in leadership training. *Personnel Journal, 29,* 412–416.

Locke, E. A., Shaw, K. N., Saari, L. M., & Latham, G. P. (1981). Goal setting and task performance. *Psychological Bulletin, 90,* 125–152.

London, M. (1991). Practice in training and development. In D. W. Bray (Ed.), *Working with organizations.* New York: Guilford Press.

London, M., & Bassman, E. (1989). Retraining midcareer workers for the future workplace. In I. L. Goldstein (Ed.), *Training and development in organizations.* San Francisco: Jossey-Bass.

Lorge, I. (1930). *Influence of regularly interpolated time intervals upon subsequent learning.* Teachers College Contributions to Education, No. 438. New York: Teachers College Press, Columbia University.

Lowman, R. L. (1991). Ethical human resource practice in organizational settings. In D. W. Bray (Ed.), *Working with organizations.* New York: Guilford Press.

Luthans, F., & Kreitner, R. (1985). *Organizational behavior modification and beyond.* Glenview, IL: Scott, Foresman.

Lysaught, J. P., & Williams, C. M. (1963). *A guide to programmed instruction.* New York: Wiley.

Mabe, III, P. A., & West, S. G. (1982). Validity of self-evaluation of ability: A review and meta-analysis. *Journal of Applied Psychology, 67,* 280–296.

Mager, R. F. (1984). *Preparing instructional objectives.* Belmont, CA: Pitman Learning.

Maier, N. R. F., & Zerfoss, L. R. (1952). MRP: A technique for training large groups of supervisors and its potential use in social research. *Human Relations, 5,* 177–186.

Manz, C. C., & Manz, K. P. (1991). Strategies for facilitating self-directed learning: A process for enhancing human resource development. *Human Resource Development Quarterly, 2,* 3–12.

Manz, C. C., & Sims, Jr., H. P. (1989). *Superleadership: Leading others to lead themselves.* Englewood Cliffs, NJ: Prentice-Hall.

Marx, R. D. (1982). Relapse prevention for managerial training: A model for maintenance of behavior change. *Academy of Management Review, 7,* 433–441.

Marx, R. D., & Hamilton, E. E. (In press). Beyond skill building: A multiple perspective view of personnel training. *Issues and Trends in Business Economics,* 703.

Mathieu, J. E., & Leonard, Jr., R. L. (1987). Applying utility concepts to a training program in supervisory skills: A time based approach. *Academy of Management Journal, 30,* 316–335.

Mathieu, J. E., Tannenbaum, S. I., & Salas, E. (In press). An influence of individual and situational characteristics on training effectiveness measures. *Academy of Management Journal.*

Mayer, R. E. (1975). Different problem solving competencies established in learning computer programming with and without meaningful models. *Journal of Educational Psychology, 65,* 725–734.

Mayer, R. E. (1989). Models for understanding. *Review of Educational Research, 59,* 43–64.

Mayer, R. E., & Bromage, B. K. (1980). Differential recall protocols for technical texts due to advance organizers. *Journal of Educational Psychology, 72,* 209–225.

Mayer, S. J., & Russell, J. S. (1987). Behavior modeling training in organizations: Concerns and conclusions. *Journal of Management, 13,* 21–40.

McCall, Jr., M. W., & Lombardo, M. M. (1979). Looking Glass Inc.: The first three years (Vol. 8, Technical Report No. 13). Greensboro, NC: Center for Creative Leadership.

McCall, Jr., M. W., & Lombardo, M. M. (1982). Using simulation for leadership and management research: Through the Looking Glass. *Management Science, 28,* 533–549.

McCann, P. H. (1975). *Training mathematics skills with games* (Technical Report 75-28). San Diego: Navy Personnel Research and Development Center.

McCauley, C. D., Lombardo, M. M., & Usher, C. J. (1989). Diagnosing management development needs: An instrument based on how managers develop. *Journal of Management, 15,* 389–403.

McCauley, M. E. (Ed.) (1984). *Research issues in simulator sickness: Proceedings of a workshop.* Washington, D.C.: National Academy Press.

McClelland, D. C. (1976). *The achieving society.* New York: Wiley.

McClelland, D. C. (1978). Managing motivation to expand human freedom. *American Psychologist, 33,* 201–210.

McClelland, D. C., & Winter, D. G. (1971). *Motivating economic achievement.* New York: Free Press.

McEnery, J., & McEnery, J. M. (1987). Self-rating in management training need assessment: A neglected opportunity. *Journal of Occupational Psychology, 60,* 49–60.

McEvoy, G. M., & Cascio, W. F. (1989). Cumulative evidence of the relationship between employee age and job performance. *Journal of Applied Psychology, 74,* 11–17.

McGehee, W., & Thayer, P. W. (1961). *Training in business and industry.* New York: Wiley.

McGehee, W., & Tullar, W. L. (1978). A note on evaluating behavior modification and behavior modeling as industrial training techniques. *Personnel Psychology, 31,* 477–484.

McIntire, R. W. (1973). Behavior modification guidelines. In T. C. Tuttle, C. B. Grether, & W. T. Liggett (Eds.), *Psychological behavior strategy for accident control: Development of behavioral safety guidelines.* Final report for National Institute for Occupational Safety and Health (Contract No. HSM-99-72-27). Columbia, MD: Westinghouse Behavioral Safety Center.

Meyer, H. H., & Raich, M. S. (1983). An objective evaluation of a behavioral modeling training program. *Personnel Psychology, 36,* 755–762.

Michalak, D. F. (1981). The neglected half of training. *Training and Development Journal, 35,* 22–28.

Miller, R. W., & Zeller, F. A. (1967). *Social psychological factors association with responses to retraining.* Final Report, Office of Research and Development, Appalachian Center, West Virginia University (Research Grant No. 91-52-6656), U.S. Department of Labor.

Miner, J. B. (1961). Management development and attitude change. *Personnel Administration, 24,* 21–26.

Miner, J. B. (1963). Evidence regarding the value of a management course based on behavioral science subject matter. *The Journal of Business of the University of Chicago, 36,* 325–335.

Mirabal, T. E. (1978). Forecasting future training costs. *Training and Development Journal, 32*(7), 78–87.

Miron, D., & McClelland, D. C. (1979). The impact of achievement motivation training on small businesses. *California Management Review, 21,* 13–28.

Mitchell, F. G. (1981). Developing an international marketing training approach. *Training and Development Journal, 35,* 48–51.

Mitchell, T. R. (1982). Motivation: New directions for theory, research, and practice. *Academy of Management Review, 7,* 80–88.

Mobley, W. H., Hand, H. H., Baker, R. L., & Meglino, B. M. (1979). Conceptual and empirical analysis of military recruit training attrition. *Journal of Applied Psychology, 64,* 10–18.

Moore, L. F. (1967). Business games vs. cases as tools of learning. *Training and Development Journal, 21,* 13–23.

Morgan, Jr., B. B., Glickman, A. S., Woodard, E. A., Blaiwes, A. S., & Salas, E. (1986). Measurement of team behaviors. (Technical Report No. 86-014). Orlando, FL: Naval Training Systems Center.

Moses, J. L. (1978). Behavior modeling for managers. *Human Factors, 20,* 225–232.

Mumford, M. D., Weeks, J. L., Harding, F. D., & Fleishman, E. A. (1987). Measuring occupational difficulty: A construct validation against training criteria. *Journal of Applied Psychology, 72,* 578–587.

Nagle, B. F. (1953). Criterion development. *Personnel Psychology, 6,* 271–288.

Nash, A. N., Muczyk, J. P., & Vettori, F. L. (1971). The relative practical effectiveness of programed instruction. *Personnel Psychology, 24,* 397–418.

National Center for Research in Vocational Education. (1978). *Occupational adaptability and transferable skills.* Information Series No. 129. Columbus, OH: National Center for Research in Vocational Education.

Naylor, J. C. (February 1962). Parameters affecting the relative efficiency of part and whole practice methods: A review of the literature. (Technical Report No. 950-1). United States Naval Training Devices Center.

Naylor, J. D., Pritchard, R. D., & Ilgen, D. R. (1980). *A theory of behavior in organizations.* Orlando, FL: Academic Press.

Nester, O. W. (1971). *Training the hard core: One experience.* Pittsburgh Technical Institute Report. Undated. Review of work also appearing in *Training and Development Journal, 25,* 16–19.

Newman, D. (1985). *The pursuit of validity in training: An application.* Ph.D. dissertation. College Park: University of Maryland.

Noe, R. A. (1986). Trainee attributes and attitudes: Neglected influences on training effectiveness. *Academy of Management Review, 4,* 736–749.

Noe, R. A., & Schmitt, N. (1986). The influence of trainee attitudes on training effectiveness: Test of a model. *Personnel Psychology, 39,* 497–523.

Nord, W. (1970). Improving attendance through rewards. *Personnel Administration, 33,* 37–41.

O'Brien, G. E., & Plooij, D. (1977). Comparison of programmed and prose culture training upon attitudes and knowledge. *Journal of Applied Psychology, 62,* 499–505.

Odiorne, G. S. (1963). The trouble with sensitivity training. *Journal of the American Society of Training Directors, 17,* 9–20.

Odiorne, G. S. (1980). Training to be ready for the 90's. *Training and Development Journal, 34,* 12–20.

Offerman, L. R., & Gowing, M. K. (1990). Organizations of the future: Changes and challenges. *American Psychologist, 45,* 95–108.

Office of Technology Assessment. (1990). *Worker training: competing in the new international economy.* Report No. OTA-ITE-457. Washington, D.C.: U.S. Printing Office.

Ohmann, O. A. (1941). A report of research on the selection of salesmen at the Tremco Manufacturing Company. *Journal of Applied Psychology, 25,* 18–29.

O'Leary, V. E. (1972). The Hawthorne effect in reverse: Effects of training and practice on individual and group performance. *Journal of Applied Psychology, 56,* 491–494.

Olson, H. C., Fine, S. A., Myers, D. C., & Jennings, M. C. (1981). The use of functional job analysis in establishing performance standards for heavy equipment operators. *Personnel Psychology, 34,* 351–364.

Orlansky, J., & String, J. (1977). Cost-effectiveness of flight simulators for military training. Vol. 1: Use and effectiveness of flight simulators. *Inst. Def. Anal. Tech. Pap. P-1275.* Arlington, VA.

Oser, R., McCallum, G. A., Salas, E., & Morgan, Jr., B. B. (1989). *Toward a definition of teamwork: An analysis of critical team behaviors.* Technical Report TR-89-004. Orlando, FL: Naval Training Systems Center.

Ostroff, C. (1991). Training effectiveness measures and scoring schemes: A comparison. *Personnel Psychology, 44,* 353–374.

Ostroff, C., & Ford, J. K. (1989). Assessing training needs: Critical levels of analysis. In I. L. Goldstein (Ed.), *Training and development in organizations.* San Francisco: Jossey-Bass.

Panell, R. C., & Laabs, G. J. (1979). Construction of a criterion-referenced, diagnostic test for an individualized instruction program. *Journal of Applied Psychology, 64,* 255–261.

Patten, Jr., T. H., & Stermer, E. P. (1969). Training foremen in work standards. *Training and Development Journal, 23,* 25–37.

Pearlman, K. (1980). Job families: A review and discussion of their implications for personnel selection. *Psychological Bulletin, 87,* 1–28.

Pedalino, E., & Gamboa, V. U. (1974). Behavior modification and absenteeism: Intervention in one industrial setting. *Journal of Applied Psychology, 59,* 694–698.

Personick, V. A. (1985). A second look at industry output and employment through 1995. *Monthly Labor Review,* 26–41.

Pfister, G. (1975). Outcomes of laboratory training for police officers. *Journal of Social Issues, 31,* 115–121.

Phillips, D. (1991). Terror at zero feet: A crew's simulated brush with death. *Washington Post,* January 1, A3.

Pinto, P. R., & Walker, J. W. (1978). What do training and development professionals really do? *Training and Development Journal, 28,* 58–64.

Pintrick, P. R., Cross, D. R., Kozma, R. B., & McKeachie, W. J. (1986). Instructional psychology. In *Annual Review of Psychology.* Palo Alto, CA: Annual Reviews.

Pratzner, F. C. (1978). *Occupational adaptability and transferable skills.* (Information Series No. 129). Columbus, OH: National Center for Research in Vocational Education.

Pressey, S. L. (1950). Development and appraisal of devices providing immediate automatic scoring of objective tests and concomitant self-instruction. *Journal of Psychology, 29,* 417–447.

Prien, E. P. (1977). The function of job analysis in content validation. *Personnel Psychology, 30,* 167–174.

Prien, E. P., Goldstein, I. L., & Macey, W. H. (1985a). *Multi-method job analysis: Methodolo-*

gy and applications. Unpublished paper. Memphis, TN: Performance Management Associates.

Prien, E. P., Goldstein, I. L., & Macey, W. H. (1985b). *Needs assessment: Program and individual development.* Paper presented at the 89th Convention of the American Psychological Association, Los Angeles.

Prien, E. P., Goldstein, I. L., & Macey, W. H. (1987). Multidomain job analysis: Procedures and applications in human resource management and development. *Training and Development Journal, 41,* 68–72.

Pritchard, R. D. (1969). Equity theory: A review and critique. *Organizational Behavior and Human Performance, 4,* 176–211.

Pursell, E. D., & Russell, J. S. (1990). Employee development. In K. N. Wexley (Ed.), *Developing human resources,* Washington, D.C.: BNA Books.

Raia, A. P. (1966). A study of the educational value of management games. *The Journal of Business, 39,* 339–352.

Ralphs, L. T., & Stephan, E. (1986). HRD in the Fortune 500. *Training and Development Journal, 40,* 69–76.

Randall, L. K. (1960). Evaluation: A training dilemma. *Journal of the American Society of Training Directors, 14,* 29–35.

Randall, J. S. (1978). You and effective training. *Training and Development Journal, 32,* 10–19.

Raser, J. R. (1969). *Simulation and society: An exploration of scientific gaming.* Boston: Allyn and Bacon.

Raynor, J. O. (1970). Relationships between achievement-related motives, future orientation, and academic performance. *Journal of Personality and Social Psychology, 15,* 28–33.

Raynor, J. O., & Rubin, I. S. (1971). Effects of achievement motivation and future orientation on level of performance. *Journal of Personality and Social Psychology, 17,* 36–41.

Reich, R. B. (1981). *The work of nations: Preparing ourselves for 21st-Century Capitalism.* New York: Knopf.

Reilly, R. R., & Israelski, E. W. (1988). Development and validation of minicourses in the telecommunications industry. *Journal of Applied Psychology, 73,* 721–726.

Reilly, R. R., & Manese, W. R. (1979). The validation of a minicourse for telephone company switching technicians. *Personnel Psychology, 32,* 83–90.

Report of the National Advisory Commission on Civil Disorders. (1968). New York: Bantam Books.

Rhodes S. R. (1983). Age-related differences in work attitudes and behavior: A review and conceptual analysis. *Psychological Bulletin, 93,* 328–367.

Robertson, I., & Downs, S. (1979). Learning and the prediction of performance: Development of trainability testing in the United Kingdom. *Journal of Applied Psychology, 64,* 42–50.

Robertson, I. T., & Downs, S. (1989). Work sample tests of trainability: A meta-analysis. *Journal of Applied Psychology, 74,* 402–410.

Ronen, S. (1989). Training the international assignee. In I. L. Goldstein (Ed.), *Training and development in organizations.* San Francisco: Jossey-Bass.

Rosen, B., & Jerdee, T. H. (1976). The nature of job-related stereotypes. *Journal of Applied Psychology, 61,* 180–183.

Rosenberg, B. D. (1972). *An evaluation of computer-assisted instruction in the Anne Arundel County School System.* Master's thesis, University of Maryland.

Rosenthal, R. (1966). *Experimenter effects in behavioral research.* New York: Appleton-Century-Crofts.

Rosenthal, R. (1978). How often are our numbers wrong? *American Psychologist, 33,* 1005–1008.

Rotter, J. B. (1966). Generalized expectancies for internal vs. external locus of control of reinforcement. *Psychological Monographs, 80,* 1–609.

Rouillier, J. Z., & Goldstein, I. L. (1990). Determinants of the climate for transfer of training. Paper presented at the meeting of the Society of Industrial and Organizational Psychology, St. Louis.

Rubinsky, S., & Smith, N. (1973). Safety training by accident simulation. *Journal of Applied Psychology, 57,* 68–73.

Russell, J. S. (1984). A review of fair employment cases in the field of training. *Personnel Psychology, 37,* 261–276.

Russell, J. S., Terborg, J. R., & Powers, M. L. (1985). Organizational performance and organizational level training and support. *Personnel Psychology, 38,* 849–863.

Russell, J. S., Wexley, K. N., & Hunter, J. E.

(1984). Questioning the effectiveness of behavior modeling training in an industrial setting. *Personnel Psychology, 37,* 465–482.

Ryman, D. H., & Biersner, R. J. (1975). Attitudes predictive of diving training success. *Personnel Psychology, 28,* 181–188.

Saari, L. M., Johnson, T. R., McLaughlin, S. D., & Zimmerle, D. M. (1988). A survey of management training and education practices in U.S. companies. *Personnel Psychology, 41,* 731–743.

Salas, E., Dickinson, T. L., Tannenbaum, S. I., & Converse, S. A. (1991). *A meta-analysis of team performance and training.* Technical Report. Orlando, FL: Naval Training System Center.

Salinger, R. D. (1973). Disincentives to effective employee training and development. Washington, D.C.: U.S. Civil Service Commission, Bureau of Training.

Salipante, Jr., P., & Goodman, P. (1976). Training, counseling, and retention of the hard-core unemployed. *Journal of Applied Psychology, 61,* 1–11.

Salvendy, G., & Pilitsis, J. (1980). The development and validation of an analytical training program for medical suturing. *Human Factors, 22,* 153–170.

Sanders, P., & Yanouzas, J. N. (1983). Socialization to learning. *Training and Development Journal, 37,* 14–21.

Saretsky, G. (1972). The OEO P.C. experiment and the John Henry effect. *Phi Delta Kappan, 53,* 579–581.

Sawyer, C. R., Pain, R. F., Van Cott, H., & Banks, W. W. (1982). Nuclear control room modifications and the role of transfer of training principles: A review of issues and research. (NUREG/CR-2828, EGG-2211). Idaho Falls: Idaho National Engineering Laboratory.

Scardamalia, M., Bereiter, C., & Steinbach, R. (1984). Teachability of reflective processes in written composition. *Cognitive Science, 8,* 173–190.

Schein, E. H. (1980). *Organizational psychology.* Englewood Cliffs, NJ: Prentice-Hall.

Schendel, J. D., & Hagman, J. D. (1982). On sustaining procedural skills over a prolonged retention interval. *Journal of Applied Psychology, 67,* 605–610.

Schmitt, N. (1987). Principles III: Research issues. Symposium conducted at the meeting of the Society for Industrial and Organizational Psychology, Atlanta.

Schmitt, N., & Cohen, S. A. (1989). Internal analysis of task ratings by job incumbents. *Journal of Applied Psychology, 74,* 96–104.

Schneider, B., & Bowen, D. E. (In press). Personnel/human resources management in the service sector. In K. R. Rowland & G. R. Ferris (Eds.), *Research in personnel and human resources management,* Greenwich, CT: JAI Press.

Schneider, B., & Konz, A. M. (1989). Strategic job analysis. *Human Resources Management, 28,* 51–63.

Schneider, B., & Schmitt, N. W. (1986). *Staffing organizations.* Glenview, IL: Scott, Foresman.

Schramm, W. (1962). Learning from instructional television. *Review of Educational Research, 32,* 156–167.

Schramm, W. (1964). *The research on programmed instruction: An annotated bibliography.* Washington, D.C.: U.S. Printing Office.

Scriven, M. (1967). The methodology of evaluation. In *Perspectives of curriculum evaluation.* American Educational Research Association Monograph, No. 1, Chicago: Rand McNally.

Seltzer, R. A. (1971). Computer-assisted instruction—What it can and cannot do. *American Psychology, 26,* 373–377.

Sheppard, H. L. (Ed.) (1970). On age discrimination. In *Toward an industrial gerontology: An introduction to a new field of applied research and service.* Cambridge, MA: Schenkman.

Sheridan, J. A. (1975). *Designing the work environment.* Paper presented at the annual meeting of the American Psychological Association, Chicago.

Shiffrin, R. M., & Schneider, W. (1977). Controlled and automatic human information processing: II. Perceptual learning, automatic attending and a general theory. *Psychological Review, 84,* 127–190.

Shoemaker, H. A., & Holt, H. O. (1965). The use of programmed instruction in industry. In R. Glaser (Ed.), *Teaching machines and programmed learning: Data and directions.* Washington, D.C.: National Education Association.

Siegel, A. I. (1983). The miniature job training and evaluation approach: Additional findings. *Personnel Psychology, 36,* 41–56.

Silverman, R. E. (1960). *Automated teaching: A review of theory and research* (NAV-

TRADEVCEN Technical Report 507-2). Port Washington, NY: U.S. Naval Training Device Center.

Singer, I. (1968). CAI in the ghetto school. *CAI Newsletter of the Institute for Computer-Assisted Instruction, 1,* 3.

Sjogren, D. (1977). *Occupationally-transferable skills and characteristics: Review of literature and research.* Information Series 105. Columbus, OH: National Center for Research in Vocational Education.

Skinner, B. F. (1954). Science of learning and the art of teaching. *Harvard Educational Review, 24,* 86–97.

Smith, B. D. (In press). *Psychology: An introduction.* New York: Wiley.

Smith, E. A. (1990). Theory and practice in training videos: An exploration. *Human Resource Development Quarterly, 1,* 409–412.

Smith, P. B. (1975). Controlled studies of the outcome of sensitivity training. *Psychological Bulletin, 82,* 597–622.

Snow, R. E., & Lohman, D. F. (1984). Toward a theory of cognitive aptitude for learning from instruction. *Journal of Educational Psychology, 76,* 347–376.

Society for Industrial and Organizational Psychology (1987). *Principles for the validation and use of personnel selection procedures* (3rd ed.). College Park, MD: Author.

Speroff, B. J. (1954). Rotational role playing used to develop managers. *Personnel Journal, 33,* 49–50.

Spool, M. D. (1978). Training programs for observers of behavior: A review. *Personnel Psychology, 31,* 853–888.

Stake, R. E. (1967). The countenance of educational evaluation. *Teachers College Record, 68,* 523–540.

Steadham, S. V. (1980). Learning to select a needs assessment strategy. *Training and Development Journal, 30,* 55–61.

Steers, R. M., & Porter, L. W. (1983). *Motivation and work behavior.* New York: McGraw-Hill.

Sterns, H. L., & Doverspike, D. (1989). Aging and the training and learning process. In I. L. Goldstein (Ed.), *Training and development in organizations.* San Francisco: Jossey-Bass.

Stewart, L. (1962). Management games today. In J. M. Kibbee, C. J. Kraft, & B. Nanus (Eds.), *Management games.* New York: Reinhold.

Sticht, T. G., Armstrong, W. B., Hickey D. T., & Caylor, J. S. (1987). *Cast-off youth.* New York: Praeger.

Strauss, G. (1972). Management by objectives: A critical view. *Training and Development Journal, 26,* 10–15.

Sugawara, S. (1991). Study: Firms holding back women and minorities. *Washington Post,* August 9, B1–3.

Sullivan, R. F., & Miklas, D. C. (1985). On-the-job training that works. *Training and Development Journal, 39,* 118–120.

Suppes, P., & Jerman, M. (1970). Computer-assisted instruction. *National Association of Secondary School Principals Bulletin, 54,* 27–40.

Suppes, P., & Morningstar, M. (1969). Computer-assisted instruction: Two computer-assisted instruction programs are evaluated. *Science, 166,* 343–350.

Swezey, R. W. (1981). *Individual performance assessment: An approach to criterion-referenced test development.* Reston, VA: Reston Publishing.

Swezey, R. W. (1982–1983). Application of a transfer of training model to training device assessment. *Journal of Educational Technology System, 11,* 225–238.

Swezey, R. W., & Salas, E. (Eds.) (1991). Guidelines for use in team training development. In *Teams: Their training and performance.* Norwood, NJ: Ablex.

Swoboda, F. (1991). GAO finds job training discrimination. *Washington Post,* July 17, A21.

Tannenbaum, S. I., Mathieu, J. E., Salas, E., & Cannon-Bowers, J. A. (1991). Meeting trainees' expectations: The influence of training fulfillment on the development of commitment, self-efficacy, and motivation. *Journal of Applied Psychology, 76,* 759–769.

Tannenbaum, S. I., & Yukl, G. (1992). Training and development in work organizations. In *Annual Review of Psychology.* Palo Alto, CA: Annual Reviews.

Teahan, J. E. (1976). Role playing and group experiences to facilitate attitude and value changes among black and white police officers. *Journal of Social Issues, 31,* 35–45.

Thayer, P. W., & McGehee, W. (1977). On the effectiveness of not holding a formal training course. *Personnel Psychology, 30,* 455–456.

Thorndike, E. L. (1927). The law of effect. *American Journal of Psychology, 39,* 212–222.

Thorndike, E. L., & Woodworth, R. S. (1901).

(1) The influence of improvement in one mental function upon the efficiency of other functions. (11) The estimation of magnitudes. (111) Functions involving attention, observation, and discrimination. *Psychological Review, 8,* 247–261, 384–395, 553–564.

Thorndike, R. L. (1949). *Personnel selection.* New York: Wiley.

Thornton, III, G. C., & Cleveland, J. N. (1990). Developing managerial talent through simulation. *American Psychologist, 45,* 190–199.

Torrence, D. R., & Torrence, J. (1987). Training in the face of illiteracy. *Training and Development Journal, 41,* 44–48.

Triandis, H. C., Feldman, J. M., Weldon, D. E., & Harvey, W. M. (1974). Designing pre-employment training for the hard to employ: A cross-cultural psychological approach. *Journal of Applied Psychology, 59,* 687–693.

Triandis, H. C., Feldman, J. M., Weldon, D. E., & Harvey, W. M. (1975). Ecosystem distrust and the hard-to-employ. *Journal of Applied Psychology, 60,* 44–56.

Trowbridge, M. A., & Cason, H. (1932). An experimental study of Thorndike's theory of learning. *Journal of General Psychology, 7,* 245–260.

Uhlaner, J. E., & Drucker, A. J. (1980). Military research on performance criteria: A change of emphasis. *Human Factors, 22,* 131–139.

Underwood, B. J. (1964). The representativeness of rote verbal learning. In A. W. Melton (Ed.), *Categories of human learning.* New York: Academic Press.

U.S. Civil Service Commission. (1970). *Programed instruction: A brief of its development and current status.* Washington, D.C.: U.S. Printing Office.

U.S. Civil Service Commission. (1971). *Computer-assisted instruction: A general discussion and case study.* Washington, D.C.: U.S. Printing Office.

U.S. Department of Labor, Manpower Administration. (1972). *Handbook for analyzing jobs.* Washington, D.C.: U.S. Printing Office.

U.S. Department of Labor. (1979). *Dictionary of occupational titles* (3rd ed.). Washington, D.C.: U.S. Printing Office.

U.S. Department of Labor, Commission on Achieving Necessary Skills (SCANS). (1991). *What work requires of schools.* Washington, D.C.: U.S. Printing Office.

U.S. Equal Employment Opportunity Commission. (1991). *The Americans with Disabilities Act: Your responsibilities as an employer.* Report No. EEOC-BK-17.

U.S. President's Commission on the Accident at Three-Mile Island (1979). *Report of the President's Commission on the Accident at Three-Mile Island.* Washington, D.C.: U.S. Printing Office.

Van Brunt, R. E. (1971). Supervising employees from minority groups. *Education Exchange: Insurance Company Education Directors Society, 111,* 1–5.

Van Maanan, J. (1976). Breaking in: Socialization to work. In R. Dubin (Ed.), *Handbook of work, organization, and society.* Chicago: Rand McNally.

Vobejda, B. (1987). The new cutting edge in factories. *Washington Post,* April 14, A14.

Vroom, V. H. (1964). *Work and motivation.* New York: Wiley.

Wallace, R. S. (1965). Criteria for what? *American Psychologist, 20,* 411–417.

Wanous, J. P. (1977). Organizational entry: Newcomers moving from outside to inside. *Psychology Bulletin, 84,* 601–618.

Wanous, J. P. (1980). *Organizational entry: Recruitment, selection and socialization of newcomers.* Reading, MA: Addison-Wesley.

Wards Cove Co. v. *Antonio,* 109 S. Ct. 2115 (1989).

Warmke, D. L., & Billings, R. S. (1979). A comparison of training methods for altering the psychometric properties of experimental and administrative performance ratings. *Journal of Applied Psychology, 64,* 124–131.

Washington Post. (1983). How not to retrain workers. Editorial. November 12, A18.

Watkins, K. E. (1990). Tacit beliefs of human resource developers: Producing unintended consequences. *Human Resource Development Quarterly, 1,* 263–275.

Webb, E. J., Campbell, D. T., Schwartz, R. D., & Sechrest, L. (1966). *Unobtrusive measures: Nonreactive research in the social sciences.* Chicago: Rand McNally.

Weidenbaum, M. L. (1978). The cost of government regulation of business. Hearings before the Subcommittee on Economic Growth and Stabilization of the Joint Economic Commission, 95th Congress, 2d Session, April 11 and 13.

Weiss, E. C. (1975). Evaluation research in the political context. In E. L. Streuning & M. Guttentag (Eds.), *Handbook of evaluation research*. Beverly Hills, CA: Sage.

Weiss, H. M. (1990). Learning theory and industrial psychology. In M. D. Dunnette & L. M. Hough (Eds.), *Handbook of industrial and organizational psychology*. Palo Alto, CA: Consulting Psychologists Press.

Wexley, K. N. (1984). Personnel training. In *Annual Review of Psychology*. Palo Alto, CA: Annual Reviews.

Wexley, K. N., & Latham, G. P. (1981). *Developing and training human resources in organizations*. Glenview, IL: Scott, Foresman.

Wheaton, G. R. (1976). *Evaluation of the effectiveness of training devices: Validation of the predictive model.* Alexandria, VA: U.S. Army Research Institute.

Wherry, R. J. (1957). The past and future of criterion evaluation. *Personnel Psychology, 10,* 1–5.

White, B. Y., & Frederiksen, J. R. (1986). *Progressions of higher psychological processes.* Cambridge, MA: Harvard University Press.

White, M. C., Crino, M. D., & DeSanctis, G. L. (1981). A critical review of female performance, performance training and organizational initiatives designed to aid women in the work-role environment. *Personnel Psychology, 34,* 227–248.

Williams, T. C., Thayer, P. W., & Pond, S. B. (1991). Test of a model of motivational influences on reactions to training and learning. Paper presented at the meeting of the Society for Industrial and Organizational Psychology, St. Louis.

Wood, R., & Bandura, A. (1989). Social cognitive theory of organizational management. *Academy of Management Review, 14,* 361–384.

Wulfeck, II, W. H., Ellis, J. A., Richards, R. E., Wood, N. D., & Merrill, M. D. (1978). *The instructional quality inventory: I. Introduction and overview.* (NPRDC Technology Report 79-3). San Diego, CA: Navy Personnel Research and Development Center.

Yukl, G. A., & Latham, G. P. (1975). Consequences of reinforcement schedules and incentive magnitudes for employee performance: Problems encountered in an industrial setting. *Journal of Applied Psychology, 60,* 294–298.

Zenger, J. H. (1981). Career planning: Coming in from the cold. *Training and Development Journal, 35,* 47–52.

Indexes

AUTHOR INDEX

Subject Index

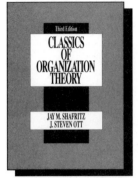

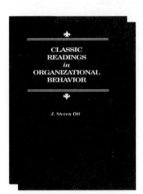

TO THE OWNER OF THIS BOOK:

We hope that you have found *Training in Organizations, Third Edition*, useful. So that this book can be improved in a future edition, would you take the time to complete this sheet and return it? Thank you.

Instructor's name: ______________________________

Department: ______________________________

School and address: ______________________________

Year in school: ______________ Major: ______________

1. The name of the course in which I used this book is: ______________________________

____

2. What I like *most* about this book is: ______________________________

____

____

3. What I like *least* about this book is: ______________________________

____

____

4. What I would have liked *more of* in this book is: ______________________________

____

____

5. What I would have liked *less of* in this book is: ______________________________

____

6. Were all of the chapters of the book assigned for you to read? Yes No

   If not, which ones weren't? ______________________________

7. On a separate sheet, please tell us anything else you would like us to know about the book. Thank you.

Optional:

Your name: ______________________________ Date: ______________________

May Brooks/Cole quote you, either in promotion for *Training in Organizations, Third Edition*, or in future publishing ventures?

Yes: ________ No: ________

Sincerely,

Irwin L. Goldstein

FOLD HERE

NO POSTAGE NECESSARY IF MAILED IN THE UNITED STATES

BUSINESS REPLY MAIL

FIRST CLASS PERMIT NO. 358 PACIFIC GROVE, CA

POSTAGE WILL BE PAID BY ADDRESSEE

ATT: *Irwin L. Goldstein*

Brooks/Cole Publishing Company
511 Forest Lodge Road
Pacific Grove, California 93950-9968

FOLD HERE